P9-EDD-662

+

CHRISTIAN CRITICS

209.73
M126

CHRISTIAN CRITICS

RELIGION AND THE IMPASSE IN MODERN AMERICAN SOCIAL THOUGHT

Eugene McCarraher

WITHDRAWN

CORNELL UNIVERSITY PRESS

ITHACA AND LONDON

LIBRARY ST. MARY'S COLLEGE

Copyright © 2000 by Cornell University

All rights reserved. Except for brief quotations in a review, this book, or parts thereof,
must not be reproduced in any form without permission in writing from the publisher.
For information, address Cornell University Press, Sage House,
512 East State Street, Ithaca, New York 14850.

First published 2000 by Cornell University Press

Printed in the United States of America

Librarians: A CIP catalog record of this book
is available from the Library of Congress.

Cornell University Press strives to use environmentally responsible suppliers and materials
to the fullest extent possible in the publishing of its books. Such materials include
vegetable-based, low-VOC inks, and acid-free papers that are recycled, totally
chlorine-free, or partly composed of nonwood fibers. Books that bear the logo of the
FSC (Forest Stewardship Council) use paper taken from forests that have been inspected
and certified as meeting the highest standards for environmental and social responsibility.
For further information, visit our website at www.cornellpress.cornell.edu.

Cloth printing   10 9 8 7 6 5 4 3 2 1

LIBRARY ST. MARY'S COLLEGE

✠

To Alecia

i love you much (most beautiful darling)
more than anyone on the earth and i
like you better than everything in the sky

       —sunlight and singing welcome your coming

Then I saw a new heaven and a new earth;
for the first heaven and the first earth had passed away,
and the sea was no more.
And I saw the holy city, new Jerusalem,
coming down out of heaven from God,
prepared as a bride adorned for her husband;
and I heard a loud voice from the throne saying,
"Behold, the dwelling of God is with men.
He will dwell with them, and they shall be his people,
and God himself will be with them;
he will wipe away every tear from their eyes,
and death shall be no more,
neither shall there be mourning nor crying nor pain any more,
for the former things have passed away."

And he who sat upon the throne said,
"Behold, I make all things new."

Revelation 21: 1–5

✝

CONTENTS

+

ACKNOWLEDGMENTS

I've waited for quite a long time to write this part of the book, and it's a pleasure to finally give thanks and praise to colleagues, friends, and loved ones who supported and guided me along my way. While I sympathize with those who complain that acknowledgments have become like Oscar speeches—or even worse, invocations of the high and mighty to disarm criticism—I still believe that gratitude (one of the most under-appreciated of virtues) must be given.

To my parents, Eugene Thorne McCarraher and Eleanor Marie Mc-Carraher, I can never fully convey my love and thanksgiving. In passing on the gifts of life and love, they taught me more than any book about the real meaning of things. I talked for hours with my brother Michael Patrick McCarraher about many of the issues in this book, and benefited enormously from his hard skepticism about my enthusiasms. My in-laws, Robert and Geraldine D'Alonzo, generously provided housing, child care, financial support, and patience for over a decade.

Many friends, colleagues, and mentors either discussed ideas with me or read all or part of this book as it progressed from dissertation to book. Jackson Lears, Philip Greven, John W. Chambers, and Leigh Eric Schmidt comprised a perfect dissertation committee at Rutgers, giving me just the right combination of freedom and chastisement. I also valued the support of Victoria De Grazia, David Oshinsky, and Maxine Lurie. Thanks also to fellow apprentices David Hyde, Julie Zayon, Regina Gramer, and Carol Helstosky.

At the University of Delaware, Christine Heyrman, Lawrence J. Duggan, John Bernstein, Suzanne Alchon, Carole Haber, Eric Miller, Monica Spiese, and Sara Montejo either read or listened to my musings about history, religion, and culture. At Villanova, Thomas Greene and Sally

Griffith have been faithful friends and invaluable sources of inspiration, while John Doody offered me employment in the humanities program at times when I needed it.

I also extend thanks and blessings to scholars and friends elsewhere. Patrick Allitt was so taken with my dissertation that he pitched it to Cornell and gave the penultimate manuscript an extremely fine reading. The inimitable James T. Fisher also read the manuscript with exceptional care. Casey Blake took my ideas about the therapeutic seriously enough to invite me to write for the *Intellectual History Newsletter*, a privilege for which I will always be grateful as well as the start of a friendship. In addition to offering unceasing encouragement, John T. McGreevey has been a keen, skeptical but sympathetic critic. Though far away, Catherine Tumber and Elizabeth Lasch-Quinn have been kind and challenging comrades-in-arms. Finally, Paul Baumann and Peggy Steinfels at *Commonweal* allowed a freshly minted Ph.D. to contribute to their venerable enterprise—long may it prosper.

In the Pew Program for Young Scholars in American Religion I benefited enormously from the criticism and support of Philip Gleason, Beth Schweiger, and Beth Wenger. The Cushwa Center for the Study of American Catholicism at the University of Notre Dame was a home away from home as well as a scholarly oasis; thanks there to John Haas, R. Scott Appleby, and Barbara Lockwood. The Princeton Center for the Study of American Religion gave me a forum to test my ideas about the therapeutic ethos, and I received great encouragement and searching criticism there from R. Marie Griffith, Diane Winston, and Robert Wuthnow.

At Cornell University Press, Peter Agree has been a model of editorial stringence and saintly patience, calmly explaining to me that I could forgo a lot of the adjectives I love so much. As my copyeditor, Marty Tenney of Textbook Writers Associates performed an exceptionally fine job.

Jackson Lears deserves special mention. As a mentor, he has always insisted on high literary and scholarly standards, and has never failed to provide unsparing criticism and unalloyed support. As a friend, he has always been there for me (even when he showed up late at Sneddon's) in good times and bad. May grace, luck, and fortune be his.

My daughters, Alexandra and Gabrielle, neither read this book nor debated its contents. I spent many days and nights either away from them or only physically at home, and I can only pray that some day they will read this book and decide that their father's distractions finally amounted to something. Their curiosity, vitality, and hope remind me, every day, of what it means to make all things new.

To my wife, Alecia Rose D'Alonzo, I dedicate this book. Alecia set aside her own artistic career to put me through graduate school, help raise our daughters, and persevere through the trials of tenuous employment. Though this book does not even begin to measure up to her love and endurance, it's all this rosy-eyed lover can offer.

EUGENE McCARRAHER

Ardmore, Pennsylvania

✛

CHRISTIAN CRITICS

✝

Introduction

"Another great change is at hand," wrote the architect and social critic Ralph Adams Cram near the end of World War I. Before the war, he recalled, the Western middle classes had ridden on the "chariot wheels of the new Juggernaut" of industrial capitalism. Confident of their power and merit, they had mangled the virtues of Christianity in the spokes of accumulation, national pride, and imperial grandeur. But now the Juggernaut had crashed, and Cram, pointing to the "signs and wonders" that portended a turning of the times, heralded the end of secular, capitalist modernity. If some saw the times as pregnant with secular possibilities—renewed commitment to reason and science and the fledgling socialist experiment in the Soviet Union—Cram perceived that within the secularism of modernity there lay "no powers of regeneration," and he insisted that only Christianity could identify and transform the prospects of the future. The wellsprings of renewal in modern civilization lay in whatever remained of Christianity: that "spirit of real communism" (one very different, Cram noted, from "the bastard thing that now bears the name") that fostered a "brilliant development of personality." Men and women would produce "a new prophet, son of Saint Benedict"—garbed, he cautioned, "in a new habit" and beholden to "an amended rule"—and release modernity from secular captivity, breaking shackles with Christ to make "all things new."[1]

The desire to make all things new compelled a number of Christian intellectuals to create a body of theological reflection on capitalist modernity in the United States. For many liberal Protestants and Roman Catholics, theology became neither a hoary liberal art nor a recondite conviction, but rather a mode of critical attention to political economy,

1

social relations, cultural life, work, and technology. This book traces these intertwined lineages in the modern American moral imagination. It offers a historical interpretation of Christian social thought and cultural criticism that sheds light not only on the course of religion but also on the vicissitudes of selfhood, intellectual life, and progressive thought in modern America.

The dramatis personae of this study turned to theology not as a supplement to secularized forms of critical reflection but as the language of a distinctly Christian social and cultural criticism. Seeking to position the expertise of social scientists in a religious framework, they recovered traditions of social thought grounded in Protestant republicanism and Catholic medievalism. Addressing the quandaries of selfhood in modern culture, they contended that the only reliable therapy lay in the liberating disciplines of a beloved community devoted to God. They identified the church as the home of genuine radicalism and the virtues of faith, hope, and charity as the lineaments of a redemptive political identity. They believed that social and cultural revolution would come not from the dialectic of class struggle or the ingenuity of social engineers but from the therapeutic political practice of Christianity.

Yet many of these figures were cultural workers in the professional-managerial bloc spawned in the rise of corporate capitalism. While they upheld religious community as the model of a redeemed modernity, they also provided ambiguous but legible seals of legitimation for the corporate order. While they challenged the social sciences on behalf of a distinctly Christian social tradition, the deference they enjoined to the sociological tradition rendered theology an eloquent but disabled alternative and served to separate the religious intelligensia from any popular roots. When they separated the therapy of religious faith from participation in religious community, they sanctioned the cultural power of psychologists, psychiatrists, and other secular doctors of the soul.

The "new class," "knowledge class," or "cultural apparatus" that occupies crucial terrain within the professional-managerial world provides an important backdrop for this story. Encompassing a broad spectrum of occupations ranging from corporate executives to doctors, professors, advertisers, engineers, and lawyers and possessing a cultural capital that ranges from technical expertise to skills in the arts, humanities, and sciences, the professional middle class has perceived itself not only as a mediator between capital and labor but also as an explorer of the human prospect. As specialists in the creation of ideas, symbols, and knowledge, intellectuals in the cultural apparatus have continually drawn, erased, and redrawn the conceptual and imaginative boundaries of American culture, particularly its notions of identity, truth, and morality. Indeed, the control of intellectuals over the means of cultural production warrants bestowing on them the title of a new clerisy, one with "secular vocations" analogous to those of an older clerisy beholden to religious traditions.[2]

In their effort to make all things new in Christ, my subjects—who wore the modern mantles of this older religious clerisy—engaged their secular rivals in a prolonged and contentious relationship that produced much of the evolving critical universe of twentieth-century America. It is wrong, I think, to see the history of Christian social thought as a record of obscurity and failure. In contrast to the declensionary narratives recounted by intellectuals (religious and secular), I maintain that the history of the American "progressive" or "left" tradition offers copious, brilliant, and compelling evidence of the persistence of religion and theology as modes of moral and political discussion. The progressive tradition has been marked indelibly by religious ideas and movements, and many "secular" intellectuals, from John Dewey to Michael Harrington, have felt obliged to define the American left in some relationship to the "religious." And while the religious is largely, I will suggest, a reified form of religion, the more conventionally committed intellectuals I study posed worthy critiques of both the secular left and corporate capitalism. If only because religion has contained the most exalted vision of human possibility, the study of theology is indispensable to the cultural and intellectual history of modern America.

In recovering theology for historians, I hope to enter and possibly reformulate several interrelated debates. Impatient with the impasse reached in the conflict between modern and antimodern, between partisans and critics of progress, I hope to strike out in a new direction by envisioning tradition, and Christian tradition in particular, as an unfinished, creative, and animated historical conversation. As Alasdair MacIntyre asserts, a tradition is not a monolithic burden passed on by successive generations but rather an only partially entailed inheritance, a "historically extended, socially embodied argument," an argument "in part about the goods which constitute that tradition" and in part about the "future possibilities which the past has made available to the present."[3] Emphasizing versatility and contingency, MacIntyre underscores the intellectual and moral fecundity of a robust tradition.

At the same time, I hope to establish the existence in twentieth-century America of a critical, progressive lineage rooted firmly in Christian theology and to locate it in relation to the broader history of progressive public intellectuals. Up to now, historians have honored secular pedigrees of dissent in this century, erecting a pantheon whose niches contain an almost exclusively secular statuary: the "Young Americans," the "New York intellectuals," academic or journalistic observers of corporate life, and a corps of independent radicals.[4] Given the contemporary state of progressive thought and politics, perhaps the time has arrived to carve out new and more prominent spaces for religious witnesses of American culture and society.

The last decade has in fact witnessed a refurbishment of this American critical pantheon. Turning to the pragmatist tradition of William James and John Dewey, several historians have attempted to revive its affirmation of experience over dogma, its sense of unbounded potential, its confidence in the promise of democracy.[5] My subjects constituted a pragmatist tradition of sorts. They did not repudiate science; rather, they warned that reliance on the optics of science provides only a restricted view of available forces and future development. Christian theology, in their view, discerned a wider field of available historical forces— namely, the practical political virtues of faith, hope, and love—and thus envisioned a broader range of historical possibilities. They suggested that bereft of the optical principles provided by theology, pragmatism could circumscribe rather than enlarge our democratic vistas.

While some scholars find the redemption of democracy in pragmatism, others have discovered it in populism or "communitarianism." Against the expertise of cosmopolitan, secularized professionals, they uphold a wisdom anchored in proprietorship, obligations to family and locality, protocols of civility, and religion.[6] Yet, even when, as in the work of Christopher Lasch, religious faith is taken with great seriousness and respect, the "religion" invoked is an altogether nebulous and generic affair. While it may be true, as Lasch asserted, that religion teaches the limitations of human striving, our dependence on forces outside our control, and our need for humility in our assertions of knowledge and virtue, many a "secular humanist" could agree without feeling any need to consider such notions as pearls of revealed wisdom. Moreover, while laudably eager to remind the left of the moral standards and insights that religious Americans could bring to cultural and political debate, partisans of "the people" or "community" forget that religion also can stand against the idols of family, country, community, and common sense so frequently venerated by populists and communitarians.

Others beckon toward the realms of craftsmanship and art. In Casey Nelson Blake's view, the "Young Americans' " artisanal critique of industrial capitalism heralded a rebirth of democracy through the remarriage of work and art in daily life. Yet Blake also recognizes an important religious dimension to this artisanal critique. Not only does Blake demonstrate that Lewis Mumford in particular drew on religious conceptions of work and community, but he also concludes that the artisanal critique proved abortive in part because, as in the case of Van Wyck Brooks, the Young Americans often proved "too modern to appreciate the persistence of republican and biblical traditions of politics and culture." For his part, Jackson Lears invites us to embark on an even more expansive enterprise: the reenchantment of the human and material worlds through art, play, and recovery of the "carnivalesque" imagination from its impressment in the service of corporate advertising. From early practitioners of magic and the occult, through evangelical Protestants, down to modernist writers and artists, Americans have always harbored a desire to avert the spiritual death of commodity culture through a "transfiguration of the commonplace," the creation of a playful connection between human beings and the rest of the material world.[7]

Still, "Young Americans" and modernist *bricoleurs* sparked no enduring projects of social and cultural politics, remaining lone critics with only the most tenuous connections to broader popular movements. If, as Leon Fink has argued, the central "dilemma of democratic commitment" on the part of progressive intellectuals has been their social and psychic alienation from a wider public,[8] then the historical inadequacy of the aesthetic-artisanal critique resides not in any poignant restatement of possessive individualism but in the lack of a clear and invigorating connection to people and movements outside the epiphanies of intellectuals and artists.

The Christian intellectuals in this book believed—often self-deceptively—that their fellowship in religious communities offered them a uniquely auspicious opportunity to cross the chasm between intellectuals and other people. Certainly not all shared this conviction. Reinhold Niebuhr—perhaps the most venerated religious star in the American progressive firmament—will emerge from these pages as an unhappily but unmistakably elitist public intellectual. Yet others—Walter Rauschenbusch, Vida Dutton Scudder, H. Richard Niebuhr, Dorothy Day—will step forth as acolytes of a more democratic style of religious criticism.

They insisted on popular and religious moorings for progressive politics because they adhered to a particular therapeutic ethic, a project of moral selfhood that fused personal felicity and social justice. By examining the concept of personality in Christian social thought, I hope to recast the history of "the therapeutic" in modern American culture. Relying on the work of Philip Rieff, I contend that the "triumph of the therapeutic" has consisted not of a straightforward shift from religion to therapy but of a triune metamorphosis of religious therapeutics into what Rieff calls the "purely therapeutic"—a redefinition of therapy and personality from moral and religious to psychic and secular terms, a transferal of therapeutic powers from religious authorities to secular experts, and an uncoupling of personal therapy from aspiration toward a broader collective destiny. In religious terms, personality denoted the human glory of likeness unto God, whereas therapy meant the transformation of desire in accordance with a community directed toward the "otherworldly"—a radically different world anticipated through practice in this one. In secular, "purely therapeutic" terms, personality marks the varieties of desire and facade, whereas therapy entails evasion of moral commitment—an evasion enabled by a market society that registers rather than transforms desire—and a simultaneous indenture to professional expertise and cultural fashion. Because the purely therapeutic partakes of what Jean-Christophe Agnew has called "the consuming vision"—a "cognitive appetite" aroused by the commodity form that tears objects "from their conventional associations and contexts and accumulate[s] them as resources, as capital"—I argue that the detachment of therapy from the concrete practices of religion produces not just psychological expertise but a "commodity spirituality," a mix-and-match collage of beliefs appropriated from various sources that is the signature religious consciousness of consumer society, the contemplative mysticism of commodity culture.[9]

"There are days at the end of winter when the increasing brightness of the sun does not so much promise the coming of spring as reveal the shabbiness and uncleanness of the wintry scene," H. Richard Niebuhr wrote in the middle of the World War II. "Our day in history is something like that. Reflection and feeling apprehend the morbidity of secular civilization, but the promise of newness of life they do not discern."[10] While pronouncements of the end time are almost certain to be premature, I offer this book as a gift to the parties of hope and memory. Surely, at the turn of both a century and a millennium, the markets in hindsights and portents promise to be brisk, voluminous, and grossly overvalued. Yet, if, in the wake of a secular radicalism spectered by socialist failure, splintered by identity politics, and overwhelmed by a brawny and agile capitalism, religion may well become the last refuge of hope for a world beyond the rule of Mammon, we will need to retrace the wellsprings of the Christian critical tradition and find our way to a fervent, sophisticated, and imaginative restatement of redemptive hope. Seeing through the eyes of this communion of critics, we may find that redemption was always the secret name of our desire.

CHAPTER ONE

"This Day Is the Scripture Fulfilled":

Liberal Protestantism, Roman Catholicism, and the Social Gospel of the Professional-Managerial Class, 1900–1919

"This day is the Scripture fulfilled." With a thunderous flourish redolent of Isaiah, Methodist minister Frank Mason North concluded his report titled "The Church and Modern Industry" to the Federal Council of Churches on December 5, 1908. Assembled in Philadelphia, the spellbound men of the cloth broke into loud, sustained applause. Revised and adopted as "The Social Creed of the Churches," the document presented the broadest and most ambitious program of social reform ever envisioned by American Protestants: collective bargaining, social insurance, and shorter hours to release workers from "continuous, demoralizing toil." Indeed, the Council believed that if modern industry were brought under the "final authority" of Jesus Christ, it might ameliorate and even annul the ancient curses on Adam and Eve, creating for future generations a land abundant in milk and honey for "the highest human life."[1]

The Council's creed convened a host of Protestant social energies scattered for over a decade, energies no less powerful and dispersed among their Roman Catholic brethren. Two years before the Council met, Monsignor John Ryan, professor at Catholic University in Washington, D.C., argued on scriptural and scholastic grounds for a "living wage," social welfare provision, and government regulation of corporations. Protégé of John Ireland, bishop of St. Paul, who had urged Catholics to "seek out social evils, and lead in the movements that tend to rectify them," Ryan quickly became the knight of faith for a generation of clerics eager to take up arms against a legion of industrial troubles. Like the Protestant prophets, Ryan believed that a Christian reconstruction of modern industry promised not only justice but also the more abundant life, the opportunity to "pursue perfection through the harmonious development of all faculties."[2]

The crusaders ventured into battle with a new and portentous conception of God's authority and its derogation in the modern world. The conditions demanded in the social creed required arbitration, education, sanitation, and technological innovation—all, increasingly, domains of trained professionals whose expertise the ministers considered a modern vehicle of charity. Ryan, while framing his demands in the language of natural law, relied on the data of the social sciences, offering precisely the "scientific statement of their faith" for which many educated Catholics had longed for more than a generation. His mentor, Ireland, had predicted that modern Catholicism would christen technology and expertise as the modern vessels of Providence. If "old-fashioned, easygoing methods mean defeat," in Ireland's view, then "steam and electricity in religion cooperating with divine grace will triumph."[3] For Catholics and Protestants, the authority of God in modernity inhered in slide rules and thermometers, clipboards and blueprints, professional associations and fields of expertise, as well as in the Bible or the *summas* of the Middle Ages.

Still, the new America that beckoned at the turn of the century posed enormous, if not insurmountable, challenges to the modern apostles. Like other Progressives, liberal Protestant and Catholic social gospelers faced a hostile, suspicious, or indifferent working class, as well as businessmen and professionals firmly entrenched, by and large, against the social witness. At the same time, the forces of science, technology, and urbanization that social gospelers celebrated were generating ideals of truth, identity, and virtue potentially or substantially at odds with older verities. These social and cultural crises raised an explosive issue for social gospelers: the meaning and agency of the church, the community of Christian believers. Would the church or some other body officiate at the baptism of American modernity?

The first generation of Christian social intellectuals wrestled with dilemmas that would reverberate down through the twentieth century. Liberal Protestant social gospelers—parties to a broader Protestant covenant with the nation's traditional and emerging elites—along with "Americanist" Roman Catholics—parties to a Catholic concordat with the dominant culture—heralded an American Christian modernity they believed to be gestating in the womb of corporate capitalism. Champions of a prodigal but still redeemable working class, the modern prophets also were evangels of an aborning corporate order and shared with other Progressives a commitment to harnessing the social and technological possibilities residing in the expertise of the professional-managerial class. Yet, more so than other Progressives, the social apostles displayed a deeply conflicted cultural and political identity. Tying the social gospel to the emerging communities of technical, managerial, and cultural expertise, liberal Protestants and Catholics also looked to the churches as salient if not primary sites of social and cultural transformation. They insisted that the new conditions of personal and social identity—the implements of the new "social selfhood" emerging from the crucible of the corporate order—required the scrutiny and sanctification of religion so as to be liberating rather than beguiling. Eager to avoid elitist schemes of social reform, they measured and labored to bridge the chasm opening between intellectuals and other Americans.

While many Progressives exhibited a vaguely "religious" consciousness of their situation and task, the divergent trajectories of Progressive thought had their origins in the various meanings of "religion." Informed by an ideology of "religion," liberal Protestant social gospelers and their imperfectly secularized Progressive brethren turned toward the professional middle class as the vanguard of social progress. Under a vaulted arch of modern medievalism, Americanist Roman Catholics articulated a medievalist Progressivism that, while serving to assimilate Catholics into the corporate order, also pointed toward a decentralized industrial democracy that better fused mental and manual labor, personal and social regeneration, religion and political identity.

COVENANT: LIBERAL PROTESTANTISM, RELIGION, AND THE SOCIAL GOSPEL OF THE PROFESSIONAL-MANAGERIAL CLASS

If the United States at the beginning of the twentieth century was, as G. K. Chesterton wrote, "a nation with the soul of a church," it had been christened mainly in the waters of evangelical Protestantism. Defined by their tenets of biblical authority and personal conversion by the Holy Spirit, evangelicals stressed the utility of Christian faith in procuring the fruits of republican virtue, political democracy, and market competition. Until well after the Civil War, the nation's political culture and cultural politics formed an evangelical dispensation that sanctified proprietary capitalism, buttressed male supremacy while sparking women's resistance, fueled reform movements from temperance to abolition, suffused the major newspapers and magazines, permeated education from the common schools to the universities, sponsored and mediated American science, and inflected the rhetoric of industrialists, advertisers, Knights of Labor, and Populists. When articulated by the northeastern middle classes who dominated the nation's politics and culture, the evangelical dispensation became what Henry F. May has called "progressive patriotic Protestantism," a vision of America as the redeemer of civilization.[4]

Emerging from this forward-looking evangelical order, liberal Protestantism had, by 1900, supplanted its ancestor as a lingua franca for the nation's postbellum Protestant establishment, a covenant theology for the vanguard of modern, industrial America. Crowned by a network of personal and institutional relationships that linked the nation's business, political, and cultural elite, the Protestant establishment included capitalists, politicians, professionals, managers, intellectuals, and social reformers. Its clerisy—an increasing number of whom were social gospelers—clarified the ways of God to humanity from the lecterns and pulpits of Harvard, Yale, Chicago, and Rochester Divinity Schools, as well as Andover and Union Theological Seminaries. While this edifice of Protestant power contained stresses and conflicts that belied its monolithic white exterior, it remained united by its evangelical devotion to a Christian America and its commitment to a liberal, even "modernist" religion as the new ark of the evangelical covenant.[5]

Until quite recently, historians have obscured this intimate connection between liberal and evangelical Protestantism, making the point of rupture harder to identify and understand. Liberal Protestant theologians—whose differences with "conservatives" did not become pronounced or acrimonious until the eve of World War I—clearly approved a greater latitude of biblical interpretation, altered or abandoned selected orthodoxies, and incorporated modern intellectual equipment (most notably evolutionary biology and the "higher criticism" of the Bible) into their scholarship. The bone of greatest contention was not over science or the Bible but over the authority given to secularized scientific disciplines. While evangelicals had enthusiastically supported science and even pioneered in the release of scientific investigation from overt religious prescription—that is, in its secularization—liberals extended this quest to a point where evangelicals could not follow: the complete secularization and professionalization of the sciences and humanities. Preaching what David Hollinger has dubbed an "intellectual gospel" that ascribed salvific significance to scientific labor and professional knowledge, liberals sanctioned a cognitive and social bifurcation of "ideals" and "facts" in which the former were assigned (with decreasing warrant) to theologians and ministers, while the latter became the bailiwick of the growing postbellum academic and professional intelligentsia. Thus, in the still strongly religious universities that were the main stations of expert training at the beginning of the twentieth century, the secular vocations of the new professional-managerial class received their baptism in the font of liberal Protestantism.[6] Sanctifying the arrogation by accredited experts of technical skills and cultural authority possessed by artisans and ministers in the evangelical dispensation, the liberal Protestant covenant was a cornerstone in the corporate reconstruction of American capitalism.

Trained and employed in seminaries, colleges, universities, and church bureaucracies, liberal Protestant intellectuals—and social gospelers in particular—constituted a clerical arm of this professional-managerial class. Yet the value of their cultural capital was being reassessed in the new and wider market of knowledge called into being by corporate capitalism. Their cultural dislocation was bound up with the formation of the modern U.S. intellectual stratum, a development that marked, as James Livingston has written, the resolution of a "vocational crisis" among gifted but disaffected young people whose ambiguous social roles sensitized them to "the possibilities residing in both the disintegrating past and the impending future." Progressivism emerged from this vortex, this movement of what Robert Crunden has called "innovative nostalgia" through which Progressive intellectuals sought to recreate the ambience of the evangelical, republican dispensation on new foundations. As Progressives, social gospelers sought to reconstruct liberal Protestant cultural authority in the midst of this fluid, open-ended moment. Indeed, their "religious" grasp of the signs of the times can shed light not only on the history of the social gospel but also on the subsequent course of the "progressive" or "liberal" tradition. What difference did religion make in the development of Progressivism, and particularly of the social gospel? What did liberal Protestants and other Progressives mean by "religion"? What hath John Dewey to do with Walter Rauschenbusch?[7] Progressive social and cultural criticism points to religion and theology as determinative forces in the intellectual life of modern America.

Progressive intellectuals recognized that the crisis they sensed at the beginning of the twentieth century was at once social and religious—the unraveling of a "pattern of evasive banality," as Jackson Lears has described it, that both camouflaged business avarice and warded off the fears provoked by science and secularization. "The great industrial forces, the aggregations of capital, the combinations of enormous physical power" afforded undeniable progress, Josiah Royce reflected in 1908, but also deprived us of "formerly accessible opportunities for loyalty." When Royce looked skyward, he saw the firmament veiled by the vapors of prosperity. "The smoke of our civilization hides the very heavens that used to be so near, and the stars to which we were once loyal." Walter Lippmann surmised in *Drift and Mastery* (1914) that without a "Rock of Ages . . . all of us are immigrants spiritually" with "no authority to lean on." Randolph Bourne—who as a student in his Bloomfield, New Jersey, Bible class had argued for socialism as "applied Christianity"—captured best the religious longing that could fuse the antimodern spirit and Progressive social politics. Liberal Protestantism, he complained in "This Older Generation" (1915), was a religion "as pleasant and easy as could be devised," full of "pious exhortations to good conduct" but bereft of the fire and brimstone, the sensuality, the clarifying fervor of religious passion in which the "heated weapons" of social reform must be forged. Progressives, he warned, must not discard the religious inheritance of the West. "In spite of its scientific clamor," Bourne opined, the modern world was "far from ready to surrender itself to prosaicness." Still "haunted with the dreams of the ages," modern America needed to clear the smoke and study the heavens again.[8]

Liberal Protestants inspected the heavens and the earth and discovered religion everywhere. To them, "religion" was not a private sanctum but the plenitude of experience and ideals, an ever-widening search for the hand of God in the midst of the world. "No wall of partition separates religious values from other values, religious experience from other experience," the renowned Union educator George C. Coe asserted in 1909. "Human consciousness as such is religious consciousness." Since liberals stressed the experiential and ethical dimensions of human life, religion became almost entirely an effort to bring reality into harmony with the ideal. As Coe's Union colleague Eugene Lyman explained, religion lay precisely in "the underlying relations between reality and value." The key fundamental of liberal theology was not its erasure of the line between sacred and secular but its effacement of Christian particularity, its reformulation of "religion" as a realm of universal sentiments and ideals. As the theologian George Lindbeck writes, liberal Protestantism exhibited an "experiential-expressive" conception of religion as a domain of feelings and aspirations, not a particular historical community with "distinctive patterns of story, ritual, belief, and behavior."[9] Although social gospelers enlisted this ever-more amorphous religiosity in the cause of social reform, it gradually would erode the theological foundations of the Protestant social witness.

For liberal Protestant social gospelers and unchurched Progressives, the social nature of "religion" became incarnate in one of the most hallowed ideals of social criticism: *personality*. Personality carried the hope treasures of many Progressives at the beginning of the century. One of the central terms in the lexicon of the liberal Protestant social gospel, "personality" denoted the highest achievement of humanity: sensitivity of feeling, rationality of judgment, and capacity for spiritual insight, all nurtured in a supportive communal setting. The therapeutic ideal of the social gospel was at once moral, physical, psychological, and religious, and its therapeutic ethic fused devotion to God and the reconstruction of society. According to Frances Willard, the Women's Christian Temperance Union was an exponent of "a religion of the body" that incarnated "Christ's wholesome, practical, blessed religion of the soul." Personality, Grinnell College's George D. Herron wrote, embodied " . . . the holiness of God . . . [and] the perfect moral, mental, and physical wholeness of man." Indeed, the cultivation of personality was a project of "sanctification," Rauschenbusch claimed in *A Theology for the Social Gospel* (1917), a process of "spiritual education and transformation" by which an individual or a society became "a willing organ of the spirit of Christ." Rauschenbusch insisted on the irreducibly religious foundations of personality—"our human personalities may seem distinct, but their roots run down into the eternal life of God"—and deemed the emancipation of personality the *summum bonum* of all religious striving, the touchstone of all Christian criticism and political struggle. Moreover, Rauschenbusch argued, the creation of personality was "bound up with the Kingdom hope," the other prominent social gospel ideal. For the Kingdom, Rauschenbusch declared, would be "a social order which will guarantee to all personalities their freest and highest development."[10] Beholden to a conception of human personality as the image and likeness of God, social gospelers envisioned an indissoluble marriage of therapy and religion, personal fulfillment and social justice.

The social gospel rhetoric of "personality" and "the Kingdom" had secular counterparts among unchurched Progressives. Just as Progressive hopes for a new "social selfhood" arising from the interdependence fostered by corporate capitalism partook of the liberal Protestant ideal of moral personality, so Progressive religiosity formed a new rhetoric of community, a new sacral order for a consolidated, professionalized democracy. When Royce beckoned in *The Problem of Christianity* (1913) toward the "Universal" or "Beloved Community" that would mark the consummation of Progressive reform, or when Bourne in "Trans-National America" (1915) declared as the goal of multicultural, cosmopolitan democracy "the good life of personality lived in the Beloved Community," they echoed the liberal Protestant social gospel. When Jane Addams urged social settlement workers in *Democracy and Social Ethics* (1902) to "love mercy," "do justly," and "walk humbly with God," she made clear that the Christian spirit lay not in the manger of organized religion but in a recognition of mutuality that sought "simple and natural expression in the social organism." Lippmann vouchsafed that science and reform would provide a sense of "modern communion," recover "the old sense of cosmic wonder," and kindle a "luminous passion" to make the human condition more gentle and beautiful. The immediate locus of this communion was the democratic nation-state. Herbert Croly—founder of the *New Republic* and a lifelong dabbler in religious enthusiasms—concluded *Progressive Democracy* (1914) with the exalted peroration that democracy, "like the faith of St. Paul, finds its consummation in a love which . . . [is] a spiritual expression of the mystical unity of human nature." Royce's "religion of loyalty" epitomized the benevolent nationalism that issued from Progressive religiosity. The "religion of loyalty"—the fulfillment of the individual self through devotion to a community—mandated a "wise provincialism," a salvific dedication to the Progressive reconstruction of America into a Beloved Community.[11]

Thus Progressive religiosity—a mutation of liberal Protestant religion—ratified the cultural power of the professional and managerial elite. Under this Progressive aegis of religion, the "intellectual gospel" baptized by liberal theology slowly degraded the authority of the Protestant intelligentsia and promoted a secular mode of legitimacy for the professional-managerial class. "Whatever may hereafter be the futures of Christian institutions, or of Christian traditions," Royce conjectured in *The Problem of Christianity,* the religion of loyalty was the vehicle of beloved modernity. And this emerging "Beloved Community," he noted happily, now employed in the social and psychological sciences "methods distinctly analogous to the methods that now prevail in the sciences of nature." Science thereby functioned as "one of the principal organs of religion." Although later admirers of Royce have identified his "religion of loyalty" as an antidote to the rootlessness and utilitarianism fostered by cosmopolitan modernity, it bathed specific religious ties in a solvent of religiosity.[12]

By the same token, pragmatism, the singular philosophical achievement of Progressive intellectuals, thrived on a religious residue, diluted and filtered by a new clerisy of professioanls. As William James's work on religion made clear, Dewey's assertion that democracy was the modern "means by which the revelation of truth is carried on" rested on two foundations: a purely interiorized conception of "religion" and a set of criteria for the assessment of "revelation" that were insulated from specific religions. The radical subjectivity of James's definition of religion in *The Varieties of Religious Experience* (1902)—"the feelings, acts, and experiences of individual men in their solitude . . . in relation to whatever they may consider the divine"—detached religious experience from its social context, delivered it to secular professional surveillance, and transmuted its therapeutic significance. Convinced that philosophy (itself an increasingly professionalized discipline) could broker a "consensus of opinion" among religious adherents by distilling "the common and essential from the individual and local elements of religious beliefs," James in effect invested academic experts like himself as a new clerisy. Indeed, theology, in his view, would have to evolve from the expression of a particular tradition to a generalized "science of religions." James's conversion of religion from a code or community into a "will to believe" heralded a shift from theology to psychology as the key therapeutic arbiter of moral selfhood. If, as he contended, "the process of remedying inner incompleteness and reducing inner discord" was "a general psychological process which may take place with any sort of mental material, and need not necessarily assume the religious form," then religious therapy was both unessential and subordinate to other, secular moral projects. "Whether God exist, or whether God not exist . . . we form at any rate an ethical republic here below," as James wrote in *The Will to Believe* (1897)—the "rate," however, being precisely the point at issue for religion. Under the pragmatist aegis, religion—or more precisely, "which type of religion is going to work best in the long run," as James put it in *Pragmatism* (1907)—gained access to the public realm only as a privatized, denatured, purely therapeutic mode of moral discourse, and depended purely on its ministration to secularized modes of psychological and social utility.[13] Pragmatism offered the new stratum of intellectuals a claim to cultural authority borrowed from traditional religion.

Yet the promise of pragmatism as a form of moral deliberation was challenged by none other than Bourne, a former student of Dewey's at Columbia, whose wartime critique of his mentor in "Twilight of Idols" (1917) reads like a bull of apostasy, the outraged theses of a believer discovering that his church is not the rock of ages. Bourne studded the essay with religious phraseology, from his Nietzschean title to his account of "the pragmatic dispensation" in which his generation of intellectuals had been immersed. To some of those like himself "who have taken Dewey's philosophy almost as our American religion," Dewey's support for the war, as well as the facility with which "a younger intelligentsia" had undertaken its prosecution, had exposed the nihilism at the core of the pragmatic dispensation. Not only did pragmatism buckle when faced with the unruly passions of avarice and bloodlust; it lacked, in Bourne's view, a conception of ends that made moral or even logical sense of practicality. Although Dewey meant to "start with values," there was always, Bourne wrote mordantly, "that unhappy ambiguity" as to "just how values were created." Still, despite the title, Bourne forsook only one idol, invoking James as the founding and now redeeming spirit of pragmatism. James's exuberant embrace of the unfinished and the indeterminate appealed to Bourne both as the sort of value-creating "poetic vision" absent from Dewey and as the model of the "malcontent-edness" he considered the indispensable critical stance for Progressives.[14] Yet Bourne could not explain how aesthetic epiphany or irreverence, bereft of roots in an ideal, would prove any more creative of values than instrumentalism.

From where, then, would come what Bourne called "the allure of fresh and true ideas" that wedded values and technique? Alienated from his Bloomfield roots, Bourne never considered the liberal Protestant social gospel as the bearer of a new "dispensation" that fused social intelligence and spiritual ideals. The liberal religious covenant chartered American social science as a Protestant form of social criticism, a mode of prophetic declamation. To many among the first generation of social scientists, their disciplines were branches of Protestant moral theology. As Richard T. Ely, doyen of liberal Protestant economists, put it in 1889, the love commandment, "when elaborated, becomes social science or sociology." Much early U.S. social science was housed not only in the new departments of secular universities but also in liberal Protestant seminaries. Courses in "Christian sociology," "ecclesiastical sociology," and "applied theology" abounded in liberal seminaries by 1900, indelibly impressing on fledgling clergy the image of social science as a modern vehicle of personality. Rauschenbusch expressed buoyant confidence in the amalgamation of Protestantism and social science. Convinced that the social sciences "confirm[ed]" Christ's "social egalitarianism," Rauschenbusch harbored few doubts that the direction of "religious energy by scientific knowledge" promised "a comprehensive reconstruction of social life in the name of God."[15]

Rauschenbusch's clear but increasingly tenuous assumption that theology would position and guide professional expertise pointed to the role of the church in liberal Protestant social thought. Social gospelers assigned to the church a salient role in the social witness, and ecclesiology—reflection on the nature and structure of the church—assumed a prominent place in their work. Willard mingled arguments for temperance with challenges to secularization, asserting that the "correlation of New Testament religion with civilization, and of the church with civilization, furnishes the only sufficient antidote to current skepticism." Since the church was "the chief of the social forces in this country," Ely claimed that reformers could "by no possibility be without her assistance." W. D. P. Bliss, Christian Socialist and editor of the *Dawn*, dubbed the church "the social base of Christian Sociology." Reverdy Ransom, cofounder of the National Association for the Advancement of Colored People and a leader in the settlement movement, considered the church "the mother institution" of the small but zealous racial cohort of the social gospel. Because the early Christian church was, in his view, the prototype of a racially integrated socialist order, black preacher George Woodbey, author of "The Bible and Socialism" (1904), one of the most popular social gospel pamphlets, reasoned that convincing the churches would be "the greatest step yet made in the cause of socialism."[16]

The most theoretically astute and politically sensitive social gospelers remained ambivalent about the relations between social science and theology, professional communities and the churches, intellectuals and people. As American social science in the manner of Ely evolved, in the university departments and professional associations, from prophetic witness to policy expertise, social gospelers such as Herron and Rauschenbusch strove to embody religious criticism in a popular democratic politics. "The new civilization will not be the creation of the merely intellectual forces at work upon a science of social origins, phenomena, and diseases," Herron warned Protestant *enrages* in 1896. It would flower as "the political outgrowth of a religious evolution of the common life." Herron chastised university and seminary reformers for routinely dismissing "the social value and creative power of the more common feeling of the people after justice." In a "rude mining town" or one of the "mortgaged farms of the Dakotas," prophets could divine the "natural and untutored sense of divine justice" unavailable in courses on "ecclesiastical or social science." Herron's romantic populism suggests that the social gospel, while fostering the legitimacy of experts, also represented a religious solution to the problem of building a popular democratic left that united progressive intellectuals and the rest of the people. If unchurched intellectuals lacked, in Leon Fink's words, any "obvious or enduring vehicle that would translate progressive ideas into progressive measures," social gospelers aspired to bestow that historical agency on the church.[17] The basis for a beloved democratic modernity lay, they believed, in Christianity as a political identity and in the church as a political community.

As a small but highly visible and prolific phalanx of ministers, professors, journalists, and reformers, social gospelers were well situated to bear the ark of the covenant. They occupied key positions in the leading liberal seminaries and in denominational social service departments. They created numerous "Christian Socialist" groups—the Christian Social Union, the Church Association for the Advancement of the Interests of Labor, the Church Socialist League, and the Church League for Industrial Democracy—and joined secular political organizations ranging from the Socialist Party to the Women's Trade Union League. They headed scores of "people's churches," "labor churches," and "labor temples" and spearheaded the settlement and "institutional church" movements that combined traditional charity work with education and political agitation. From the editorial offices of the *Christian Socialist, Christian Advocate, Zion's Herald, The Dawn, Church Review,* and eventually *Christian Century,* the social gospel entered the homes of thousands of ministers and laity. In a torrent of letters, speeches, books, and movements, Protestant social gospelers made the most democratic promise of Progressivism: the union of pulpit and pew in a pentecost of social redemption. While Rauschenbusch surely exaggerated the social passion's pervasiveness when he claimed that "the social gospel has become orthodox," it had certainly become inescapable.[18]

Of all social gospelers, Rauschenbusch theorized this religious politics with the greatest passion, sophistication, and wealth of experience, having gone from ministerial work in New York's Hell's Kitchen to academic life at Rochester. The church, Rauschenbusch stated in *Theology for the Social Gospel,* was "the social factor in salvation," possessing a "composite personality" replete with "a collective memory stored with great hymns and Bible stories and deeds of heroism, with trained aesthetic and moral feelings, and with a collective will set on righteousness." Yet such broad and exquisite sensitivity to sin and injustice developed, he maintained, only as churches attended closely to their own internal cohesion and vitality. "The church in maintaining its own life is the nursery of Christian revolutionists," he wrote in *The Righteousness of the Kingdom,* an early, posthumously published rumination on the social gospel. Impressed by the disciplined solidarity of the Jesuits and the Salvation Army, Rauschenbusch insisted that by setting exacting standards of study, conduct, and observance for their members, churches became beacons shining light toward a new social order, radiating "that revolutionary influence which consecrated men exercise upon the world."[19] The church, then, was the material force linking spiritual reality and political action, the nexus of charity and history.

Intellectuals played a leading but not mandarin role in Rauschenbusch's strategy of social and cultural politics. Respectful but wary of academic reformers, Rauschenbusch prevailed on a new generation of Protestant intellectuals to acquire the erudition and sympathy necessary for a revolutionary religious intelligentsia. "A compelling evangel for the working class," he asserted in a 1904 call for "a new evangelism," would arise only from those "who love that class, share its life, understand the ideals for which it is grasping, penetrate those ideals with the religious spirit of Christianity, and proclaim a message in which the working people will find their highest self." Noting that the early churches—"democratic organizations of plain people"—had "no official clergy distinct from laity," he warned young Protestants to avoid making theology into "an affair of experts" as their ancient forebears had with the *coup d'eglise* of the Roman upper classes. Indelibly marked by his youthful pastorate in New York's Hell's Kitchen, Rauschenbusch himself tried to close his own distance from the subaltern, lecturing frequently both in churches across the country and at the "People's Sunday Evenings" sponsored by Rochester's Protestant churches. In 1910, he published *For God and the People: Prayers of the Social Awakening*, a book of common prayer for the social gospel that contained numerous vignettes-cum-supplications for industrial workers, artists, musicians, and "women who toil."[20] Rauschenbusch labored for a democratic, religious left, a union of progressive intellectuals and people accomplished under the sign of the cross.

The "Kingdom of personality" hastened by this awakening would recover what Rauschenbusch called "primitive communism" on a higher material and spiritual plane. "The city water-works," he mused in *Christianity and the Social Crisis* (1912), "are the modern counterpart of the communistic village well to which Rebekah and Rachel came to fill their water jar." Rauschenbusch beheld in the rise of corporate capitalism a new therapeutic opportunity, an auspicious episode in the history of moral selfhood, a moral economy with more generous prospects than those entertained in the proprietary, evangelical dispensation. "The evolution of a cooperative economic organization as wide as society," he declared in *Christianizing the Social Order* (1907), was laying the foundation for "the miraculous power of human personality." Yet social gospelers could not, as secular radicals did, limit themselves to possibilities imagined from within the bounds of capitalism. Rauschenbusch never wavered in the belief that Christianity was fundamental to the left. Secular socialism, he argued in the *Christian Socialist* in 1914, was "raw and undeveloped socialism" that had "angrily flung aside some of the most precious possessions of humanity." Only an awakened church composed of workers, farmers, and their bourgeois allies could discern the situation and possibility of the corporate moment. Through the agency of the church, the leaven of love became a "spiritual power along the existing and natural relations of men," a practical virtue bestowed "to direct them to truer ends and govern them by higher motives."[21]

However, Rauschenbusch undercut the democratic potential of Protestant Progressivism to the extent that he bound its energies to professional expertise. If there had been no institution like the Christian church, he argued in *Theology for the Social Gospel*, a "great religious mind" would have had to invent it, especially "if he understood psychology and social science." Rauschenbusch placed great faith in the idealism and sagacity of professionals, looking especially to their presumed capacity for disinterested mediation between classes, their talent for "interpreting each to the other." Because Rauschenbusch considered legal ownership and the distribution of wealth to be the key issues before socialists—to the exclusion of the division of mental and manual labor—his communism amounted to the moralization of professional power.[22] As Rauschenbusch's ambiguity shows, the Protestant social gospel broached the most populist and democratic solution to the dilemmas of Progressive intellectuals while auguring a more elitist project of social engineering by benevolent policy experts.

CONCORDAT: AMERICANIST CATHOLICISM, MEDIEVALISM, AND THE SOCIAL GOSPEL OF THE PROFESSIONAL-MANAGERIAL CLASS

If liberal Protestant intellectuals saw themselves as the acolytes of a new Christian witness, Roman Catholics appeared to cradle relics from the Middle Ages. They spoke the language of a fallen empire and wore the vestments of hierarchy and mystery. Surveilled closely from the Vatican, Catholic clerics defended a tradition inscribed with the names of saints, councils, and dogmas and embellished with a host of rituals, chants, and images. Catholic intellectuals navigated by the constellation of Scripture, encyclical, and a patristic tradition that, by the end of World War I, featured St. Thomas Aquinas at the north star of Catholic reflection. The Church's Code of Canon Law, revised and promulgated in 1917, required all professors of "the sacred sciences" to "adhere religiously" to "the method, the doctrine, and the principles of the Angelic Doctor."[23] Thus, while proclaiming their devotion to America, American Catholic intellectuals exhibited a strongly European and medievalist inclination, channeling European and neomedievalist religious ideas directly into the mainstream of American cultural and intellectual history.

Supposedly introduced into Catholic intellectual life as an antidote to modernity, neoscholasticism and medievalism allegedly induced a prolonged state of triumphalist smugness, mental paralysis, emotional repression, and spiritual asphyxiation that was cured only by the zephyrs of Vatican II.[24] Yet this account obscures the complexity and significance of American Catholic medievalism. Far from being a refuge, neomedievalism was a form of social and cultural criticism that sought to divide the wheat from the chaff in the promises of American modernity.

In 1879, Pope Leo XIII bestowed his official blessing on the study of scholasticism in the encyclical *Aeterni patris* and enjoined Catholic intellectuals to study the scholastic corpus and apply its wisdom to the world of science, technology, and industrial capitalism. The new scholasticism's relative openness to science enabled modern scientific and humanistic learning to enter Catholic cultural and intellectual life with greater facility than previous popes had allowed. Twelve years later, Leo issued *Rerum novarum* (1891), which declared that "no practical solution" to modern social problems could be found "apart from the intervention of religion and the Church." Anxious to counter the appeal of socialism to European workers, Leo opened the epoch of social encyclicals by outlining the rights and duties of labor and capital, the duties of the state, and the ideal of a wide diffusion of property ownership. Leo used the Middle Ages as a standard of moral measurement in social and economic life, arguing that economic life was a communal and religious affair that could not be left to the free individual and the free market.[25] Landmarks in the Catholic engagement with modernity, *Rerum novarum* and *Aeterni patris* laid the groundwork for a neomedievalist form of social and cultural criticism.

At the time, American Catholicism held very mixed promise as an outpost of neomedievalism. Over the nineteenth century, "Catholic domesticity" and "evangelical Catholicism"—both centered firmly in the largely Irish entrepreneurial and self-employed professional classes—had given a Victorian complexion to much of American Catholic religious culture. Anchored in the home and the parish, they regulated the oscillation between "separatism and subculture"—between "the ghetto" and "Americanization"—that shaped the informal concordat between American Catholics and their Protestant countrymen. By emphasizing individual responsibility for salvation and defining moral evils as personal problems amenable to individual, family, or parish remedies, domestic Catholicism reinforced the bourgeois ideal of accumulation and militated against any Catholic reconstruction of the social order. Eager to "make his fortune both in this life and in the next," the middle-class Catholic, George Santayana believed, "seems to take stock in his church as he might in a gold mine"—a church, moreover, in which religion was "private and sacred, with no political implications."[26]

Yet Catholic religious culture also harbored challenges to the accumulative ethos and the ideology of "Americanization"—"a thousand denials and menaces," as Santayana described them. Although it articulated the fears and resentments of clerics contending with the new locations of moral authority in expertise and mass culture, Catholic moral theology—which had long stressed the spiritual perils of capitalist enterprise—dovetailed with widespread popular anxiety over the market's demolition of traditional securities and customs. Catholic immigrants arrived in the United States with notions of moral economy that conflicted with the older ideal of entrepreneurial individualism and the newer icon of corporate industrial discipline. Catholicism could never quite escape the status of alien in a land dedicated, so it seemed, to the erasure of memory and the enshrinement of novelty. The *Baltimore Catechism*, rosary beads, incense, saints and prayers for all occasions and vocations, *l'art Saint-Sulpice*, Marian statues in imitation grottoes, blessed throats on the feast of St. Blaise—the symbolic universe of American Catholicism remained a world difficult to reconcile with the evangelical, pragmatic sensibility of American business culture.[27]

Other compelling pockets of Catholic resistance to that culture lay in the pronounced femininity of the Church's symbology and in its ethnic and spatial parochialism. While it sanctioned both male supremacy and resignation to injustice, the maternalism of Catholic gender ideology also cradled a powerful dissent from the ethic of accumulation and the mania of productivity. Virgins, saints, mothers, swaddled babes, and sacred hearts comprised a devotional iconography that set a world of charity, miracle, and fecundity against the impersonality and technomania of the marketplace. Even a lapsed Protestant such as Henry Adams could turn to this maternalism, as in his "Prayer to the Virgin of Chartres" (1901), where he juxtaposed the destructive masculine obsession with science and power with the feminine wisdom of faith and forgiveness. Salvation, for Adams, lay "not in the future science" but in "the mystery of Maternity."[28]

Catholic maternalism had a counterpart in a "sacramental" sensibility generated by the patterns of urban settlement among immigrant Catholics. The imposing exterior of the American Church concealed a more decentralized lattice of dioceses and "national" parishes with different languages, customs, and degrees of amity. Since, as John McGreevey puts it, each parish acted as "a small planet whirling through its orbit, oblivious to the rest of the ecclesiastical solar system," the parish boundaries of school, church, and neighborhood marked the spaces wherein Catholics encountered the sacred in the routines of daily life. This inclination to fuse the local and the sacred could both reinforce racial bigotry and enable resistance to the market's whirlwind indifference to place.[29]

Seen against this backdrop, the "Americanist" and "modernist" controversies that racked Catholic intellectuals at the turn of the century represented not just discrete theological disputes but a broader imbroglio over the impact of corporate capitalism.[30] "Conservatives" such as Archbishop Michael Corrigan of New York—protectors of doctrinal orthodoxy and ethnic religious cultures—could be seen not only as defenders of "tradition" but also as critics, however narrow-minded, of the emerging corporate order. On the other hand, "liberals" or "Americanists" such as Bishop John Ireland of St. Paul affirmed the progress of science and corporate industry.

Ireland was the most tireless missionary of the Americanist project. Like Rauschenbusch, Ireland waxed prophetic on the possibilities incubating in the scientific and managerial reorganization of capitalism. Addressing the World's Auxiliary Congress of the Columbian Exposition in Chicago in 1892, Ireland hailed the harnessing of nature's forces to those "chariots of science and industry" rushing onward and upward. We need not fear the concentration of capital, he told a Labor Day 1903 assembly of St. Paul's AFL leaders—leaders of workers whose skills and shop cultures were marked for extinction by corporate capital—for without them "the wonderous enterprises which characterize our country and create exhaustless sources of wealth would have been impossible." The power and abundance conferred on Americans by the corporate coupling of knowledge and technology would enable them to resolve the vexing "woman" and "labor" questions. By fostering a broader awareness of interdependence and an expanded social sympathy, the new corporate order mandated an "enlargement of the sphere of woman's influence." In addition, Ireland advised labor leaders to organize workers and demand social legislation but also to cautiously embrace the nascent culture of consumption. Like many in the immigrant working class, Ireland both feared and desired the pleasures of the new consumer culture. After dutifully sermonizing on the spiritual dangers inherent in "luxury," Ireland noted that spending on pleasure fueled a rising volume of business activity and labor income. "More to be feared than the extravagant man or woman," Ireland warned the Labor Day gathering, "is the miserly hoarder of wealth, who is always accumulating and never spending."[31]

The Americanist benediction of the corporate order sanctioned Catholic entrance into the professional-managerial class. Catholics, Ireland demanded, should seize the reins of modernity's chariots, stimulating "deeper researches, more extensive surveyings" and leaving "untouched no particle of matter . . . no incident of history, no act in the life of humanity." "Let us be the most erudite historians," Ireland urged the flock, "the most experienced scientists, the most acute philosophers." Informing an audience at Notre Dame in 1895 that Catholics must lead "wherever intelligence is at work," Ireland identified "scientific inquiry, the management of large enterprises, [and] statesmanship" as the prime venues of apostolic modernity.[32] However friendly to labor, Ireland and other Americanist prelates became point men for the technical and administrative intelligentsia.

This hosanna to "intelligence" sheds light on the Americanist support for a greater "lay" presence in the American Church. Lay power had been a contested issue ever since the antebellum "lay trustee" controversy, when middle-class advocates of a "Republican Church" were vanquished by the hierarchy. The issue surfaced again in the late 1880s in the form of "lay congresses" through which, as one of their spokesmen said, the laity hoped to inspire "confidence in the intelligence and motives of laymen." Ireland endorsed the lay congresses when he complained that there was "too much dependence upon priests" among the laity, especially among immigrants.[33] Dismissing the critical resources available in Old World ethnicity, Ireland turned instead to a "laity"—a corporate stratum—inured to the protocols of professionalism.

Thus the Americanist zeal for social reform assumed a clearly elitist cast. In the 1880s, Ireland and Bishop Samuel Gibbons of Baltimore had been instrumental in the Vatican's condemnation of Henry George's *Progress and Poverty* and had kept silent when Edward McGlynn, New York's fiery single-tax cleric, was censured and excommunicated. More than a decade later, Gibbons warned against the "paternalism and caesarism" he saw lurking in the Progressive movement and supported (along with Ireland) the National Civic Federation's call for "moderate" unionism and "cooperation" between labor and capital. Ireland distrusted Peter Dietz's Militia of Christ, the Catholic wing of the American Federation of Labor, which, by the 1910s, contained multitudes of skilled Catholics. When Ireland voiced a very thinly veiled criticism of Leonine medievalism by declaring that "the age of democracy" meant that "the days of princes and feudal lords are gone," he immediately advanced the ambiguous maxim that "he who holds the masses, reigns."[34] Ireland pithily stated the tension between democracy and elitism that ran through Catholic Progressivism.

Americanists initiated the Catholic dialogue with the culture of professionalism, especially its social science precincts. Writing to Keane in 1896, Father William Kerby, future director of Catholic Charities, conceded the attraction of socialism to workers and advised that in order to "captivate the multitude of American Catholics," Catholic leaders had to show that they "clearly understood their need" and that they grasped "the principles by which they shall be met." Catholic social activists thus could "head off demagogues" and show that "we are at heart their best friends." Later, writing in 1900 in the *Catholic University Bulletin,* Kerby asserted that the priest had an "exceptional advantage" in the study of social science because, in scholasticism, he constantly beheld "a complete theory of human existence, human society, and revelation." The social sciences, Kerby continued, must be incorporated into scholasticism "as an integral portion" and "become part of the theological formation" of priests, at the same time that they had to submit to "the limitations which healthy traditions impose." Mindful of the quandaries faced by liberal Protestants in their enthusiasm for the social sciences, Kerby insisted on the centrality of theology for Catholic social professionals. "The social intelligence must be formed in the theoretical truths of revelation, and the social will must conform to its practical truths."[35]

Kerby's plea for professionalized social services was complemented by John Ryan's initial forays into social and economic policy, condensed into *A Living Wage* (1906). A native of rural Minnesota's volatile political climate—Populist agitation, labor radicalism, and Irish nationalism—Ryan had studied for the priesthood in Ireland's diocese and aspired to synthesize the motley ideas of Ireland, Henry George, Ignatius Donnelly, and Leo. He did so by recasting his rural Catholic producer ethic in the mold of liberal Protestant professionalism, using Ely's work (whose influence was, Ryan later wrote, "very large, indeed") as a model of Christian social science. While he paid his required respects to Leonine medievalism—the basis of economic principles in natural law, the (rather sparse) citations of Aquinas, the primacy of the male-headed and fecund nuclear family—Ryan relied heavily on social science to mediate Catholic moral prescription. Although Ely characterized *A Living Wage* as the outline of a "Roman Catholic political economy," other observers captured this more telling significance. "Mr. Ryan's economics are stronger than his ethics," one hostile critic scowled, "and economics fills three-fourths of his pages." The modernist *New York Review* lauded Ryan's "scientific exposition" of what had been left for too long "a vague theological view." Ryan complemented social science with confidence in the prospect of industrial concentration. "The resources of the nation in capital, invention, and labor are now so great," he believed, that "the one want of the time is organization." *A Living Wage* catapulted Ryan into the advance guard of Americanist Catholics and into more nationally connected Progressive circles, where he worked with the National Child Labor Committee, Florence Kelley's National Consumers' League, and some of Minnesota's Progressive professionals and businessmen.[36]

The Americanist blend of medievalism and social science puzzled liberal Protestants such as Rauschenbusch, who observed in 1912 that American Catholicism included "a complexity of the most ancient and modern elements, a mixture of reactionary and progressive forces." Catholicism held an even greater fascination for Progressives such as Bourne, who expressed admiration for the "Catholic ideal of a living, universal Church, founded on a rock of historical and spiritual community." Bourne was especially attracted to the sensuous and communal features of Catholicism, whose "ecclesiastical organization is the bony structure of the Church, the laity the flesh and muscle, and the priesthood the life-blood bringing nourishment to all the cells and organs of the body." Searching for a secular synthesis of spiritual values, social-scientific knowledge, and beloved community, Bourne lit on Catholic modernism as a model for the reconciliation of spirituality and expertise. Like a modernist Catholic priesthood, intellectuals—"modern heroic medical scientists"—would use "all the resources of modern science" to provide nourishment to the secularized laity. Five years later, disappointed by Dewey and other Progressives whose faith in expertise had not inoculated them against martial fever, Bourne looked once again on Catholicism and applauded not the modernist openness to science but the "uses of infallibility." While liberal Protestants wandered through the "vague twilight realm of modernity"—a "spiritual limbo," as Bourne called it—Catholics preserved the "wild accuracy" of Christian belief through resort to dogma.[37]

Taken together with the hopes of Ireland, Kerby, and Ryan, Bourne's use of Catholic modernism as a model for professionalized social science suggests a new kind of significance for the inquisitorial resolution of the "Americanist" and "modernist" controversies. The heavy-handed Vatican reaction—embodied in encyclicals, dismissals from seminaries, and the creation of diocesan "committees of vigilance" to patrol Catholic intellectual life—appears at first to be a frosty Thermidor conjured to kill the tender spring plants nurtured by Leo. Yet the draconian treatment did not in fact impose a new Ice Age on all quarters of American Catholic intellectual life. While the Vatican's strictures paralyzed dogmatic theology for sixty years, they also decisively forced Catholic Progressivism into the ambit of neomedievalism and thus ensured that American Catholics would engage American modernity from a potentially more creative critical location than that occupied by their liberal Protestant counterparts.

Indeed, American Catholic social critics spoke in much more overtly medievalist terms in the 1910s. Medieval and scholastic allusions, references, and praises abounded in Ryan's *Distributive Justice* (1916), as well as in *The World Problem* (1919) and *Democratic Industry* (1919) by Joseph Husslein, editor of the Jesuit weekly *America*. "We Catholics are fond of contrasting the modern industrial system with the organization of industry that prevailed in the Middle Ages," Ryan wrote, because "the principles underlying it can and ought to become the foundation of a reformed industrial order." Both Ryan and Husslein were especially concerned to uphold this neomedievalist perspective against socialism, which they considered a stolen set of "Catholic principles seen through the distorted Marxian lens," in Husslein's words.[38]

Although Ryan eventually garnered the lion's share of influence and historical attention, Husslein concentrated more frequently and explicitly on the indispensable religious foundations of social and cultural criticism. In Husslein's view, the root of modern malaise lay in the sundering of religion from other areas of life, a divorce decreed in the nuptial rites of liberal individualism and "post-Reformation capitalism." Religion, Husslein argued, was not "a private matter" sequestered in the recesses of interiority. Religion concerned the whole person, and its separation from work, sex, family, and politics withered and disfigured the organic unity of human life. "All our social and economic disorders," Husslein declared in *Democratic Industry*, could be traced ultimately to "godlessness." The erosion of humanity's divine image and likeness began, Husslein argued, with Protestantism and culminated in modern secularism. Indeed, Protestantism and its secular offspring had sent the medieval Catholic synthesis of religion and life into an obscurity so profound that "commonplaces of Catholic tradition"—the priority of the common good over individual profit, price controls and living wages, labor organization and government regulation of economic activity—were now "proclaimed as modern discoveries."[39]

Only Catholicism could reunite the estranged partners in the felicitous union ordained by God. "There can be no assurance of a true and lasting universal brotherhood without a universal faith." Without religious foundations, Husslein warned, the new social movements of the turn of the century—labor unions, consumer groups, feminists with their wisdom that woman's place was in the home, "hospital, workshop, school, or office . . . wherever Providence has given her duties to perform"—would lose sight of their coveted goals and "degenerate into wrongful and dangerous developments." Husslein too often caricatured secular radicalism with nightmare portraits of nihilistic, psychopathic anarchists, boorish Wobblies, and sinister socialists. Still, Husslein remained adamant that, if rooted in secularism, social movements not only would fail but also would exacerbate the corruption and injustice they protested.[40]

Husslein's contention that secularism disabled democracy by eroding the virtues that made it possible partook of a broader Anglo-American medievalist current. Because popular alienation from the means of production loomed large in this transatlantic discourse as a main culprit in moral drift and cultural disarray, issues of culture and the workplace merged in Anglo-American medievalism. In Britain, socialists such as

G. D. H. Cole, put off by the technocratic temper of Fabianism, looked to the medieval guild system as a prototype for a decentralized industrialism that restored workers' direct control over production and revitalized their aesthetic, intellectual, and political powers. Cole, as well as the Americans Croly, Mary Parker Follett, and Lewis Mumford, hoped to emulate this medievalesque "guild socialism" without sacrificing the scientific knowledge, technological advance, and secular *mentalite* of modernity. With greater fidelity to the religious character of medieval guilds, English Catholics such as G. K. Chesterton, Hilaire Belloc, and A. J. Penty argued that socialism represented merely the culmination of capitalism's collectivization of production. In their view, Fabians, Social Democrats, or Progressives only accelerated the triumph of a "servile state" in which the propertyless depended on a small stratum of technicians and administrators. The only solution, they believed, lay in "distributism," the radical disassembly of capitalism and the dispersal of productive property among families. Often dismissed as "merrie England" Luddites, distributists favored not the elimination of technology but rather its redesign in a manner consonant with the maintenance of proprietorship, craftsmanship, and community. "It was not machinery that lost us our freedom," Belloc wrote in *The Servile State* (1912), the historical manifesto of distributism, "It was the loss of a free individual"— a subject whose freedom, republican and religious rather than liberal and secular, was both enabled and limited by strong communal bonds.[41]

Ryan and Husslein acknowledged a great debt to distributism, claiming that some Americanized and technically more advanced version constituted the "only effective alternative to socialism," in Ryan's view. Debating the Socialist Morris Hillquit in 1913, Ryan identified industrial education and the abolition of private monopolies as the two indispensable and inseparable elements of a Catholic program of social reform. "Private organizations" rather than the state had, Ryan insisted, to "make the mass of wage-earners, in some degree, owners and managers of capital." Supplemented by minimum wage laws, social insurance, a family-centered agricultural policy, and the creation of industrial and farming cooperatives, Ryan's agenda represented an American guild industrialism with "religion as the unifying and guiding principle of our economic life."[42]

Husslein advanced a similarly medievalist but more pronouncedly artisanal critique of industrial capitalism, endorsing workers' reclamation of skill and ownership as a religious duty. Especially in *Democratic Industry*, Husslein linked a progressive politics of the workplace to a renaissance of religious fervor and practice, producing a Catholic intervention in the "industrial democracy" debates that animated intellectuals, labor and corporate leaders, and policymakers. Cavalierly dismissing the Protestant social gospel as "mere humanitarianism," Husslein called for a reconstruction of the workplace along the lines of medieval craft guilds. Workers—meaning "all engaged in mental as well as in manual occupations"—should organize all enterprises and professions along guild lines, recapturing ownership and daily operation from the clutches of capitalists. Husslein distinguished his version of industrial democracy from socialism, defining his guild ideal as "wide private ownership and management by the workers" rather than state control. Yet, if the rhetorical idealization of private ownership constituted a nod toward the distributists and indeed toward Pope Leo, Husslein drew the bounds of the "private" sufficiently wide to make neomedieval guilds into sites of a Catholic "social selfhood." "The persistence of private productive property" meant, to Husslein, the absence of state power; guild control of the workplace entailed "ownership and management vested . . . in the workers themselves."[43]

While Husslein acknowledged the affinities of his plan with the ideals of syndicalists and guild socialists, he reiterated that secular social thought owed many of its ideals and much of its moral force to the Catholic Middle Ages. Most brands of secular radicalism, he argued, bore "germs of the guild idea" but lacked the "belief in God" that alone could win and sustain industrial democracy. Medieval guilds emerged from Husslein's pages as idealized religious bodies, fusions of ritual and social witness. The guilds, he asserted, demanded strict adherence to "faith, dogma, and external worship." Moreover, the selection of patron saints for guilds and a calendar of holy days and liturgical celebrations kept workers aware of "the great spiritual realities of life" whose neglect eventuated in "the degradation of labor."[44] The guild's essentially liturgical configuration of economic life both bridled the sinful drive to amass riches—and hence to subdivide and deskill labor in the interests of accumulation—and encouraged attention to the aesthetic and communal dimensions of labor.

Yet, despite their espousal of "industrial democracy," Husslein and Ryan opposed the erasure of class distinctions. Ryan candidly characterized his reform program as "paternalistic," whereas Husslein brushed aside all "fatuous delusions" about "a Socialistic abolition of classes"—a "mad utopia," he scoffed in *Democratic Industry*. Having rejected the classless society as a pagan chimera, Husslein advanced the ideal of a "Christian Democracy"—"the highest expression of social science illuminated by the light of faith"—wherein classes practiced "mutual love and consideration" rather than class warfare.[45] Figured in the faithful artisan who combined mental and manual labor, Catholic industrial democracy hinted at a solution to the Progressive dilemma of democratic commitment. Yet, like Rauschenbusch, Husslein and Ryan denatured the popular Progressivism envisioned in Christian social criticism to the degree they highlighted the managerial acumen of the social sciences.

The Catholic and Protestant social gospels crossed and fertilized in the mind of the Anglo-Catholic socialist Vida Dutton Scudder. A professor of literature at Wellesley, Scudder shuttled tirelessly among Progressive circles, pouring her enormous energy into writing, church work, social reform, and political agitation. Member of the Episcopal Church's Commission on Social Service, the Christian Social Union, and the American branch of the Church Socialist League, founder of the College Settlement Association, president of the Church League for Industrial Democracy, board member, with Addams and Lillian Wald, of the National Women's Trade Union League, *outré* theorist of the Socialist Party, speaker in churches, lecture halls, editorial offices, union meetings, and settlement houses—Scudder seldom rested her head in the maelstrom of modernity. Indeed, her continuing search for a place of psychic and spiritual respite—her "antimodern," medievalist quest for meaning in the midst of secularization—paralleled those of other sensitive bourgeois at the turn of the century.[46] Yet Scudder's antimodernism also fueled a Christian socialism that both represents a consummate statement of religious progressivism and merits her inclusion among the premier Progressive intellectuals.

Entering Oxford University in 1883 as one of its first female students, Scudder attended John Ruskin's lectures; frequented the Toynbee Hall settlement house, imbibing its ethos of service but rejecting its genteel secularism; and witnessed the heyday of Christian Socialism, especially of the Church Socialist League that combined doctrinal orthodoxy, opposition to secularism and political accommodation, and respect for working-class culture. Her political and ideological excitement coincided with her discovery of the Oxford Movement from which John Henry Newman argued for a disciplined but historically sensitive orthodoxy. Growing ever more aware of "the plethora of privilege in which my lot had been cast," Scudder suffered an "intolerable stabbing pain" from which she sought relief in literature, socialist politics, and Anglo-Catholic religion.[47]

Scudder rued the secularity of modern socialism, arguing that its abandonment of heavenly hopes narrowed and corrupted its imagination. Dubbing Shelley the bard of radicalism in *The Life of the Spirit in the Modern English Poets* (1895), she noted how the poet's atheism replaced faith in the supernatural with a keen consciousness of a natural world whose life was "abounding but elusive." Dante, on the other hand, enraptured by the "Beatific Vision of the Most High," possessed thereby "an audacity impossible to the poet of revolution." Prometheus unbound could never rival the face of Beatrice. Moving to the present, Scudder worried that secular radicals both simplified the complexity of human identity and entangled their hopes in the liberal individualism they aspired to transcend. Her objection to the "violent individualism" of the sexual freedom advocated by August Bebel and Emma Goldman—whose views struck Scudder as "hideous and foolish"—rested, she explained in a 1914 *Yale Review* essay, not on male supremacy but on the Pauline conviction that our bodies were not our own. If the body was a gift from God and an indispensable part of social existence, then sexual life was always "the business of the whole community." Scudder castigated secular radicals in the belief that feminism and socialism so clearly approximated the Christian ideal that the religious transfiguration of these movements was imperative. Otherwise, she warned presciently in *Socialism and Character* (1912), the left would erect monolithic, repressive regimes, substitute bureaucracy for beloved community, and occasion "the worst disaster of any experiment in collective living that the world has ever seen."[48]

The only hope against barbarism lay, she maintained in *Socialism and Character,* in reconciliation of "conservative Christianity and revolutionary socialism." Yet Scudder neither collapsed religion into socialism nor dissipated theology into socialist theory. In her view, Christian orthodoxy supplied the bedrock of the social witness as a theory of religious materialism. "Ordinary socialist analysis," she explained, "over-simplifies by construing all life in terms of class psychology." Scudder opposed not the idea that material forces determine the course of history but a circumscribed delineation of material forces themselves. Since the material world was a "sacrament ordained to convey spiritual life to us," then religion, and especially Christianity, was a particular mode of material force, a "spiritual power" arising as "the natural product of a concrete situation." Moreover, Scudder's socialist theology was resolutely Trinitarian, sacramental, and ecclesiastical. The doctrine of the Trinity, she reasoned, underlay the ideal of personality, "an equal interchange of love." Sacramentalism, by affirming "an imperative craving for the sanctification of the flesh," countenanced the enjoyment of abundance and the dignity of labor. Finally, as she argued in *Social Ideals in English Letters* (1898), the church was the *beau ideal* of beloved modernity, "the ideal expression of the human race." While faith was prior to politics— "the social impulse in the Church is always effect and not cause of her deepest life"—Scudder insisted that the disciplined and apparently apolitical spirituality of the Oxford Movement had prepared the way for the militance of the Church Socialist League.[49]

As orthodox radicals, Christian Socialists undertook "the great task that lies before the modern world: the spiritualizing of that mighty democracy which is our fate and our future." Although Scudder often was characterized as an elitist, the imagery of union between intellectuals and the toiling masses recurred throughout Scudder's work. Middle-class academics, socialists, and professionals were, she complained in her novel *A Listener in Babel* (1902), "Utopists all," estranged from "actuality." Scudder's medievalism combined a republican-proprietary ideal of union between hand and brain, her "anti-modern" animus against secularity, and her modern commitment to a popular progressive politics. Medieval monasteries, she wrote in *Social Ideals,* anticipated a "pure Christian communism, vowed to democratic fellowship," while William Langland's *Piers Ploughman* represented a Christian social criticism figured in a "workman-Christ" who merged the laborer and the prophet, the worker and the intellectual. Lamenting the contemporary lack of such "a common intellectual consciousness between manual workers and the privileged classes," Scudder conceived of a democratic church as a "shrine of social practice" in which "thinkers and laborers," bound by "personal ties and spiritual faith," forged a political identity that prefigured a classless, beloved world.[50]

World War I halted the march to beloved community. Like Dewey and other Progressives, Protestant and Catholic social gospelers supported American entry into the war in the hope that wartime mobilization would promote more rational forms of social organization. Catholics such as Michael Williams (a recent convert and future founder of *Commonweal*) marveled how the Church, an institution "incomparably well-adapted" for "the dissemination of spiritual inspiration," could become a chaplaincy of the wartime state. Williams celebrated the new organizational branches of American Catholicism spawned by the war, especially the National Catholic War Council, which, morphing quickly into the National Catholic Welfare Council, neatly traced the link between warfare and welfare in modern democracy. The Council's Committee on Special War Activities distributed prayer and devotion, Williams wrote, by "the laws of system and with the maximum of efficiency," while the Council as a whole cut through "unnecessary duplication of effort" and "overlapping authority." "Living religion," Williams concluded, possessed a "scientific exactitude" honed in the crisis of war and readied for the challenges of peace.[51]

Indeed, right after the war, the social gospel appeared to have reached a pentecost of opportunity. Within a year of each other, Catholic and

Protestant leaders issued sweeping statements on the need for "reconstruction": the National Catholic War Council's "Bishops' Program for Social Reconstruction" (1919) and the Federal Council of Churches' *The Church and Industrial Reconstruction* (1920). In both reports, church officials exhorted political and economic leaders to redistribute wealth, erect a generous and centralized welfare state, and devise "some form of cooperation in the ownership of productive wealth," in the Federal Council's words.[52]

Yet the Great War and its aftermath soon proved inimical to the social gospel—a "pentecost of calamity," as Susan Curtis has described it.[53] The butchery wrought by the marshaling of men, resources, and expertise prompted a long moment of despair, retrenchment, and crisis in the North Atlantic world. If the war quickened the reconstructive ambitions of religious Progressives, its aftermath forced a revision of their hopes, their methods, even the knowledge they believed they possessed. The prophets entered a melancholy but creative period of drift.

✝

CHAPTER TWO

After Such Knowledge:

The Modern Temper and the Social Gospel, 1919–1932

"After such knowledge, what forgiveness?" Surveying the rubble of nations and spirits left by World War I, T. S. Eliot searched for the well-springs of absolution and hope. If the dreams of reason had been dispelled at Ypres, Verdun, and Versailles, Eliot saw new, more insidious reveries of deliverance stalking through the ruins. If reason had not prevented slaughter, if faith seemed too deluded or self-conscious to inspire action, and if, as F. Scott Fitzgerald declared, all Gods were dead, all faiths in men shaken, after such knowledge, what forgiveness?[1]

Having supported the war as an auspicious occasion to reconstruct the social order, American progressive intellectuals fell under the same shadow. On discovering that Mars could not lie lissomely with Minerva, many progressives—reborn as "liberals"—decamped from their prewar positions. Some followed John Dewey in a chastened but renewed commitment to a scientifically informed democracy, or Walter Lippmann down the path of elite manipulation, or H. L. Mencken in bilious declamation about what rubes these mortals be.

Liberal Protestant and Roman Catholic intellectuals shared this yearning for renewal. The young Detroit pastor Reinhold Niebuhr wrote acridly in 1919 of liberalism's "gray spirit of compromise"—"the philosophy of the middle-aged," as he echoed Randolph Bourne—and welcomed the opportunity to "tear down old houses and build new ones." Yet Niebuhr's youthful bravado matched the counsel of the middle-aged John Ryan, who observed in the "Bishops' Program of Social Reconstruction" (1919) that while the war's end had brought peace, "the only safeguard of peace is social justice and a contented people," neither of which was possible without "ultimate and fundamental reforms." These changes, Ryan believed, had to be informed by a "Christian view of work and wealth"—something Ryan and others in the Catholic hierarchy clearly considered absent from American life.[2]

Historians, however, tell us that the social witness itself was absent or muffled in the decade after World War I. Just as "labor's great war" for industrial democracy ended in the truce of welfare capitalism, so the social gospel legions retreated in disarray. Certainly, when the social gospeler Sherwood Eddy addressed Protestant students during Christmas week 1919, he was shocked at their open disdain for his social gospel verities. The students, he wrote, derided his gospel as "piffle . . . old shibboleths . . . worn-out phrases."[3]

Yet the Protestant and Catholic "enthusiasm for humanity," as one historian puts it, did not wane in the 1920s.[4] Confronted with unprecedented challenges, in high and mass culture, to the intellectual and moral authority of Christianity, Christian intellectuals remained adamant in their prewar social witness while reconsidering the social tradition. Loyal to the shibboleths of personality, industrial democracy, and beloved community, many social gospelers preserved the hopes of prewar progressivism more steadfastly than their secular brethren. Some brought the social gospel more closely into line with the protocols of an aggressively and thoroughly secularized intelligentsia that was itself claiming clerical status in American culture. Others—often Protestant and Catholic champions of some "new medievalism" or medievalist modernism—reasserted the centrality of theology and church to the social gospel.

THE MODERN TEMPER: AMERICAN INTELLECTUALS, RELIGION, AND THE CRISIS OF CLASSICAL MODERNITY IN THE 1920S

Throughout the North Atlantic world, the war and its aftermath precipitated what Detlev Peukert has called "the crisis of classical modernity." With old verities in morals and religion discredited, and with the Enlightenment ideal of rational progress hollowed, intellectuals longed for the end of the existing order without a clear sense of what would follow. The spectrum of innovation in letters, the arts, and intellectual life— from Dada to psychoanalysis to Frankfurt School Marxism—encompassed an explosive but aimless liberation of energy and imagination that portended but could not deliver the new. "The modern temper," as Joseph Wood Krutch dubbed it in 1929, this volatile and politically elastic sense of drift, was a witness to despair in the midst of possibility, to stasis in conditions that cried out for revolutionary transformation. As

Modris Ecksteins put it plainly, "a profound sense of spiritual crisis" brooded through the first postwar decade.[5]

In unpropitious times, European Christian writers set about redeeming the modern temper. In his "crisis theology," the Swiss theologian Karl Barth sounded the death knell of liberal enlightenment, secular and religious, and argued that the times testified to the truth of sin's ubiquity and intransigence. Only this wisdom, he contended ironically, could sustain socialist politics in a dark age. Paul Tillich's "religious socialism" drew even more directly on the modern temper. In his "theology of culture," Tillich embraced the modernist ferment of Weimar Germany and enlisted it to rejuvenate Christianity. While flirting with the protofascist *Action Française* and settling among the "new Catholic left," the French Catholic philosopher Jacques Maritain wedded scholastic thought to Henri Bergson's celebrations of flux and vitality. Eager to "restore all things in Christ," Pope Pius XI made a fateful concession to the modern temper in 1922 by blessing "the participation of the laity in the work of the apostolate"—the "lay apostolate" or "Catholic action"—and inaugurating a long revolution in the Roman Catholic Church.[6]

As the new elite of the Fordist order, professionals received considerable and not always flattering attention in European Christian social thought. Tillich condemned the secularism of this "exclusive, educated aristocracy," while Maritain, reflecting French anxiety about "the American cancer" of scientific management and assembly lines, maligned technical experts in *Art and Scholasticism* (1920) for their love of the "chronometrized and taylorized gesture." On the other hand, the British Labour historian R. H. Tawney maintained that professionals constituted an "intellectual proletariat" capable of redeeming *The Acquisitive Society* (1920). Imbued with Christian virtues and devoted to service rather than profit, Tawney's new socialist professionals would leaven expertise with responsibility and charity. Deference to professional authority was not "the submission of one man to another," Tawney reasoned, but rather "that of all men to the purpose for which industry is carried on."[7] While Christian intellectuals differed over the import of Fordist professionalism, they agreed that it was a novel form of cultural authority rooted in efficient and abundant production.

In the United States, debate over "civilization" likewise revealed two clerisies girding for battle over cultural leadership. As Warren Susman has observed, civilization connoted the symbolic environment generated by radio, film, advertising, and mass-circulation newspapers and magazines. Faced with the "hieroglyphics of a new civilization," as Vachel Lindsay called them, intellectuals labored to create modes of authority compatible with the new culture of communication and consumption. "Symbols control sentiment and thought," Dewey noted in *The Public and Its Problems* (1927), "and the new age has no symbols consonant with its activities." Dewey, along with other intellectuals, looked to science and expertise—"intelligence work," as Walter Lippmann termed it in his study of *Public Opinion* (1922)—to provide the gravitational principles of that new symbolic universe.[8]

Debate over those principles ignited a new round of struggle in the politics of American culture, as spokesmen for a scientific, corporate-sponsored, secularized modernity made bolder claims to cultural authority. In *Whither Mankind?* (1928) and *Toward Civilization* (1930), a representative two-volume panorama of reflection on science, technology, the arts, and morals edited by the historian Charles Beard, numerous intellectuals and experts—"authorities of outstanding competence"—supplied reasons for what Beard hoped would be a "cheerful outlook upon the future of civilization." Over and above the conventional recitals of "how far we have come," the essays exuded the missionary fervor and priestly assurance that animated the scribes of the professional-managerial class. In the conclusion to the second volume, Beard reasoned that just as the Church Fathers had "rationalized the best elements of the feudal order and idealized them," so technicians and their intellectual celebrants would do likewise for the modern order. Indeed, Beard asked rhetorically, "is a saint more of a saint because he rides in an ox cart, rather than in an automobile or airplane, to spread the gospel or to do good to them that are sick or in prison?" Other contributors showed a similar facility in donning the robes of a new clerisy. In an essay entitled, "Religion," James Harvey Robinson capped an overview of historical criticism of religious belief by transferring sacrality to the modern class of social and biological experts. "The effort to engineer life in the light of already existing intelligence" was itself "as holy a task as any hitherto assayed by saint or martyr."[9]

Yet, if, during the 1920s, "all the gods trembled," they were shaken by intellectuals whose unbelief often was less than proud and robust. There was certainly no lack of militant secularism. H. L. Mencken's vituperative reportage on the Scopes trial, as well as his *Treatise on the Gods* (1930), Sinclair Lewis's portrait of the roguish revivalist *Elmer Gantry* (1927), Harry Elmer Barnes's hopeful meditation on *The Twilight of Christianity* (1929)—all seemed to confirm Edmund Wilson's bumptious claim that "few first-rate men take religion seriously anymore."[10] However, other intellectuals, nurtured in the mental universe of liberal Protestantism and progressivism, could not be so dismissive. Their farewells to traditional religion were more rueful, even "religious," and they held their newly assertive secularism with as much trepidation as confidence. In their reflections on religion, American intellectuals marked a crisis of classical modernity that belied the sureness of Mencken or Wilson.

Walter Lippmann, whose prewar hope for "modern communion" had borne the trademark of progressive religiosity, illustrated this ambivalence. His portrait of William Jennings Bryan in *Men of Destiny* (1925) championed secular cultural elites against the Protestant democrats of Dayton, Tennessee. "Guidance for a school," he insisted, should come not from benighted citizens but "ultimately only from educators." Yet later, in *A Preface to Morals* (1929), Lippmann noted sadly how liberal clergymen, unable to hurl fire and brimstone at rapacious employers, had to "inquire courteously of the president's secretary" to schedule a meeting at which (if they got an appointment) they had to argue "on secular grounds" with data on health, efficiency, and working conditions "worked up for them by economists." Modern churchmen, Lippmann concluded, had brokered away "the great provinces of the human soul." These realms could be reclaimed, he felt, through recourse to a rarefied "high religion," a distillation of religion and philosophy purified of doctrinal and ecclesial impurities. Having "no thesis to defend," the devotees of high religion would eschew the inanities and insularities of the multitude and instead seek "excellence wherever it may appear."[11]

Other intellectuals sought a similarly "high religion" to replace the lowly form of traditional faith. Dewey reminded readers of the *New Republic* in 1922 that "the church-going classes" had long been the backbone of "philanthropic social interest, social reform, . . . pacifism, and popular education." This evangelical public reappeared in a secularized form in *The Public and Its Problems* (1927) as "the Great Community" (or "democracy") whose "life of free and enriching communion" recalled the prewar hopes of progressive religiosity. Such a community, Dewey hoped, would take hold of the mass media and, like the God of Genesis, "breathe life into it." Still, Dewey demanded in his 1929 Gifford Lectures that religion "surrender once for all commitment to belief about matters of fact, whether physical, social, or metaphysical" and "leave such matters to inquirers in other fields"—inquirers, he made clear in *Individualism Old and New* (1930), such as "sociologists, psychologists, novelists, dramatists, and poets." Dewey's demarcation of the zones of religion and science echoed the Harvard mathematician-philosopher Alfred North Whitehead's attempt in *Science and the Modern World* (1925) to draw up articles of peace and lines of sovereignty. Warning that "the future course of history" depended on "the decision of this generation as to the relations" between science and religion, Whitehead proposed a partition in which science governed "physical phenomena," while religion ruled "the contemplation of moral and aesthetic values."

Whitehead's delineation replicated the pragmatist conception of religion as exalted subjectivity—"what the individual does with his solitariness," as he wrote in *Religion in the Making* (1926), "the art and theory of the internal life of man" whose highest virtue was "a penetrating sincerity." Detached from specific rites or codes, relocated in private subjectivity, and recast as "sincerity," both high religion and pragmatist exaltation constituted a purely therapeutic form of religion that was, as Whitehead realized, a flat denial that religion was "primarily a social fact."[12]

By the end of the decade, some secular writers had grown impatient not only with traditional religion and unbelief but also with the sort of compromises struck by Whitehead, Dewey, and their liberal religious admirers. Lippmann cashiered liberal theology in *Preface to Morals* as a "revered collection of hypotheses," while Krutch, though "disillusioned with the laboratory," recoiled both from Catholic efforts to beguile the modern world "back to Saint Thomas" and from what he considered liberal Protestantism's "flabby pseudo-religion." The idiosyncratic indictment of secularism and its religious cousin was John Crowe Ransom's *God Without Thunder* (1930). Though an avowed unbeliever who embodied the passage from Victorianism to modernism in southern intellectual life, Ransom (the prodigal son and grandson of theologians) declared his preference for the "stern and inscrutable" God of traditional Christianity against the "Amiable Rotarian" of liberal theology. Ransom shrewdly identified the yoke placed on humanity by the liberalization of God: a religion of "service" that reinforced an already insidious work ethic. "Now that it is God's will that mankind be served, it becomes holy living if mankind proceeds to serve itself as hard as possible." Defining culture in religious terms, Ransom perceived its inextricable tie to the politics of production. "The religion of a people," he wrote, was "that background of metaphysical doctrine which dictates its political economy." A religious economy, Ransom explained, stresses limits and emphasizes worship, whereas a secular economy was a "wartime economy" that mobilized against nature, multiplied and intensified desire, and conscripted human labor and intelligence in an unending pursuit of power. The only antidote to the martial ardor of secularism was a revival—not out of metaphysical conviction but out of pure "psychic necessity," as Ransom put it bluntly—of traditional religion and obedience to a "virile and concrete God." Paradoxically, the recovery of God's virility and thunder required a recovery of "the feminine gender," the "demonic and irrational aspect of his being" that disrespected the pathetic power lust of human beings. No *mater dolorosa*, this "Mother Ghost," but the spirit of utter clarity and realism, "the peace that passeth understanding."[13]

Liberal Protestant and Catholic intellectuals were equally at sea in this crisis of classical modernity. "Contemporary human life and contemporary religion have been drifting apart," the Union professor and Riverside Church pastor Harry Emerson Fosdick observed in 1926, accounting for "the present turmoil in the churches." This sense of drift without prospect of mastery coincided with shifts in the cultural climate and institutional arrangements of American religion in the 1920s. Expecting a pentecost of reform spirit after the war, Protestants quickly encountered a "religion depression" in the mainline churches, marked by lower attendance, waning enthusiasm, and lower financial support. The apathy and hostility of college youth in particular vexed Protestant intellectuals. "A typical college youth spurns faith," Fosdick observed, adding lamely that "the students would never dream of saying so, but they want a theology—an intelligible idea of God in which they can honestly believe." While Catholics avoided a "depression," the immigrant enclaves spawned a generation seeking greater autonomy in marriage, work, and residence and finding in mass culture a plethora of possibilities unimagined, frowned on, or proscribed in the local parish church and school.[14]

Catholic and Protestant youth slowly embraced postwar modernity as their higher educational institutions emulated the shape and ethos of the corporate world. As mainstream Protestant leaders in higher education sought the advice of the Rockefeller and Carnegie Foundations, they increasingly measured their goals and curricula by corporate standards. The deterioration of liberal Protestant hegemony in higher education paralleled an organizational revolution in American Catholicism. Urban bishops and cardinals asserted greater control over parish priests, seminaries, and diocesan services and promoted greater centralization and administrative efficiency. Catholic higher education moved in the direction of rationalized curricula, centralized administration, and research orientation, using as models both corporate philanthropic foundations and professional organizations such as the American Council of Learned Societies and the Social Science Research Council.[15]

Determined to rekindle an "enthusiasm for humanity" among their more lukewarm brethren, social gospelers remade their prewar vows to social reconstruction. Protestant advocates of "industrial democracy" and Catholic partisans of the "lay apostolate" tried to preserve a more democratic conception of social reform than those proffered by more secular intellectuals. Yet they embarked on the mission with a more conflicted temper than their prewar forebears had possessed. Shailer Mathews of the University of Chicago, for instance, studded his manifesto, *The Faith of Modernism* (1924), with warnings to the "near-sighted optimist" who regarded "social change as always social progress" and conceded that religious liberalism, like political liberalism, often lacked power because "it fails to count life's fears." Harry Emerson Fosdick devoted an entire book, *Christianity and Progress* (1922), to rescuing the social gospel from "the amiable idiocies of evolution, popularly misinterpreted." Downtown from Fosdick's Riverside Church, George Shuster, an editor of *Commonweal* (founded in 1924 as the first lay journal of American Catholic opinion), was almost alone in identifying the lingering ideologies of progress and secularism as forms of class politics. Marking "the change of the Protestant ministry into a professorate," Shuster saw Mencken as the nadir of this declension, discerning in his vitriol "a marked form of class consciousness" arising from his membership in a new elite. For all his apparent iconoclasm, Mencken represented, in Shuster's view, a reliable spokesman for a scientific and technical clerisy in whom Americans now invested an "awe . . . which a more primitive time always associated with religious teachers."[16]

The modernist controversy in postwar Protestantism exemplified the modern temper among Christian intellectuals. Despite the anathema pronounced by fundamentalists such as Princeton's J. Gresham Machen in his *Christianity and Liberalism* (1922), liberal Protestants often were acutely conscious of what Fosdick admitted were "the dangers of modernism." Unless they recognized the gravity and form given to spiritual life by places, images, creeds, and churches, Fosdick warned, liberals would turn that life into "a disembodied wraith, without a local habitation and a name." Harry F. Ward, professor of social ethics at Union and one of the most prolific Protestant socialists, saw even more clearly the class politics inscribed in religious modernism. Urging Protestant churches to reflect on their links to "the upper fringe of the middle class"—those in "engineering, teaching, medical service, law, finance, and business management"—Ward contended that modernism was an adjustment to this bloc, "not to the needs of the masses." Since experts had been "trained in universities it has funded and endowed," Ward surmised that liberal Protestantism faced a moment of truth in the moral and political direction of the professional middle class.[17]

Still beholden to the ideal of self-denial, Christian intellectuals found it hard to decipher the hieroglyphics of the new civilization. Writing in the *Ladies Home Journal* in 1926, Fosdick mused that popular recreations were "too good to be monopolized by the devil." Looking toward urban Catholic workers newly enfranchised in the consumer republic, the editors of *Commonweal* dismissed "threadbare wiseacres" and their virtues of economy and thrift. "We should have every good and truly ornamental thing that we are able to pay for," they insisted, for the real values of life—"comfort, enjoyment, decorum, beauty"—would wither under a regime of self-denial. George Shuster pronounced a genteel benediction on mass culture, asking only that the bread and circuses of the "simple, workaday folk" be made of "honest grain" and "more than tedious orgies." Yet Shuster remained more sensitive than many other religious critics to the political nature of the culture industry. He bemoaned the waste of professional intelligence in the production of mass culture and lamented the "committee of governors" who, with their "barometric devices" such as books-of-the-month, carefully regulated the cultural climate.[18]

Shuster's reference to orgies pointed to the encapsulation of social gospel misgivings about postwar consumer culture in discussions of the accelerating sexual revolution. The emancipation of women was one of God's "new blessings upon the conditions of the age," *Commonweal* opined in 1929, and contained the possibility of "sturdier spiritual expression." Yet Catholics and liberal Protestants judged the new woman in terms of her contribution to religious revitalization. "Unless we can get out of the new system motherhood as consecrated, spiritual quality as fine, idealism as exalted, religious faith as cleansing and ennobling" as that allegedly possessed by previous generations, Fosdick cautioned, then the woman question will have been resolved for the worse. *Commonweal* qualified its enthusiasm for feminism by warning that women's entrance into offices and factories might lead to "irresponsibility" and to their immersion in a swill of injustice that already engulfed men.[19] While this wariness of feminism surely signaled the persistence of Victorian conventions, it also conveyed unease about the conditions of corporate work and the amorality of consumption.

If the "new woman" embodied the ambivalence of Christian progressives about the prospects of capitalist modernity, new developments in contraceptive and reproductive technology also provoked alarm at the prospect of a new regime of experts. Again, while social gospelers were anxious about the uncoupling of pleasure from reproduction, they also addressed more fundamental issues of human identity and destiny. Fosdick shuddered at the implications of eugenics for human freedom and dignity. Recoiling from the biological elitism and moral parsimony of eugenists, Fosdick argued that Christian reverence for personality, rooted in faith that humanity reflected the image and likeness of God, cultivated a far more generous and democratic sense of the possibilities residing in common folk. While upholding the Catholic prohibition of contraception as a defense of women as well as matrimony, John Ryan also suspected that "overpopulation" camouflaged an effort by "bourgeois advocates of birth control" to "shift the blame for the awful conditions of the working classes from their own shoulders." Convinced that economic hardship was a political issue of distributive justice, Ryan denounced the class and racial politics he discerned in neo-Malthusian defenses of contraception and eugenics. "The magic circle of fitness," as he labeled it sarcastically in 1927, could be contracted until it included "only Nordics, or Class A in the army intelligence tests" and excluded anyone "whom the social experts or the politicians may regard as a social liability." The oft-cited G. K. Chesterton elaborated Ryan's suspicions into a broader aspersion on professional supervision of personal life. Coupling eugenics to the lethal efficiency of "Prussianism" in *Eugenics and Other Evils* (1922), Chesterton linked it to a wider conspiracy of "stuffy science . . . bullying bureaucracy, and . . . terrorism by tenth-rate professors" to violate "the sanctuary of sex." Contraception and eugenics represented, in Chesterton's view, both an industrial colonization of the body and a corruption of pleasure by the spirit of calculation.[20]

The fear that consumer culture held more serious terrors than materialism surfaced often in religious cultural criticism. While inveighing against greed ("the hogs become refined and like clean sties with pictures on the walls," in Ward's overworked metaphor), Harry F. Ward and John Ryan in particular drew up other counts of indictment. Ward feared the ecological despoliation wrought by consumerism. Ryan always harbored a distrust of consumption and leisure that reflected his Irish Jansenism, producerist suspicions of luxury, and masculine fears of feminization. Pleasures beyond the carefully policed bounds of health and "moderate comfort," he wrote in 1919—cosmetics, jewelry, rich foods, furnishings—distracted from "health, virility, [and] good morals," fostered "effeminacy, artifice, and vulgarity," and engendered a bevy of "unlovely and unchristian qualities." Ryan's frugality (shared with his fellow Minnesotan Thorstein Veblen) slighted the longing for bodily redemption in a land flowing with milk and honey that resided in the theatricality and materialism of consumer culture. Yet it also pointed to the illusory sense of community conjured by mass culture, its mystification of the destructively private character of consumer fulfillment. Contradicting a line of economic philosophy running from Adam Smith to Simon Patten, Ryan perceived the commodity form's power to constrict rather than enlarge the range of human sympathy, its capacity to "diminish the feelings of disinterestedness and generosity" by narrowing the bounds of moral personality.[21]

The tensions in the postwar social gospel appeared even more clearly in the interrelated Protestant discussions of personality, industrial democracy, and socialism. Despite contentions that liberal Protestants acquiesced in corporate managerialism and sponsored a transit "from salvation to self-realization," social gospelers preserved a theological conception of personality that retained a close, socially critical fusion of personal *and* social renewal, therapy *and* morality, and salvation *and* self-realization. The social Christian—the "personalist"—cleared the path for the *imago dei*, according to Francis J. McConnell, Methodist bishop of New York, and furthered the "progressive advance of human personalities to likeness with the Infinite Personality." Personality remained "the highest value in the universe" as the Fellowship of Reconciliation's Kirby Page argued in *The Personality of Jesus* (1932), a value realized, as Fosdick wrote in *Twelve Tests of Character* (1923), through "finding your real self and then having it set free" in a liberation that released its "full power and abundant fruitage." These fruits would ripen in what Ward called "the Beloved Community" in *Which Way Religion?* (1931), a fellowship wherein, according to the Boston personalist theologian Edgar S. Brightman (later a major influence on Martin Luther King, Jr.), persons "cooperate with others in the production and enjoyment of shared values."[22]

Cursing the obstacles to this beloved community as threats to personality, Protestants mandated commitment to social reform and endorsed postwar versions of "industrial democracy" and socialism that were at least ostensibly democratic. Fosdick condemned child labor, low wages, and degrading factory and residential conditions as a cumulative "sacrilege" that "debauches . . . the personalities of men and women." Importuning social gospel legions to embark on an *Adventurous Religion* (1926) that promoted "the real sanctity—human personality," Fosdick charged them to "fight with all the fierceness of the crusaders against its profanation." Protestants usually pronounced "industrial democracy" or socialism as the vehicle of personality. Synthesizing a Taylorist scientific ethos, assembly-line discipline, and the vestigial remains of artisanal work culture into what Steve Fraser has called a "Marxism of the professional middle class," many postwar labor intellectuals transformed the prewar ideal of industrial democracy into a Fordism with a human face. Protestant social gospelers—especially those associated with the Church League for Industrial Democracy and the Fellowship for a Christian Social Order (1922)—argued for more a more "representative government in industry," in Kirby Page's words, in consonance with "the development and enrichment of human personality." Others such as Ward committed themselves more explicitly to socialism. Since property, Ward reasoned in *The New Social Order* (1919), was the "base upon which man stands" for "the increase of personality"—for the "nourishment," that is, "of his spiritual development"—then only in a Christianized beloved community of socialized production would there reign "a true conception of the relation of property to personality."[23]

Despite the persistence of personality as a mode of Protestant social thought, many social gospelers also harbored a dogged and even increasing respect for the authority of secular experts, especially in the social and psychological sciences. As R. Laurence Moore has written, enthusiasm for the social sciences rested on "the questionable assumption that American sociologists would continue . . . to regard Christianity as laying down the normative terms for a good society." Indeed, many postwar social scientists eschewed moral judgment in favor of an idealized "objectivity" that left power relations undisturbed. While rewriting and often forsaking the vows of their discipline's marriage to liberal Protestant theology—a separation tied to the wider divorce of higher education from Protestant religious hegemony—social and political scientists slowly reimagined democracy itself as a species of elite orchestration. As Robert Westbrook has observed, postwar students of society and politics began to redefine democracy itself as "government for the people by enlightened and responsible elites." Enthralled by the new objectivism of social scientists eager to move beyond their discipline's religious origins, Protestants followed a similar trajectory. Marshaling experts from around the University of Chicago, Shailer Mathews anticipated Beard's *Whither Mankind* by parading the *Contributions of Science to Religion* (1924) in thirteen essays by physicists, astronomers, botanists, geologists, and eugenicists. Exulting in *Faith of Modernism* at the prospect of a social order that relied on "good will and expert authority" and thus folded democracy into benevolent expertise, Mathews proved the most unrestrained but not atypical Protestant acolyte of the social sciences. Ward's democratic socialism, for instance, reflected the technocratic potential of the Protestant social witness. "Democratic cooperation of life," he declared in *The New Social Order,* entailed both fellowship among "technicians and administrators and laborers"—who presumably possessed unequal degrees of power and knowledge—and "scientific discovery in the realm of human living." Ward bypassed the knotty issue of professional power by fusing the engineering ideal and the Sermon on the Mount, commending engineers in 1919 for their commitment to social progress through maximum production and referring to the Soviet Union in *Which Way Religion?* (1931) as an exemplary feat of "human engineering."[24]

Protestants also embraced more secularized forms of psychological therapy. Though rejecting the more grotesque versions of "mental hygiene" and "success" psychologies that proliferated after the war, they welcomed equally secularized modes of psychological expertise. Fosdick, for one, was a fervid champion of secularized psychological knowledge and its uses for pastoral counseling. In *Living Creatively* (1932), Kirby Page included a chart by which Christians could measure the progress of personality. Under headings such as "relieving human misery" and "transforming unjust social conditions," readers could mark off time and quality of achievement: "S = Substantial, M = Moderate, N = Negligible."[25] Despite their faith in personality, social gospelers increasingly exhibited deference to secularized canons of selfhood.

Catholic social thinkers—still mainly priests—followed a similar course. George Shuster's coeditor Michael Williams provided the most striking homage to expertise, comparing the Trappist order to the emerging institutional structure of scientific research. As "experts in prayer" whose monasteries functioned as "laboratories and experimental stations for the study and application of spiritual forces," the monks were to religion "what the Rockefeller and Carnegie Foundations, and the departments in universities, . . . are to science." After the war, the American Church witnessed the formation of a scientifically informed, nationally oriented cohort of clergymen, many of whom had been baptized in the fire of the Americanist and modernist controversies: John Ryan (director of the National Catholic Welfare Council's Social Action Department at Catholic University), William Kerby (director of the National Council of Catholic Charities), Raymond McGowan, and Paul Hanly Furfey. Espousing a "science of charity," they advocated nationwide social reconstruction as well as with local relief. Furfey, a Catholic University sociologist, preached fervently that "through exact measurement and mathematical analysis the study of human behavior could move nearer and nearer to the exact sciences." The Catholic social worker, Kerby argued in *The Social Mission of Charity* (1921), should be "a specialist who is familiar with literature, problems, and methods in the field of relief" and a manager with a "passion for efficiency." "The progress of our charities," Kerby believed, "is in [the] last analysis a question of qualified leadership and technical skill."[26] Catholic social thought embarked on a road paved by liberal Protestants and patrolled by secular social scientists.

Ryan distinguished his own version of industrial democracy from other antidemocratic "corporatist" notions circulating among European and American Catholics in the 1920s, especially those bound up with the distributist ideas that had influenced him before the war. Invoking the

Chesterbellocian specter of the "Servile State," Ryan considered industrial democracy a "third way" that was more democratic than fascism or socialism and more industrial than the artisan-agrarianism of distributists. More consistently than other postwar industrial democrats, Ryan criticized managerial and professional monopolies on skill, power, and authority and demanded the extension of workers' control over production. Workers, he argued, "should take part in all those phases of industrial management which concern them directly": not merely wages, hours, and conditions but also "installing of new machinery, improvement of industrial processes and organization, . . . industrial experiments and scientific management."[27]

Yet Ryan's industrial democracy retained a Fordist regime of work and technology that had already gone far in transforming production into a deskilled, mechanized, repetitive process. Indeed, Ryan and other industrial democrats never explained how the democratic management and improvement of repetition would rescue work from degradation. Shuster, after noting the "solidarity of circumstance" among workers in factories and offices, could only remark lamely that the solution was to make the solidarity "vital and significant." Though never suggesting anything this therapeutically evasive, Ryan openly expressed doubts that, in the end, most workers had anything worthwhile to contribute to the technical and administrative aspects of production. "Most of our industrial population," he suspected, was not "competent" enough to be citizens of an industrial democracy, since only a "small number of men have superior abilities of management." In Ryan's own estimation, industrial democracy would flourish with only a minimum of democrats—citizens, he wrote elsewhere, whose incentives remained the more conventional imperatives of productivity and profit: "the traditional American philosophy," as Ryan put it. Industrial democracy would make workers into "business men," he hoped, capable of competitively obtaining "indefinitely large gains as the rewards of efficiency and success."[28] At the very moment that Ryan's progressivism heralded a more decentralized, democratic political economy, it also augured the incorporation of workers into the competitive, accumulative mores of corporate capitalism—suggesting that its third way was but a repaving of the first way.

Fluid but still hierarchical in structure, putatively but far from effectively democratic in governance, competitive but compassionate in ethos—Ryan's industrial democracy defined the postwar Catholic progressive vision as a socially responsible capitalism, a vision well suited to the interests of managers and professionals. Ryan's contraction of industrial democracy reflected a conception of the lay apostolate that dovetailed with a benevolent form of managerialism. In his scheme of industrial democracy, worker participation in management, like the greater lay participation in the salvific work of the Church, would remain subsumed under the authority of professionals. As Williams made clear, the lay apostolate would be undertaken by the "intelligent, well-instructed laity," those who "mingle with the world, and know its language."[29]

The modern temper of postwar Christian social thought found its best exemplary exponent in Reinhold Niebuhr. Raised (along with his younger brother Helmut Richard) as a preacher's son in the pietist but relatively liberal Evangelical Synod, Niebuhr had been wary of the social gospel long before his appearance on the liberal Protestant scene shortly after World War I. "Many ministers of the gospel," he complained in a student journal in 1911, treated poverty, family breakdown, business avarice, and alcoholism "as an economist or a practical statesman would treat them," more as "a detriment to the state and nation" than as "obstacles to eternal life." Yet only two years later, as a divinity student at Yale, Niebuhr harbored doubts about that eternal life. The closing words of the Apostle's Creed about forgiveness of sins, bodily resurrection, and life everlasting were, he later recalled, "an offense and a stumbling block to young theologians . . . [of] my generation." Meanwhile, Niebuhr's Evangelical piety faded on exposure to Jamesian pragmatism by D. C. Macintosh, Yale's most thorough-going modernist. Religious ideas arose from our needs and values, Niebuhr asserted in his B.D. thesis, and "in so far as we can verify our needs and values we have a certainty that they are true."[30] The future scourge of secular and religious optimism left Yale in 1915 indelibly impressed with the emblems of liberal Protestant religious culture: the conception of religion as a realm of ideals and the containment of faith in the strictures of scientific discourse.

Niebuhr's subsequent tenure as pastor of Detroit's Bethel Evangelical Church, usually seen as the moment of his departure from liberal theology and the prewar social gospel, actually marked his debut as the last elder of the liberal Protestant covenant with the nation's elites. In his diary (published in 1929 as *Leaves from the Notebook of a Tamed Cynic*), he confided his dissatisfaction with a rationalized faith and his admiration for the piety of "unschooled people" educated by pain, hope, and endurance. He was "too cautious to be a Christian," he confessed, despairing that Christian love might "be no more than a leaven" in human affairs. Asking in 1927 "Why I Am Not a Christian" (a reference to Bertrand Russell's widely read essay), he reflected that the compromise he struck in his mind between "the religious strategy" of transcendence and the "scientific strategy of transforming nature" appeared all too reasonable. It was, he acknowledged, "the very basis of my spiritual bondage."[31]

Yet Niebuhr also acknowledged another warden of incarceration: his professional middle-class flock. Though at first his Bethel congregation consisted mainly of local businessmen, by the late 1920s it had attracted a large and younger class of professionals who, more liberal in religion and politics, supported Niebuhr in his celebrated attacks on Henry Ford. Niebuhr noted the concordance of his religious and political views with those of professional workers. "I have come . . . to be very dependent upon the reactions of the public to my message," he admitted in the *Christian Century*. Niebuhr continued to believe, as he sermonized in 1928, that religion required "the best social intelligence"—an assertion welcome to the ears of his professional congregation. Remarking on the eight-hour day in one sermon, he attributed its attainment not to legislation or class struggle but to the "labor-saving machinery" furnished by technical expertise.[32] Niebuhr's enduring hope that industrial workers would unite with "enlightened" professionals against employers was rooted in his experience as a pastor to the upper middle class in the holy city of Fordist capitalism.

Throughout the 1920s and early 1930s, liberal theology and its deference to expertise served as the basis of Niebuhr's criticisms of liberal optimism. "Those spiritual values which religion conserves" would survive in the modern world, he wrote in an Evangelical Synod magazine, only if "we are wise enough to interpret spiritual affirmations in the light of scientific discoveries." In lectures to the New York School of Social Work in 1930, Niebuhr averred that religion lacked the "detailed knowledge of human motives and of the intricacies of human personality" that only "the science of psychology" possessed. Echoing James in defining religion as "an affair of the emotions," Niebuhr not only placed religious experience under the scrutiny of psychology but also opined that the "therapeutic value" of religion lay not in the "dogmatic and traditional variety" but rather in a more individualized form. "The more purely personal the religious symbol," he claimed, "the more powerful is the emotional force" quickened by religion.[33]

Niebuhr's first book-length reconsideration of his liberal Protestant inheritance, *Does Civilization Need Religion?* (1927), presaged the rest of his career. Throughout the text, Niebuhr mixed romance and pragmatism. At one point he waxed that "religions grow out of real experience in which tragedy mingles with beauty," whereas elsewhere he became the iconoclast arguing for the retention of prophetic power through streamlined design. Religion had to eliminate "maladjustments" so as to provide its "indispensable resources" to "serve the needs of men in modern civilization." Niebuhr even speculated à la Mathews that Protestants might have to "make some concessions which even modern liberalism seems still unwilling to make."[34]

Bowing to the apparent indifference of the Detroit working class to liberal religion, Niebuhr settled on an enlightened minority—a "movement of detachment," a "layman's movement"—as the agent of social reconstruction. This movement's "ministers" would be laymen—"spiritualized technicians," as Niebuhr christened them in a strongly Veblenesque phrase—endowed with the technical skills necessary for industry and politics. Though "religious teachers" might inspire the movement, its "efficacy" depended on this new soviet of religious engineers. Thus, even as Niebuhr characterized liberal Protestantism itself as a product of the "growing intelligence of the privileged and therefore educated classes," his dismissal of the church as a political site left him with the professional middle class as the only available agent of the social gospel. When he left Detroit for New York in the summer of 1928 to assume a post in Christian ethics at Union, the *enfant terrible* so eager to rattle teacups in the social gospel vicarage remained ambivalent about his own allegiances. "I have the uneasy feeling that I belong to those forces that are undermining religion," he wrote in his diary.[35]

"THE IDEALISM OF THE LEVELER": THE SOCIAL GOSPEL AND THE MEDIEVALIST MODERN TEMPER

If he had lived (and cared) to read Niebuhr's diary, William Jennings Bryan might have agreed. In his undelivered speech to the Scopes trial jury, the "Great Commoner" had gathered the religious and populist energies of his career into a final, prescient remonstrance against the technicians, spiritualized or not, of capitalist modernity. Hoping to transform the trial from a showcase of cultural conflict into "a renewal of the issue in Pilate's court"—the struggle between power and love—Bryan pitted force, embodied in Pilate and evolution, against the "meek and lowly Nazarene," the "Apostle of Love." Pointing to the "distinguished educators and scientists" who comprised an "irresponsible oligarchy of self-styled 'intellectuals,' " Bryan warned that the lack of a "heavenly vision" among academics, technicians, and other experts ensured their ministration to the interests of the strong—especially to the state. The state's use of more powerful and efficient military technology in the Great War represented, in Bryan's view, only a glimpse of humanity's impending crucifixion on a cross of secular reason.[36]

The absence of a "heavenly vision" among intellectuals also appalled Lewis Mumford, much of whose cultural criticism in the 1920s traced the results of what he described in *Sticks and Stones* (1924) as "the great heresy of modern life": the inability to revere any "Lords of Life" greater than mechanical power and ingenuity. Mumford's sardonic critique of pragmatism in *The Golden Day* (1926) pointed to the essential failure of moral imagination that James, Dewey, and their epigones were helpless to redeem. Conceding that a distance lay between James and "modern professors" who worked as admen, bond traders, and publicity agents, Mumford still held that "the line that connects them is a fairly clear one." Likewise, Mumford's complaint that Dewey's prose style was "formless as lint" applied more generally to the shapeless, amoral quality of pragmatism itself. "Without vision," Mumford chided, "the pragmatists perish." Mumford had found ample imagery for his own vision in the Middle Ages. In *The Story of Utopias* (1922),[37] he praised the medieval era's "two great international cultural vehicles," the Catholic Church and its Latin language, for fostering a universalist ideal that nonetheless incorporated local and regional differences. The demise of this Christian cosmopolitanism had inflicted a festering wound on the Western moral imagination, Mumford rued, and "nothing that nationalism has done since has repaired this loss."

Mumford's admiration for the Middle Ages (which he displayed occasionally in the pages of *Commonweal*) converged with the medievalist modernism that remained a salient feature of Christian social criticism after World War I. Ralph Adams Cram's claim in *The Great Thousand Years* (1918) that medieval monasticism had encouraged a "brilliant development of personality" and a "spirit of real communism" reflected the persistence of this prewar medievalist current. Jacques Maritain, whose *Art and Scholasticism* and *The Angelic Doctor* (1930) became urtexts among the Catholic intelligentsia, appealed for a modern incarnation of "the spiritual principles and eternal norms of medieval civilization." Medievalism surfaced among Protestants as well, especially in H. Richard Niebuhr, who did not share his brother's hopes for a spiritualized technical class. Likening the postwar moment to the twilight of imperial Rome, Niebuhr urged Protestants in a remarkable 1925 *Christian Century* piece to look "back to Benedict" and consider his order's discipline of prayer, asceticism, and simplicity.[38]

Niebuhr and other medievalists did not, however, countenance retreat from the field of social politics. Though brooding gothically on the apparent fall of Christendom, medievalist moderns placed hope in diminutive prospects for a renewal of civilization. Looking to art, ritual, and small community, Niebuhr, Maritain, and others continued the prewar quest of Walter Rauschenbusch and Vida Scudder for the grail of a Christian modernity. Medievalist moderns insisted that theology occupy the center of social criticism and sought to bestow on the churches a primary agency in social and cultural politics. In a 1927 *Christian Century* essay, Niebuhr prevailed on Protestants to end the "sterile union" of psychology and theology; two years later, in *The Social Sources of Denominationalism* (1929)—a book often cited as a masterpiece of religious sociology—he urged them to annul the marriage of social science and Protestant theology. Frustrated by the intransigence of Protestant racism, Niebuhr concluded that "something more than a sociological cure seems necessary for the healing of this wound in the body of Christ"—implying that something more than a social weapon had inflicted the mutilation. In *The Angelic Doctor,* Maritain echoed Niebuhr in blasting "the imbecile dogma of positivist sociology" that religion was a product of other social forces rather than a social force in its own right.[39]

Medievalist criticism of the modern tradition in religious thought did not, however, entail outright rejection. Christopher Dawson, a British Catholic historian much favored by American Catholic intellectuals, chided liberals for their platitudes about "the liberation of religion from dogma" while demanding that religion "offer some solution to the social and intellectual problems of the modern world." Dogma, Dawson held, was a historical tradition that provided intellectual and political flexibility. Thomism, Maritain insisted, was "a progressive and assimilative philosophy" capable of incorporating modern scientific knowledge while maintaining the integrity of revealed truths. Though Niebuhr wrote scornfully in 1925 of the social gospel's degeneration into a "soup-kitchen caricature" drained of evangelical fervor, he conceded in 1931 that a new Protestantism would have to incorporate the achievements of the social gospel or risk failing to "relate theology vitally to one of the sources of real life in the present." Another source of vitality, he told his Yale students, lay in the working class, over whose "progressive alienation . . . from religion" liberals had presided. In Niebuhr's view, the eschatological wisdom that only catastrophe forced fundamental change resonated more deeply with the experiences of American workers than liberal faith in reason and orderly progress. Though not conversant in the medievalist idiom, Howard Thurman, a young minister and theologian, and the first black board member of the Fellowship of Reconciliation (FOR), contended that the cause of racial justice hinged more on spiritual force than on bureaucratic effort and more on the wealth and texture of African-American memory than on rational enlightenment. If the spirit of Jesus spread by "contagion" rather than "organization," Thurman told his fellow preachers in 1928, then the black minister must "read, though through tears, the story of the spiritual strivings of his people."[40] Though affirming the obvious need for knowledge and organization, Thurman, Niebuhr, Maritain, and Dawson trusted even more in memory to educate and embolden the social passion.

Convinced that "the religious impulse" drew sustenance not primarily from "the arid and narrow region of the discursive reason" but from the ground of history—"faith in an historical person, an historical community, and an historical tradition," as Christopher Dawson argued in *Progress and Religion* (1929)—medievalists echoed prewar social gospelers in affirming "church" as the model of beloved community. Pointing in a leftward political direction, medievalists bore a distinctive set of political virtues, upheld a religious internationalism, and beckoned toward a renewal of artisanal democracy. Niebuhr invoked "Beloved Community" in *Social Sources* to counter Barth's aspersion on the redemptive value of human action, asserting that the church possessed political relevance "as a society" and not as a junior partner to other social forces. The church, Niebuhr cautioned, meant not the churches as they stood—divided by denomination, nation, race, and class—but "the church within the churches," a movement or communion of saints dedicated to a "communism of love" practiced by the first Christians, the Franciscans, and the Quakers. Niebuhr coupled his "communism of love" with respect for the ideological and organizational acumen of the Marxist left. Christian communism, he clarified, relied not on the "cynical counsel of self-interest and class warfare" but on the virtues of patience, self-sacrifice, repentance, and trust in God. In "Back to Benedict," however, he had argued that the monastic orders had been a prototype of modern socialist parties, a "Black International" in the theoretical and social vanguard of their times. Niebuhr's own Socialist Party membership, as well as his 1930 trip to the Soviet Union with brother Reinhold and Sherwood Eddy, evinced a commitment to class struggle.[41] Thus the "communism of love" was a gesture toward some form of social theory (akin to those of Rauschenbusch or Scudder) that set class politics in a broader religious movement.

Maritain, writing of the Church as the "Mystical Body of Christ" in the ecclesiological parlance favored by north Atlantic Catholic intellectuals after the war, speculated that a revival of the social witness depended not on the reinstatement of Christendom but on a new kind of church, a "network of hearths . . . disseminated among the nations" that doubled as communities of worship and production. Shuster proposed that Catholic architects and urban planners design updated medieval villages, replete with basilicas, churches, central apartment houses, factories, and offices decorated with religious art, all centered around a cathedral, "the place around which all of [medieval] life—including economics—pulsed strongly."[42]

This liturgical emphasis reflected both the endurance of prewar Catholic industrial democracy and the indigenous impact of the "liturgical renaissance" present in European Catholicism for over a generation. Convinced that attention to ceremony would revitalize Catholic faith, liturgical revivalists rummaged through the Catholic past for art, music, prayers, vesture, architecture, and ritual. As the renaissance moved to America in the 1920s, it revivified the medievalist Catholic discourse of industrial democracy, surrounding the artisanal ideal with the incense of liturgy and aesthetics. The Liturgical Arts Society, founded in 1928 at Portsmouth Abbey, Rhode Island, by a group of young, disaffected lay artists, draftsmen, and architects, sponsored the study of medieval art, vestments, architecture, plain song, and Gregorian chant, berating the sentimentality of American Catholicism's copycat Gothic, Byzantine, and Romanesque churches. In its journal, *Liturgical Arts,* members often railed against mass production for its erosion of aesthetic intelligence and dexterity, drawing on Maritain's work as well as that of the British Catholic engraver, sculptor, and essayist Eric Gill, whose writings on art, technology, and religion—as well as his life with other artisans in a "cell of good living" at Ditchling Common—held out the promise of a world transfigured in beauty, craft, democracy, and Christian love.[43]

The exemplary exponent of medievalism was G. K. Chesterton, who acquired an almost cultish following among American Catholic intellectuals after the war. Combining an unshakable commitment to democracy with a suspicion of modern professions of emancipation, Chesterton—feeling "the attraction of the red cap as well as the red cross, of the Marseillaise as well as the Magnificat"— produced a penetrating corpus of cultural criticism. His account of his travels in the United States, *What I Saw in America* (1922), contained some of the decade's most trenchant reflections on the future of secular, capitalist modernity.[44]

In two essays, "A Meditation in Broadway" and "The Future of Democracy," Chesterton examined the impact of mass culture and modern science on democracy and spiritual health. In modern America, Chesterton thought, the Enlightenment had blossomed disappointingly into a culture of rampant triviality, misplaced enthusiasm, and perverted religious longing, a glittering wasteland epitomized in Broadway. Walking under the "artificial suns and stars of this tremendous thoroughfare," Chesterton attested to the majesty and beauty of the modern metropolis: the Manhattan skyline, studded and draped with ads and lights, beckoned any sensitive soul to contemplate "a brotherhood broader than Broadway." But to what trinity of hopes did those lights and towers testify? Not liberty, equality, and fraternity—and certainly not faith, hope, and charity—but "Tang Tonic Today, Tang Tonic To-Morrow, Tang Tonic All The Time." Only a people gulled by "a sort of mesmerism" could laud the squandering of such energy, treasure, and imagination on so petty a concern.[45]

Chesterton objected as a democrat to the servility enjoined by Broadway's advertising and architecture—its refulgence, he wrote, "does not come from any popular enthusiasm at all"—but he objected as a Christian to the bogus salvation offered on the broad and easy way. Broadway was a phony Eden, planted with "groves of fiery trees . . . golden foliage and fruits," and strewn with sights to rival "the flaming sword or the purple and peacock plumage of the seraphim." As hypnotists holding the means of "pyrotechnic violence," the adman and the financier inscribed "their commands in heaven with a finger of fire," while the industrial and mercantile priesthood emblazoned a "beautiful superstition" in the skies. Chesterton reproved the enthusiasm of consumer modernity with a stark reminder that all glory was fleeting. "Nothing remains at last of a flaming rocket, but a falling stick."[46]

If the undemocratic avenue of Broadway led to the false religion of capitalism, the cultural authority of science suggested to Chesterton the need to root democracy in religious not secular ground. Against Dewey, Mencken, and other acolytes of a post-Christian order, Chesterton argued that the most insidious enemy of democracy was not religion but science, the very discourse to which liberal and socialist intellectuals had always pinned their hopes. Pointing especially to racialist and eugenic theories, Chesterton rejected the argument that the scientific method supplied an unimpeachable basis for a democratic culture. Because it could demonstrate indisputably wide variations of intelligence, skill, and merit, science undermined belief in human equality and buttressed the leadership of elites. A democracy rooted in religion, on the other hand, rested on a belief in divine parentage that made men brothers as well as equals and could thus assure its citizens that "its indestructible minimum of democracy really is indestructible." Thus, Chesterton reasoned, revolutionary élan pulsed more strongly and surely through religious rather than secular channels. "The idealism of the leveler," he reflected, "could be put in the form of an appeal to Scripture, and could not be put in the form of an appeal to Science."[47]

Democracy had no reliable foundation, Chesterton concluded, but in the narrow and certain way, "a dogma about the divine origin of man." Any secular groundwork was a "sentimental confusion, full of merely verbal echoes of the older creeds." American democracy would remain truly democratic, and its citizens would eschew the beguiling light and plumage of Broadway, only if they remained religious—which in Chesterton's view meant Catholic Christian. Chesterton skirted the problem of religious diversity, lamely dismissing it as another of modernity's ruses. Still, he underlined the perennial quandary of secular democrats: how a democratic community (especially a "beloved" one) could survive if its convictions were recognized as purely human—hence fallible, contestable, and revocable. In Chesterton's view, there was neither security nor meaning—save, perhaps, those acquired in a Hobbesian struggle for power—if the universe lacked "a centre of significance and authority that is the author of our rights."[48] To Americans increasingly informed that progress and freedom depended on the abandonment of religious illusions, Chesterton reasserted the orthodox basis of republican democracy.

A short time after Chesterton rued the unbrotherly future of American democracy, the Benedictines of St. John's College in Collegeville, Minnesota, led by Virgil Michel, a former "worker-priest," published the first issue of *Orate Fratres* ("speak, brothers") in April 1926. Illustrated by Eric Gill, the inaugural cover bore an epigram—"to restore all things in Christ"—that acquired a special urgency three years later when the temples of the moneychangers buckled.[49] As the fault lines of Western capitalism opened and widened, as the noxious gases of fascism and reaction spewed from the cracks, as the ministrations of experts proved ineffective—talk of "reconstruction" faded quickly. Restoring all things in Christ required a mandate for revolution.

✛

CHAPTER THREE

The Permanent Revolution:

Christianity, Moral Economy, and Revolutionary Symbolism, 1932–1941

In March 1932, shortly after the Japanese invasion of Manchuria, the Niebuhr brothers sparred in the *Christian Century* over the proper response to the episode. Seeking "the grace of doing nothing," Richard argued that Americans should desist from high-minded but helpless outrage and abjure the civic arsenal of letters, resolutions, marches, and petitions. Admitting impotence in the face of crisis, Christians should instead choose between different kinds of inactivity, since in not acting "we are also affecting the course of history." Richard held up the apparent indifference of Communists to the fate of Manchuria as a model. Maintaining a "long vision [and] steadfast hope," they engaged in "the slow laborious process of building up . . . those cells of communism which will be ready to inherit the new world" after the collapse of capitalism and nationalism. Christians, too, needed to create small communities of partisans—cells—as organizers and evangelists for the cause, since like Communists they recognized a force making for righteousness in history that works not primarily through our "slow accretion of better habits"—the delusion of religious and secular liberals—but through "revolutionary change which will involve considerable destruction." Christians, Richard advised, should build "cells of those within each nation" who, renouncing their loyalties to capitalism and the nation-state, are united in a higher loyalty that transcends "national and class lines of division." This "radical Christianity" eventually might constitute a "Christian international"—the "Third Christian international," Richard emphasized, following on the first of Rome and the second of Geneva, itself already well on "the way of the Second Socialist International."[1]

A few weeks later, Reinhold Niebuhr reprised the argument of *Moral Man and Immoral Society*, just published to the consternation of the social gospel community. Admitting that Richard's "ethical perfectionism and apocalyptic note" captured the spirit of the gospels better than his own *realpolitik*, he nonetheless dismissed inactivity as irresponsible—not, he conceded, naïve. As a fellow socialist, Reinhold heard the Marxist chords of Richard's argument, affirming that his brother advanced a "realistic interpretation of the facts of history." Still, he insisted, if any justice could be attained in a sinful world, then violence and coercion were worthy, if not perfect, methods for the political Christian.[2] Activity, for Reinhold, encompassed the available array of social forces: state power, class war, and physical and political intimidation.

In the same year, Catholic intellectuals faced a similar if less pronounced conflict over the nature of Christian political commitment. The year before, Pius XI had issued *Quadragesimo anno* on the fortieth anniversary of Leo's *Rerum novarum*. Like its predecessor, this encyclical was deliberately opaque: Pius' reference to "occupational groups," for instance, could be construed either as a simple endorsement of labor unions or as a call for a corporatist political economy. Distancing himself from right-wing advocates of "the corporate state" in Italy, France, and Spain, John Ryan, the doyen of Catholic liberalism in 1932, took the encyclical as an imprimatur for "industrial democracy." Yet Ryan saw no immediate political prospects for the papal plan. Unimpressed by both President Herbert Hoover and his Democratic challenger Franklin Roosevelt, Ryan lukewarmly supported the Democrats.[3]

Yet other Catholics drew closer to a program of cells. Covering hunger marchers in Washington in December 1932, journalist Dorothy Day— veteran of the lyrical left, contributor to *Commonweal* and the *New Masses*, and recent convert to Catholicism—wearily endorsed the crowd's demands for social legislation as "temporary panaceas for the evils of the depression." She warmed, however, to a banner inscribed with the slogan "WORK NOT WAGES"—a call, she believed, for an anarchist system of complete workers' "ownership of and responsibility for the means of production." Day herself had long revered both the syndicalism of the Industrial Workers of the World (I.W.W.) and the anarchism of Peter Kropotkin.[4]

Still, Day left the marchers nonplused, admiring the ability of the Communists to organize the marchers but bemoaning the apparent indifference of the Catholic hierarchy. "Where was the Catholic leadership in the gathering of bands of men and women," she remembered asking herself, for the "works of mercy that the comrades had always made part of their technique in reaching the workers?" Wandering into the National Shrine of the Immaculate Conception, Day prayed for the grace to do something. "I offered up my prayers . . . that some way be shown me to do the work that I wanted to do for labor." On returning to New York, Day found the short, stocky Peter Maurin in her apartment, "as ragged and rugged as any of the marchers I had left." Sent there by George Shuster, Maurin had, like Day, combined the erudition of hard knocks with that of the library—itinerant labor in France, Canada, and America; study of Aquinas, Kropotkin, Marx, Lenin, and Maritain; and authorship of "easy essays" that excoriated industrialism. Over the next few days, Maurin harangued Day on three points: a Catholic radical newspaper for the masses, communities of "cult, culture, and cultivation," and a theology of radicalism, invoking Lenin's dictum that "there is no revolution without a theory of revolution."[5] Day's prayer, apparently, had been answered.

These episodes illustrate the conflicts provoked among Christian intellectuals in the 1930s. The decade has been seen as the end of a "Protestant search for political realism," a vindication of Reinhold Niebuhr's divorce of Christian love from political morality. Another story relates how Catholic liberals such as John Ryan successfully educated their brethren in a "badly needed realism" about the shortcomings of capitalism and the possibilities of the state. Through narrowing the expansive hopes of the social witness, the realism of Niebuhr and Ryan sanctioned a New Deal order that marked the most enduring achievement of social gospel ideals. Yet realism, both as political strategy and as cultural politics, was precisely what was at issue in the controversies of the 1930s.[6] What were the most effective responses to the catastrophes of depression and fascism? What were the most truthful and provocative modes of representing these calamities?

Conceiving of material life and culture as parts of a larger sacral order, social gospelers linked the struggles for a moral economy and revolutionary symbolism, stamping the 1930s as a distinctive chapter in the history of the modern American moral imagination. By declaring religion of no special or immediate relevance to social and political strife, the "realism" of Reinhold Niebuhr and his partisans licensed the political, corporate, and military elites of the New Deal order. Richard Niebuhr's "realism"—articulated in a Trotskyite argot of "cells" and "permanent revolution"—both portended the direction of his brother's gospel and posed an alternative to Protestant *realpolitik*. Catholics forged a twofold, conflicted "labor Catholicism." On the one hand, John Ryan and Philip Murray, of the Congress of Industrial Organizations (CIO), espoused a democratic corporatism that demanded organized labor's tenure on the directorate of the Fordist order. On the other, Dorothy Day and the Catholic Workers sketched a more far-reaching vision of social reconstruction that beheld the transcendence of the Fordist regime in favor of a more decentralized, anarchosyndicalist moral economy. These debates over political economy converged with conflicts over moral language and imagery, the contents of what Kenneth Burke dubbed the "revolutionary symbolism" required to elicit popular recognition and commitment. Catholic medievalism, together with Protestant notions of mythology and history, comprised religious-popular strategies to fuse intellectuals, workers, and others with a common imagery and identity.

"Secular Prayers": The Search for a Common Faith in the Years of Depression and Fascism

Historians have long recognized that the Depression witnessed both an upheaval in the nation's social life and political economy—the rise of the "New Deal order" in "the age of the CIO"—and a seminal moment in its cultural history. As Warren Susman has observed, the idea of culture itself received unprecedented attention at this time from scholars of anthropology, literary history, and "folk culture.". When aligned on the left, cultural workers in publishing houses and magazines, the cultural projects of the Works Progress Administration, and the maturing mass-culture industries joined what Michael Denning has called a "cultural front" that extended across a number of conflicts, especially over the nature of "the people": the "national-popular," as Antonio Gramsci called it, the most coveted cultural and political prize of the period. Intellectuals on the cultural front sought, in Susman's words, not merely commitment but also "a special collective relationship in which all Americans might share a new sense of common belief, ritual observance, common emotional sharing."[7]

On both sides of the Atlantic, this political attention to culture led intellectuals to religion. Frightened by the success of fascism, European Marxists studied religion to clarify both the nature of "cultural hegemony" and the revolutionary dimensions of culture. Antonio Gramsci, for instance, recommended the Catholic church as a model for the Communist party. Church leaders, he explained, preserved "the doctrinal unity of the whole mass of the faithful" with an "iron discipline" on intellectuals and a careful cultivation of "strong mass movements"—popular fronts, so to speak—that issued in "the creation of new religious orders." Even as Gramsci insisted on fluid channels between party and people, his assertion that the party's main duty was to "lead [the people] to a higher conception of life" implied a clerical status, however secular, self-critical, and temporary, for Marxist intellectuals.[8]

While Gramsci studied religion largely for tactical wisdom, Walter Benjamin—whose work before the 1930s had contained numerous theological motifs—hoped to refashion Marxism itself into a new ark for the messianic desires long encased in Judaism and Christianity. In his 1936 essay on the mechanical reproduction of art, Benjamin identified the use of the earliest art in magical and religious ritual as the source of its "aura," its capacity to legitimate social life. Eager to realize the liberating possibilities of mass communication, Benjamin argued that the Fordist production of images finally "emancipates" art from this "parasitical dependence on ritual." Thus his call for a "progressive intelligence" to "politicize art" asked, in effect, for the bestowal on art of a new, secular aura. Yet, as the European situation worsened, Benjamin concluded that theology must become the very soul of historical materialism. Marxism could be "a match for anyone," he mused in his "Theses on the Philosophy of History" (1940), if it procured "the services of theology," for "our image of happiness is indissolubly bound up with the image of redemption." Redemption, he argued, entailed the salvation of all previous generations, who must not be consigned to oblivion by the acolytes of "progress." The writing of history became a crucial battle site, for "even the dead will not be safe" from "the Antichrist" and his strictly forward-looking sense of time and significance. Benjamin saw a different history and politics in "chips of Messianic time," fragments of hope which, carried along in the temporal stream, made the present rich in revolutionary, redemptive possibilities. The Jews, Benjamin reminded himself, lived by such remembrance, knowing that every second could be "the strait gate through which the Messiah might enter."[9]

Like Benjamin, some American left intellectuals discerned a religious quality in their struggles against capitalism and fascism. Sharing an inchoate sense that some religious or sacral cultural order was necessary, they urged intellectuals throughout the cultural apparatus to create this new structure of meanings. When Lewis Corey urged professionals to endorse the Communist ticket in his eloquent 1932 pamphlet *Culture and the Crisis,* he called on "the teacher, writer, and artist"—not the minister, rabbi, or priest—to "fashion the creative ideology of a new world and a new order."[10]

Kenneth Burke, John Dewey, and Thurman Arnold clearly connected the quest for a new, common, sacral culture and the cultural politics of professionals. Burke's Marxist work of the 1930s not only abounded in references to religion but also propounded a theory of culture as the history of clashes over sacred symbols. In his controversial address on "Revolutionary Symbolism in America" to the American Writers' Congress in 1935, Burke likened cultural workers to "the best artists of the religious era [who] recommended or glorified their Faith." Urging his comrades in good "national-popular" fashion to enlist American symbols and traditions in the cause of socialism, Burke also recalled the cunning of the early Church. Ancient and medieval Christians, he noted, had "invariably converted pagans by making the local deities into saints." Burke's analogy was not facile, as he demonstrated in *Permanence and Change* (1935), *Attitudes Toward History* (1937), and *The Philosophy of Literary Form* (1941). Defining culture as a form of "secular prayer," Burke cast cultural history as the story of successive sacral orders and "impieties," challenges to the reigning symbols that became new orders in their turn. The "priests" and "spiritual bankers" of capitalism resided in the culture industries, technical cadres, and intellectual bureaucracies. Revolutionary writers and artists comprised, Burke believed, the latest agents of impiety, busily crafting the credos of a secular, communist culture from within the culture industry itself. Indeed, Burke ended *The Philosophy of Literary Form* with a "Dialectician's Hymn" to dialectical materialism—the "god-function" term that summarized revolutionary aspiration—that expressed the utopian hope that "how things are / And how we say things are / Are one."[11]

While Burke longed to recite a new breviary of secular prayers, Dewey pleaded for *A Common Faith* (1934), "a religious faith that shall not be confined to sect, class, or race." Recently characterized by Robert Westbrook as an ideal of "consummatory experience," a kind of beatific vision for a secular, radical democracy, the pragmatist sacrality of *A Common Faith*, though it weakly recalled the religiosity of progressive intellectuals, certainly ratified the clerical status of experts. In Dewey's view, faith and culture were inseparable. Faith—"the unification of the self through allegiance to inclusive ideal ends"—depended on symbols, especially of persons and events imaginatively idealized so as to "enlist devotion and inspire endeavor." These symbols required the approval of a "final arbiter," a group (like Burke's priests) endowed with cultural authority. Dewey conferred these powers of culture and sacrality on the professional middle class, whose relocation of cultural power in the mass cultural and intellectual institutions marked both a shift in "the social center of gravity" and a "revolution in the seat of intellectual authority." Their cultural production now exercised "the greater hold upon the thought and interest of most persons—"even," Dewey emphasized, "of those holding membership in churches." Eager to appropriate religious "ideals" while discarding dogma and superstition, Dewey proposed "the significant achievements of men in science and art" as the objects of the common faith.[12] Although Dewey rejected a technocratic politics, *A Common Faith* concluded his lifelong endeavor to preserve Christian virtue without Christian theology under the auspices of a modern, scientific clerisy.

Marxists and radical democrats were not the only intellectuals eager to create a new sacral language. Thurman Arnold, professor of law at Yale and head of the Treasury Department's antitrust division, devoted considerable attention to the politics of culture and belief, the "spiritual government" of society as he called it in *The Symbols of Government* (1935). While insisting on a formal separation of "spiritual government" from the practical organization of society, Arnold highlighted the importance of symbols and symbol-making institutions. The spiritual government always promoted and chastised the temporal order, Arnold believed, as when "the partnership of feudal states and the Church during the Middle Ages" resembled that of "the great corporations and our National Government." Against the pernicious folklore of laissez-faire capitalism ("folklore" connoting for Arnold both popular myth and the ill-informed opinion of nonexperts), a new class of "business and social technicians"—engineers, social workers, economists, political scientists, and lawyers—was developing "a creed of its own." Though Arnold was no man of the left, his characterization of the New Deal and its professional supporters as a "spiritual government" heightened the significance of the "laboring of American culture" undertaken by Popular Front workers in the Works Projects Administration (WPA) art, theater, and writers' projects.[13]

The Nerve of Action: Mythology, Realism, and the Secular Politics of Reinhold Niebuhr

As tenuous claimants to the "spiritual government" of the nation, liberal Protestants fretted incessantly during the 1930s about the continuing "religious depression" and its impact on the social witness. "This period of depression has brought forth no revival of religion," the *Christian Century* observed in 1935, and the churches were "wholly unprepared to take account of it, and to minister to the deepest human need which it discloses." Secular observers agreed. Modern churchmen, Kenneth Burke observed in 1935, were now vicars of spiritually gutted churches with "broken windows and littered doorways." The radical journalist James Rorty noted ruefully in 1936 that "Protestant and Catholic churches" were "culture-makers and culture-bearers . . . without effect."[14]

The demoralization and political inertia of the Protestant mainline often was lamented by social gospelers. When Walter Marshall Horton complained in 1934 that liberal churches had "no corporate life, no common consciousness," and when F. Ernst Johnson wrote a year later that the liberal churches lacked "a group conscience that will support the action we propose to take," both men registered a drift and lethargy throughout liberal Protestant religious culture just when a social gospel was needed most urgently. As Samuel C. Kinchloe, of the Federal Council of Churches, declared in his sobering 1937 report on religious life, "the time was overdue for men again to be reminded of the need to let the spiritual dominate the material order."[15]

At this point in most histories, Reinhold Niebuhr takes command of the moment, dismissing those liberal social gospelers who lacked (it is often argued) the clear-eyed, hard-boiled realism that dictated a revolutionary program of social transformation, the discomfiture of middle-class congregations, and the abandonment of pacifism. Ensconced at Union, Niebuhr became the social gospel's most fearsome warrior. Although a member of such organizations as the Socialist party, the Fellowship of Reconciliation (FOR), the League for Industrial Democracy, and the League for Independent Political Action, Niebuhr grew restless among his fellow progressive professionals, divining their naiveté as he noted the pride of secular radicals. Thus historians have routinely praised Niebuhr's neoorthodox rejection of liberal idealism and socialist secularity for bringing a new tough-mindedness to the American progressive tradition. With his neoorthodox reminder of human intransigence and his realism about the limits of Christian love, Niebuhr forced liberal Protestants and other progressives to relinquish the vertiginous ideals once associated with "personality" and assume a more sober and tragic responsibility for the vagaries of human affairs. Niebuhr, in the words of Richard Fox, delivered "a telling blow to the progressive faith in history and expertise."[16]

Yet historians have misconstrued the debate over realism among liberal Protestants in the 1930s, for the conflict pivoted not simply on the issues of socialism and violence but on theology and especially the political nature of Christianity. Far from introducing a more religious sense of sin that invalidated the power of experts, Niebuhr actually inhibited the creation of a popular, democratic left precisely in so far as he *devalued* the importance of religion. Niebuhr's neoorthodoxy—the most advanced modernist expression of liberal religious idealism—served to weaken religion as a distinctive political identity and to cede the terrain of social and cultural politics to professional and managerial elites. In his role as a Protestant socialist, Niebuhr rehearsed his part as *pontifex maximus* to Cold War liberals.

Niebuhr's reputation as a tablet-smashing prophet rests on his own brash and brawny declamations. Railing in *Moral Man* that "our religious inheritance has been dissipated by the liberal culture of modernity," Niebuhr berated all wallowers in the "sentimentality" of good will, education, and civility concocted by Dewey. Too many progressives wanted, in his estimation, "a mild capitalism, joined with a mild democracy, garnished with a mild philistinism and perfected with a genteel religion." Recanting much of his work from the 1920s in a 1939 *Christian Century* symposium—work powered, he confessed, by "all the theological windmills against which I tilt my sword"—and arming himself with what he called in *Reflections on the End of an Era* (1934) the "bizarre and capricious" weaponry of "radical politics and conservative religious convictions," the Protestant Quixote rode with a lance directed at the twin enemies of liberalism and capitalism.[17]

Niebuhr's gendering of the political world into a soft, sentimental, heretical liberalism against a martial, realistic, orthodox socialism stimulated other young Turks keen on smashing tea cups in the social gospel parsonage. Yet it also concealed the umbilical cord that still connected Niebuhr to the liberal Protestant social gospel. As he confided later to Harry Emerson Fosdick, he had always believed that there were "many values in what is generally called liberal Protestantism that must be preserved." H. Richard Niebuhr—always Reinhold's best critic—perceived more clearly than his brother's adversaries the underlying liberalism of *Moral Man* and other works. "You think of religion as a power," he chided Reinhold in response to *Moral Man*—"dangerous sometimes, helpful sometimes—that's liberal." Contrary to his casting as the neoorthodox specter haunting liberal Protestantism, Reinhold Niebuhr provoked an internal debate among liberal Protestant social gospelers, one through which most of them persevered, in Yale theologian Robert Calhoun's words, "bandaged but unbowed." Writing in the same 1939 *Christian Century* symposium as Niebuhr and Calhoun, John C. Bennett, one of Niebuhr's closest friends and comrades, declared that he was "a changed liberal—but still a liberal," while Georgia Harkness took pride in her own "unashamed and unrepentant" liberalism.[18] Neoorthodoxy was the grim face of liberal Protestantism, and the Niebuhrian moment marked the immersion of the social gospel in the muddied waters of liberal religious idealism.

If the social gospel seemed "lacking in thrills and moral splendor," as Calhoun put it, Niebuhr sought to electrify it by emphasizing the pragmatic value of illusion. Anticipating both Burke's call for a "revolutionary symbolism" and Dewey's plea for "a common faith," Niebuhr stressed forcefully in *Moral Man* the need for "necessary illusions" in social conflict, "the right dogmas, symbols, and emotionally potent oversimplifications" that supplied "morale" for combat. (Niebuhr in fact praised Dewey's book in the *Nation* for exemplifying "the kind of faith which prophetic religion has tried to express mythically and symbolically.") Revolutionaries required a strapping spiritual musculature, for only those who had "substituted some new illusions for the abandoned ones" could be "effective agents" of social transformation. Partisans of dispassionate reason, he warned in *Reflections,* would only "lame the nerve of action." Religion was one such illusion or, in Niebuhr's words, a myth. A myth was not a fable in a pejorative sense. Niebuhr distinguished between "primitive" myths—prescientific accounts of natural and historical events—and "permanent" myths, which illustrated enduring truths and ultimate longings. Myth inhabited a foggy but creative zone between fiction and literal truth; in fact, Niebuhr felt, the question of whether or not religious statements were literally true had "no particular significance."[19]

As for the Niebuhr of Detroit, religion remained a "resource," a leaven to socialist politics and a tool in the struggle for cultural power. Niebuhr seconded St. Paul's remark that preachers were deceivers, yet true, for they proclaimed "a great truth in the interest of which many little lies are told." "The truest visions of religion are illusions," he asserted, because they move believers to act as "if the truth is not doubted." While all the great religious and political leaders told noble lies, the religious believed their own illusions—even Jesus, in whose "sublime naiveté" the Christian myth was born.[20]

This modernist idealization of religion—foreshadowed in his 1930 lectures on the therapeutics of religious faith—set Niebuhr's subsequent ideological and political trajectory. For all his sound and fury about the bankruptcy of secular progressivism, he demonstrated toward secular political culture a deference validated by the notions of illusion and mythology. Convinced that, as he wrote in *Moral Man,* "pure religious idealism does not concern itself with the social problem," Niebuhr did indeed shift Protestant social criticism from personality to responsibility, as Richard Fox has argued.[21] However, in banishing personality "to an ideal realm beyond society," in Fox's words, Niebuhr disarmed personality of its critical force, delivered society to the sway of *realpolitik,* and sanctioned rather than challenged the authority of political and managerial elites.

Niebuhr offered no clear religious alternatives in cultural and social politics. He could only cavil, as he did in *Moral Man,* that middle-class blacks hampered the progress of their race by their "identification . . . with the more privileged white race" or that unionized workers shared the acquisitive ideal of their employers. Looking at Germany, Niebuhr attributed much of the success of fascism to its cultic and mythological ingenuity. The average American industrialist, he observed in *Reflections*, "cut a very poor figure as a social liturgist" because he had no "effective ritual" that draped his avarice in the garments of morality or beauty. The fascists, while diabolical, were not prosaic, exhibiting a genius for "pageantry" and "political liturgies." Niebuhr's final dismissal of fascist liturgies as "cheap theatricality," however, suggested both the capacities and limitations of his cultural criticism. Tracing the rise of mass culture to the Fordist homogenization of work, Niebuhr decried the "morbid eagerness" with which individuals sought out sports events and public spectacles to provide collective illusions of abundance and solidarity. Embodied in "standardized cinema and conventionalized amusements," mass culture distracted its consumers as it integrated them into capitalism's "great mechanical slaughtering enterprise." Yet, despite his insight into the sacral nature of fascist and capitalist pageantry—consumer culture, he observed, was the "effective ritual" constructed in the culture industries—Niebuhr could not point to an alternative cult.[22]

By the same token, Niebuhr could offer only a less forceful version of the "democratic social engineering" that pervaded liberal and socialist thought. Niebuhr often leavened his criticism of reason with praise for "social intelligence." Reason, he wrote in *Moral Man* (which contained an entire chapter on "rational resources" for social change), could align impulses with "an inclusive social ideal." Three years later, in *An Interpretation of Christian Ethics* (1935), he expressed confidence that inequality could be overcome by "an intelligent control of social life." Throughout most of the 1930s, Niebuhr felt that the socialist left possessed a keener social intelligence than liberals. When Niebuhr marched in the front lines of a "radical religion" embodied in the Fellowship of Socialist Christians and theorized in *Radical Religion*, Marxism served as his ideological and political compass. "Radicalism," he judged in *Reflections*, was more realistic than liberalism or religion in "gauging the social forces of the contemporary situation." Echoing Rauschenbusch, Niebuhr lauded the "vast social progress" ushered in by capitalism and argued for socialism as the legitimate historical offspring of corporate capitalism—"the next step forward," as he wrote in *World Tomorrow* in 1936. Marxism, he argued, was the "only possible property system compatible with the necessities of a technical age"—the necessities, that is, of the Fordist order.[23] Braced by theological modernism, Niebuhr conferred political relevance only on those identities and possibilities generated from within the secular bounds of capitalism.

Niebuhr's default was evident in his evaluation of the Delta Cooperative, an interracial agrarian cooperative in Mississippi. Delta residents considered themselves a prefigurative community of "socialized abundance" and "prophetic religion." Niebuhr (one of the farm's trustees) called Delta "the most significant experiment in social Christianity now being conducted in America." Yet his realism served at almost every turn to diminish that very significance. Although the tenants came from among the "religiously disinherited" who realized that "the organized church as such does not serve them," they still possessed a relatively "undissipated religious inheritance," especially the prophetic heritage prominent among black farmers and preachers. Niebuhr also noted the ecclesial character of meetings of the Southern Tenant Farmers' Union, where members performed a "Ceremony of the Land" replete with biblical passages giving sanction to demands of "Land for the Landless." Yet the ever-chary Niebuhr declined to confront southern white ministers who defended Jim Crow, explaining to northern liberals who condemned racism "rightly but simply" that the desire to preserve "racial integrity" was a "collective will-to-live as potent as any individual impulse of survival."[24] This vague and troubling concession to race devalued the religious energy Niebuhr himself recognized as the catalyst of the Delta experiment.

This kind of pragmatism led Niebuhr to anoint the professional middle class as the bearer of the social gospel. Professionals had been the most supportive members of his Detroit congregation (as well as the basis of his hopes for "spiritualized technicians"), and Niebuhr now moved in New York's socialist political culture and liberal Protestant seminary world—circles composed almost entirely of college-educated workers. Although Niebuhr was ambivalent about these "more intelligent portions of a community," he nonetheless foreshadowed his definitive turn toward professional and managerial elites during and after the war. In *Moral Man,* he speculated that "professional people, clerks, small retailers, and bureaucrats," however "ambiguous in membership and social outlook," might still hold "the clue to the riddle of the future of western civilization." What socialists needed to radicalize professionals, he wrote in an oracular and tantalizing way, was "some new radical force and interest . . . introduced into the political situation." As he moved from Marxism to a kind of left populism over the 1930s, Niebuhr cast the middle class as a key player in the revolutionary drama. "Enlightened" professionals, for instance, figured prominently in the farmer-labor coalition he championed just before World War II.[25]

Those pacifists who suffered Niebuhr's scorn often suggested that the churches constituted the "new radical force" he sought in *Moral Man*—a suggestion Niebuhr routinely brushed aside. Niebuhr's fellow *enrages* sometimes pointedly upbraided him for his inattention to the church as a political force. As Francis Miller, head of the World Student Christian Federation (and later an editor of Niebuhr's *Christianity and Crisis*), wrote to him in 1933, Niebuhr had no conviction that "Christianity has a unique function to fulfill" in social revolution because he had "no theory of the Church or of its function and task in the midst of modern civilization." John C. Bennett argued in *Christian Realism* (1941) that the churches needed to "develop among [their] own people a mind that understands the social implications of Christianity." "If we cannot change the mind of the constituency of the Church," Bennett wrote, "we cannot change the mind of the world."[26]

For Niebuhr, however, the full force of Christian faith appeared either among sects such as the Quakers or in "intimate religious communities" that "do not conquer society." Niebuhr himself acknowledged the power of his critics' position. His invocation in *Moral Man* of the "spiritual discipline against resentment" came in a discussion of nonviolence, and he concluded—pointing to Gandhi's achievements in South Africa and India as models for American blacks—that "there is no problem of political life to which religious imagination can make a larger contribution than this problem of developing nonviolent resistance." Still, Niebuhr's dismissal of pacifists as a "Quaker canticle" when he left the FOR in 1934 reflected his profound aversion to the notion of religious community as the fulcrum of a radical culture and politics.[27]

Unwilling to act through Protestant churches as cultural and political sites, liberal Protestant social gospelers were overtaken by evangelical and fundamentalist churches whose remarkable growth at this time reflected an élan and tenacity comparable with that of organizers in the CIO. The engagement of numerous Protestant ministers, seminarians, and laity in the labor struggles of the 1930s only underscored this problem. Many liberal Protestants supported strikes, organized workers and farmers, and agitated for civil rights. Others produced remarkable artifacts of labor reportage and sociological reflection, especially Howard Kester's story of the Southern Tenant Farmers' Union in *Revolt of the Sharecroppers* (1936) and Liston Pope's *Millhands and Preachers* (1942), the classic account of religion and class conflict in Gastonia, North Carolina.[28] Yet the failure of liberals, realist or otherwise, to launch a coordinated movement on the social and cultural fronts—a failure epitomized in the refusal of the Federal Council of Churches to take political positions—ensured that liberal Protestantism would play at best an adjunctive role in the remaking of the nation's moral economy.

This failure pushed liberal Protestantism toward Niebuhr's secularized politics, which, in casting the problem of political morality in terms of "moral man" and "immoral society," ignored churches as sites of the "spiritual discipline" necessary for a popular religious left. Bereft of any specifically religious discipline, Niebuhr's ideal of the moral man could sanction the use of violence and other unsavory means to achieve justice. The "moral man"—a brooding virtuoso of amorality—would appeal to an emerging cohort of liberal intellectuals and national security managers eager to demonstrate their virility and moral flexibility.

"No Connection Except by Elevator": Labor Catholicism and the Wayward Journey of Democratic Corporatism

Unlike Protestants, Catholics appeared blessed with a unity of purpose that was the envy of liberal Protestants. "The Church knows where it stands, and why," Walter Marshall Horton marveled in 1938, "and so holds steady in a world that is being shaken to its foundations." Indeed, Catholic intellectuals possessed a definitive, if opaque, social encyclical—the oft-cited *Quadragesimo anno*—and a triumphal (even smug) conviction that Catholicism was a culture, an all-encompassing way of life, as well as a creed.[29]

Partisans of this Catholic culture explicitly likened their handiwork to the cultural front of the secular left. Francis Talbot, literary editor of the Jesuit periodical *America,* considered the trans-Atlantic literary revival a "united front," while Calvert Alexander, surveying "operations on the literary front," praised Burke's address on revolutionary symbolism and exhorted Catholics to produce a similarly revolutionary literature. This Catholic cultural front formed part of a larger "lay apostolate," "Catholic action," or "social Catholicism" that linked social reform with spiritual renewal. Robert Pollack, a young philosopher at Fordham, celebrated "the dream of a people's commonwealth" in a widely praised volume entitled, *Man and Modern Secularism* (1940), while Father Luigi Ligutti of the National Catholic Rural Life Conference described the struggles of rural Americans against a "mechanistic plutocracy" as "America's Third Struggle for Liberty."[30]

Yet the partisans were never as unified as they appeared or imagined. When the Michigan branch of the Association of Catholic Trade Unionists (ACTU) asserted that the Church had a social program "as complete and well-developed as the 'party line' of the communists," they obscured the conflicts that roiled under the medievalist tent of Depression Catholicism. Even though John Ryan, Dorothy Day, and other social Catholics could sign a 1936 pamphlet entitled *Organized Social Justice* that included a call for "self-governing, democratically organized membership of the industries, of farming, of trade, and of the professions," the joint statement concealed sharp and obdurate differences.[31] The "labor Catholicism" that defined American Catholic social thought at this time was torn between democratic corporatists, represented by Ryan and other supporters of the New Deal, and more decentralist personalists, such as Day.

Though formulated in a French milieu, Jacques Maritain's influential "integral humanism"—contained in *Freedom in the Modern World* (1935) and *Integral Humanism* (1936)—indicated the ambiguities of American labor Catholicism. The social and cultural politics of integral humanism must be, in Maritain's view, unreservedly popular. "It is not the leisure of a few lovers of plain chant but the life of the mass of people . . . the common works of men that should be crowned with fetes and liturgies and hymns and canticles." This popular Catholic moral economy rested on a medievalist theology of labor and property. "The foundation of labor ethics," Maritain asserted, was the Incarnation, since God's assumption of human form confirmed "the human person . . . as the image of God." Through labor, persons participated in God's own creative power and acquired a right to property only in so far as they used that power rightly. While the producer—the "artist"—could appropriate resources, "the use of goods . . . ought to be common," a communism of consumption arranged through families, workers' associations, technicians, shareholders, and state institutions. Such communism flourished best (indeed only, Maritain implied) in the Church, the "Mystical Body of Christ," where men and women learned charity, the godlike virtue of giving without thought of return and the "most human mode of sharing goods."[32]

Maritain called for the restoration of small-scale family proprietorship on the land and for a system of "co-ownership" among workers, technicians, and "sleeping partners" in industry. Yet, while arguing that "technical necessities" made direct control by workers impractical, Maritain also implied that the moral economy could ensure personal and social felicity only with the erasure of distinctions between mental and manual labor—hence the abolition of class. If "technical competence and effective work go hand in hand with ownership," as Maritain wrote, and if "the co-ownership of the means of work" released "that which is fundamentally and inalienably the property of the worker: his personal forces, his intelligence, his arms," then the ideal moral economy was an artisanal republic suffused by Christian charity. While Maritain and others shied away from the term "corporatism" because of its fascist connotations, the structural arrangements he outlined represented a democratic variant on what scholars have identified as a corporatist element in the politics of North Atlantic nations.[33] This democratic corporatism—

a form of nationwide economic planning that fused political democracy with the collaborative governance of industry by capital and labor—recycled the prewar ideal of industrial democracy.

Yet, like "industrial democracy," corporatist labor Catholicism articulated an unclear vision of moral economy. Maritain's evasiveness on the issue of class stemmed in part from his scholastic insistence that the spiritual and temporal orders were "distinct . . . but not separate" spheres each with its own "proper carnal law."[34] This reservation of an area for "proper carnal law," like Niebuhr's segregation of religious idealism from social problems, legitimized secular professional expertise. At the same time that advocates of integral humanism could raise the standard of a decentralized, artisanal moral economy, they also might support a liberal politics of managerially orchestrated antagonism.

In the United States, democratic corporatists labored on the basis of a relatively clear delineation of the temporal and the spiritual, the natural and the supernatural—demarcations akin to the separation of religion and politics in Niebuhr's Protestant socialism. John Ryan, for example, summarized his theology in a letter to a friend in 1937. "Of course I do not regard the supernatural order as a kind of second story, built as if by afterthought on top of the natural order," he wrote. Still, he went on, "the assumption of no connection between the two except by elevator has always seemed to me rather logical."[35] Inscribing this vertical imagery of natural and supernatural onto their labor Catholicism, democratic corporatists forged an ideological template for the managerial liberalism of the New Deal order.

The modified reproduction of clerical authority provided one revealing illustration of corporatist labor Catholicism. Certainly, clerical leadership in "Catholic action" did not equate with reaction. Labor priests such as Charles Owen Rice and George Higgins regularly mounted soapboxes for the CIO, fended off attacks from Catholic conservatives, and directed labor schools that promulgated Catholic social thought among Catholic workers and exhorted them to join the labor movement. Yet, as the surveillance of working-class thought and politics by the labor priests demonstrated, "Catholic action" and the "lay apostolate" fenced off an enlarged but still carefully circumscribed demesne of lay autonomy. In a widely used collection of essays entitled, *A Call to Catholic Action* (1935), Fr. Joseph Schrembs reiterated that the Church could not be entrusted to anyone other than to "those who have received the divine commission to shepherd the sheep and the lambs of the flock of Christ." All Catholic action groups, he stated, must work "under the direct guidance and control of the bishops." While Schrembs hastened to explain that this did not imply a "vainglorious domination" by the clergy, he reminded lay readers that in the Mystical Body, "as in all other living bodies," subordination of the members "to the higher centers of control is the very law of corporate existence." Both the ACTU and the Young Christian Workers (founded in 1938) exhibited this deference to the clergy in their refusal to press for a full-scale industrial democracy. The ACTU's statement of principles, for instance, exemplified the simultaneous challenge and accommodation to managerial prerogative that defined democratic corporatism. Calling for a living wage, just prices, job security, and collective bargaining, the ACTU urged cooperation with "decent employers" to create "guilds" and cooperatives in which the worker "shares as a partner" in the ownership and direction of the enterprise.[36]

Corporatist intellectuals were equally ambiguous about their political trajectory. Father Raymond McGowan, Ryan's top assistant in the Social Action Department, argued that control over production should reside in an "economic nation within a nation"—a system of guilds, each one a "cooperating, democratically organized industry and profession," all coordinating their activities through complex planning structures subject to overarching government mandates. During and for some time after the war, the National Catholic Welfare Council (NCWC) and many leading hierarchs advanced an "industry council" plan calling for the establishment in all large industries of triumvirates comprised of capital, management, and labor. CIO president Philip Murray echoed the bishops' ideas in the "Victory Plan" he outlined in 1941 as labor's production strategy for impending American involvement in war. Announcing that "the sons of labor are fully aware of their responsibilities in this present emergency," Murray also explicitly referred to the plan as a Catholic blueprint for the postwar political economy. Industry councils, he argued, would embody the "perfection of cooperation between labor and industry" decreed in *Quadragesimo anno*.[37]

Yet the democratic corporatist moment was not to be, and it was John Ryan, venerable nestor of industrial democracy, who traced the path of labor Catholicism toward the New Deal. The New Deal, he flatly asserted in 1936, was "the only existing social force that is likely to bring about any reforms." "Never before in history," he proclaimed in *Commonweal* in 1939, "have government policies been so deliberately, formally, and consciously based upon conceptions and convictions of moral right and social justice." Ryan scoffed at opponents of the New Deal as "unrealistic" radicals or as "Bourbons," "retainers of plutocracy." Yet, as Ryan lauded the legislative accomplishments of the New Deal, his corporatism atrophied, especially as the prospect of an extensive state presence in the economy quickly eclipsed the ideal of workers' participation in management. As early as 1934 Ryan was asserting that the National Recovery Administration's industrial codes augured "an industrial system . . . in complete accord with the social order proposed by the Holy Father." By 1941, the occupational groups that held a central place in *Quadragesimo anno* had virtually disappeared from Ryan's work. The primary object of the state's social and industrial legislation, he now believed, was the provision for workers of "reasonable opportunities of obtaining a living and advancing their material welfare"[38]—a pronouncement opaque enough to convey the old ideal of industrial democracy but which more directly indicated the impending demise of workers' control in the discourse of Catholic corporatism.

Sharing with New Dealers a commitment to social reform and class reconciliation through the concerted action of social experts, organized interest groups, and state bureaucrats, Ryan and other Catholic leaders soon hid the light of the corporatist gospel. When the NCWC issued a 1940 statement entitled, "The Church and Social Order," it combined a clerical conception of the Church as "teacher of the entire moral law" with a refusal to hold "employers as a class" responsible for the Depression. Writing one sentence on occupational groups into a document largely devoted to wages and security, the NCWC included an offhand but portentous endorsement of professional and managerial power. Matters of "scientific organization, production, cost accounting, transportation, [and] marketing," the NCWC declared, were not political issues but rather "a technical problem proper to economic science and business administration."[39]

The cultural politics of corporatist labor Catholicism augured this deference to managerial prerogative. A strong current of antiurban producerism ran through much of corporatist cultural criticism. Recalling the virtues of a sturdy and fecund yeomanry, Luigi Ligutti referred to cities as "graveyards of the family" and lamented that the Founders would be "sad to learn how we have left the fields and piled ourselves up around the smokestacks of great factories." Even John Ryan turned briefly from his labors on behalf of industrial workers to declaim that farmers had "more independence, more self-reliance, more room for children . . . and better opportunities for decent home life" than urban dwellers. This "producerist" moralism competed, however, with a consumerist rhetoric that went far in determining the liberal trajectory of the corporatist social gospel. Catholic skilled workers who joined the CIO found in the corporatist gospel a defense of a workplace status, tied firmly to church, neighborhood, ethnicity, and family, that was being lowered progressively by technological change. Scions of several generations of non-Anglo ethnics, these workers embraced the "producerist" and anticommunist strains of labor Catholicism. Yet their semiskilled Catholic brethren were less securely fixed in the primordial webs that held their comrades. They were, as Steve Fraser describes them, "quintessentially urban, with a functional and instrumental but not existential relationship to their work, far more integrated as consumers into the mass market and more influenced by the media of mass culture"[40]—and also, one could add, less responsive to producerist moralism and less averse to the Fordist managerialism of the New Deal order.

Moreover, these workers were often second-generation non-Anglos who saw in unionization a vehicle for what Gary Gerstle has called a "working-class Americanism," a form of national identity that eased assimilation by linking traditionalist paeans to frugality and family to a progressive celebration of industrially generated abundance. The consumerist element in corporatism—marked by the subtle change from living wage to fair wage and minimum wage—lubricated the passage of this new working class into an American culture increasingly defined as a democracy of consumption. The corporatist gospel held in suspension the moralist and consumerist currents of industrial militance. However, the consumerist mode would come to prevail in the political circumstances of postwar recovery, the preponderance of the semiskilled working class, and the constriction of organized labor's social imagination within the bounds of what Lizabeth Cohen calls a "moral capitalism."[41]

Thus, by the eve of World War II, many Protestant and Catholic intellectuals had converged on a humane Fordism as the epitome of moral economy. Yet others in the ranks posed troubling questions. Was there anything identifiably Christian about this solution to the conflicts of capitalist modernity? Did industrial technology and mass-mediated culture not undermine the technical skill, generosity, and spiritual vitality necessary for a moral economy of friends?

Was there a place—indeed, a central place—for religion in the social and cultural revolution?

"Ours Is Indeed an Unpopular Front": Permanent Revolution, Personalism, and Sacramental Radicalism

For these Christians, Christianity embodied the exemplary revolutionary community, and they adopted a rhetoric of ecclesial militance that abounded in comparisons to labor unions and Communist cadres. A. J. Muste, Dutch Reformed minister, seasoned labor organizer, and firebrand of the American Workers' party, believed that the churches constituted a potential revolutionary vanguard. Christians comprised "the

Body, the incarnation of Christ in the world," he argued in *Non-Violence in an Aggressive World* (1940), and were a polity akin to "the Leninist's idea of the Party or the Internationale." H. Richard Niebuhr set *The Church Against the World* (1935) as a "revolutionary community in a pre-revolutionary society," a network of cells that housed "the rank and file of the church." Paul Hanly Furfey identified "the Mystical Body of Christ" in *Fire on the Earth* (1936) as the vessel through which "Christianity has social and political significance," just as Dorothy Day declared in the *Catholic Worker* that the Church was, "as always, the True International." "The Catholic social ideal," Furfey explained in *Three Theories of Society* (1937), was "to reproduce heaven on earth," a paradise that other Catholic radicals described as "utopian, Christian communism," in Peter Maurin's words. "Communism is a good word, a Christian word originally," Day asserted in *From Union Square to Rome* (1940), maintaining that "it is only through religion that communism can be achieved." Both Day and Richard Niebuhr couched Christian theology in Trotskyite terms through their advocacy of "permanent revolution." Day and other Catholic workers often used this phrase to characterize their labors, while Niebuhr, in *The Meaning of Revelation* (1941), employed it as a translation of the Greek *metanoia,* or "repentance."[42]

Though not nearly so influential as their socialist or corporatist brethren, the "permanent revolutionary" cohort of Christian intellectuals preached varieties of revolutionary symbolism and moral economy that put religion more firmly at the center of social and cultural politics. Especially in the personalism or sacramental radicalism of the Catholic Worker movement, they fused a religious-popular cultural strategy with a decentralist, artisanal social ideal that aimed at the transcendence, not the moral uplift, of the Fordist order.

The permanent revolutionaries demanded a new symbolic language for a partisan church and urged their comrades on the cultural front to lessen or end their dependence on the secularized culture of professionalism. Richard Niebuhr excoriated his fellow liberals in *The Kingdom of God in America* (1937) for their deference to academic and managerial expertise, upbraiding their gratitude "for every sop which men of science threw their way . . . every kind word which the mighty, in universities and halls of government" pronounced in their favor. Social science especially constituted, in his view, a vocabulary of managerial manipulation, replete with "adjustments and maladjustments" that reduced men and women to "undernourished bodies or maladjusted carburetors." Furfey more directly linked social science with the culture industries and corporate hegemony. The "positivist" mentality of capitalism recognized only the truths of prediction and control, of "system and efficiency in office management." The positivist leaders of business controlled the entertainment industries, advertising agencies, mass-circulation magazines, and higher education and exercised a shimmering tyranny over the moral imagination of the working class. "The thought of success lightens the burden of his toil and sweetens his minor triumphs," Furfey wrote of the industrial worker. "The life of the success-class dominates his phantasy." The interconnected networks of business and cultural elites—a "Kingdom of Satan," in Furfey's fiery, if overwrought, phrase—included "rich men . . . endowing our universities . . . our intellectual leaders, from professors, publicists, writers, dramatists . . . poets, artists, and musicians."[43]

For Christianity to present a "sign of contradiction" to the corporate regime, Christian theology had to reclaim its place as the Archimedean point of social and cultural criticism. "Theology," Niebuhr declared, "must take the place of the psychology and sociology which were the proper sciences of a Christianity . . . dependent on the spirit in man." Theology, however, could not be a "universal religious language"—that is, neither the bland Esperanto of liberal Protestantism, the modernist "mythology" of brother Reinhold, nor the "common faith" of Dewey. Christians proclaimed and practiced "a particular faith, since there is no other kind," and hence theology must always be a confession of a distinct point of view. In what he called "supernatural sociology" (or what other Catholics dubbed "Christian sociology"), Furfey undertook the task of vindicating Christian theology as social theory. "The supernatural life," he asserted, "is the very essence of any truly Christian sociology." Christians possessed a venerable language of social thought in the forms of "Revelation, Scripture, and Tradition" and traced their heritage back to Aquinas's *Summas* and Augustine's *City of God*. Niebuhr and Furfey contradicted the claims of other clerics and discourses: the democratic social engineering championed by Arnold, Dewey, and the Lynds of *Middletown in Transition* (1935); Reinhold Niebuhr's politically and ideologically plastic Protestant socialism; and the "revolutionary symbolism" sought by Burke and others in the Popular Front.[44]

This concern with theology led revolutionists to creed and ritual as the twofold bond between culture and commitment. Just as secular radicals explored the political possibilities of art and theater, some Protestants and Catholics sought to shape political consciousness through creeds and ritual performances. Insisting that doctrines and rituals were "not confining but liberating," Richard Niebuhr emphasized their necessity for disciplined and fruitful thought. Reminding his fellow social gospelers that religion was cult as well as morality, *Christian Century* editor Charles Clayton Morrison chastised them for their delinquency in linking *The*

Social Gospel and the Christian Cultus (1933). Since the social gospel, he noted, had made great headway among the clergy but little among the laity (who heard "only enough of it to be irritated by it"), Morrison called for "new hymns, new prayers, new denominational activities expressive of social idealism" that would give the social passion "an organic place in the liturgy of communal worship." The creation of such a liturgical order would produce "a fellowship which stands over against the secular order—over against the state, and the economic order."[45]

Morrison's book appeared in the midst of a small but suggestive liberal Protestant liturgical movement. The Federal Council of Churches (FCC) established a Committee on Worship in 1932 whose first substantial work appeared in 1937 with the publication of *The Christian Year*, a liturgical calendar designed by Fred Winslow Adams, a Methodist minister and Boston University theology professor. A Sabbath work schedule for "the uncompleted task of building a Christian world," the calendar included an entirely new season, "Kingdomtide," and represented numerous social gospel causes: World Peace Sunday, Race Relations Sunday, Nature Sunday, Rural Life Sunday. Although widely adopted and even reissued in 1940, it indicated the problems in linking the social gospel to liberal Protestant liturgy. Since the *Christian Year* was, as the FCC stressed in the subtitle, only "a suggestive guide," it lacked the authority inherent in Catholic liturgy, while the focus on *time* obscured the need to reform ritual itself. Morrison himself had noted that the traditional prominence of the sermon in Protestant worship had diverted social gospelers' attention from the visual and musical elements of ritual.[46]

Catholic liturgical reformers associated with Virgil Michel and *Orate Fratres* linked liturgical and social concerns more easily and compellingly than their Protestant brethren. Catholic liturgists advocated a number of far-reaching reforms: a more streamlined church architecture, use of the vernacular, evening services for industrial workers, and greater participation of the laity—especially of women—in ritual practice. All these reforms were couched in terms of labor Catholicism. Father Gerald Ellerd's description of the Mass as "collective bargaining with the Lord," along with Eric Gill's oft-cited proposal of a "Mass for the masses"—a Mass-in-the-round centered on an altar in the middle of the church—illustrated this connection of ritual and social politics. The Catholic Worker artist Ade Bethune, calling for smaller churches in "home-like buildings," charged that the "mammoth pseudo-basilicas" of the brick-and-mortar era were akin to industrial factories, leaving "the masses of the people without any sense of ownership. . . . they are proletarians in their own church."[47] In the pages of *Orate Fratres*, the *Catholic Worker*, the *Christian Front*, and *Commonweal*, liturgists enjoined a regimen of prayer, reading, meditation, reception of the sacraments, and liturgical performance as indispensable disciplines for the political will and imagination.

For all Catholic radicals, the Mass provided the model of a sacral social order. Catholic social action depended, Furfey believed, on frequent and informed observance of Catholic ritual. "Facility in charity of the social kind is acquired by participation in the Liturgy." Social reform without this spiritual integrity represented "a dangerous innovation, something alien to Catholic tradition and likely to lead to disastrous results." For Catholic radicals, this fusion of sacramental ritual and social witness was most apparent in the Eucharist, which served, one liturgist wrote in *Orate Fratres*, as the "centrifugal and centripetal core" of a truly Christian moral economy. This liturgically centered social order (referred to variously as "Christocracy," "the liturgical economy," or "the New Testament economy") resembled a communion banquet. Catholics receiving the Eucharist do not each enjoy Christ as an exclusive possession, Michel asserted; rather, they are "all contained in one and the same Christ." Since supernatural goods were held in common, natural goods should likewise be shared. "What belongs to all belongs to each and what belongs to each belongs to all."[48]

These creedal and ritual concerns comprised elements of a broader strategy of cultural politics. Where the secular left attempted to forge a people's front through a national-popular mobilization of symbols and sentiments, Niebuhr, Day, Furfey, and their comrades envisioned a religious-popular vanguard aligned on the basis of a shared religious history and destiny. Zealous to collect Walter Benjamin's "chips of messianic time," Niebuhr recalled a mode of history as hopeful remembrance. From Carl Becker's reminder to historians of their kinship with "that ancient and honorable company of wise men of the tribe, of bards and story-tellers and minstrels, of soothsayers and priests," to histories of slave revolts and black Reconstruction by Herbert Aptheker and W. E. B. Du Bois, secular historians were themselves reviving a conception of their craft as an avowedly moralized endeavor. The Christian historian, Niebuhr argued, should assess historical action not merely in terms of "valency or strength" but in terms of "what is noblest"—a practice which, he admitted, might commemorate failure more often than victory. Still, Niebuhr remained adamant about the political energy afforded by the knowledge of history. "No great change in political or economic life has ever taken place without a recollection of the past," he declared in *The Meaning of Revelation*. "No new freedom has ever been won without appeal to an old freedom, nor any right established save as an ancient right denied by intervening tyranny."[49]

For Niebuhr, historical memory—participation in what Benedict Anderson would call an "imagined community"—enlarged the bounds of identity, taught lessons in humility and charity, and lowered the barriers of race and class—providing, in other words, the "spiritual discipline against resentment" sought by his realistic brother. Just as fledgling Communists received indoctrination in Marxist theory, so Christians, Niebuhr implied, should obtain an ideological and political education as novices in a revolutionary community. Rebuking the sinful twins of Protestant racism and American nationalism, Niebuhr contended that by virtue of the historical consciousness mandated by conversion, "Christians of all races recognize the Hebrews as their fathers," became "immigrants into the empire of God which extends over all the world," and assumed kinship with crucified apostles, medieval friars, shackled slaves, all dispossessed and disenfranchised peoples.[50]

Niebuhr's sort of commitment to a religious-popular cultural politics spawned a recovery of American religious history that unearthed a mother lode of critical resources. In their rehabilitation of Puritanism, Niebuhr, Joseph Haroutunian, and Perry Miller labored to rescue the Puritans from the clutches of Vernon Parrington, H. L. Mencken, and assorted bohemians. Haroutunian's *From Piety to Moralism* (1932) clearly troped the history of New England as a degeneration from Calvinist rigor to accommodation. Miller saw in Puritan New England "the innermost propulsion of the United States" and used its history as a vehicle of cultural commentary over the 1930s and 1940s, especially in *Orthodoxy in Massachusetts* (1933) and *Jonathan Edwards* (1949). Theology, Miller argued in *Jonathan Edwards*—now "nearly a lost art" except in "fairly sheltered groves"—had once been "the proud possession of all Protestant Americans," a critical language mastered by clerics but accessible to all. Indeed, Miller hoped that Americans, if they harkened to Edwards and the Puritans, would realize that "applied science and Benjamin Franklin's *The Way to Wealth* seem not a sufficient philosophy of national life."[51]

Tying together the national-popular and religious-popular banners of cultural politics, Niebuhr himself recast the nation's past as an "experiment in constructive Protestantism" in *The Kingdom of God in America* (1937). Rather than simply oppose Christianity to culture—the stale contrast so often set up by neoorthodox Protestants and their retainers—Niebuhr made Protestantism the dynamic principle of American history, the engine of a permanent revolution whose progression was his generation's appointed task. The "Protestant movement," as Niebuhr called it, bore all the signs of a popular insurgency. Performing a "New World symphony," the Protestant virtuosi—Jonathan Edwards, Roger

Williams, Charles Grandison Finney, Horace Bushnell, and Walter Rauschenbusch, among others—joined in a popular front with simpler fiddlers whose notes emanated, as in the Second Great Awakening, from "crude instruments, fashioned in the backwoods and played by amateurs." Relishing the homespun theology of the unlettered that appalled secularized historians from Vernon Parrington to Richard Hofstadter, Niebuhr praised evangelical social reformers on their disrespect for the "safe," "practical," "intellectual rationalism" of Lyman Beecher and Timothy Dwight, court musicians of the well appointed.[52] A contemporary evangelical revival would, Niebuhr implied, mount a similar assault on the dominant conventions of discussion.

Yet Niebuhr was not uncritical of the popular element in American Protestantism. Acknowledging that evangelical religious culture could indeed foster complacency and political indiscipline, Niebuhr modified his praise for homespun Protestantism with references to Catholicism. Throughout *Kingdom of God,* Niebuhr employed Catholic images to describe the corporate discipline of cadres in the Protestant movement. Roger Williams became a "Protestant monk"; Edwards and George Whitefield changed into "Protestant friars"; Quakers, Mennonites, and Congregationalists emerged as "Protestant orders"; Methodists appeared as "Franciscans or Dominicans in a new incarnation"; and revivalists resembled "the friars of the twelfth and thirteenth centuries."[53] In these striking phrases, Niebuhr attempted not only to reconcile his democratic sympathies with the medievalism that continued to attract him but also to suggest models for a resurgent Protestant movement.

However, if Niebuhr's religious-popular work constituted a singular contribution to the social and political thought of the 1930s, it offered little in the way of a concrete program for a Protestant rank and file. Contending against Max Weber that "the spirit of capitalism and the spirit of Protestantism remain two wholly different things," Niebuhr lauded early Puritan and Quaker moral economies in which property had been seen as a bulwark of virtue. Capitalism, he protested, had "corrupted and perverted" this system of "early democracy and Puritanism." But Niebuhr offered no glimpses of a reconstructed Puritan moral economy, asserting weakly that private property was not "an adequate basis for the modern economic structure." Though a member of the Fellowship of Socialist Christians (FSC), Niebuhr lacked the relish of battle that inspired his brother. Thus when the *Christian Century* complained that Niebuhr "sound[ed] a trumpet call to nothing in particular" in *The Church Against the World;* they underscored the same isolation of liberal Protestant elites that precluded the mobilization of a popular religious left on the basis of realism.[54]

Like Niebuhr's Protestant religious-popular, Catholic medievalism contained a revolutionary symbolism and an alternative history, but it also included a more concrete social program. The medievalism of Catholic radicals was always more pronounced than that of their corporatist brethren. "Why are we afraid to be called medievalists?" Dorothy Day once asked rhetorically in the *Catholic Worker*. Catholic radicals' "invention of the Middle Ages" drew on numerous European writers: Jacques Maritain, the French philosopher Etienne Gilson, G. K. Chesterton, Christopher Dawson, Nicholas Berdyeav (whose *The End of Our Time* heralded a "new Middle Ages"), and especially Eric Gill and Peter Kropotkin (whose admiration for medieval guilds appealed to Maurin, Day, and other Catholic Workers). Radicals agreed with the illustrator and writer Constance Mary Rowe when she reflected in the *Christian Front* that "we cannot do better" than recall St. Dominic and St. Francis and "the mighty examples of these two Medieval Saints." When the engraver and distributist writer Graham Carey (whose grandfather Arthur had been a leader in the arts and crafts movement at the turn of the century) saw redemption from mass culture's "artistic sin" in "the Medieval or Christian view" of art as craft organized around guilds dedicated to saints, he both connected radical medievalism to an earlier antimodernism and demanded a social reconstruction unimagined by its forebears. Still, Catholic radicals realized that medievalism could be dismissed easily as evasive exoticism unless it were fused with American republican hopes. Catholic social thought, Michel asserted, expressed better than other traditions "our traditional Christian and American ideals of democracy."[55]

Under the banner of medievalism, sacramentalists sought, as Warren Susman has written of many left intellectuals in the 1930's, "to become 'an unlearned class,' " so as to reconnect intellectuals with industrial workers, farmers, and other powerless groups. Catholic radicals highlighted the role of intellectuals and other cultural producers in creating a new cultural hegemony. To Paul Hanly Furfey, medievalism shaped a healthy fluidity between intellectuals and the people dismissing the ideal of the autonomous intellectual and endorsing instead "the medieval ideal of social scholarship" that charged the learned Christian to "express with clarity and precision the ideas of the group." Furfey enjoined Catholic cultural workers to become, like the medieval artist, "absorbed in a great social truth" and discover individuality in the course of expressing truths that remained "common property." As Dorothy Day later recalled, Catholic Workers perceived that "it was the scholar's inability to communicate except to his peers that prevented the workers from following him."[56] Eager to avoid both elitism and condescension, sacramental radicals attempted to act as a democratic clerisy, a vanguard of a religious-popular movement against capitalist modernity.

Sacramental radicals conducted their cultural politics on several sites. In contrast to corporatists, Catholic Workers blurred the line between clergy and laity. "The laity were looked upon as second class citizens," one Catholic Worker later recalled, "whose main function was to fall upon their knees and open their purses." Catholic Workers often regarded the hierarchy with a mixture of respect, camaraderie, wariness, and impatience. Though she "loved the Church for Christ made visible," Day also admitted that the institutional Church "was often a scandal to me" and that she lived in "a state of permanent dissatisfaction with the Church." Still, Michel, Furfey, and other clerical sympathizers seldom pulled their clerical rank, while the liturgical movement longed for a laity as well informed as the regular clergy.[57]

Day's skepticism of officialdom dovetailed with attempts to foment an intellectually serious and popularly accessible criticism that would appeal, Day hoped, to "those who worked with hand or brain, those who did physical, mental, or spiritual work." Recalling the medieval friars and scholars who walked the roads or depended on fees from students, Furfey urged contemporary Thomist radicals to take scholasticism into the streets with "the preparation and distribution of literature, speeches on political topics, the organization of study clubs." The names of Catholic radical publications indicated their courtship of a broad audience: the *Catholic Worker* (an obvious counter to the *Daily Worker*), the *Christian Front* (an allusion to the Popular Front), *Orate Fratres* (which, translatable as "pray brothers" or "speak brothers," suggested a fusion of religious and political concerns), or the *Christian Social Art Quarterly* (renamed the *Catholic Art Quarterly* in 1938 and which published pieces on the social character of the arts for artists and art teachers at all levels).[58]

The apostolate of art figured highly in sacramental cultural politics. Sacramental radicalism had a notable appeal to younger Catholic engravers, painters, and illustrators, especially when conveyed in the pages of *Orate Fratres* or *Liturgical Arts* or in the essays and drawings of Eric Gill. While the prospect of contributing to the aesthetic resplendence of a medievalist tradition was part of the appeal of the apostolate of art, Catholic radicals also emphasized the social mission of artists. Furfey, stressing that "we need novels and poetry and mural paintings no less than we need handbooks of sociology," pointed to the work of Popular Front artists and writers—"the present proletarian movement in the drama, in fiction, in mural painting, and even in music"—as worthy of study and emulation. Yet he also warned Catholic experimentalists against a "Catholic adaptation of modern progressive art" that re-produced the "separation of art from life." Ceramist Ade Bethune—a fa-vorite illustrator of Catholic radicals and editor of the *Catholic Art Quar-terly*—criticized the " 'artiness' that seems nowadays to cling to the craft like a leech" but cautioned Catholic artists to be "not against being mod-ern, but against modern*ism*." Modern*ism*, in her view, fetishized obscu-rity and complexity, thereby severing the vital link between the aesthetic sensibility of the artist and the social use of objects. Rather than simply reject or embrace modernism, Catholic artists should, Bethune thought, refashion modernism in a "hieratic" religious art that appropriated cer-tain formal features of modernism while retaining both social utility and representational, "sacramental" fidelity.[59]

Catholic radicals also envisioned new forms of intellectual life de-signed to destroy the authority of professionals as a class by erasing the distinction between mental and manual workers. For Day, Furfey, and other university-educated radicals, roundtable discussions in the houses of hospitality were an elementary step in this direction. Open to anyone, they provided spaces for informed conversation and friendship while ac-quainting intellectuals, workers, and sympathetic professionals with so-cial, political, and religious problems. Likewise, the agronomic universi-ties endorsed by Day and Maurin (and attempted on Catholic Worker farm communes) aimed to abolish the distinctions between intellectuals and others by fostering discussion in a craft and agricultural setting.[60]

These attempts to decentralize intellectual life merged with efforts to reintegrate learning around a theological center. The *autodidact* Maurin dismissed most colleges and universities as "fact-factories" churning out "fact-foolish" and morally paralyzed specialists. The elective system, he believed, hastened the disintegration of intellectual life by promoting a market ideal of culture and abetting the onslaught of technical and busi-ness education. While Maurin's indictment of the university resembled those of humanists such as Robert Hutchins and Mortimer Adler (who shared with Maurin a fondness for Aristotle, Aquinas, and John Henry Newman), his own pedagogical ideal drew more on John Ruskin and especially Kropotkin, whose support for an "integral education" com-bining technical training and humanist learning resonated with Catho-lic notions of integrity. Moreover, while Hutchins and Adler looked to scholasticism's cohesive potential apart from any serious religious im-port, Maurin insisted both that theology had to integrate the disciplines and that education had to mold religious personalities in a larger beloved community.[61]

These beloved communities—especially the "farm communes" of the Catholic Workers—best exemplified the vocation of sacramental radicals. Running abreast of New Deal Resettlement Administration green-belt ventures that sought to restore greater balance between country and city, Catholic radicals both transfigured the republican producer ideal of unified mental and manual labor and grounded what Maurin called the green revolution in religious community. Since property, radicals argued, was a social space for creative work—work that could be creative only when hand and brain, production and planning, were indissoluble incarnations of God's own image and likeness—proprietorship was a social trust defined and regulated in religious terms. The republican proprietor became a Catholic Worker within a beloved community, a "liturgical economy" that embodied what *Christian Front* editor Deverell called "the communal nature of private property." Both Maurin's trinity of "cult, culture, and cultivation" and Day's program of "ownership by the workers of the means of production, the abolition of the assembly line, decentralized factories, the restoration of crafts, and ownership of property" encapsulated a moral and political economy rooted in religious life.[62]

At the same time, in calling themselves personalists and their religious social theory personalism, Catholic radicals retrieved the standard of personality discarded and trampled underfoot in the Protestant stampede for realism. For personalists, the restoration to work and technology of a sacramental quality desecrated by industrial capitalism became a paramount therapeutic duty as well as a social commitment. Uniting spiritual, therapeutic, and physical longings, "a man who works with his hands as well as with his head is an integrated personality," Day believed. Labor, in Day's view, was a vocation in which the worker—properly speaking, an artist—"shares in God's creative activity." Indeed, the worker-artist's greater proximity to matter occasioned a greater intimacy with God. "Using mind and brain to work on beautiful things," she wrote, gave men and women "a sense of the sacramentality of life, the holiness, the symbolism of things." This ideal of spiritual fulfillment through sacramental work lifted Catholic Worker imprecations against materialism from platitude into criticism. In their view, the Fordist production and consumption of riches required a division of labor that both weakened the bond between hand and brain and lamed the sensuous capacities of the body itself. Thus "the worst materialism of all," Day declared, resided in a lack of creative exuberance, "when this dear flesh of ours is denied."[63]

The pronounced agrarianism of the Catholic Worker, exemplified in its farm communes, must be understood in this light. Without a doubt, these communes were, as James Fisher has judged, "unmitigated disasters." Yet far from merely replaying Brook Farm's futile exercise in pastoralism, Catholic Worker agrarianism offered solutions to problems much more pressing than the jading of metropolitan intellectuals. For one, the revival of the nation's agrarian economy and rural culture was a widespread concern in the 1930s. The work of Herbert Agar, Ralph Borsodi, and the Twelve Southerners, for instance, aimed not simply at recovering "the simple life" but at recovering the cultural and political power of the producer tradition. Catholics, especially those in the Catholic Rural Life Conference (CRLC), saw the resuscitation of agrarian life as an important religious mission. The CRLC addressed (often presciently) issues ranging from biodynamic farming to the impact of racism and mechanization on southern black sharecroppers. Most Catholic agrarian activists looked to the revival of farming as a reversal of the undemocratic effects of professionalization under corporate auspices. Thanks to the subdivision of labor, Luigi Ligutti wrote in 1940, millions were "managed in every detail of their work, [and are] soon in a position where they look for management in government, in play, in education, in social affairs, in all situations."[64] Far more than a moment in the history of rural idiocy, Catholic Worker agrarianism critiqued both the distributive injustice of the Fordist order and its estrangement of mental from manual labor.

Still, Catholic Workers' implacable animus toward industrial technology proved injurious intellectually and politically. Could work be artisanal, fulfilling, and sacramental outside the ambit of traditional handicraft and farming? Could technology develop so as to preserve and even enhance worker's direct control of production? Raising these questions, Catholic Workers never confronted them in any sustained or nuanced fashion, leaving the field open to corporatists and liberals whose answers, more amenable to the Fordist order, would prevail among Catholic social activists during and after the war. Workers differed notably from Kropotkin—who had promoted both modern forms of handicraft production and biodynamic farming—and from critics of industrialism such as Lewis Mumford and Simone Weil—who shared with Catholic Workers a desire to effect, as Mumford wrote, "the fresh integration of work and art and life." Like the Catholic Workers, Mumford hoped to recover "those vital and historic and organic attributes that had been deliberately eliminated from the concepts of science and from the methods of the earlier technics." Yet he also looked in *Technics and Civilization* (1934) to an electrically and biodynamically centered "neotechnics" controlled by "a new worker," an "all-around mechanic" characterized by "alertness, responsibility, [and] an intelligent grasp of the operative parts." Across the Atlantic, Weil, while advocating decentralized factories and workshops, also embraced the possibilities of newer, more sophisticated forms of production technology.[65]

Unwilling to face these issues, Catholic Workers routinely retreated into a facile antimodernism. "The symbolism of the machine is ugly and devilish," Day once snarled, while Maurin's "Easy Essays" obscured and even dismissed important issues of productivity and design. Day appeared at times to see this. Maurin, she once conceded, "never filled in the chasms, the valleys, in his leaping from crag to crag of noble thought."[66] Yet Day's deference to Maurin ensured that Catholic radicalism would plunge headfirst into these abysses. Her concessions to Maurin also reflected her own lack of prolonged experience in a factory—experience Weil used to compose a critique of Fordism at once theologically informed, empirically textured, and theoretically sophisticated.

Other failures compounded the theoretical shortcomings of Catholic radicals. Betraying their own educational ideals, Catholic Workers failed to forge connections to the labor movement, depriving themselves of a needed critical audience. Privileging hardship and renunciation as hallmarks of genuine Catholic identity, radicals were never sure what to do with second-generation ethnic Catholics emerging from immigrant ghettos and venturing into the voluptuous agora of consumer culture. Faced with the appeal of commodified culture, Catholic radicals retreated into asceticism, forsaking the very sacramental vision of life through which they might have seen the redemptive longing in the love of abundance. This failure of imagination bore the residue of culture and class, particularly in Day, whose literary skill and highbrow reading tastes marked her as a middle-class intellectual. Determined to be refugees from university and professional milieus, Catholic radicals found it difficult to make a home among the unlettered pursuers of happiness.

As a result, Catholic radicals never developed fluid, ongoing relationships with farmers or industrial workers, especially in the CIO. Day hoped at one time that unions could be cells for the sacramental gospel, arguing in 1938 that they could be "indoctrinated and taught to rebuild the social order." But while they supported the CIO's organizing efforts and economic demands, sacramentalists lamented both its insouciance about industrial technology and its social-democratic statism. Thus, sacramentalists cultivated only tenuous links to labor, ensuring that their ideals seldom underwent the sort of scrutiny that would have occasioned self-criticism and renewed engagement in a vigorous movement culture. "Ours is indeed an unpopular front," as Day once sighed.[67] Beholden more to an idealized Catholic Worker than to Catholic workers, radicals jettisoned an opportunity to translate the sacramental vision into a durable politics of work, technology, and social relations.

Just as debilitating was the chasm that separated radicals from corporatists who had stronger ties to the labor movement as well as contacts with New Deal experts and politicians. John Ryan wrote privately in 1937 that the New Deal partisans in the Social Action Department (SAD) provided "the only adequate and effective leadership in social problems" for American Catholics, while his Catholic University colleague Paul Hanly Furfey swiped at what he considered Ryan's haste to "make . . . our social agencies as much like [the New Deal's] as we can."[68] As this sniping indicated, labor Catholics never composed their differences for the sake of a united movement, one that could very well have mobilized legions of Catholic workers and set the course of the CIO. Thus Murray's "Victory Plan," as well as his open invocation of papal encyclicals, suggested that democratic corporatism held wide popular appeal and therefore stood as a genuine political possibility at the turn of the decade, perhaps the best hope of the democratic left. Sacramentalists such as Dorothy Day need not have been chagrined, for labor Catholicism might have entailed a corporatist stage which, by introducing more democratic governance into the Fordist order, laid the groundwork for a decentralized, artisanal moral economy. Still, an array of forces precluded such a composure: the decision of corporatists to fight communists as zealously as they did employers, the working-class Americanism of CIO workers, and the countercultural complacency of Catholic radicals.

World War II and its inauguration of an American imperial order would settle these differences for a generation. The defeat of fascism in warfare and the lifting of depression in war production and consumer abundance would send radicals hastening to catacombs where they waited for better days. Those who taught the lessons of realism would learn to render unto a new American Caesar.

✛

CHAPTER FOUR

Rendering Unto Caesar:

The American Century, the Covenant of Containment, and the Gospel of Personalism, 1941–1962

In February 1941, publisher Henry Luce announced the dawn of "the American Century." Son of a Presbyterian missionary, Luce reproved his fellow citizens for their dereliction of historical duty. Americans, he claimed, had not "accommodated themselves spiritually and practically" to their power, stature, and opportunity. In order to further "the growth of American life," they required a searching of their souls commensurate with the global scale of their historical moment. Yet Luce feared that Americans might postpone or cancel their appointment with this redemptive destiny. Their "educators and churchmen and scientists," preoccupied with the Depression and fearful of the implications of an American imperium, had softened and even paralyzed the national will. Undaunted, Luce challenged the guardians of culture, religion, and science to welcome the perils of global reach as "great creative opportunities" and to ready the nation through an extensive project of cultural fertility and purification. They must save souls, find a remedy for the "virus of isolationist sterility," and restore vigor to the body politic, for the United States could not undertake its mission as "the Good Samaritan to the world" unless there coursed "strongly through its veins . . . the blood of purpose and enterprise and high resolve." With strapping sinews and clean blood that flowed without contagion through the national vessels, the United States could lift humankind above the beasts to a level "the Psalmist called a little lower than the angels."[1]

Over the next generation, a great deal of blood would be spilled as the United States embarked on a course of imperial expansion uncharted even in Luce's fevered imagination. Spreading treasure and legions from the Danube to the straits of Formosa; rerouting and commanding the waves of financial capital; establishing retainers and clients from Chile to the Congo to Iran and Indonesia; slaying the minions of communism in the hills of Korea, the jungles of Guatemala, and the paddies of Vietnam; forging an arsenal of chariots and catapults unparalleled in destructive power—the American Century marched onward from its baptism at Pearl Harbor.

Just as the American Century required its craftsmen, proconsuls, and centurions, it needed scribes and priests to survey the state of the imperial culture. This "new class" of cultural workers became a hegemonic historical bloc after World War II, a coalition of producers in higher education, the entertainment industry, journalism, and other sites. Akin to the political and managerial brokers of the New Deal order, these "cultural arbiters," as Daniel Bell dubbed them, possessed the power to grant or withhold seals of cultural approval, delineate the boundaries of common sense, and quarantine the microbes of vulgarity, conformity, and totalitarianism. As "cultural health professionals," they embarked on a project of cultural containment analogous to the policies pursued by George Kennan, John Foster Dulles, and other Cold Warriors. Discovering, in Bell's words, the wisdom of "pessimism, evil, tragedy, and despair" and charting the world by the latitude and longitude of "irony, paradox, ambiguity, and complexity," this well-mannered, liberal, mature, disenchanted guild failed Luce's standards of nationalist exuberance. Indeed, Bell's own announcement of *The End of Ideology* (1960) consecrated this gray flanneled stoicism as the wise middle way between the kitschy sentiments of the masses and the utopian enthusiasm of the left.[2]

Yet Bell could not deny the persistent attraction of utopia. The end of ideology, he cautioned, "is not—should not be—the end of utopia as well." More than ever before, there was a need for some vision "fusing passion and intelligence" in a "City of Heaven." But Bell quickly reverted to technocratic form. The ladder to the heavenly city could not be a "faith ladder," he warned, but rather an empirical one, with rungs detailing costs, materials, and terms of payment.[3] Shorn even of the expansive progressive hopes that animated William James and John Dewey, Bell's constricted utopian impulse marked the managerial denouement of secular pragmatism.

Bell's reference to the heavenly city and his dismissal of faith ladders typified the measured respect secular liberals displayed toward religion in the postwar period. Abjuring barbs at cretinous believers and forswearing attempts to make a common faith out of science and progressive politics, postwar liberal intellectuals tolerated religion so long as it remained locked within the realms of emotion and imagination. As David Hollinger has argued of the modernist literary canon that helped to define liberal intellectual life in the 1940s and 1950s, the texts of religion and theology retained among secular liberals an aesthetic character, suitable for imaginative or critical appreciation but without significance for daily life. When religious enthusiasm did seek political form, Bell warned, it became either murderous or ineffective, disrespectful as it allegedly was of mundane realities. A religious movement could "live in but not of the world," Bell wrote in Weberian fashion; "a political movement cannot." Beyond both religion and ideology, Bell and other liberals settled into the secular clerisy, with greater opportunities than their forbears to effect a modest utopia. Indeed, as Adolf A. Berle remarked of the postwar liberal intelligentsia, they constituted a clerical class of "Lords Spiritual . . . keepers and developers of the public consensus" who followed in the steps of Elijah, "demanding redress for known wrongs."[4]

Among those Bell described as "intellectual nestors" strode Reinhold Niebuhr, a "prodigal son" who had returned home after venturing into the far country of radical politics. Niebuhr's shadow loomed long and dark over Bell's generation, providing a welcome cover for many secular "atheists for Niebuhr," as Morton White labeled them. As *New Yorker* pundit Richard Rovere wrote in 1960, Niebuhr was the "theologian for the Establishment," the *pontifex maximus* of the postwar state who appeared before Senate committees and attended meetings of the Policy Planning Staff.[5] Moreover, as Niebuhr—along with John Courtney Murray, a Jesuit and Niebuhr's colleague in several intellectual venues— graced the cover of Luce's *Time,* the stoical religious message of postwar liberalism extended from the temples of cultural arbiters into the hearths of middlebrow culture.

Niebuhr and Murray, together with other liberal Protestant and Roman Catholic intellectuals, constructed a covenant of containment, a "public theology" or "civil religion," for the New Deal–Cold War order. Consonant with the cultural politics of liberal intellectuals and the policy designs of corporate and political elites, this covenant was an indispensable item in the postwar liberal arsenal of cultural and international containment. Emerging out of an ecumenical New Deal religious order and a cultural détente between religious and secular intellectuals, the covenant of containment ratified the managerial authority of Bell's cultural arbiters, stigmatized the indecorous enthusiasms of radical politics, and christened the "corporate commonwealth" unequally shared among corporate capital, organized labor, and the welfare-warfare state.[6]

Yet this covenant was not recognized by all the "nestors" of Bell's generation. Terrified by the behemoth scale and violence of the corporate commonwealth, postwar personalists refused induction into the pantheon of moderation. Although personalists such as Dwight Macdonald often borrowed religious ideas while insisting on the secularity of their opposition to the postwar order, others contended that only religion could properly channel the cultural and political energies of the left. Indeed, by preserving personality as the grail of radical criticism and politics, religious personalists such as Dorothy Day, A. J. Muste, and Thomas Merton comprised the vanguard of the postwar "new left."

A DECENT MEASURE OF RESTRAINT: THE DEMISE OF RADICALISM, THE NEW DEAL IN AMERICAN RELIGIOUS CULTURE, AND THE CLERICAL DÉTENTE

Most liberal Protestant and Catholic intellectuals saw World War II as a providential moment for the social gospel. The struggle against the Axis, Jacques Maritain argued in *Christianity and Democracy* (1944), augured for the West a "recovery and purification" that was "more urgent than ever." John Cort, now *Commonweal*'s labor journalist, speculated that wartime cooperation would raze all the "great, towering black walls of indifference" to Catholic social thought and hasten the erection of a sturdy "bridge across the abyss that now separates management from labor." The editors of Reinhold Niebuhr's *Christianity and Crisis* believed that wartime sacrifices offered Christians a moment of charity, "a new knowledge of the privilege of giving [them]selves away." Indeed, Niebuhr's coterie of "realists" envisioned a global hegemony of American Protestant benevolence. Francis Miller, reflecting in 1942, likened the impending American imperium to the world dominion of the Romans. Just as "the Pax Romana and the Roman roads . . . made the journeys of St. Paul possible," so American preeminence would further the nation's "God-given mission" to "realize freedom and security" throughout the world. Niebuhr himself opined in the fall of 1943 that the United States had received "a special measure of the divine mission." God, concluded the future sage of irony and humility, "has chosen us in this fateful period of world history."[7]

If his brother saw favorable auspices, H. Richard Niebuhr could gesture only weakly to a hope beyond the carnage. Surveying "the wild and disturbed actions of men and nations" in *The Meaning of Revelation*, Richard concluded that "we do not know what we are doing by our aggressions." Later, in a remarkable series of articles in the *Christian Century*, Richard explained the war as a "crucifixion" of the combatants whose redemption lay only in a penitential postwar dedication to social

reconstruction. While Catholic Workers accepted the war as a penitential discipline, they also considered it "a confused war between Mars
and Mammon" whose propaganda camouflaged "the sordid military
expeditions of capitalism and national imperialism with a profession of
high ideals." Dorothy Day saw in domestic mobilization an ominous
portent of popular disengagement from social and material reality.
Americans' willingness to accept conscription and rationing "like
sheep" and to "throw themselves over cliffs" in the service of abstractions—Country, Flag, Freedom, etc.—convinced Day that people longed
to "escape from matter, from flesh, from life."[8]

Day's suspected rightly that the war augured badly for the religious
left, as Reinhold Niebuhr confirmed in his imprecations against "a too
simple social radicalism" in *The Nature and Destiny of Man* (1941).
Marked by his newfound caution, Niebuhr's words also reflected his
awareness of a new politics of knowledge forged in the smithy of war.
The Allied landings in North Africa, he wrote in *Christianity and Crisis*
in 1942, afforded a "revelation of the relation of technical-military to political aspects of war in a democracy." The "absolute necessity" for se-
crecy boded ill for the postwar relationship between democracy and expertise. "In a technical age," Niebuhr predicted anxiously, "the hiatus
between public knowledge and the skill of experts, who are in charge of
the mechanisms of the social process, will tend to widen."[9]

Niebuhr's anxieties lessened over the 1940s as he, along with
Catholics such as Maritain, moved away from radical religious circles
toward more secularized, liberal reform milieus. By 1941, Niebuhr had
effectively ended his association with the Fellowship of Socialist Christians, working instead with the Union for Democratic Action, a coalition
of labor leaders and prolabor intellectuals that served as a stop for many
radicals on their passage from socialism to liberal anticommunism. By
1944, Niebuhr had disembarked at the *Fortune* station, joining Luce's
Commission on the Freedom of the Press along with Arthur Schlesinger,
Jr., Archibald MacLeish, Robert Hutchins, and Maritain. Maritain, after
traveling extensively in the United States in the 1930s, settling in New
York after the fall of his homeland in 1940, and making broadcasts to
Vichy France for the Office of War Information, entered American academic life at Chicago, Columbia, and Princeton, where he received a permanent post in 1948.[10]

By the time they shook hands under the auspices of Luce, Niebuhr and
Maritain had muffled their apprehensions about a postwar hegemony of
experts in a celebration of liberal democracy. Published in 1944,
Niebuhr's *The Children of Light and the Children of Darkness* and Maritain's
Christianity and Democracy both exemplified the gathering fear of totali-

tarianism among liberals and others on the left and offered new sanctions for professional and managerial authority. Totalitarianism, Niebuhr observed, had prompted the Western democracies to "view all collectivist answers to our social problems with increased apprehension." Besides, Niebuhr now believed, the "property issue" was a problem of managerial finesse rather than class politics or radical religion. "The economic, as well as the political process" required "the best possible distribution of power for the sake of justice and the best possible management for the sake of order." This judicious management would come from "the professional class"—comprised, he wrote, of "the most intelligent portions" of American society—which stood in "a position of relative detachment from the ideological struggles of owners and producers."[11]

Long a more incisive critic than Niebuhr of industrialism and expertise, Maritain endorsed a similar, if somewhat more populist, version of liberal managerialism. Waxing eloquent about the plain people who perform "the great elementary and anonymous work of daily life," Maritain also made subtle concessions that presaged the restricted scope of the postwar social settlement. Asserting that scientific and technological advances required "an increment of soul . . . to become true instruments of liberation," Maritain now defined the primary problem of "the machine" not as its redesign or redeployment in a democratic workplace but rather the regulation of "its use for truly human needs"—a worthy but also indistinct goal.[12] Maritain's emphasis on "use" and "increment of soul" legitimated the placement of technical issues under professional and managerial control.

The thinning of Christian socialist and corporatist ranks proceeded quickly through the late 1940s, especially after the Taft-Hartley Act demonstrated the extent of corporate power and determination. Catholic corporatists abandoned or considerably tempered their hopes. Despite both Congress of Industrial Organizations' (CIO) leader John Brophy's dogged advocacy of the Murray plan and the U.S. Conference of Catholic Bishops' 1948 endorsement of industry councils as "the basic organs of a Christian and American type of economic democracy," the postwar corporate offensive against labor forced John Cort and others to retreat and demobilize. While paying his respects to the industry council ideal, Cort recommended a pragmatic acquiescence in the corporate commonwealth. The ACTU and the CIO should jettison the Murray plan, he argued in a series of articles over 1947 and 1948, defer to managerial authority, and focus on high wages and job security, even if these depended on military production. Anyone demanding redistribution of wealth or worker participation in management "is a crackpot, because he is going too far."[13]

Cort now saw consumption rather than industrial democracy as the key issue. Rejecting the Catholic Workers' insistence on the centrality of religion and the sacramentality of work, Cort offered a counterideal of "Christian industrialism" that ratified the new Fordist moment. Mass production, he argued, was a neutral "technique of producing things in large quantities," not a desecration of human skill. Employing some of the newest weapons in the rhetorical arsenal of maturity and pluralism, Cort derided "young zealots" entranced by "romantic and intolerant editions of agrarianism"—a clear shot at the Catholic Workers. Zealots should hasten to the urban factories, Cort advised, where they could labor for the fruits of mass-produced abundance under the benevolent watch of "decent employers" and "democratic union leaders."[14] Through this "Christian industrialism," Catholic corporatists—ever reluctant to abolish class, ever torn between republican propriety and consumer pleasure—commended their spirits into the hands of New Deal liberalism, to rise again as denatured ideologues for the Democratic coalition.

Meanwhile, Reinhold Niebuhr cast off his already threadbare socialist raiment and donned the robes of Protestant liberal. Like Cort's turn to Christian industrialism, Niebuhr's turn to what he termed the pragmatism of the New Deal reflected both concordance with the corporate moment and the end of a long ideological metamorphosis. "Technical advance," he wrote in 1948, "has made it impossible for the worker to own either his own tools or the place of his work." Although this invocation of technical advance—the reification of professional-managerial power—implied the impossibility of socialism, Niebuhr (along with his comrades in the Frontier Fellowship, the liberal precipitate of the disbanded Fellowship of Socialist Christians [FSC]) arrogated the word and drained its political substance. "We continue to be socialists," he claimed, "in the sense that" they believed both that capitalism stood "under divine judgment" and that "justice in modern technical society" required "a completely pragmatic attitude toward the institution of property." Niebuhr's newfound pragmatism tempered and eventually ended his animus toward New Deal reforms. The reformism of the New and Fair Deals, he speculated in 1949, provided a satisfactory "answer to the problem of justice in a technical age."[15]

Two years later (as the Frontier Fellowship became the more blandly named Christian Action), Niebuhr defined his politics in terms of "the effect of this or that policy in this or that situation"—a far cry from the galvanizing, albeit ambiguous, mythology of *Moral Man*. Niebuhr's *Christianity and Crisis* followed the same line, with one writer declaring that a "Christian attitude" in economics concerned not "the title deeds to any piece of property" but rather "the motives of those who 'own,' control, or manage it."[16] This shift from power and class to attitude and motive (akin to the corporatist move from industry councils to Maritain's "increment of soul") defined the political trajectory of Christian realism. With this deference to technical competence—hedged with his signature invocation of complexity, ambiguity, and other staples of neoorthodox discourse—Niebuhr completed a journey he had begun with his call for "spiritualized technicians."

As the moment passed for socialism and corporatism, racial injustice received greater attention from Christian social thinkers. Nazi anti-Semitism, the anti-Japanese racism of wartime propaganda, and heightened racial tensions in the cities provoked an unprecedented response from leading liberal Protestants and Catholics. American Protestantism would have to eradicate segregation, *Christianity and Crisis* editorialized in 1942, or else cease to consider itself "an instrumentality of redemption." Niebuhr urged that "every stratagem of education and every resource of religion" be used to abolish racism. One of the most difficult problems for democracy, he asserted in *Children of Light,* was to arrange the relations among "ethnic, religious, and economic groups" so that the "richness and harmony of the whole community will be enhanced and not destroyed." Maritain (whose marriage to Raissa, a Catholic convert from Judaism, and whose youthful flirtation with the French right made him especially sensitive on the matter of Catholic anti-Semitism) called in similar fashion in *Commonweal* for an "intercultural fellowship," a "personalist and pluralist democracy" embracing "diverse groups and traditions."[17]

This celebration of racial and ethnic pluralism, while marking both the commencement of a shift from class to race in Christian social thought and a renewed enthusiasm for liberal democracy, also hinted at what Mark Silk has called a new era in the nation's "spiritual politics."[18] As many liberal Protestants and Catholics withdrew from class politics in favor of class reconciliation, they began, warily and haltingly, to forsake their old antagonisms in favor of an uneasy, unequal, but nonetheless substantial religious settlement that paralleled the postwar social truce between capital and organized labor. This coalition, bound by the adhesive rhetoric of a Judeo-Christian tradition, was a "New Deal" in American religious life and became an indispensable foundation of postwar American culture and the covenant of containment.

As corporate capital and organized labor struck a tense truce, leading liberal Protestants and Catholics laid the groundwork for a new American religious order. In tandem with their call for the cessation of class hostilities, Niebuhr and Maritain drafted articles of religious détente. Soon after declaring in 1941 that "a vicar of Christ on earth is bound to be, in a sense, Anti-Christ," Niebuhr relented, arguing in 1944 that liberal democracy needed a reconstructed "religious culture" in which each religion proclaimed its highest insights while "preserving a humble and contrite recognition" of its limits. Faith itself, he reasoned, encouraged men to "moderate their natural pride" and "achieve some decent consciousness of the relativity of their own statement of even the most ultimate truth." While Maritain could not second Niebuhr's account of relativity, he asserted in identically liberal nationalist fashion that "America's problem" was to "raise the religious and spiritual potential of its democracy to the height of the cross." Maritain even invoked the fissiparous nature of American Protestantism—formerly a scandal to Catholic intellectuals—as evidence of the potential for a new era of multicreedal, antitotalitarian democracy. The "diffuse and diluted shapes" of American Christianity, he believed, contributed to a greater fusion of "the democratic principle and the religious principle." The people's war against fascism, having issued in a "powerful religious revival," demonstrated the essential unity of "all the believers of the great Judeo-Christian family, not only the faithful of the Catholic Church and those of the Protestant Churches, but also those of Judaism"—a unity exemplified in Niebuhr's invitation to Maritain to publish in *Christianity and Crisis*, as well as in their shared labors on the Luce payroll.[19]

Skeptics, especially among Catholics, pointed to the wartime origins of pluralism and tolerance as grounds for suspicion. Without arguing for uniformity and intolerance—the "totalitarian" indictments of radicalism hurled by liberals in the postwar period—critics of ecumenism saw concessions to national pride and corporate prerogative in the emerging civil religion. Urging blacks in 1943 to resist invocations of the melting pot in war propaganda, the editors of *Orate Fratres* also warned Catholics and Protestants to avoid the melting pot of wartime ecumenism as an idolatrous substitution of "supreme faith in the country" for faith in God. Paul Hanly Furfey linked the rise of a new civil religion with the decline of radicalism. Agreeing that intercreedal cooperation was justified when restricted to limited social or economic goals, Furfey feared that the erasure of religious distinctiveness from social thought would clear a larger space for the spuriously nonideological forces of managerial power. Since the labor question was, in his view, "primarily moral and religious and not primarily economic," Furfey upheld explicitly socialist or communist labor unions as models for Catholic workers, praising "the European type of labor organization which is vastly more ideological."[20]

The Protestant-Catholic détente was complemented by a clerical settlement that contained hostilities between religious and secular cultural leaders. Appalled by the savagery of World War II, terrified by the new prospect of atomic annihilation, and faced with an officially atheist state as the incarnation of totalitarianism, many leading secular writers found a new and compelling resonance in once-forsaken notions of fall and original sin. During the war, the prospects for peace between the clerisies looked gloomy. Delivering his notorious scholastic diatribe "God and the Professors" to participants in Rabbi Louis Finkelstein's Conference on Science, Philosophy, and Religion, the philosopher Mortimer Adler argued in 1940 that behind the polite discourse and insulting tolerance of the assembled secularists lurked a stiff-necked refusal to credit religious faith in any form. Adler's polemical intemperance (professors, he snapped, were more dangerous to democracy than Hitler) obscured his larger point that the uncritical acceptance of a "multiplicity of technical jargons," by fostering a one-dimensional concern with means, eroded the cultural foundations not only of democracy but also of moral life in any form. Maritain agreed, openly blasting Deweyan pragmatism in his Yale Terry Lectures in 1943 as a "technocratic denial of the objective validity of any spiritual need."[21]

While Maritain was denouncing Dewey, Dewey's Marxist protégé Sidney Hook was dismissing Maritain, Adler, Niebuhr, and others in *Partisan Review* as agents of a "new failure of nerve." Opposition to totalitarianism necessitated a tough-minded Deweyan pragmatism, Hook argued, not the presumably flaccid musculature of religion. After the war, *Partisan Review* editor Philip Rahv, ridiculing the confessions (spiritual and otherwise) of Whittaker Chambers, warned against assigning to religion "the radical task of re-organizing the world." Social and cultural reconstruction, Lionel Trilling made clear in *The Liberal Imagination* (1950), would have to proceed along secular lines. Taking as his realm "the politics of culture," the secular intellectual—who was more and more, Trilling noted, a university cultural worker—was a secular cleric directing "human life toward some end or other." Modernist literature demonstrated that the fullest exploration of "variousness, possibility, complexity, and difficulty" could be found not in religion or theology but in fiction. In fact, Trilling opined, the "historical-literary mind" was "the best kind of critical and constructive mind that we have"—"better," he insisted, "than the theological."[22]

Trilling's confidence in the clerical capacity of secular intellectuals paralleled that of atomic scientists eager to establish what James Gilbert has called a "republic of science" in which scientists would play a leading role in political and cultural life. As James B. Conant—physicist, president of Harvard, and tireless public intellectual—wrote in 1947, American democracy needed "a unified, coherent culture" in a "new age of machines and experts." While the primary obstacles to the emergence of this culture were orthodox believers resistant to "broadening or purifying their religion," Conant also chastised secular intellectuals who denied the validity of all religions. Conant's view of the conflict recalled the prewar class antagonism of capital and labor, just as his advocacy of an intelligent interchange of views mirrored the postwar social settlement. Moreover, like the social peace that dictated labor's acceptance of corporate control, the reconciliation of science and religion mandated religion's relinquishment of power to set the basic terms of cultural life. "The doctrines of Christianity or Judaism," Conant declared in *Science and Common Sense* (1951), must be "subject to the same critical examination as the boldest would apply to the scientific explanations of man's origin and development."[23]

While light-years apart in sensibility, Conant the physicist and Trilling the critic—a distinction replicated in the scientific-technical and humanist divisions of the new class of cultural professionals—shared a commitment to secularized expertise as the criterion of cultural life. Their assertions of secular primacy rested on expansion of the corporate cultural industries as well as on the growing enrollments, resources, and prestige of universities after World War II. Riding the rising wave of enrollments and corporate media expansion, cultural workers found, as Trilling wrote in 1952, that "the needs of our society" had brought "a large class of people of considerable force and complexity of mind" close to "the top of the social hierarchy."[24] This new group of cultural arbiters, as Bell later called them, supervising cultural production from classrooms, broadcast suites, magazine offices, and foundation conferences, emerged from a university culture supportive of innovation and dissent. Many of the former adversaries of corporate capitalism were now ensconced in remunerative managerial positions.

Still, despite the unprecedented cultural authority and material prosperity enjoyed by secularized intellectuals after World War II, many continued to draw, often heavily, on the cultural capital accumulated by the old religious clerisy. Leslie Fiedler, pointing to movies, comic books, and dime novels as the ritual artifacts of an American folk religion of "innocence and achievement," called on the American writer in 1952 to assume a clerical role as "the recorder of the encounter of the dream of innocence and the fact of guilt." Consumers of mass culture, he reminded his readers, worship in "the catacombs of movie theaters" and genuflect before "the images of saints on the news-stands." Trilling characterized the preoccupation with the self in modern literature as a "revival of the concepts of religion." The presence of prominent scientists such as Harlow Shapley in Finkelstein's pantheon of luminaries attested to the continuing significance of religious concerns with ethics and ends among secularized cultural and scientific workers.[25]

Over the course of the 1940s, in tandem with the tentative steps toward ecumenism, Christian and secular intellectuals took halting steps toward a settlement between the religious and secular clerisies. Like the nascent triumvirate of Protestant-Catholic-Jew, this rapprochement was conceived under the aegis of totalitarianism and gestated in the womb of religion. The outlines of this clerical settlement could be seen in Lewis Mumford's *Faith for Living* (1940). A friend of Niebuhr and an admirer of Maritain, Mumford shared their belief that the "religious faith" of fascism could not be countered without "a faith equally strong, equally capable of fostering devotion and loyalty, and commanding sacrifice." Looking to religion as an Arnoldian "repository for the best that has been thought, felt, imagined, divined, in each age," Mumford emptied the particular codes and practices of different religious into a universal solvent of high-mindedness. Invoking "the universal distinction that all religions have made" between good and evil, truth and falsehood, Mumford declared that the chief mission of religion was to preserve those "ideal points of reference" without which life became "savage, degraded, and brutish."[26] By smoothing the edges and diluting the contents of particular religions, Mumford prepared a blueprint for the postwar clerical détente.

Christian intellectuals met Mumford and other secular "fellow travelers" of religion at several points during and after the war. The Committee on Science, Philosophy, and Religion (set up, as Finkelstein explained, as a "united intellectual front" against fascism) was a working model of religious-secular cooperation, supplying what Gilbert has illuminatingly described as "the outline of a functioning democratic intelligentsia." Luce's Committee on Freedom of the Press, the Union for Democratic Action and the Americans for Democratic Action, the Congress for Cultural Freedom, the Ford Foundation, and Robert Hutchins' Fund for the Republic all emerged as sites for clerical rapprochement. In all these venues, Christians were enjoined to practice "a decent measure of restraint in expressing the Christian hope," as Niebuhr urged in 1943. Anxious to avoid Christian obscurantism, Niebuhr cautioned Protestants in 1949 to affirm "the obvious truths about life and history" revealed by "the social, political, psychological, and historical sciences," just as Maritain now praised the "secularized Christian feeling" of liberalism—formerly a nemesis—as the agent of most of the modern world's technical, intellectual, and humanitarian achievements. Moreover, Christian faith would be enriched, Niebuhr believed, by the "constant commerce" in "specific insights" between religion and the sciences—a reified and revealingly mercantile way of describing theologians' *entente cordiale* with the growing numbers of experts in the expanding universities.[27]

By the winter of 1950, when *Partisan Review* began its four-part symposium on religion and the intellectuals, the discursive architecture of the clerical settlement was in place. Hook and Dewey repeated their already boilerplate indictments of religious obscurantism; William Barrett more keenly suspected the attempts of intellectuals to "think themselves back into religion"; and Allen Tate began his essay by reciting the first line of the Apostles' Creed. However, the most striking overall features of the symposium—its wary civility and the generous indulgence given to religion by the predominantly secularized participants—emerged out of a common opposition to totalitarianism and a fungible definition of religion. The fear of totalitarianism was a clear incentive for the entire enterprise, as the editors demonstrated when they asked if religion was necessary to counter "the new means of social discipline we all fear." Alfred Kazin, after dismissing much of liberal Protestantism as tissue thin, lauded Catholics for their prodemocratic, anticommunist resolve. "I can disagree with Catholics," he wrote, but "totalitarianism permits no argument."[28]

The earnestness that pervaded the *Partisan Review* symposium suggests its significance as a postwar cultural artifact. Defined by the absence of definite beliefs and practices and occasioned by the derailment of socialism as the vehicle of a new sacral order, a nebulous "jargon of authenticity," as Theodor Adorno called it—the argot of dread, alienation, authenticity, and other keywords often but not exclusively associated with existentialism—melded with religion for many among the first generation of New Deal cultural professionals. It also served as a bridge between religious and secular intellectuals employed in the expanding cultural institutions. As many symposiants realized, the evacuation of the particular contents of religion enabled secular intellectuals to appropriate both the aura of religious sensibility and the cultural authority of religious traditions. The editors received numerous affirmations that certain aspects of a religious attitude could be viable without the constraints imposed by religious beliefs. James Agee, for instance, recommended religion's "incomparably well-equipped gymnasium" for an exercise regimen in muscular humanism—a workout to be undertaken, he cautioned, by "individualists." Sweaty from his own exertions on the bench press of the spirit, William Barrett (later prominent as a leading American expositor of existentialism) urged a "creative waiting" for the return of some vaguely "primitive simplicities." By the early 1950s, interest in religion appeared to be downright fashionable in secular circles. Recalling in a *Saturday Review* essay in the winter of 1951 that "no self-respecting intellectual would have been caught dead with a religious interpretation of anything" before the war, the historian H. Stuart Hughes observed that now "religion . . . is the latest thing." Although skeptics such as Meyer Shapiro implicitly compared religious enthusiasm with Popular Front commitment by deriding "fellow travelers" of religion, this scorn only underlined the pronounced turn toward religion among secular intellectuals after World War II.[29]

Only Tate appeared to dissent from this clerical truce. His recital of the Apostles' Creed conveyed not only his faith but also his fear that important distinctions were being drowned in a bland vat of seriousness. The religious consciousness to which the editors alluded could not be very conscious, Tate pointed out, if it lacked "something to be conscious of"—namely, "a definite religion."[30] Tate's insistence on the specificity of traditions was overwhelmed by the more widely recognized need to present a common cultural front in the face of totalitarianism.

H. Richard Niebuhr had made similar criticisms of liberal religion before the war, and his own course over the 1940s exemplified the broader drift of the liberal Protestant and Catholic social gospels. Near the end of the war, Niebuhr glimpsed an ambiguous redemptive possibility. "There are days at the end of winter when the increasing brightness of the sun does not so much promise the coming of spring as reveal the shabbiness and uncleanness of the wintry scene," he wrote in 1944. "Our day in history is something like that. Reflection and feeling apprehend the morbidity of secular civilization, but the promise of newness of life they do not discern."[31]

Yet later, in *Christ and Culture* (1951), a panoramic survey of styles in Christian social thought and cultural criticism, Niebuhr seemed to hold out such a promise of rebirth. Assessing the virtues and vices of several ideal critical types, Niebuhr issued both a warning and an invitation to Christian intellectuals signing up in the corporate commonwealth. Rebuking the consumerist inclination in the postwar social gospel—justice was not, he scoffed, about "improving the quality of the husks served in the pigsty"—Niebuhr also chastised the conservatism he detected in his brother's realism, which advocated little more than "improvements within an essentially unchanged context of social habit." Richard's preferred "conversionist" approach—"Christ the transformer of culture"— rested on the doctrine of the Incarnation. "The Word that became flesh and dwelt among us, the Son who does the work of the Father in the world of creation, has entered into a human culture that has never been without his ordering action." Turning to Augustine, Niebuhr explained that culture was "perverted good, not evil; it is evil as perversion, not as badness." Rejecting the stark polarity of church and world that defined his position in the 1930s, Niebuhr now promoted a leavening of the world by the church. "The problem of culture," he asserted, is "the problem of its conversion, not of its replacement by a new creation," even though "the conversion is so radical that it amounts to a kind of rebirth." This conversion would still be accomplished, as before, by a popular front of believers—church—who lived as "men and women, parents and children, governors and governed, teachers and learners, manual and intellectual workers."[32]

Yet Niebuhr himself realized that this resolution of the problem of Christianity and culture remained almost entirely rhetorical. Indeed, the subtle shift in Niebuhr's language—from "church against the world" to "Christ the transformer of culture"—registered the marginality of Christian radicalism. Noting the absence of a "widespread and profoundly serious radical Christianity," Niebuhr identified "Christians of the center" as "the main movement of the Church," the only remaining site for a religious cultural politics.[33] Moreover, by concentrating on culture without a complementary attention to society, politics, and economics, Niebuhr underwrote a Tory politics of managerial liberalism situated in the professional and managerial sectors. Frozen in the Cold War, satisfied by the truce between capital and labor, and committed to the new cultural dispensation of religious pluralism and clerical détente, most liberal Protestant and Catholic critics now confronted the new quandaries of power, affluence, and religious enthusiasm. If the social order could not be restored in Christ, then perhaps it could be contained in Caesar.

THE SAINT IN THE GRAY FLANNEL SUIT: CONTAINING CHRISTIANITY IN THE CORPORATE COMMONWEALTH

While the rhetoric of containment relayed the designs of American foreign policy elites, it also conveyed the tone of domestic life in the two decades after World War II. A culture of containment—exemplified in the varieties of anticommunism and the fierce reassertion of "traditional" sexual and family mores—both legitimated the Cold War and bounded the symbolic universe of the corporate commonwealth. To the blue-collar worker, the gray flannel suit, and their comradely wives and children—a people of plenty in the balmiest Gilead of Fordist modernity—the culture of containment promised imperial strength, steady abundance, and the quotidian grandeur of suburban domesticity, even as the threat of atomic destruction lurked in the background to tarnish the golden age of capitalism.[34]

The culture of containment also leavened the critical mood of liberal intellectuals. Weary of battle on the fronts of depression and war, many intellectuals demobilized from the battalions of the left, purchased lots in the growing cultural industries, and built new homes (with tasteful siding) on the modest estates of consensus. In mildly discordant tones of resignation and critical affirmation, liberal intellectuals urged the composure of old grievances, preaching a tasteful, discriminating deference to corporate imperatives and aestheticizing social conflicts as matters of taste rather than matters of power and morality. If the man who strode through the pages of postwar social criticism was incarcerated in the organization, he could, he was told, take heart in small, apolitical, but personally liberating acts of resistance.[35]

This devotion to cultural containment put many liberals on guard against the postwar religious revival. Both bemused and horrified by Billy Graham and Fulton Sheen, liberals discerned a kind of right-wing Popular Front in the revival, a noxious blend of passion, credulity, and aesthetic mediocrity. As scholars in search of the origins of "the new American right," liberals identified evangelical Protestants in particular as forerunners of kitsch, moralism, and political repression. In *The New American Right* (1955), Daniel Bell traced the origins of McCarthyism directly to evangelical moralism. Frontier Methodists and Baptists, he wrote, were charged by "high-voltage confessing" that lit the dim bulbs of "egalitarianism and anti-intellectualism." Richard Hofstadter, doyen of the American historical profession, showered evangelical Protestantism with even more unremitting derision. In *Anti-Intellectualism in American Life* (1963), Hofstadter portrayed the heroes of Niebuhr's *Kingdom of God* as braying rubes of the heartland who had "repudiated a learned religion and a formally constituted clergy" and dispensed with "trained leadership"—an unmistakable reference to the postwar liberal clerisy. *Anti-Intellectualism in American Life* was the apex of a scorn first articulated in *The Age of Reform* (1955), where Hofstadter's aversion to populism had been fueled in part by his loathing of its evangelical character. The Protestants Hofstadter did applaud were the liberals, whose dedication to professionalism and social science had cleared the way for their supercession by the experts Hofstadter admired. Progressivism, he argued, was a "latter-day Protestant revival" sponsored by a "full complement of chaplains" whose enthusiasm for expertise prefigured the New Deal's secularized indifference to moral issues.[36] Licensing both disparagement of popular democracy and confidence in the acumen of social scientists, postwar liberal secularism was a key element in the culture of containment.

The mainstream of Christian social thought and cultural criticism over the 1950s, while developing in tandem with the secular idiom of cultural containment, also refracted the oft-maligned religious revival. The late 1940s and 1950s witnessed a wave of denominational mergers and coalitions in mainline Protestantism, cresting in the formation of the World Council of Churches in 1948 and the National Council of Churches in 1950. This ecumenical consolidation, by fostering what Paul Harrison called a "managerial revolution," created new ecclesial structures, added new layers of bureaucracy, and expanded the professional-managerial cohort of American Protestantism. Just as the expansion of the university system sustained Bell's cultural arbiters, the corporate reconstruction of American Protestantism supported a new bloc of what Robert Wuthnow has dubbed "religious specialists: counsellors, educators, educational consultants, news writers, church growth specialists, missions planners," and other experts. When H. Richard Niebuhr wrote in 1956 that Protestant churches resembled "the political structures of Canada and the United States" and that the ministerial status aped "political, educational, and economic executive or managerial authority," it was apparent that the mainline Protestant future lay with the managerial parsonage.[37]

American Catholicism saw not a wave of mergers but a great Diaspora as large numbers of the faithful left the urban immigrant ghettoes and dispersed, college degrees in hand, among the professional and managerial denizens of the suburbs. John Cogley, an editor of *Commonweal*, pronounced the postwar exodus the dawn of a brave new epoch in American Catholicism. Catholics who had picketed factories were now "helping to build Park Forest and Levittown," he wrote in 1958. Catholic liberals were confident that the ranch house and not the house of hospitality was the new abode of the Catholic social witness and that from corporate suites and suburban sidewalks a new Catholic would bear cross and briefcase in the cause of Christ. "The sun now rises over Larchmont, not Mott Street," Cogley declared, while the young priest and sociologist Andrew Greeley located the "seedbed for future prophets" amid *The Church and the Suburbs* (1959). "Can an organization man be a saint?" Greeley asked. "Of course he can."[38]

Catholic liberals exhibited an almost unrestrained enthusiasm for these gray-flannel saints. The emergence of the layman as a key figure in postwar Catholic discourse both signaled the entrance of Catholics into the professional middle class and marked the acceptance by many Catholic intellectuals of the New Deal's social and cultural order. "A successful, educated, and independent man," as Greeley described him, the lay-

man was a figure of credentialed proficiency and ready mobility—
"judged," as *Commonweal* editor Daniel Callahan wrote in *The Mind of the
Catholic Layman* (1963), "in terms of his professional skills" and "free to
live where he likes, and change jobs if he likes"—as well as a corporate
climber with vaunting but sober ambition, "a junior executive-type busi-
nessman on his way up," as *Ave Maria* editor Donald Thorman observed
in *The Emerging Layman* (1962). These corporate knights of faith would
be missionaries, Jesuit Walter Ong believed, in an "apostolate to the business world," the gabardine redemption of the organization man.[39]

The managerial revolution in liberal Protestantism, together with the
suburban Diaspora of Catholicism, set the stage for the *religious* vilifica-
tion of the religious revival that marked the two decades after World
War II. More than an episode in the nation's "spiritual politics," religious criticism of popular piety implicated religious liberals in the project of cultural containment. Neoorthodox liberals in particular followed
the *Christian Century* in dismissing much of the postwar religious revival
as "a tightly clutched camouflage, hiding driving fear beneath pseudo-
serenity." Reprising its role as the Sanhedrin of Protestant sanity, the
Christian Century regularly vilified Billy Graham and other Protestant
evangelicals as Popular Front masters of "skillful manipulation" designed to "exploit the churches." Catholic liberals were no less vigilant
in containing unsophisticated piety within the bounds of enlightened
decorum. Daniel Callahan, for instance, scorned the more feminine,
working-class spirituality of Marian devotions, rosaries, and novenas as
unsuitable for the sophisticated, publicly accountable Catholicism he
considered indispensable for the new laity.[40]

Not all critics of the revival rushed to burn the suburban church and
the imitation grotto. Reinhold Niebuhr conceded that Billy Graham's
success, together with the widespread idealization of family and church,
answered needs for "asylums of fellowship" from the impersonality of
technological civilization. Ong observed that the much-maligned foot-
ball teams, sewing clubs, bowling leagues, and church picnics both anchored faith in daily life and sustained a "camaraderie or good-fellow-
ship" that knit together the newly settled pilgrims of suburbia. Will
Herberg, whose *Protestant, Catholic, Jew* (1955) framed much of contemporary and subsequent historical understanding of the revival, likewise
vouched for the authenticity of postwar spiritual striving. The widespread interest in religion stemmed, in Herberg's view, from the longing for "an indispensable citadel for the self" against the "depersonalizing pressures" of contemporary life."[41]

These concessions to the spirit of the revival usually preceded inter-
diction and containment on the grounds of intellectual and aesthetic in-

eptitude, however. Complimenting Billy Graham as an untutored, albeit "photogenic exemplar of Christian virtues," Niebuhr borrowed from Clement Greenberg in condemning the blandness of the entire religious revival. Herberg's undisguised contempt for the crassness of popular piety—epitomized for him in Jane Russell's image of God as "a livin' Doll"—foreclosed any serious engagement with the desires for self-transformation and beloved community that accompanied the glitter and banality.[42] By invoking, like Niebuhr, the standards of taste common to "responsible and discriminating secularists," religious critics of the religious revival both missed the significance of the "livin' Doll"— the desire for God as an intimate, tactile presence, a concrete power in the present—and renounced the progressive dream of a united front as a nightmare of sentimentality.

Their renunciation stemmed from the public theology that united covenant and concordat in a baptismal certificate for the corporate commonwealth. A critical but friendly complement to the liberal consensus, the fundamentals of this New Deal public theology were the magnanimity of American imperialism, the benediction of corporate power, and the need for an "orderly revolution" in the nation's race relations.

"The United States is an imperialism, like it or not," John Courtney Murray stated candidly in *We Hold These Truths* (1960), echoing Reinhold Niebuhr's allusion to "our vast American empire" in *Christian Realism and Political Problems* (1953). Protecting and extending this *pax Americana* required Christians both to prefer death to communism and to live mired in patriotic gore. "We are right in preferring death to [the] annulment" of "our cherished values of individualism," Niebuhr maintained in *The Irony of American History* (1952). Murray appraised the imperial musculature as "sinewy beyond comparison" with arms "getting dirty beyond the wrists." Both recommended the classical Christian virtues as nutrients for the imperial system. Humility, Niebuhr wrote in 1953, supplied a necessary ingredient in the compound of qualities to which the United States would owe its success in "maintaining our political hegemony in the free world."[43] Gracing the cover of *Time* and attending the Ford Foundation's perennial mandarin circuit, Niebuhr and Murray proved that he who humbled himself for Caesar's sake would be exalted by Henry Luce.

Since much of that free world needed technical and economic assistance, Niebuhr and others preached the gospel of modernization so siren sweet to the ears of postwar academic, government, and corporate circles. Walter Ong wrote appreciatively of the sense of mission and the "impulse to 'reform' whatever it encounters [that] marches with American capitalism around the world." Often cited as a trenchant critic of

American imperial self-delusion, Niebuhr harbored profound illusions about the impact of American power in the underdeveloped world. Dismissing the "prejudice of the Asian world against our alleged capitalistic imperialism" and bristling at the position of the United States as "residuary legatee of their resentments," Niebuhr brushed aside indigenous resistance to Western modernization schemes as the surliness of "sleep-waking cultures" among whom "the drama of human history is not taken seriously." Conceding that it was impossible to "transmute an agrarian culture into a technical civilization without vast cultural and social dislocations"—to make an omelet without cracking eggs, in other words—the communist menace placed the United States under the moral necessity of "telescoping developments which required four centuries in European history."[44]

Niebuhr's endorsement of modernization reflected a broader consecration of liberal managerialism as the culmination of Christian tradition. Reading Augustine's *City of God* as a primer in political realism and social thought, Niebuhr cast the conflict between the cities of God and man not as a struggle between two kinds of social order but as a battle between "love and self-love . . . in every soul." Murray, drawing on the scholastic distinction between natural and supernatural that had structured the corporatist social gospel, likewise denied that religious communities constituted social alternatives to the corporate liberal order. The Church, Murray asserted, exercised only a "spiritual jurisdiction" in liberal capitalist democracies, wherein social life and government had "relatively autonomous" ends in the "temporal and terrestrial order."[45]

Murray exemplified most clearly and haughtily the adoption by Christian intellectuals of the liberal containment mentality. Although he argued in 1955 that Western civilization had been "eroded, eclipsed, [and] discarded" by secular intellectuals, his unease obscured his affinity with the gatekeepers of the postwar consensus. One of the key diplomats in the ongoing postwar negotiation between secular and religious cultural elites, Murray espoused a liberalism that was most evident not in his beleaguered advocacy of church-state separation but in his suspicion of popular politics. Politics, he wrote in 1960, was "a good argument among informed and responsible men" insulated from the contentiousness of popular democracy. Like Hofstadter and Bell, Murray associated popular politics with the unwashed, irrational masses who inhabited the "barn" or "toolshed" rather than the "mansion" that was democracy's proper abode. Murray saw a corps of cultural professionals setting and patrolling the perimeters of public discussion, guardians of the "public philosophy" invoked by lords spiritual such as Walter Lippmann. The wisdom of this menagerie of academic, corporate, and political arbiters—"the conclusions of careful university professors, the reasoned opinions of specialists, the statements of responsible journalists, [and] the solid pronouncements of respected politicians," all delivered in the mien of senatorial *gravitas*—was for Murray "the real tribunal to which the American system is finally accountable."[46]

Murray's tribunal exercised extensive jurisdiction over the social and economic agendas of Catholic and Protestant liberals in the 1950s. Reviewing an American Business Leaders' booklet entitled "Human Relations in Industry" in 1951, Loyola sociologist Edward Marciniak (a former Catholic Worker) lauded its effort to "state in the language of American industry the basic moral principles governing economic life." Ong, rejecting the Ruskin-Morris-Gill tradition of the Catholic Worker, urged his fellow business apostles to seal a "Church-business world alliance" so as to redeem the commercial world "in terms of the persons involved in it." The Niebuhrian John Bennett agreed, writing testily in 1958 that the only Protestant social statements "worth the paper they were written on" were those reflecting a consensus constructed by management experts, social scientists, labor leaders, and—trailing last— "theologians and pastors." Jacques Maritain, convinced that America stood poised to "pass beyond capitalism," proclaimed an end to "the old merciless struggles between management and labor" in his *Reflections on America* (1958). Aligning himself with management theorist Peter Drucker, *Fortune* magazine avatars of capitalism as "permanent revolution," and liberal intellectuals such as Daniel Bell, John Kenneth Galbraith, Adolf Berle, and David Lilienthal, Maritain asserted that the avarice of corporations had been bridled and that the separation of management from ownership heralded a society in which firms conformed to socially beneficent principles. "You have no Bourgeois," he informed Americans. In Maritain's view, the new social apostolate entailed the sentimental education of the professional-managerial class through a regimen of middlebrow culture and industrial relations. Maritain hailed the Great Books "Fat Man" programs of Adler and Hutchins, along with Hutchins' Fund for the Republic and Center for the Study of Democratic Institutions, as exemplary venues for the transformation of executives and technicians into a corps of philosopher-managers. Plato, Aristotle, and Aquinas would be supplemented by "applied psychology" utilized by "instructors in human relations," whose sagacity Maritain found distilled in a Johnson & Johnson guide on executive development.[47]

Maritain's identification of race as the one remaining stain on the national soul pointed to the new focus of liberal energy in the postwar social witness. Long overshadowed by class in Christian social thought, race attracted greater attention from religious intellectuals with the apparent settlement of class differences. Even so, the gospel of containment checked liberal enthusiasm for the nascent civil rights movement. Christian liberals hoped to inspire and guide an "orderly revolution," in David Southern's words, a transformation of the nation's race relations that would somehow both attain justice for nonwhites and respect the stability of social and political institutions—a spectacular feat of managerial orchestration if there would ever be one.[48]

The containment mode in the racial gospel appeared most clearly and disappointingly in Reinhold Niebuhr and John La Farge, both of whom proved all too prudent about investing their moral capital in the enterprise of racial justice. Niebuhr (whose speculations in *Moral Man* on the possibilities of nonviolence proved prescient in the 1950s) reminded his fellow liberals in 1948 that racism was "finally a religious problem," the most insidious guise of pride, "the final form of human evil." Yet Niebuhr joined secular liberals in overestimating the significance of judicial and legislative achievements. The 1954 *Brown* decision proved to Niebuhr's satisfaction that American racial problems were "on the way of being resolved," since the declarations of human equality in the nation's founding documents had now acquired "political reality and relevance"—but not, evidently, too quickly real and relevant. Invoking the Burkean argot of custom and organic change, Niebuhr urged Martin Luther King, Jr., and other black leaders to decelerate the civil rights crusade. While it was "politically unwise to advocate 'gradualism,' " Niebuhr mused, it was still "morally wise to practice it" so long as it was "genuine in giving blacks "hope for the future." Niebuhr's garbled counsel matched that of La Farge, who argued in *The Catholic Viewpoint on Race Relations* (1956) that pleas for "moderation, patience, tolerance, and mutual good will" could never be too frequent and earnest. ("Ignatius hurries no one," the Jesuit reminded readers of the *Interracial Review* in the same year.) The Catholic bishops' 1958 pastoral letter on "Discrimination and the Christian Conscience," while it condemned a "gradualism that is merely a cloak for inaction," also hastened to admonish any "rash impetuosity."[49]

As race received unprecedented attention in the social gospel, liberal Protestants and Catholics turned to the culture industries as new frontiers in the Christian witness. One *Christian Century* contributor argued late in 1957 that liberal Protestants needed not a social gospel but a "culture ethic" appropriate for the new conditions of widespread abundance. Niebuhr, for instance, focused almost exclusively on the tawdry and effeminizing effects of mass culture. "The arts of mass communication," he opined in 1952, produced a "vulgarization of culture" that reached its nadir in television, "a threat to our culture analogous to the threat of atomic weapons to our civilization." A comparable danger lay in prosperity itself—"the lady of our dreams . . . most opulent and desirable."[50] Yet Niebuhr—whose own visibility as the Protestant conscience of the postwar mandarinate owed much to the middlebrow press—never wavered in supporting the very New Deal order that generated the opulence he decried. Besides marking the persistence of the Protestant reluctance to embrace the spiritual possibilities disclosed in material life, Niebuhr's gendered anxiety about the enervating effects of prosperity also deflected his criticism of corporate capitalism into the realm of style.

With more of their brethren visiting the consumer agora, Catholic liberals were more receptive to the opportunities afforded by mass culture. Mass cultural production, in their view, was a corrupted but genuine vessel of redemptive longing to be embraced and "impregnate[d] with Christ," in Walter Ong's words. Noting in *The Mechanical Bride* (1951) that the "folklore of industrial man" was not a genuinely folk culture at all but rather a product of "the laboratory, the studio, and the advertising agencies," Marshall McLuhan—a convert and neomedievalist enthusiast of Chesterton, Maritain, scholastic philosophy, and distributist economics—also discerned in industrial folklore the secular heir of medieval culture, a vehicle of spiritual aspiration. Luce's *Fortune,* for instance, appeared to McLuhan as a "Bayreuth festival," a "major religious liturgy . . . celebrating the feats of technological man," while Superman, embodying the dreams of corporate moguls and technical experts, emerged as "the comic-strip brother of medieval angels." Meanwhile, the Jesuit literary scholar William Lynch argued in *The Image Industries* (1959) that the corporate-generated symbols of abundance pointed beguilingly to "a hidden glory, the *deus absconditus,* the hidden God." Just as the previous generation of Catholic intellectuals had fought for social justice, so a new generation must struggle, Lynch wrote, for "the very inward shape of the soul itself as it is inundated by our everyday images." Rejecting the "snobbish detachment" of Dwight Macdonald and other contributors to Bernard Rosenberg's anthology *Mass Culture: The Popular Arts in America* (1958), Lynch argued that the religious intellectual should pursue a popular, emancipatory critical mission that enabled "the people" to "respond and even to leap ahead of . . . [themselves] in their insights." Lynch prevailed on artists, theologians, critics, university intellectuals, and corporate media professionals to muster a "common act of intelligence and competency" against "the great commercial interests" who controlled the culture industries.[51]

Without a larger base either in the image industries or among the growing Catholic middle class, however, these Catholic critics could only aspire to join the cultural apparatus and hope for the best. McLuhan wed the mechanical bride by accepting a chairmanship with the Ford Foundation, whereas Ong (a former student of McLuhan's), searching for a "real Christian *mystique* of technology and science," promised lamely that television ensured "better personal rapport" among its users.[52] Relatively insouciant about corporate control of the media, Ong exemplified the Christian mystique of the corporate commonwealth, urging a mannered equipoise in what appeared to be the best of all sinful worlds.

NOT A PINCH OF INCENSE: POSTWAR CHRISTIAN PERSONALISM AS THE FIRST NEW LEFT

While Niebuhr, Murray, and other Christian liberals wrote the religious clauses in the charter of the corporate commonwealth, some of their brethren refused to notarize the postwar social contract. In their view, the public theology of the American Century was a pact with the devil, an amalgamation of Christianity with the national-security state and the military-industrial political economy. Surveying the American scene in 1962, A. J. Muste invoked one of the oldest of Christian specters by declaring that "we are indeed in Rome," a power before whose altars Christians should burn "not a pinch of incense." Muste rescued his analogy from moralistic cliché by focusing not on self-indulgence but on the sway of American power. "Slaves, merchants, adventurers, sophisticates, evangelists, intellectuals" all trod their Appian Ways in the *pax Americana* of money and markets. More rootless than ever, Americans brayed loudly of their freedom as they accepted their vassalage to the state and the corporation. "People [are] now individuals," Muste mused—nomads with increasingly attenuated and utilitarian ties to region, work, tradition, or God—"but not persons" anchored in historical communities and in God. The most frightening specimens of depersonalization lay among the country's professional and cultural elites. "The great minds have become a munitions factory," Muste asserted in *Not By Might* (1947), echoing Dorothy Day's aspersions in the *Catholic Worker* on "scientists, army officers, great universities . . . captains of industry" for their complicity in atomic murder. Worse still, the churches had become temples of "the operative religion," a Constantinian worship of "the Empire, or of the State," in Muste's view. "In the final analysis, the crisis is religious," Muste intoned, and "only a religious rebirth can save the world now."[53]

This religious critique of the postwar order paralleled those of freelance radicals—secular personalists, as James J. Farrell has called them—

aghast at the colossal and unfathomable scale of modern social organization. Taking the person as their standard of criticism and action, personalists such as Paul Goodman, Dwight Macdonald, and Kenneth Rexroth, writing in periodicals such as *politics* and *Liberation*, sought to restore smaller and more humane proportions to modern life through decentralized factories, ecologically sensitive urban development, and greater attention than radicals had previously paid to the quality of individual experience and identity. By espousing more diminutive, intimate, and libertarian alternatives to New Deal liberalism, social democracy, and state socialism, personalists cleared the way for the postwar "new left."[54]

Personalists often conveyed their fears of scientific hubris and technological amorality in religious language. Although often attracted to Asian religions they thought untainted by Western desires for mastery and progress, they drew most often on Judaism and Christianity for moral and intellectual resources. When many of them came together in *Liberation* to advocate "experiments in creative living," they identified as the first of their moral and intellectual roots the "ancient Judeo-Christian prophetic tradition." Goodman, exploring the problems of "drawing the line" after the war, faulted advertising and state propaganda for inducing a "state of continuous alarm" that dulled the "religious, eschatological sense of emergency" he thought indispensable for personal and political transformation. Later, in *Communitas* (1947) and *Growing Up Absurd* (1960), Goodman asserted that subdivided labor and leviathan scale had, in making people "ignorant by specialization," rendered them "superstitious of science and technology." Only in smaller-scale societies, he argued, could they recover the medieval understanding of work as vocation and make a "moral selection of machines." Macdonald, despite his own professed indifference to religious questions, frequently turned to figures such as Dorothy Day and Simone Weil. Macdonald's 1952 *New Yorker* portrait of Day was a model of secular reverence. (He told Michael Harrington that the roundtable discussions reminded him of Trotskyite debates, "except that the points of reference were Augustine and Aquinas, not Marx and Engels.") As editor of *politics,* Macdonald introduced American readers to Weil's reflections on what she called "the Apparatus," the gargantuan, technocratic industrialism that engulfed the capitalist and socialist worlds while warping and breaking the soul in the gears of military and factory routine.[55]

However, where many personalists invoked the "Judeo-Christian" lineage only vaguely and fragmentarily—indeed, often as aesthetically as their liberal counterparts—Christian personalists claimed full title. Historians often have noted the prominence of religious figures in the early years of the "new left": Muste's leadership of the War Resisters League and Day's maternal charisma in the civil defense protests of the late 1950s. What needs to be emphasized is that the irreducibly religious character of their politics distinguished them from their secular descendants. Inheriting the bequests of personality, industrial democracy, and permanent revolution in the age of Cold War and corporate commonwealth and setting examples for a subsequent wave of religious and secular firebrands, Christian personalists composed the first new left of postwar radicalism.[56]

Against Christian "realists," Christian personalists denied the theological basis for the covenant of containment. Realists deliver us over to corporate and imperial power, Muste thought, by transmuting Christianity into a form of stoicism that sanctioned managerial command. Christian realism robbed men and women of agency—and hence relieved them of responsibility—by declaring that "the important decisions have all been made, or are being made, but always by something or someone else." Even when they acknowledged the reality of divine grace, Muste noted, realists did so almost grudgingly, always adding swiftly that sin lurked over and behind any moment of redemptive possibility. "Where grace abounds," as Muste condensed Christian realism, "sin still also persists." But this was not the final word, Muste maintained—at least not for real Christians. *"Where sin abounds,"* Muste quoted Paul, *"grace much more abounds."* And this abundance of grace could be discerned only by a community—"the Body of Christ . . . a living cell of the new Divine order"—devoted to a "passion for perfection," not resigned to the management of mediocrity.[57]

Opposing the abundance of grace to the poverty of realism, personalists rejected the rhetoric of containment and adopted a discourse of personal authenticity. The Catholic convert and Trappist monk Thomas Merton, whose best-selling *The Seven Storey Mountain* (1948) marked his trail of wild oats to the doors of the monastery, wrote most notably in the personalist vein. In *Seeds of Contemplation* (1949), Merton asserted that holiness and salvation depended on "finding out who I am" and "discovering my true self." "For me to be a saint means to be myself." The genuine, authentic self was always shadowed by a false self, a private self who lurked "outside the radius of God's will and God's love." Indeed, the false individualism of American life, he wrote in *Disputed Questions* (1960), was a prison of commodity fetishism, a jailhouse constructed and guarded by "engineers of the soul" who bound personal experience with the gossamer chains of advertising and entertainment. Unlike other postwar critics of conformity, Merton saw that escape from inauthenticity required "unselfish devotion to a common cause." Even if they declined the liberating discipline of monastic life, men and women could still enroll, Merton believed, in some "school of charity," a beloved community of instruction in the good life of personality.[58]

Founding several "schools of charity," Christian personalists conducted several communal experiments after the war, establishing decentralized, racially integrated communities—"communities of friendly men" as Howard Thurman described them—in which they erased the color and assembly lines. As James Farmer, secretary for race relations of the Fellowship of Reconciliation (FOR), pleaded to Muste in 1942, a new Congress of Racial Equality (CORE) should create "common environments," entering both "the industrial and the racial fields of conflict" and conducting their battles from "a religious base." Farmer's own sketch for a network of CORE cells recalled the Delta Cooperative and the Catholic Worker garden communes. Each cell, Farmer hoped, would be a "carefully planned cooperative community" producing "folk craft and art by Negroes and Whites alike."[59]

First inspired by a pilgrimage through India, Burma, and Ceylon in the early 1930s, Howard Thurman left a tenured position at Howard University in the summer of 1944 to become a pastor of the Church for the Fellowship of All Peoples, an ecumenical and racially integrated religious community in San Francisco. Hoping to establish "a beachhead in our society in terms of community," Thurman and the fellowship grounded their class and racial politics in a common spiritual and liturgical life. The church's lecture series and its "intercultural workshops" on literature, art, music, and cuisine were designed to act as transparent windows through which the "spiritual landscape could be seen and sensed." Throughout his tenure there from 1944 to 1953, Thurman insisted that the church's worship serve as the heart of the fellowship's wider social and cultural politics, the strong and resilient chamber of "one systolic and diastolic rhythm." In *Jesus and the Disinherited* (1949), which grew directly out of his fellowship pastorate, Thurman argued that similar islands of beloved community, if multiplied, could topple an order he clearly perceived as imperial and depersonalizing. Just as Jesus sought out Jews and Gentiles, even the soldiers and tax collectors of the Roman order, so "the privileged and underprivileged" must create "common environments for the purpose of providing normal experiences of fellowship."[60]

Meanwhile, the ex-Union student David Dellinger and his friends modeled their farming cooperative in Glen Gardner, New Jersey, directly along Catholic Worker lines. In shabby conditions enchanted by zeal, the Glen Gardners aimed to restore a unity of mental and manual labor. Including a print shop where "everyone . . . took his or her share of both intellectual and physical work," from writing and editing to cleaning presses and stapling the magazines (among which was *Liberation*), the Glen Gardner cooperative abolished "artificial distinctions between owners, managers, skilled craftsmen, and laborers." In the mid-1950s, Staughton and Alice Lynd lived in the Macedonia Cooperative Community in northeastern Georgia. Employed in a dairy and a shop that supplied children's play equipment for schools, the Macedonians shared a "common religious experience," the Lynds recalled, that "different persons might use quite different words to describe." While neither the Glen Gardners nor the Macedonians had any institutional links to established denominations, their sense of themselves as what Dellinger called a "Christian colony" attested to the persistence of liberal Protestantism as a political identity.[61]

Catholic personalists often were more stringent in their criticism of liberal accommodation. Berating both the industry council plan and Cort's Christian industrialism in an acerbic series of "Reflections on Work" in the *Catholic Worker* over 1946 and 1947, Dorothy Day denied "that Christ is present in the factories." Huffing that she was "tired of hearing our Lord compared to a modern factory worker," Day belittled the improvements in wages, hours, and working conditions won by unionized workers. Day and other Catholic Workers validated her technophobic invective by mechanically celebrating (and often reprinting) Maurin's "easy essays" long after his death in 1949.[62]

Yet other Catholic personalists moved reluctantly but perceptibly away from Day's loom-and-hoe Luddism and reappraised the sacramental gospel of work and technology. Ed Willock, editor of *Integrity* and cofounder of the (disastrous) Marycrest, New York, farming commune, published numerous essays in the middle and late 1940s on factory work, consumer culture, and the cult of expertise, devoting the entire January 1948 issue to the subject of mass production. Redefining distributism away from family proprietorship toward functional teams consisting of "small groups of workers," the *Integrity* circle both speculated about social as well as more strictly individual forms of craftsmanship and suggested that technological innovation was not prima facie evidence of artisanal and spiritual degradation. *Catholic Worker* contributors often invoked Martin Buber's praise of decentralized but technically advanced factories in *Paths in Utopia* (1949) or referred to the French communities of work described in Claire Huchet Bishop's *All Things Common* (1950) as personalist enclaves for sacramental production. Small, decentralized, and conducive to family stability and happiness, the *communités du travail* also were decidedly advanced technologically, with all workers receiving thorough technical training and management experience. The French communities also featured greater sexual equality, leading one writer to compare them favorably with secular Israeli kibbutzim. The kibbutzim, in defining labor as wage labor, devalued women's domestic work, while the French workers' wives performed housework "as valuable as the husband's factory work" that was "paid accordingly." While the wage system itself remained odious, this relative sexual equality arose, she argued, from the sacramental regard for all forms of material life that stemmed from the work community's religious character.[63]

Thomas Merton could be a particularly eloquent expositor of personalist economic philosophy. For Merton, the sainthood of personality was inseparable from the charity of a Christian communism. God, he opined in *Seeds of Contemplation*, had instituted his own economy of salvation, a "communism of charity and grace," an authentic communism that preceded and shamed "the spurious communism of the Marxists." In a deliberate provocation of his Cold War readers, Merton declared that "a man cannot be a perfect Christian—that is, a saint—unless he is also a communist." Since "everything belongs to God," men enjoyed property rights only in so far as they were "administrators of God's possessions, instruments of His Providence in sharing with others what they themselves do not need." If you have money, Merton suggested to his middle-class readers, "consider that . . . God allowed it to fall into your hands . . . that you might find joy and perfection in throwing it away."[64] Merton's romantic exhortations reveal that personalists, while disdaining consumer culture, implicitly presumed an abundance whose charitable dispersal they considered both right and possible.

Less renowned but more rigorous than Merton, *Catholic Worker* columnist Robert Ludlow was the most trenchant and comprehensive theorist of Christian personalism. In his "Pax Column" that appeared in the late 1940s and early 1950s, Ludlow fashioned a philosophy of "radical personalist democracy" that recycled the anarchosyndicalist tradition through Catholic theology. Although "relegated to the literature of clichés," anarchosyndicalism—in Ludlow's view, "the principles of revolutionary labor as taught by the I.W.W."—was a base secular metal transfigured through the alchemy of Christianity.[65]

While Ludlow restated Catholic Worker agronomy—decentralized factories, a preference for rural, small-scale village communities, pacifism—he recognized more clearly than Day that it too closely resembled the bucolicism of the right. Carefully distinguishing the personalist ideal from the chauvinism of existing villages, small towns, and neighborhoods, Ludlow argued that as catholic "citizens of the world," personalists were Christian cosmopolitans who eschewed all that was "penny-pinching and provincial." To his left, Ludlow conceded that the theoretical and practical elements of personalism amounted to a "hodge-podge . . . a plank here and there from the various radicalisms," but he justified his eclecticism as a genuinely catholic bricolage. Since Catholics believed that truth in a sinful world lay scattered everywhere, they could freely appropriate it wherever it was and gather it back to the bosom of Christ. More pointedly, Ludlow saw the only prospects for justice in "a union of Catholicism and the Left"—a left purged of "materialism and atheism, remnants of bourgeois life."[66]

Both the secular left and the chauvinist right joined in obeisance to a coven of modern demons that Ludlow cursed as "the State:" capitalism, socialism, imperialism, industrial work, and lesser deities. Larger than the bureaucratic apparatus of government, the State comprised the serpentine network of corporate, military, political, and educational institutions—C. Wright Mills's power elite and managerial demiurge—whose "vast hideous apostasy brings doom and sin and everlasting death." Ludlow's rhetoric was more than pyrotechnic flourish, for the State and its left opposition converged in a denial of supernatural life, a life that, conscious of God's presence, required neither exponentially expanding wealth nor the violence necessary to protect or expropriate it. Because both liberal and socialist states did not recognize a divine purpose in creation, they wrought two kinds of havoc. Plundering the material world in search of a never-ending and hence pointless abundance, they desecrated "the sacramentality of the earth." Worse, their repudiation of teleology as a regulative principle of social order delivered them over to technocracy—the impersonal, bureaucratic organization of social life made necessary by the profusion of conflicting desires—and alienated them from *grace*—a gift freely bestowed and always transferable in charitable, personalist communities. In the apparently liberating mobilization of technology, Ludlow discerned a containment within schedules, regulations, and machines; in the apparent restraints imposed by teleology lay grace, freedom, "the possibility of deification," the attainment of personal authenticity. In so far as we "live in the supernatural," Ludlow asserted, "we achieve personality."[67]

Only Christian orthodoxy and its political incarnation in radical personalist democracy could rescue personality from the State. "Precisely as we become more Christian," Ludlow reasoned, "we approach [in] this life a governmentless society." Ludlow distinguished the coercive government of the productive, philanthropic, but fundamentally uncharitable state from the directive government glimpsed in medieval guilds and religious kibbutzim. However benign their intentions, liberal intellectuals, labor leaders, and New Deal Democrats endorsed an insupportable form of coercion, Ludlow believed, because they accepted the State's criteria of efficiency, abundance, and profit.[68] To custodians of the corporate commonwealth, Ludlow's political imagination must have seemed intemperate, even febrile. Yet the subsequent escalation of imperial violence and popular discontent arguably demonstrated the superior realism of personalist democracy. Although he retired into obscurity in the mid-1950s, Ludlow mended the tattered banners of personality, workplace democracy, and beloved community once borne by Rauschenbusch, Scudder, the younger Niebuhr, and Day.

Christian personalists wove together the search for personal fulfillment and the demand for social reconstruction. By insisting against liberal realists that grace could abound in this life without the direction or protection of the state, they preserved the ideal of church as a critical, prefigurative commonwealth. They also sounded discordant variations on the themes of personality and authenticity that resounded through postwar social and cultural criticism. In the life and work of Paul Tillich, this personalist quest for salvation found its most tormented expositor.

CHAPTER FIVE

The Gospel of Eros:

Paul Tillich, the Consuming Vision, and the Therapeutic Ethos

After settling into his cell in the Georgia state prison in late October 1960, Martin Luther King, Jr., composed a letter to his wife Coretta. He listed some books he wanted to read: the Bible, a book on Jesus' parables, a study of Gandhi. At the top of the list were the two recondite volumes of Paul Tillich's *Systematic Theology*. King had his reasons for bringing Tillich to his cell. In his Boston University dissertation, King had pronounced Tillich's God too rarefied to lead a people from the bondage of southern pharaohs. Yet later, in his "Letter from Birmingham Jail," King summoned Tillich to support his demand for the immediate appearance of justice. Tillich, King reminded his readers, had defined sin as the separation of man from God and of man from man—and what were racism and segregation but forms of sinful division?[1]

At the same time, another of King's heroes, Reinhold Niebuhr, castigated Tillich as a paladin of therapeutic self-absorption, moral irresponsibility, and political apathy. Charging Tillich with indifference to social injustice and communist tyranny, Niebuhr attacked his theology as a blend of aestheticism, sensualism, and depth psychology. Niebuhr's Tillich was a learned dandy, hardly a figure who could inspire an imprisoned prophet.[2]

Paul Tillich was a prominent, even celebrated figure in postwar American culture. His books were immensely popular with college students and intellectuals, his talks packed lecture halls, and his professorial visage appeared on the cover of *Time*. Conversant in socialism, psychoanalysis, and existentialism, Tillich provided abundant evidence that Protestant theology was not a philistine enterprise. Indeed, a German émigré who mingled Augustine, Freud, Marx, and Beckett seemed anointed to preach the Christian gospel in the cadence of modernist culture. Moreover, Tillich's compelling rhetoric of renewal and liberation—conveyed in books with titles such as *The Courage to Be, The New Being, The Eternal Now,* and *The Shaking of the Foundations*—stirred the hearts and inflected the discourse of fledgling student radicals.[3]

Yet some scholars have been far from sanguine about Tillich's impact on postwar culture and religion. To Philip Rieff, Tillich's work was a cistern of "tepid holy water" doused on secular psychology, a "default of thought in some of the highest reaches of contemporary Christian theology." More recently, Richard Fox has echoed Niebuhr's hostility to Tillich, characterizing him as "the theologian for an age of abundance, ease, and self-satisfaction," a sage well-versed in the arts of "coping with the dissatisfactions of modern existence."[4] Rieff and Fox see Tillich as a perfect post-Christian minister for the faithless but nervous libertines of our other-directed world.

Tillich's psychological (or existential) rhetoric, together with his tortured personal life, his celebrity, and his status as an unofficial mentor to many postwar liberals and radicals, makes him indispensable to an account of religion, therapy, and selfhood in modern American culture. While displaying some of the oft-maligned features of the therapeutic sensibility, Tillich's life and work also pointed toward the therapeutic nature of religious community and underlay a social gospel that linked personal fulfillment and social reconstruction. Through Tillich, liberal Protestants both sealed a devil's bargain with psychological man and glimpsed a flourishing personality redeemed in a beloved community. Following Tillich from Prussia to Chicago—from the company of army chaplains to the circles of metropolitan professionals—we may learn how a theology shaped among Junkers and Weimar bohemians could resonate with Manhattan analysts and a Baptist minister in a Birmingham jail.

From Cobbled Streets to Godless Trenches: Tillich's Years in Wilhelmine Germany

Paul Tillich was born in August 1886 in the town of Starzeddel, Brandenburg. His father Johannes, a Lutheran pastor and school administrator, subjected his gifted son to intense intellectual pressure, engaging Paul in theological and philosophical discussions from an early age and imparting a sturdy conservative rectitude in religion and politics. Johannes stimulated but also loomed over Paul, inspecting and judging him as he did the churches and schools in his district. Paul later traced his impatience with orthodoxy to his need to overcome the patriarch's inquisitorial solicitude. Indeed, as Karl Barth later remarked, Tillich always seemed to be "fighting against the Grand Inquisitor."[5]

Although Tillich attributed his intellectual daring to his father, he downplayed the equally significant impact of his mother Mathilde. While the mature Tillich seldom referred to his mother in print, the depth and desperation of his love for her were evident in Tillich's reaction to her death when he was seventeen. A brief poem he wrote resounded with terror and anger at abandonment and a yearning for the nocturnal peace of engulfment. "O abyss without ground, dark depth of madness! / Would that I had never gazed upon you and were / sleeping like a child!"[6] This poem presaged some of the enduring concerns in his life and theology: his tortured sexual relationships, his search for God as "the ground of Being," his attempt to connect salvation with sanity. The domestic ambiance of strict rule and warm emotion instilled in Tillich a perpetual and creative conflict between respect for authority and desire for experience and transgression.

When Tillich was four, his family moved to Schonfliess, whose medieval lineage was apparent in its Gothic church, cobblestone streets, and town hall, all surrounded by a high wall with gates crowned by towers. Learning and playing among the children of Junkers, Tillich idealized the liberality and cosmopolitanism he discerned in the nobility and acquired a lifelong disdain for the pettiness and provincialism of the *Kleinburger*. Meanwhile, the surrounding forest became an edenic garden of imagination for the adolescent Tillich. In the woods, he reflected later, he nurtured an aesthetic sensibility that precluded his having a purely scientific, "technically-controlling relation" to nature. "Nearly all the great memories and longings of my life," he wrote, "are interwoven with landscapes, soil, weather, the fields of grain and the smell of the potato plant in autumn, the shapes of clouds, and with wind, flowers, and woods." Tillich also remembered the family's yearly trip to the Baltic coast as "the great event, the flight into the open, into unrestricted space." The "immediate influence of the turbulent sea" elicited both the longing for union and the romantic adventurism that would animate his theology and personal life.[7]

After graduating from the local gymnasium in 1904, Tillich attended the universities of Berlin, Tubingen, and Halle, receiving doctoral degrees in philosophy and theology. While at Halle, Tillich became a leader in the Wingolf Fellowship, a Christian men's student group. Wingolf (Norse-German for "friendship house") resembled those youth and student movements characterized by historians of Wilhelmine, Germany, as "prophets of community" on both the left and the right. Composed almost entirely of bourgeois males alienated from their rationalist, commercially minded parents, the *Wandervogel* and *Burschenschaften* sought a love and solidarity they missed in the family and the marketplace. Whether hiking, singing peasant songs, or sporting mock-military uniforms, they often invoked the communal importance of Eros in opposition to what they considered the soulless impersonality of industrialism and liberal democracy.[8]

Tillich's fraternity experience augured two related tendencies in his subsequent life and work. Remembering the Wingolf fraternity as a communion, Tillich later surmised that it enabled him both to understand the appeal of fascism and to connect the personal and political dimensions of Christian faith. Yet Tillich's later relationship with his wife Hannah sheds a harsher light on Wingolf's *Volkische* Protestantism. In Wingolf, Christian love merged with a strong will to power, as male friendship both draped itself in military regalia and mandated the exclusion of women from all but festive occasions. (Tillich himself later confessed his enthusiasm at the time for the trappings of Prussian militarism, the "uniforms, parades, maneuvers, history of battles, and ideas of strategy."[9]) Tillich's later amorous résumé, stocked with seduced and abandoned lovers, betrayed a need to dominate and humiliate women. The tension within Tillich's work between the ideal of "religious eros" and a reluctance to set rules for the erotic life had roots in the gendered Christian community of Tillich's fraternity.

Shortly after his ordination and disheartening two-year stint as a pastor in a working-class quarter of Berlin—the workers, he later recalled, dismissed his liberal preaching as irrelevant and incomprehensible— Tillich, like many of his compatriots, saw the outbreak of war in 1914 as an auspicious moment of national unity. After two years of service as an army chaplain, however, Tillich lost his patriotic ardor and his conventional faith amid the carnage of Verdun. Reading Nietzsche's *Thus Spoke Zarathustra* in the smoke and butchery of the trenches, Tillich could not help but feel that the Wilhelmine God had died on the fields of France. The death of Tillich's God occasioned a new critical awareness: He saw that German imperial unity was spurious and that the workers "considered the Church as an unquestioned ally of the ruling groups." Tillich returned to Berlin in 1919 "a barbarian," a clergyman who shunned the church, a theologian shorn of his liberal Protestant optimism and respect for bourgeois conventions.[10]

In the same year, Karl Barth, himself disillusioned by the war, published his essay on Paul's letter to the Romans that inaugurated a new era in North Atlantic Protestant theology. In Berlin, the fall of the monarchy and the abortive Spartacist uprising heralded the birth of the

Weimar Republic. With the death of its Wilhelmine God, German Protestantism desperately required revitalization. Over the next fourteen years, Tillich's personal and theological odyssey converged with the paths of other German intellectuals through the maelstrom of Weimar culture.

WEIMAR THEOLOGY: TILLICH'S PROTESTANT *KULTURKRITIK*

Weimar culture at first might not seem to have provided an auspicious climate for Protestant intellectuals. Brechtian theater, expressionist painting and film, the *neue Sachlichkeit*'s fascination with the new mass culture, and Frankfurt School Marxism—Weimar modernists would not appear to have entertained anything so quaint and reactionary as the hope of redemption. Yet much of Weimar modernism, particularly in the form of *Kulturkritik,* sought ways to avert the costs of modernity— spiritual emptiness, uncritical celebration of technology, the hegemony of science and instrumental reason, a "hunger for wholeness" unsatisfied by conventional politics—while retaining its social and technical achievements. Tillich's theology was a Protestant form of *Kulturkritik*, a recasting of theology in the crucible of cultural modernism, a religious resolution of the crisis of classical modernity.[11]

Shortly after the war's end, Tillich joined with other disenchanted Protestants to form the *Kairos* circle. Taking its name from the Greek *kairos* ("moment of divine intervention"), the *Kairos* group rejected the reformist politics of Protestant bluebloods such as Ernst Troeltsch, the historian of Christian social thought, and called for new forms of political and religious life to replace those discredited in the wake of war and reaction. Indeed, like other German intellectuals such as Martin Buber, Max Horkheimer, Theodor Adorno, Ernst Bloch, and Walter Benjamin, Tillich saw the Weimar moment as a challenge to reformulate the socialist tradition.[12] At the same time, transfiguring theology into socialist theory and cultural criticism, Tillich aimed to forge a new form of legitimacy for a Protestant intelligentsia displaced by a more secularized elite of technical, managerial, and cultural workers.

Conceding that the forces of modernization had driven the churches into "a movement of retreat," Tillich recognized the "decisive spiritual type of our day" not in theologians and ministers but in technicians, scientists, and other university-trained experts. This "small, educated class," an "exclusive, educated aristocracy" in the service of monopoly capital, had disenchanted and imprisoned the world in the cage of usefulness, dissolving a "magical sense of communion" into the blandness of technical control. Repelled by the coldness and venality of the tech-nomanagerial elite, Tillich was only slightly less disappointed by social-ists who mounted a futile and equally mandarin opposition to the rule of capital and expertise. In his view, the intellectual socialism of the So-cial Democratic party replicated the managerial mentality in its social and ideological distance from the working class.[13]

Tillich was convinced that the postwar West stood in a *kairos*, anx-iously poised for a courageous leap into a new "theonomous" culture that was "open to and directed toward the divine." The modern vehicle of this theonomous culture must be a "religious socialism." Religious socialists, Tillich explained in *The Socialist Decision* (1933), engaged not only in a struggle *"for* socialism" but also in "a struggle *about* socialism," providing a "religious analysis of the secular forms of socialism" as well as a prophecy against capitalism. Secular socialism, Tillich noted, shared the narrow faith of its capitalist parent in the emancipatory sufficiency of science, technology, and power politics. Yet, if, as socialist theory maintained, the proletariat imagined its future within the moral frame-work of capitalism, it could never create a truly different world. With-out the transfiguring leaven of charity—religious eros, as Tillich called it—socialism would simply amplify and bureaucratize the rapacity of bourgeois civilization. Religious socialists envisioned more than justice; they desired a beloved community, "a unity of power and love." Rather than polar opposites, power and love were sundered partners who would be joined again when workers controlled the factories and expe-rienced their work as a sacrament, a "cultic consecration of technologi-cal production."[14] Upholding an ideal of sacramental craftsmanship and anointing charity rather than accumulation as the cardinal virtue of so-cial life, Tillich hoped to refashion socialism into a witness against the incorrigible secularity as well as the injustice of capitalism.

Under the aegis of religion, Tillich connected political economy to per-sonal fulfillment in the form of personality. Personality, to Tillich, was the capacity for theonomous selfhood. Capitalist societies, he observed, transmuted the myriad sacramental possibilities of personality into "a constant change of attitude," a marketable resource and a market for commodities. Tillich discerned especially dangerous threats to person-ality in the culture industry and in professionalized therapy. While cele-brating the cosmopolitanism afforded by mass communications, Tillich also feared the ideological envelopment of corporate-mediated experi-ence. Mass-marketed ideals of personality eroded narrow provincialism but also pulverized more immediate "sources of concrete experiences and individual formations," creating an atmosphere in which "every-thing interests, nothing effects." Anticipating Hannah Arendt's arguments about the roots of popular support for fascism, Tillich predicted that this cognitive rootlessness would be a yearning for a "new tribal existence" promising intimate community and vital experience.[15]

Even the possibilities furnished by modern psychology were compromised by secularism, in Tillich's view. Although charitably disposed toward psychoanalysis, Gestalt, and other modes of psychological expertise, Tillich claimed that a secularized therapeutic ethos left many spiritual and psychic needs unfulfilled and that modern technologies of the self could balm but not heal the damage inflicted on personality by capitalism. Despite his later reputation as a Protestant point man for psychotherapy, Tillich vigorously criticized secular therapeutic methods in *The Religious Situation* (1925) as simulacra of religious discipline. Attacking the use of religion for personal development (an oblique reference to the work of Carl Jung), Tillich rued that the psychologist's office had become a substitute for "the priestly confessional" where "all takes place in the presence of God." Although Tillich saw great promise and religious import in psychotherapy, he resisted the temptation to simplistically identify psychic health and sanctification. Moreover, he warned that modern therapeutic psychology, if unanchored in religion and uncoupled from socialist politics, would reinforce technocratic hegemony in all areas of life. If "only a priestly man can be a complete psychiatrist," then only a priestly socialist community could offer genuine therapy for the wounded personality. Personality, Tillich insisted, required "a spiritual center," a theonomous direction that a secular culture could never abide.[16]

While religious socialism remade theology as socialist theory and personal analysis, Tillich's theology of culture reconstructed it as cultural criticism. Plumbing the ultimate and deepest meaning of even the most trivial or blasphemous cultural work, the new Protestant intellectual could enlist cultural modernism as an ally in the salvation of modernity. Expressionism, for instance, aroused Tillich's interest through its break with traditional representational forms and its frank avowal of disturbing spiritual states—a bracing contrast to the banality of German Protestantism. Tillich seems to have been even more powerfully drawn to the *neue Sachlichkeit* ("new realism"). New realists such as Otto Dix and Georg Grosz conveyed the horror and promise of industrialism and mass culture by fusing expressionist formal innovation with traditional representation. Not only did the new realists "point to the spiritual meaning of the real by using its given forms," but they also carried "the battle into the very camp of the enemy" by "employing his own best weapons against him." By calling his own theological perspective " belief-ful realism," Tillich indicated a considerable debt to the *neue Sachlichkeit*.[17]

Still, though undertaken to regenerate Protestant theology as a critical force, Tillich's immersion in Weimar modernism also was a harbinger of religion's decline as a form of therapeutic integrity and cultural criticism. Tillich's marriage to Hannah sheds light on how his work could intensify rather than fill the hunger for wholeness by sanctioning purely private odysseys of therapeutic exploration. Like many of his fellow Weimar "barbarians," Tillich despised the mores of the German middle class, especially sexual conventions that appeared more ludicrous than ever in the light of urbanization, feminism, psychoanalysis, and contraception. Endorsing this "sexual revolution," Tillich urged the Protestant churches to abandon the "hypocrisy of bourgeois conventionality" on sexual matters and to create a new morality that would "point to the transcendent sphere" but avoid the "purely legal and conventional." Accepting the burdens of guilt for himself, Tillich ventured into erotic experiments that he hoped would prefigure a new Christian sexual ethic. Like Wilhelm Reich, Tillich perceived an inextricable link between sexual repression and political quiescence and argued that liberation from the capitalist political economy mandated manumission from the traditional Christian sexual economy. Praising the literary eroticism of Rainer Maria Rilke and Franz Werfel, Tillich argued that "the man who tries to impose a limit or condition upon love does not know that love is universal, cosmic, simply because it affirms and embraces everything that is real."[18] If Christian love was truly bountiful, Tillich reasoned, then its scope and occasions should be boundless, extending to the erotic as well as the working life of the redeemed.

Along with Hannah, Tillich pursued a social life in Berlin and Frankfurt that brought him into contact with Weimar's artistic and sexual bohemia. Their social life was a classic movable feast: dinner parties, ateliers, trips to the Italian coast, opera and theater engagements—all leavened with the *Gemutlichkeit* of drinking, song, and conversation. Ever the bon vivant, Tillich believed that a plethora of experiences added to the depth and perspicacity of his religious reflection; Hannah recalled that he often thought and wrote in cafés, loving the "anonymity and voyeurism in streets full of desirable crowds . . . watching the girls go by, meeting over a sherry, being in the world." The Tillichs conducted their marriage in a similarly open fashion. Paulus engaged in numerous affairs (the first one, in fact, on his wedding night); Hannah, while less prodigious, experimented with heterosexual and homosexual relationships. Although the Tillichs were well aware of their separate intimacies, Hannah was clearly more emotionally entangled in the marriage than her husband: "I turned Paulus into a little god," she wrote later, "a boy Eros." Tillich exploited his advantage in the union, openly referring to Hannah as his "second best" and constantly pleading with her to stay with him—for the sake of his career.[19] Yet Tillich also appeared to find some kind of psychological ballast in his marriage to Hannah, a safe port of return from life on the ever-receding boundaries of the erotic. Tillich's expansive, romantic ethic camouflaged both a love of power and a deep-seated irresponsibility.

Tillich's bohemian defiance of bourgeois hypocrisy and repression, though it now appears clichéd and self-serving, nonetheless addressed a genuine source of suffering. Yet, as Colin Campbell has pointed out, bohemias, with their "romantic ethic" of pleasure and novelty, often have served as laboratories for morality and consumption styles. Tillich's bohemian Protestantism was one experiment in a culture of consumption, partaking of the rootless and acquisitive "consuming vision" that increasingly defined the moral horizon of capitalist societies. The anonymity and voyeurism to which Hannah alluded encompassed his lovers—his relations with whom Tillich perceived largely in terms of his own search for transcendent experience—and his promiscuous anointment of cultural products as religious. For neither Tillich's sexual life nor his theology of culture were rooted in a distinctive religious community that countered the world of Weimar capitalism. An antidote to the emotional sclerosis of bourgeois fidelity, his sexual experiments affirmed no larger communal purpose. Suggestive and trenchant as a reading of modernism and mass culture, his theology of culture recommended no alternative universe of symbols, no alternative economy of cultural production. Tillich himself realized that his rootless brand of cultural criticism could be absorbed easily by the culture industries. The Protestant avant-garde might themselves become hollow men, Tillich feared, and create institutions "empty of substance, impotent in their social reality." The theologian of culture in particular could become a "fashionable religious prophet," an evanescent cultural commodity—a charge that would later be hurled at Tillich himself.[20]

By December 1933, Tillich and other religious socialists were clearly unfashionable in Germany. Tillich had foreseen the challenge fascism posed to liberal, secularized democracies and had warned that the fascist "tribalism" of blood and soil was a perverted fulfillment of venerable desires for community and spiritual regeneration. Dismissed from his post at Frankfurt, Tillich left his homeland for the United States, where admirers such as Reinhold Niebuhr had arranged for him to assume a position at Union Theological Seminary. Along with many of his friends, Tillich set sail for the United States, where his cultural gospel would both find a larger audience and spawn a more significant and ambiguous legacy.

You Are Accepted: Tillich and Moral Psychology in the 1940s

Tillich and his family arrived in New York in November 1933. All of Union's faculty agreed to contribute 5 percent of their salaries to finance Tillich's first year, and all the furniture in their first apartment on Riverside Drive was provided by seminary colleagues. Tillich quickly became a Manhattan boulevardier, exploring Wall Street, the Cloisters, Greenwich Village, and the Museum of Modern Art. Though Niebuhr complained about the hubris of the skyscraper, Tillich grew fond of the Manhattan skyline, admiring the clouds as they moved serenely over the spires of American capitalism.[21]

Tillich struggled with a daunting array of challenges in his new homeland: learning English, supporting a family, and climbing the academic ladder. He found his students eager and affable (if also woefully undereducated) and enjoyed the easy familiarity of students and faculty in lecture halls, elevators, dining rooms, offices, and religious services. (Tillich began attending church services again after President Henry Sloane Coffin suggested he show up.) Tillich discovered at Union something akin to the camaraderie he had known as a student in Germany, even as his one attempt at hosting a swank soiree atop one of the seminary buildings ended in embarrassment.[22] As their sexual lives and frequent excursions to Harlem's nightlife demonstrated, Paulus and Hannah endured and disdained Union's social conventions.

On an American journey that ended with his death in 1965, Tillich transformed liberal Protestant notions of personality. Eclipsing but not forsaking his religious socialism and engaging while not baptizing neo-Freudian psychoanalysis and existentialism, Tillich refashioned religious discourse on personality in a manner that both enlivened and enervated American Protestant social and cultural criticism.

While forging ties with Columbia's Philosophy Club and working with the New School for Social Research in relocating German refugee intellectuals, Tillich plunged eagerly into the city's burgeoning culture of psychology. The clustering of psychologists, psychiatrists, and psychoanalysts in New York (many of them, like Tillich, refugees from the Nazis) created a brisk market for exchange between doctors of the soul and doctors of the psyche. Along with other Protestant theologians and pastoral writers, Tillich attended the Columbia Seminar on Religion and

Health, whose participants sought uses for ministerial counseling in the latest psychological theory and therapeutic practice. During the war, Tillich joined the monthly meetings of the New York Psychology Group. The so-called New York Group brought together pastoral counselors and neo-Freudian analysts whose work soon figured prominently in Protestant counseling and secular social and cultural criticism: Seward Hiltner, David Roberts, Erich Fromm (an acquaintance from Tillich's Weimar days), and Karen Horney (with whom Tillich had a brief affair).[23]

Neo-Freudian or revisionist psychoanalysis rekindled for many Protestants the religious reformist possibilities latent in modern psychology. The revisionists' penchant for moral exhortation, their celebration of growth and self-realization as the goals of psychotherapy, and their generosity toward religion attracted numerous religious intellectuals, especially among Protestants whose notions of personality had long defined redemption as in part a release of human potential. Although often dismissed as a psychological bromide, the neo-Freudian rhetoric of growth and self-realization originally possessed a forceful critical import. While "growth" and "self-realization" were, by the 1930s, buzzwords for the consumption of goods and professionalized psychological services, they also figured as talismans for intellectuals eager to effect, under secular, scientific auspices, a reunion of personal felicity and social justice. For Fromm, Horney, and other neo-Freudians, "self-realization" meant not self-absorption but rather fulfilling work, genuine leisure, the discovery and fruition of human possibility. Fromm's work of the 1940s—especially *Escape from Freedom* (1941) and *Man for Himself* (1947)—represented a neo-Freudian attempt to harness the remaining cultural authority of religion to a secular, expert-defined project of personal and political renewal. Clearly viewing psychoanalysts as the heirs of the rabbis and priests, Fromm studded his books with sympathetic invocations of theologians, rabbis, and other religious figures. Fromm's use of religious rhetoric veiled his confidence in social and psychological expertise. The "humanistic ethics" he espoused in *Man for Himself* amounted, Fromm wrote, to "the applied science" of an "art of living" informed by a "theoretical science of man."[24]

Although Tillich conceded that "mental diseases have become epidemic" in the West and identified self-expression and creativity as two of the most daunting issues facing the postwar world, he balked at entrusting these problems to a new clerisy of doctors. Opposing Fromm and other neo-Freudians, Tillich argued that "mere psychotherapeutic psychology" could neither touch the deepest roots of evil nor supply "by itself a new system of ethics." Personal fulfillment, he reiterated, required both a theologically grounded therapy and a socialist politics.[25]

Tillich's work of the 1940s extended his quest to weave together the liberal Protestant discourse of personality, the psychotherapeutic rhetoric of self-realization, and religious socialism.

Christianity remained the cure of souls, Tillich contended, because the fundamental problems of personality were social and spiritual in nature. While rehearsing many of the standard themes of "mass society" criticism—in particular, the specter of "standardized human beings"—Tillich's wartime work stood out as one of its distinctly religious forms. Writing in *Christianity and Crisis* in 1942 on the "spiritual problems of postwar reconstruction," Tillich traced the malady of "massification" not to democracy but to "the monopolistic direction of public communication" and to the incorporation of other realms under the aegis of capital and expertise. As a result, in both capitalist and socialist societies, personality became increasingly a matter of "technical intelligence and adjustment," the prerogative of social and psychological specialists equipped with all the modern technologies of the self. Genuine community rested on faith in something beyond the community itself. Thus the only solution to the malaise of personality in mass society was salvation, not more technical proficiency, productive work, and psychological adjustment.[26]

Still, psychoanalysis supplied Tillich with a compelling representation of sin and redemption. Sin, Tillich preached in "You Are Accepted," one of his most remembered sermons at Union, consisted not in bad actions but in separation, estrangement from oneself, from others, and ultimately, from God. In a manner that recalls Melanie Klein's account of pre-Oedipal psychic life, Tillich compared sin and redemption to the early relationship of mother and child. Oneness with God resembled the blissful fusion of maternal connection, "the unity of life, which is grace." Sin—a state not of self-love but rather of "selfishness and self-hate"—was akin to the denial of maternal dependence, the desire to be one's own absolute master. Closing the chasm opened up by sin, the God whose love remained reparative and unconditional asked for nothing from us but the acceptance of love. "Do not seek for anything; do not perform anything; do not intend anything. Simply accept the fact that you are accepted!" Resonant both with his own memory of maternal abandonment and with his own compulsive, guilt-ridden conduct toward Hannah, Tillich's gospel of repose beckoned toward the amazing grace he hoped would save a wretch like him. (Indeed, on the manuscript of the sermon, Tillich wrote "for myself" next to the title.)[27]

This gospel of acceptance did not, however, countenance a self-absorbed, apolitical acquiescence to evil. The acceptance of God, Tillich believed, infused a graceful eroticism that encompassed the broader continuum of human life, from the sexual to the ecological. Rooted in the "ground of our being," we know "the grace which is able to overcome the tragic separation of the sexes, of the generations, of the nations, of the races, and even the utter strangeness between man and nature." Tillich's reparative conception of politics contrasted sharply with the pragmatism and *realpolitik* of socialists and liberals such as Niebuhr. Unlike his sponsor, Tillich understood the end of politics as graceful reenchantment, a conception potentially less available for appropriation by secularized elites. When Niebuhr once rebuffed Tillich's remark on the loveliness of the flowers in Union's quadrangle—"they were there last spring, too"—he indicated much more than aesthetic indifference. Exemplifying what Casey Blake has aptly called "the anemic conception of the relationship between culture and politics" held by left-liberal intellectuals in the 1940s, Niebuhr never fathomed Tillich's appreciation of aesthetic and natural beauty as the hallmark of an alternative way of political being.[28]

However, Niebuhr's advantage lay in his willingness to rely wholly on secular sources of power and expertise, which in lieu of religious alternatives made Christian realism the only game in the city of man. Tillich, while arguing that postwar reconstruction provided a *kairos* for a "spiritual vanguard," suspected nonetheless that Protestant religious culture lacked the resources for such an avant-garde. Preaching at Union shortly after the Nuremberg trials, Tillich wondered if Christian symbols had not lost their force by having been "too often repeated and too superficially used." Moreover, "the Protestant principle" of prophetic iconoclasm—the refusal to provide the social and symbolic mediation supplied by Catholic sacraments and ritual, the rejection of "any identification of grace with a visible reality, even the Church"—had fostered the sort of rationalized faith that underlay a wholly secular, "realist" approach to politics. Tillich's postwar collection of essays on *The Protestant Era* (1948) actually announced the end of the Protestant era, declaring that the future lay in a reintegration of the "Protestant principle" and "catholic substance," a recasting of Christian churches that wedded the social and sacramental features of Roman Catholicism with the critical energies of Protestantism.[29]

This reformation of "the Protestant cultus" would succeed, Tillich believed, only if enlightened Protestants partially seceded from the official denominations and reconfigured themselves as "an order or fellowship"—very Catholic religious forms, as he forthrightly acknowledged. Such a Christian vanguard could, Tillich speculated, become gadflies to conventional Protestants, cultural missionaries to the secular world living in "anticipation of the Kingdom of God." Tillich's notion of an order or fellowship dovetailed with similar appeals to diminutive but anticipatory community on the part of Catholic Workers, Paul Goodman, Dwight Macdonald, and other postwar personalists.[30]

Yet Tillich's complete repudiation of doctrine and ethical legalism undercut his political and therapeutic aims. In his statement of "Protestant Principles" in the spring 1942 issue of the left-liberal *Protestant Digest*, Tillich illustrated the unresolved contradictions in his attempt to unite a socially unmoored theology of culture to an equally disembodied religious socialism. On the one hand, Tillich restated his Weimar *kulturkritik* that culture had a religious foundation and could not be separated from religious transcendence. On the other hand, he affirmed the "independent structure of the different spheres of cultural life" and protested against "encroachments upon their autonomy by churches and states." Intended as a solid Sinai tablet for Protestant political action, Tillich's principles threatened to grind religious politics into the dust of the purely therapeutic. Denying to churches any role to play in class and cultural politics other than as windows on some ineffable realm of transcendence, Tillich erased from his work the social and ideological lineaments indispensable to any effective religious foundation. After the war, Tillich went even further, arguing that membership in the orders should be completely open, "without the necessity of belonging to a Protestant or even a Christian church."[31]

Shortly thereafter, Tillich expanded on this freelance religious ideal in a celebrated 1948 Union lecture upholding the "transmoral conscience" as the model of Christian moral personality. The Christian conscience, once free from "the yoke of the law," inhabited a realm of grace from which the Christian could survey and embrace the creativity of life in all of its "creative and destructive power." Here, Tillich construed moral selfhood not as adherence to the practices of a particular community but as a marketplace of moral plenitude. While often praised as an annulment of the merger of Protestantism and American culture, this neoorthodox critique of the liberal Protestant moral imagination also furthered the secularization of the therapeutic ethos. The Jehovan *gravitas* of neoorthodoxy, while it braced a powerful critical posture, also weakened the connection of Christianity to any culture or moral code whatsoever. Although careful enough to stress love as a touchstone for ethical decisions and cautious enough to affirm most conventional mores, neoorthodox ethicists nonetheless figured the individual Christian as one who stood apart from any institution, the moral man against the immoral society. The neoorthodox effort to distill faith from the dross of culture or religion—like Tillich's alchemical extraction of religion from the concrete, particular practices of religions—underwrote a vision of the moral life defined more by amplitude of possibility than by steadfastness of commitment.[32] By the same token, it potentially disabled religion as a critical force by robbing it of concrete agency and political direction.

The "transmoral conscience" was a consuming vision of moral self-hood for the New Deal political economy. Enfranchised by the erosion of restrictive moral codes and galvanized by the possibilities of good-ness, the transmoral conscience was the ideal moral imagination for a mixed economy whose abundance derived from the unimpeded minis-trations of social, cultural, and technical specialists. Despite his belief that the transmoral conscience would be a fearless critical lever, Tillich missed the possibility that it also could license an elastic, amoral self-hood—an "other-directed character," a practitioner of the "social ethic," even a "hipster"—readily tutored by professional authority and easily portable on the shifting winds of expertise and cultural fashion. Tillich's account of the Western world's postwar unease, for instance, alluded to ruminations among "statesmen, educators, psychologists, physicians, sociologists"—a distinguished panel of accredited anxiety with whom Tillich met in symposia, lecture halls, academic conferences, and profes-sional meetings.[33]

The whirlwind unleashed by a transmoral conscience clearly roared through Tillich's marriage. Though pursuing their separate sexual in-trigues, Paul and Hannah remained married, even as they chafed in the starched collars of Union's mores. They took to the city's nightclubs as hungry consumers of experience, especially of Harlem's nightlife. They often patronized Small's Paradise, a club frequented not only by blacks but also by a considerable white middle-class clientele. Along with other whites, the Tillichs relaxed as "grateful voyeurs," in Hannah's words, of the "primeval charm" of exotic dancers, jazz musicians, and assorted hipsters. The Tillichs' adventures in Harlem recalled the long tradition of white excursion into African-American culture in search of forbidden pleasure. Hannah, for instance, later described Small's as "a tropical for-est with parrots screaming, dark faces peering out of the jungle, falsetto voices, and brilliant colors." Like similar transgressions of the color line, however, this one indicated a genuine need on the part of well-placed whites to escape the emotional and sensate bondage imposed by their success. A far cry from the teas at Union ("People at the seminary," Han-nah later remarked dryly, "did not think our adventures a good idea"), Small's Paradise delivered on the promise of its name, providing the Tillichs and their companions with a redemptive vista of unashamed eros and sensual communion, an enclave where the manifold possibili-ties of personality could be imagined and even realized.[34]

Yet the Tillichs failed even to notice another such vista: Harlem's evangelical and pentecostal churches. As James Baldwin (at the time a precocious teenage minister) later remembered, black churches were no less corrupt than those of whites. However, as Baldwin also recalled of his own congregation, there were days when "their pain and joy were mine, and mine were theirs," days when in momentary ecstasies "we all became equal, wringing wet, singing and dancing, in anguish and rejoicing, at the foot of the altar."[35] Harlem's churches embodied the physical reality of sanctification, the fusion, however evanescent, of the personal and collective transformation for which Tillich pined in his ruminations on personality and socialism.

Tillich's sexual life remained a thicket of powerlust, sexual desire, and spiritual longing that he struggled to redeem in his work. In her memoirs, Hannah related one especially grotesque incident that captured the sordid quality of Tillich's own moral selfhood. On entering a room in their apartment, she discovered Paul watching a pornographic film containing numerous images of naked young women hanging on crosses, "tied and exposed in various positions," as well as scenes of women holding whips and crosses—"always, whips, crosses, whips." Tillich's idealization of erotic freedom coincided with punitive fantasies of domination and humiliation. His pornographic imagination suggested a dark underside to modern quests for self-realization, an underside best illuminated by the psychoanalytical work of Janine Chasseguet-Smirgel and Melanie Klein. Frustration of intense longings for maternal fusion can lead, they contend, to the desire to destroy not only obstacles to reunion (a psychic basis for ideological fanaticism, Chasseguet-Smirgel argues) but the mother as well (in Klein's view, envy as the psychic equivalent of original sin).[36] Tillich's repressed sadism hinted that behind the purely therapeutic ideal of erotic liberty lay an incessant struggle for power and a devaluation of the objects of love.

By the end of the 1940s, Tillich's personal turmoil contrasted sharply with his status as one of liberal Protestantism's reigning icons. Like his Union colleague Niebuhr (who was by then also an estranged rival, intimidated by Tillich's scholarly reputation and repulsed by his sexual affairs), Tillich rose to fame as a brooding prophet bearing judgment. Opening *The Shaking of the Foundations* (1948) with a post-Hiroshima sermon on Isaiah's announcement that "the earth is split in pieces," Tillich declared that the prophet spoke with unrivaled authority. "That is the religious meaning of the age into which we have entered," he observed. "This is no longer vision; it has become physics." So dark and wide was the atomic specter that it occluded from Tillich's view the light of religious socialism. The *kairos* had passed, he wrote in the *Christian Century* in 1949; history had entered a vacuum, a "sacred void" to be accepted and endured. Yet, peering into the abyss, Tillich clung to the promise of a new Protestant witness. "The prophetic spirit has not disappeared from the earth," he asserted in *Foundations*. "When the earth grows old and wears out, when nations and cultures die, the Eternal changes the garments of His infinite being."[37] Tillich's postwar fashioning of new raiment for the divine, far from representing a failure of nerve or a retreat into the recesses of the self, would extend his mission to preach the gospel of personality.

Harvest Time (I): Psychoanalysis, Existentialism, and the Postwar Gospel of Personality

During his most prolific years, Tillich reached the summit of academic prestige and celebrity. He remained at Union until 1955, when he was given a university professorship at Harvard; after eight years he moved to the divinity school of the University of Chicago, where he stayed until his death in 1965. Along the way, Tillich garnered numerous academic honors and toured the world on lecture engagements from the United States to Japan to the Middle East. Meanwhile, the mass culture he despised conferred recognition far beyond the bounds of academe. The subject of an adulatory profile in *Time*, Tillich received an invitation to the magazine's gala in 1963, where, sometime between the cocktails and the prizes, he warned the assembled luminaries that the American cultural critic was being absorbed as "another cultural good." Inundated with mail and requests for appearances and opinions, Tillich basked in the glow of the "harvest time," as Hannah put it.[38]

The harvest coincided with the appearance after World War II of a more personalist mode of social and cultural criticism that owed a great deal to Tillich. Reaping the fruit of his previous work, Tillich helped to sow the seeds of a "new left" whose critical discourse relied heavily on psychology and existentialism. Religious intellectuals in particular found in Tillich's harvest abundant justification for dismissing churches as potential political sites, thereby crippling rather than strengthening religion as a vehicle of moral imagination. Thus Tillich's postwar work both invigorated postwar radicalism and augured a triumph of the therapeutic in the nation's religious life and cultural politics. Moving among the culturally and geographically mobile class of professionals and intellectuals, Tillich distilled from his gospel of personality a religious discourse for the psychological man of the emerging postindustrial world.

In the first rank of postwar personalists, Tillich joined other writers who employed a psychological idiom to forge new modes of social vision and reconstruction. Many liberal and left intellectuals turned from the struggles of classes to the struggles of the self, offering Freud, Sartre, and Kierkegaard positions once occupied by Marx and Dewey. Psychoanalysis, existentialism, aesthetics, and social criticism all formed a loose discursive coalition that transmuted the analysis of power into the analysis of identity and collapsed political issues into matters of taste and style. Yet this turn to the personal or the existential, while it certainly eclipsed the politics of class, also extended the boundaries of political discussion by enlarging the range of political subjects and launched an attempt to remap the landscape of utopia.[39]

As the modern acolytes of personality, psychoanalytical social critics often plundered the hope treasures of religion. Lamenting the devil's bargain with reason negotiated by liberal religion, Herbert Marcuse declared in *Eros and Civilization* (1955) that "where religion still preserves uncompromised aspirations for peace and happiness, its 'illusions' still have a higher truth value than science which works for their elimination." The Harvard psychoanalyst Erik Erikson, while contributing to the vital centrist rhetoric of maturity, also christened his *Young Man Luther* (1958) a case study in revolution. In *Young Man Luther*, Erikson wrote, "the resources of tradition fuse[d] with new inner resources to create something potentially new: a new person; and with this new person a new generation, and with that, a new era." Fixing Reinhold Niebuhr in his crosshairs, Norman O. Brown wrote *Life Against Death* (1959)—a study of "the nature and destiny of man"—to provide a visionary alternative to "the politics of sin, cynicism, and despair." "What shall man do to be saved?" Brown asked of psychoanalysis. An apostate from the progressive view of history shared by liberals, Marxists, and modern Protestants, Brown touted such retrograde believers as medieval mystics and fundamentalist Protestants as the worthiest bearers of the immortal aspiration to a new heaven and earth. "Protestant fundamentalism," Brown observed, "retains the wisdom of folly," the conviction that desire and imagination preceded reason in the long march to the promised land. Since religion remained the most outlandish genre of utopian folly, psychoanalysis could fathom the secrets of the human heart, Brown surmised, only if it could "recognize religion at the heart of the mystery."[40]

However, religion had been blasphemed, Brown asserted, for the established religion of modernity was a Protestant work ethic that, however secularized, inflamed the madness of unrelenting production and accumulation. As the spiritual leaven of modern capitalism, the Protestant ethic was an especially morbid manifestation of aggressive impulses, Brown asserted, "a pure culture of the death instinct." Brown tied together the drive for mastery, the rage to accumulate, and Protestant theology in his brilliant discussion of Luther and the devil—entitled, not coincidentally, "The Protestant Era," a clear acknowledgment of a debt to Tillich. Lauding Tillich as a pioneer in the effort to "disentangle Protestantism from its alliance with capitalism," Brown recommended his theology as a model of religious social criticism, an exemplary therapeutic weapon in the struggle for life against death.[41]

Yet other psychoanalytical critics such as Erikson and Goodman attempted to reclaim the aesthetic and salvific dimensions of the Protestant work ethic. Erikson's Luther retained an artisanal conception of labor, inveighing against "holy busywork" that had nothing of "the quality of devoted craftsmanship." Such sacramental craftsmanship could flourish, however, only when the worker had faith, the central Protestant virtue to which Goodman devoted an entire chapter of *Growing Up Absurd* (1960). Indicting the organized system for its discouragement of "the religious convictions of Justification and Vocation," Goodman argued that corporate capitalism befouled rather than embodied the Protestant work ethic. The Protestant ideal, Goodman believed, was faithful, graceful labor undertaken in a beloved community. Faith was confidence that "the world will continue to support the next step" of one's life, whereas grace arose from a world plentiful in "possible ways for activity and achievement." American youth grew up "absurd," Goodman thought, because they knew that a prosperous future lay in useless, wasteful, and destructive production. "There is no justification in such works," Goodman declared in Lutheran fashion.[42]

Goodman's contention that the young were growing up absurd signaled his debt to the postwar currency of existentialist philosophy, theater, and literature. Although easily caricatured as a movement promoting nihilism and despair, existentialism had its greatest American impact in a religious form. While secular figures such as Friedrich Nietzsche, Jean-Paul Sartre, Albert Camus, Martin Heidegger, Samuel Beckett, and Eugene Ionesco were the most celebrated representatives of the movement in Europe, in the United States, religious philosophers and theologians played a comparable if not greater role in defining the existentialist sensibility. Through Soren Kierkegaard, Martin Buber, Karl Jaspers, Miguel de Unamuno, Nicholas Berdyaev, and Simone Weil, American readers encountered a moral universe full of agonizing decisions, hunger for God, and hopes of moral grandeur in a sterile technological civilization. "Existential theology"—a rubric under which a host of disparate religious figures could find themselves gathered (from the Niebuhr brothers and Tillich to Jacques Maritain, Rudolf Bultmann, and the anti-Nazi martyr Dietrich Bonhoeffer)—composed one of the most turbulent tributaries to this existentialist current. Using a parareligious rhetoric—authenticity, meaning, anxiety, being, the human condition—existentialists asserted that the intellectual and political conventions of the Enlightenment had disrespected the deepest human needs and that revolution, if it came, would have to be more far-reaching than those envisioned in the liberal and Marxist traditions.[43] Especially when cast in religious terms, existentialism fueled quests for personal transformation through political commitment.

The existentialist vogue derived in large measure from the personal tensions generated by reproduction of the professional middle class. The themes that ran persistently through existentialist discourse—the inadequacy of reason and technology, the anguish of personal decision, the inescapability of personal responsibility and engagement—resonated with special force among young men and women who, raised to honor the ideal of professional self-direction, recoiled from the corporate bureaucracies to which their skills and selves would be harnessed. Acquiring these skills in intensely competitive settings, many students harbored desires for greater intimacy and harmony. While existentialism gave voice to technical and scientific students not inseparably chained to ledger and protractor, it also appealed to humanists whose learning threatened to render them marginal to the technological and business imperatives of the corporate world. Liberal Protestant seminarians, determined to evade what Gibson Winter cursed as *The Suburban Captivity of the Churches* (1963), found in existential theology both an expression of their fears and a validation of their cultural capital.[44]

As a prominent Protestant intellectual, Tillich became an especially conductive lightning rod in this growing storm of personalist dissent. Crowning his intellectual career with the dense tomes of his *Systematic Theology* (1951–1963), Tillich spoke more accessibly in his popular collections of sermons and lectures, *The Courage to Be* (1952), *The New Being* (1955), and *The Eternal Now* (1963). More clearly than many others who spoke in the argot of personal turmoil and renewal, Tillich traced the roots of postwar anxiety to the military and technoscientific structures of modern civilization and based the recovery of moral selfhood on a religious-cultural politics that broke their monopoly on human consciousness.

Tillich continued to dispute the cultural authority claimed by the human sciences, especially by psychology. Psychology, he asserted in *The Courage to Be*, formed but one weapon in an arsenal of "controlling reason," "controlling knowledges" by which human beings are catalogued and manipulated by specialists. Despite fear on the part of many of his contemporaries that Tillich was reducing theology to psychological and existential categories, he harbored profound skepticism about both psychoanalysis and existentialism, believing both movements indispensable but inadequate allies in a religious vanguard. Writing in the leading Protestant pastoral journal *Pastoral Psychology* that the nonjudgmental acceptance integral to psychoanalytical practice was a model for Christian counseling and even for theological inquiry, Tillich insisted that it was necessary to distinguish clinical from pastoral concerns, therapy for mental illness from therapy for moral and spiritual disorders. Unlike Erich Fromm, Rollo May (his former student at Union), Victor Frankl, Abraham Maslow, and Fritz Perls—"medical moralists" who often turned to religion as a tool of therapeutic intervention or self-actualization—Tillich linked the therapeutic task to a community pointing beyond itself. Interpersonal relations required a spiritual center, he wrote in the *Systematic Theology*, without which they inexorably turned manipulative and exploitative. Personality developed as a movement of the self "that rises first toward God" and only then "returns from him to the other self." Far from blessing the postwar boom in psychology, Tillich often caviled about the extravagant redemptive hopes placed in the mental professions. As he told Robert Coles (in the early 1950s a student of Tillich's and a young, perplexed resident in psychiatry), "psychiatry, today, is a faith for the faithless."[45]

Tillich expressed similar reservations about existentialism. Praising secular existentialists for their resistance to scientific scrutiny and managerial control—launching, in his words, "the most desperate attempt to escape the power of controlling knowledge . . . which technical reason has produced"—Tillich argued that their secularism ensured their continued enslavement. The self-affirming existentialist hero, so eager to liberate himself from conformity that he could not imagine social alternatives to the meaningless world of techniques and organization, could not ultimately "escape the forces of his self which may drive him into complete loss of the freedom that he wants to preserve."[46]

Employing existentialist language, Tillich avowed that the "courage to be" came from God, the "power of being itself," who was encountered only in the church, "the mediator of the courage to be." Although Tillich regarded the existing churches of suburban Christendom as a rotting edifice of complacency and spiritual torpor, he clung to the ideal of religious community as the foundation of personal authenticity. Reflecting on the fate of "the person in a technical society" in 1953, Tillich argued that personality could resist the dehumanizing forces of managerial and technological control only by a "partial non-participation in the objectifying structures of technical society." Unlike critics of the corporate order such as David Riesman and William H. Whyte, who advocated private withdrawals from conformity and other-direction, Tillich recommended small networks of friends and believers as communities in which personality could be protected and enriched. Following Day, Buber, Goodman, and Macdonald, Tillich emphasized that one could "withdraw even partially only if he has a place to which to withdraw." This community, he concluded, was in effect a church, a "New Reality" whose criterion was "Jesus as the Christ," a place of grace and a depot of "attack on the technical society and its power of depersonalization."[47]

At the same time, Tillich's appreciation of the prospects opened up by psychology and existentialism suggested an antidote to the skinflint moralism of the Protestant republican tradition. Indeed, steeped in the cultures of classical German humanism and Weimar modernity, Tillich was uniquely positioned to release the American Protestant imagination from its indenture to producerism. In one of his more memorable sermons, Tillich pointed to Jesus's anointment at Bethany as an example of "holy waste." Although the apostles rebuked the women for wasting ointments that could have been sold to help the poor—a rebuke repeated, Tillich noted, by all the modern world's "reasonable" social and clerical experts—Jesus reminded them that such waste was a "beautiful thing." Tillich interpreted the story as a parable of abundance. Christian love, he wrote, meant precisely wasting oneself, giving of one's powers "beyond the limits of law and rationality." The wasteful love of *agape* issued from "the abundance of the heart" that "united reason and ecstasy, moral obedience and sacred waste"—God's own rationality of gratification, as Marcuse might have called it. "People are sick," Tillich explained, not simply because they fail to receive "but also because they are not allowed to give love, to waste themselves."[48] Expressed in the language of plenty that American liberals used to celebrate and disdain postwar consumer culture, Tillich's praise of self-expending folly recalled the liberal Protestant faith in the largesse of personality and offered a powerful rebuke to the self-limitation enjoined by liberal resignation, professional propriety, and market calculation.

This appeal to self-expenditure as the way to personal authenticity and fulfillment—finding one's self by losing one's self—resonated with many college students and professionals, black and white, who execrated the corporate world as a glad-handing hell. As Doug Rossinow has demonstrated, existential theology, often introduced to students through Tillich's work, saturated the intellectual atmosphere of numerous campus fellowships and student groups that became key nuclei of the New Left. Still, since many of these students had only the most attenuated connections to churches and religious traditions, their personalism eventually would degenerate into a purely therapeutic form of identity politics. The most faithful acolyte of Tillich's gospel of personality was Martin Luther King, Jr. Like Tillich, King had accumulated a rich trove of erudition in theology and philosophy. Like Tillich, King had acquired both academic and pastoral credentials. Like Tillich, King often had chastised the smugness and venality of middle-class churches, especially that of his own "silk-stocking" Montgomery congregation who epitomized the black bourgeoisie's preoccupation with status and prestige. Though praiseworthy, King thought, the entrepreneurial and professional virtues of thrift and diligence fostered a parsimony of spirit that sapped the "soul force" necessary for the social gospel.[49]

Moreover, in a manner most like Tillich, King distinguished his social gospel of racial justice from the secular racial liberalism of many of his supporters. "The humanist's hope is an illusion," he forthrightly declared in Strength to Love (1963), because belief in "salvation within a human context" rests on a "self-delusion that ignores fundamental facts about our mortal nature." When their hopes withered, secular liberals and radicals grew despairing and spiteful because they could not love their racist enemies—they could not, in other words, have faith in the redemptive power of God. Christians could struggle for justice, King explained in the Christian Century in 1957, because they knew that "the universe is under the control of a loving purpose," a love that was "the most durable power in the universe." That power, King contended in Stride toward Freedom (1958), lay in "personality," and "creation is so designed that . . . personality can only be fulfilled in the context of community." Enveloped in Christian notions of personality and love, King's political imagination conferred therapeutic powers on the civil rights movement. Blacks fought racism as much for whites as for themselves, King believed, since if "the white man's personality is greatly distorted by segregation, and his soul is greatly scarred," then "the love of the Negro" worked not only to establish justice but also to "remove [the white man's] tensions, anxieties, and fears." Thus, in King's view, the nonviolence of the Montgomery bus boycott represented "more than a method"; it betokened "commitment to a way of life."[50] Wedding evangelical ardor and liberal theology, the civil rights movement marked an unexpected denouement of the postwar religious revival.

Most unlike Tillich, King grounded his gospel of personality in the conventional church. "The Negro church"—part of a church that King acknowledged as "the Body of Christ"—represented for King the "New Reality" of which Tillich had written. Although "fundamentally a clergyman, a Baptist preacher"—that is, a member of the professional middle class—King insisted as a traditional Baptist on a radically democratic church structure and political culture. Dismissing W. E. B. Du Bois's concentration on the "talented tenth" as a "tactic for an aristocratic elite" who really wanted "no role for the whole people" either "in the struggle or in the promised land," King reminded readers of *Stride toward Freedom* that the vast majority present at church meetings during the boycott were working people. "The Ph.D.'s and the no 'D's were bound together in a common venture, physicians, teachers, and lawyers sat or stood beside domestic workers and unskilled laborers."[51] Under religious auspices, the civil rights movement became, however briefly, an incarnation of the united front that haunted the dream life of American progressivism.

Harvest Time (II): "Ultimate Concern" and the Triumph of the Therapeutic

Yet another legacy stemmed from Tillich's gospel of personality: a therapeutic ethos divorced from a religious politics of social reconstruction. While King's personalism presumed a grounded and vigorous religious culture, Tillich inhabited the footloose and bureaucratic world of a mostly white, educated, and mobile religious intelligentsia. Among them, personalism inspired an equally political but also more purely therapeutic gospel of personality that gradually weakened the symbolic and institutional structures of mainline Protestantism.

Tillich's postwar work consummated his effort to distill from the array of religions a purer element of "religion." Religion, as Tillich now defined it in an oft-cited phrase, was "ultimate concern," "the depth of all functions of man's spiritual life," "that which is ultimate, infinite, unconditional in man's spiritual life." This rhetoric of depth, infinity, and ultimacy made up in portentousness and emotional intensity what it lacked in social concreteness. Relegating the creeds, codes, and rituals of religions to a secondary importance and beckoning toward an "absolute faith" that thrived "without the safety of words and concepts, without a name, a church, a cult, a theology," Tillich pushed the liberal Protestant idiom of religion and personality to its farthest limits of discursive abstraction and psychological form.[52]

Tillich's anointment of modernist art and literature as a reservoir to replenish the wasteland of "broken symbols" indicated the therapeutic dilemma in delegitimizing traditional religious conventions. Thanks to his "method of correlation" by which he discerned Christian meanings in cultural objects and provided Christian answers to secular questions, Tillich could opine, as he did at a 1954 Union Seminary exhibition, that any art "which points toward the Ultimate Ground of our being is entitled to be called religious art." Thus Picasso's *Guernica* became, in Tillich's view, a "great Protestant painting" by capturing "the infinite distance between God and man." Frequently enlisting figures from the modernist literary and theatrical canon (Kafka's novels and Beckett's *Waiting for Godot* were his favorite examples), Tillich clearly hoped to broker exchange between religious and secular cultural producers.[53]

Tillich's own work resembled that of abstract expressionists such as Mark Rothko and Barnett Newman in seeking to express spiritual concerns without the limitations of conventional representation. Longing to transcend the corporate conformity they considered destructive of moral integrity and spiritual vitality, abstract expressionists often produced works—Rothko's color-field paintings, Newman's black-and-white abstractions bearing titles such as *Covenant* and *Stations of the Cross*—that offered "penetration into the world mystery" and depicted "absolute emotions" whose truth could not be assessed by scientists and engineers. Viewers of the *Stations*, Newman believed, avoided the kitschy renditions of the crucifixion that disgraced the walls of suburban churches and instead experienced the agony of "the first pilgrims [who] walked the Via Dolorosa." Tillich's absolute faith that supposedly flourished outside the confines of symbol and ritual was an analogous attempt to recover the original transformative power of the gospel, now weakened through attrition by middle-class mores and tired aesthetic conventions. However, Newman's own determination to make "cathedrals of ourselves" ("there are no more temples to paint," as Rothko lamented) suggested the purely therapeutic consequences of abstracting faith from the symbols and practices of religious communities and lodging it in individual subjectivity.[54] If the religiosity of abstract expressionism was William James on canvas, the absolute faith of Tillich was William James in the pews.

Tillich was not the only Protestant seeking to relieve the alleged symbolic poverty of Christian faith. Toward the end of his life in 1962, H. Richard Niebuhr began to wrestle with the problem of therapeutic modernity. "Our old phrases are worn out," he wrote in the *Christian Century* in 1960, having become clichés that constricted the spiritual experience of modern men and women. In Niebuhr's view, the longings articulated and disciplined through traditional symbols were increasingly wayward, diffuse, and therefore dangerous. The great theological problem of the future, he predicted in the Cole Lectures at Vanderbilt in the spring of 1961, would be the creation of new therapeutic symbols and symbolic activities to replace the old ones. Recalling Jonathan Edwards's Puritan conception of therapy as a moral and religious education of desire and arguing that the Scriptures themselves described the sinful life as one of disordered emotions, Niebuhr urged young Protestant intellectuals to revisit the emotions and define the spiritual life as "an emotional life redeemed, liberated, and ordered." Niebuhr guardedly welcomed existential theology and depth psychology as sources of a new Christian vernacular. They were not, he told the Vanderbilt audience, "alien intruders into a language that ought to be kept pure at all costs."[55]

Yet Niebuhr's last work published in his lifetime, *Radical Monotheism and Western Culture* (1960), demonstrated that existential and psychological notions could indeed threaten the social and therapeutic missions of liberal Protestantism. For the radical monotheist who believed that nothing except God deserved unswerving loyalty, "no special places, times, persons, or communities are more representative of the One than any others are"—an almost perfect rendition of Tillich's ultimate concern. While Niebuhr conceded that radical monotheism could dissipate into an "abstract . . . purely individual and spiritual attitude divorced from the concrete life of the people"—into a therapeutic regimen that separated spiritual and intellectual virtuosi from their brethren—he failed to explain how this fate could be averted without granting privilege to some particular historical community. Niebuhr noted that Israel's prophets had always been "legal reformers, ethical seers, . . . theological critics, political advisers, poets, . . . exponents of new types of aesthetic sensibility" and that "revelatory moments" were always "political struggles, national and cultural crises." They were always, that is, bound up with "the concrete life of the people" that a radical monotheism would evade and erode.[56] Radical monotheism thus ratified by default both the cultural authority of experts—religious communities, having no privileged access to truth, could not directly challenge expertise—and the purely therapeutic transformation of religion into privatized experience.

While Tillich and Niebuhr retained an attenuated link with a Protestant religious language, other intellectuals embarked on similar, more unfettered, and equally prefigurative quests to uncouple the therapeutic resources of religion from religious traditions and communities. In his highly regarded comparative study, *The Hero with a Thousand Faces* (1949), Joseph Campbell—an epigone of Jung, one of Tillich's Weimar psychologizers of faith—argued that myths and religions were variations on a single archetypal theme: the adventure of the hero, a sort of Nietzschean *übermensch* who, after suffering confusion, scorn, and death, rises to the knowledge of truth through his own creative powers. Modern men, incapable of strict fidelity to a single religion, would find their own heroism in a therapeutic piracy that ransacked the world's spiritual treasures. Campbell's later popularity as a spokesman for the power of myth to enable spiritual seekers to "follow their bliss" derived greatly from the symbolic consumerism heralded in Tillich's notions of ultimate concern and absolute faith.[57] In Tillich, the liberal Protestant tradition produced an artifact of the consuming vision, an embryonic stage of the "commodity spirituality" that denotes one of the purest therapeutic forms in the culture of late capitalism.

In one of his most moving sermons, "Waiting," Tillich described the tension and suffering that accompanied a cure of souls begun but far from completed. "Our time is a time of waiting; waiting is its special destiny." He did not miss the eroticism implicit in his message. Even in "the most intimate communion among human beings," lacking and waiting were necessary but revealing moments in any earthly love.[58] Tillich knew that he waited for God as he waited for Hannah, painfully conscious of the chasm that lay between his sinful self and his declarations of love.

In his final years, Tillich tried to heal the wounds he had inflicted on Hannah. On his deathbed, clutching his prized German Bible, Tillich asked once more for her pardon; Hannah granted it, being more merciful than just. After Paulus's death and cremation, Hannah had his ashes interred in a park bearing his name in New Harmony, Indiana, where, a century and a half earlier, Robert Owen had tried and failed to build a beloved community. A bust of Tillich stands near his grave, as if waiting for the final *kairos* when a New Harmony will finally encompass the earth.[59]

Yet even in death Tillich afflicted Hannah with the results of his erotic experiments. Sorting through their belongings at East Hampton after the funeral, Hannah came upon the locked desk in which Paulus stored what he called his "spiritual harvest," his complete oeuvre of book manuscripts and unpublished writings. Unlocking the drawers, Hannah watched as more unsavory grains of Tillich's spiritual harvest spilled onto the floor: letters, photographs, and other erotic memorabilia. Though she spent two days burning the harvest in the fireplace, "I was tempted," Hannah later wrote, "to place between the sacred pages of his highly esteemed lifework those obscene signs of the real life that he had transformed into the gold of abstraction—King Midas of the spirit."[60]

Tillich's golden harvest, arising from an alchemy of sexual torment and spiritual longing, helped to purchase for postwar Americans a partial release from sinful conventions. In his journey from Prussia to America, Tillich had seen the circles of hell and heaven on the battlefields of France, in the spotlights of celebrity, and in his numerous infidelities where he sought some transport into the absolute. Perhaps it was fitting that Martin Luther King, Jr.—a man possessed by his own angels and demons—should find in Paul Tillich a solace behind the bars of segregation. For King would carry the Christian message that love both fuses and liberates, atones for sin and sets all captives free.

✝

CHAPTER SIX

The Twilight of the Gods:

The Rise and Fall of the Secular City, 1962–1975

"We are post-Christian men," Paul Goodman declared in 1961. Despite the robust religious revival, Goodman held that Christianity was waning as a coherent force in American life. Since so many Christian virtues had been uprooted from the Christian churches and relocated in secular institutions—charity, for one, had become the impersonal state provision of money and services—there was no point, Goodman felt, in attributing them any longer to "a special group of believers." While Goodman affirmed this culmination, the arrival of a post-Christian America clearly troubled him. Far from raising earthly expectations, the disappearance of heaven had trivialized them, Goodman feared. Limited to the horizons defined by science and technology, men and women wandered "unable to dream awake"; their souls suffocated in a "vacuum of religious expectation." Even among professing Christians, a "failure of millenarian nerve"—a dearth of the exuberance and courage required for social reform—marked the demise of Christianity as "a living world faith." "The Church is no longer militant," Goodman sighed.[1]

Most of the church, that is, for Goodman sensed millenarian vitality in two saving remnants: "Southern Negroes and their friends" in the civil rights movement and young white Protestant intellectuals. (The newly "bourgeoisified" Catholics, he sniffed, were just "smug".) When he was young, Goodman recalled, a minister had been thought an ass, while seminarians had been ranked as morons. Now, the younger clergy and theology students were the most piquant "salt of the earth." Goodman noted shrewdly that their new boldness reflected their partial cultural dispossession. Conceding that Christian virtues might indeed be better practiced in secular forms, the new clergy remained reluctant to sign over their "valuable real estate" to "secular hands that will use it worse." Uncertain of its market value—even conscious that it might be priceless and inalienable—they clung to the ancestral property, "hoping they will learn *what* to do with it." Goodman wished them well. "Creator Spirit come," he implored.[2]

Creator Spirit came—and slouched. By the end of the decade, Goodman had been disappointed by the young clerics. Scoffing at the vogue for relevance among the Protestant and Catholic intelligentsia, Goodman criticized the pursuit of timeliness as the squandering of a precious inheritance. As a neolithic conservative, Goodman reminded the young clerisy that while burning draft cards and carrying placards were admirable modes of apostolic witness, genuine relevance hinged on having something distinctive to preach. Abandoning tradition "in their new zeal for relevance," religious intellectuals were "badly failing in their chief duty to the young, which is to be professors of theology"—in both the personal and academic senses. Sold off or sublet at the lowest rates, the estate of Christian theology lay in disrepair. Chagrined, Goodman remained hopeful. "If the chaplains stop looking in the conventional places where God is dead, and would explore the actualities where perhaps He is alive, they might learn something and have something to teach."[3]

Goodman's transit from hope to disappointment anticipated the work of recent historians who emphasize both the magnitude of expectation among left intellectuals and the limitations, even the ambiguities, of their achievements. Across the progressive spectrum, from liberal reformers to the New Left, forms of postindustrial social criticism proliferated as assessments of the possibilities residing in a society whose expertise and technology seemed to ensure a permanent plenty. New Left intellectuals believed that this postindustrial or "post-scarcity" society permitted not only an equitable distribution of prosperity but also a space for the flourishing of personal authenticity. Authenticity—a secular substitute for the ideal of "personality"— became the grail and the poison goblet of the movements that comprised the New Left. Shaped in large measure by religious existentialists such as Paul Tillich, the quest for authentic selfhood began as a search for "beloved community," splintered over issues of race, gender, and sexuality, and ended in the fragmentation and therapeutic insularity of identity politics. Thus the problem of authenticity was bound up with that of historical agency. Where, New Leftists asked, is the ultimate social location of authenticity and hence of the transformation necessary for its attainment? These problems became more acute as members of the New Left, assuming posts in the university system at the end of their "long march through the institutions," grew more distant from the public than any previous generation of progressive intellectuals.[4]

Attention to the religious thought of the 1960s might clarify the full significance of the immolation of the New Left.[5] Since authenticity and beloved community were ideals with historical roots in Christian notions of personality and church, and since the New Left itself owed a great deal to the "first new left," which had pioneered the personalist mode of social and cultural criticism, the presence of a religious center for secular radicalism could have averted precipitation of the politics of authenticity into the politics of identity. Indeed, an often highly profiled part of the New Left, a "new breed" of Christian intellectuals produced an array of theologies—from "the secular city" and "the open church" to varieties of "people's religion" such as "black theology" and "feminist theology"—that doubled as religious forms of postindustrial criticism. On one hand, this new breed of religious intelligentsia not only supplied shock troops and media stars for the civil rights and antiwar movements but also directed critical fire at secular versions of postindustrial thought. On the other hand, these individuals prefigured a more purely therapeutic religious culture that was a key part of the cultural liberalism fostered by the New Left. Their deliberate and often contemptuous repudiation of existing congregations, besides adding mightily to the disarray of liberal Protestantism and Catholicism, also betrayed the venerable hope of uniting intellectuals and people in a formidable religious progressivism.

DANCING ON THE GRAVE OF GOD: POSTINDUSTRIAL THEORY AND THE FATE OF RELIGION

The present or impending arrival of a postindustrial society excited many American intellectuals in the 1960s. "Postindustrial society" constituted a cluster of hopes, analyses, and anxieties common to liberals and left intellectuals, one that contained both celebratory and more critical accounts of contemporary social, technological, and cultural changes. It appeared in numerous analytical and ideological guises, spanning the left-liberal spectrum from "post-scarcity" anarchists, to critics of technological glut and ecological devastation, to radical students, liberal academics, and policy specialists. However diverse, most postindustrial visions shared a number of common elements. They emphasized the increasing centrality to production and social policy of automation, cybernetics, and new "intellectual technologies" such as game theory and statistical analysis. They harbored a conviction that technologically advanced societies, having achieved a capacity for widespread and exponentially expanding abundance, were ready to repeal the primacy of economics and arrange their affairs by a more benevolent social calculus. They heralded the diminution of the old industrial working class as a social factor in production and an agent of social and political reform. They identified the professional-managerial sectors of the corporate economy and the university system that trained them—dubbed variously the "new class," the "technostructure," the "educational and scientific estate," or the "knowledge class"—as the vanguards of social and cultural transformation. Postindustrial society marked, in Howard Brick's words, a "confidence in the capacity of modern society to enlarge the scope of social provision and the purview of public planning," a confidence that was "unabashedly progressive in spirit, imagining a future based on modern cosmopolitan ethics and the achievements of advanced technology."[6]

For left-liberal intellectuals, this new class comprised a "conscience constituency," in Michael Harrington's words, predisposed to social planning and possibly amenable to political alliances with racial minorities and the poor. While the importance of professional-managerial workers had been recognized and uncontested for almost a century, the early 1960s commenced what Barbara and John Ehrenreich have termed their "golden age," a quantum rise in their numbers, income, and prestige. Approaching or having reached a critical mass both in the information-dependent workplace and in the burgeoning university system, the professional-managerial class stood poised, in John Kenneth Galbraith's view, to make the corporation "responsive to the larger purposes of society." The spark igniting this velvet uprising would leap, David Bazelon predicted, from the friction of professional rationality with archaic business and military imperatives. In the frustrations of the new class, Bazelon saw the basis of a new politics in which personal fulfillment, professional achievement, and the social good would converge in "a deeper sense of community." Harrington went so far as to anoint the time as a moment when "the Western ideal" of freedom and plenty in community could be realized. The problem, he wrote in *The Accidental Century* (1965), was to "infuse the minute and calibrated technology, and the growing abundance of statistical and planning data, with the Western spirit, to marry engineering and philosophy."[7]

But who would write the vows, perform the ceremony, and christen the offspring of this union of spirit and expertise? Harrington pointed directly to a salient feature of postindustrial discourse: the implicit (and at times overt) belief that postindustrial society could very well be post-Christian or even postreligious. Bazelon, wondering "where religion went" with the cultural triumph of science, implored liberals to recover something of its essence because politics was "too important . . . to be managed without religious feeling." Whether or not religious feeling would indeed leaven the postindustrial future was a key question for many intellectuals in the 1960s. Tom Hayden of Students for a Democratic Society (SDS) and the democratic socialist Michael Harrington—both ex-Catholics—believed that many of the old Christian verities could survive in secular forms. Acquainted with the work of Reinhold Niebuhr and Jacques Maritain and well-versed in the lexicon of postwar personalism, Hayden wrote in "The Port Huron Statement" of men as "infinitely precious," possessing capacities for "reason, freedom, and love" that made their lives "personally authentic." Much like John Dewey, Hayden urged a new left to draw up secular facsimiles of religious community, "blueprints of civic paradise" as he called them in a phrase neatly evocative of the technical, republican, and religious strands in American progressivism. This civic Eden would revive what Hayden feared was the decaying humanistic enterprise of the university, its obligation to provide professionals and technicians with a higher moral education in love, fraternity, and authenticity.[8] Marching in the progressive tradition, Hayden's brothers and sisters in SDS and Southern Non-Violent Coordinating Committee (SNCC) unfurled a newfangled banner of religiosity, with "beloved community" and "authenticity" rewoven from the threads of "common faith" and "Great Community."

Harrington, on the other hand, was more ambivalent about the prospects for a secular religiosity. Though he lost his Catholic faith and turned to socialism while writing for the *Catholic Worker*, Harrington remained too much the creature of Mott Street to see things as simply or sanguinely as Hayden or Bazelon. Harrington placed postindustrial possibility in the context of an unresolved cultural (or what he called "spiritual") crisis: "the simultaneous loss of faith and unfaith," as he described it in *The Accidental Century*. Far from making the world more transparent and secure, the eclipse of God in the accumulation of techniques, knowledge, and mastery had rendered life more opaque and inexplicable. While religious people themselves, Harrington argued, "should dance on the grave of the God of hunger and fear and human impotence," religion remained necessary for "the expression of a higher anguish," the torment of a world liberated from material privation but exposed to a new dearth of purpose and direction. In this Celtic twilight of the Christian God, democratic socialism marked, for Harrington, not the crowning achievement of secularization but the ongoing resolution of the spiritual dilemmas of modernity. "The task of building Him a home in the modern city will open up the way to the genuine depths of man."[9]

The prospect that Harrington's home would in fact be a crypt worried the sociologist and moralist Philip Rieff. In *Freud: The Mind of the Moralist* (1959) and *The Triumph of the Therapeutic* (1966), Rieff displayed no inconsolable grief over the death of God. "I, too, aspire to see clearly," he wrote in *Triumph*, "like a rifleman, with one eye shut." Though he missed the gods in their apparent senescence, Rieff conceded that technology promised a life beyond the religious vale of tears and consolations. Since technical intelligence was feeding more people than compassion ever had, and since the lifting of neurotic controls over sexual and other desires might yet fulfill rather than destroy civilization, Rieff believed that conservative disparagement of science and moral remission demonstrated "a lamentable lack of imagination" in the face of a new human condition that rendered "all salvations obsolete." ("What apocalypse," he asked, "has ever been so kindly?") Signs of life in contemporary theology were the spasms of a corpse, he wrote in *Freud*, moments in "the general dying within which each specific revival must run its course."[10]

Yet Rieff, like Harrington, could not let God go gentle into the night. The attempt of secular psychological or therapeutic men and women to live without stringent moral codes was, if not quite doomed to failure, corrosive of the bonds that even the bureaucratic democracies of the West needed to survive. Yet Rieff considered those Christians active in the civil rights movement timely counters to the encroaching therapeutic ethos. Desperately seeking "fresh access of communal purpose" from the movement, theologians, clergy, and other Christian intellectuals hoped not only to see justice done but also to revive their own faith and reassert their cultural authority. Marches, sit-ins, and freedom rides betokened for this clerisy, Rieff argued, both a "rebirth of their moral demand system" and a portentous clash between the new legions of prophets and the many "nominally Christian barbarians" in the pews.[11]

Still, Rieff was not unequivocally sanguine about the religious significance of the civil rights movement. While the movement's unabashed moralism pointed toward "something greater than a place in a vaster suburbia," too many sympathetic whites saw a confirmation of their own acquisitive mores. At the same time, blacks themselves, emerging from the vale of deprivation and oppression, were more and more convinced that they too could "live by bread alone." Any effacement of its moral and religious critique of American culture would strip the movement of political energy, Rieff warned, and demote it to the status of a placable interest group—a prescient anticipation of the shift from beloved community to identity politics. To avoid this therapeutic demise, the civil rights movement would have to press for far more than the liberal ideal of civil rights and "become more profoundly cultural."[12]

The broader cultural criticism would emerge, Rieff hoped, out of the movement's specifically Christian roots. While the movement certainly challenged the nation to honor its own professed ideals, Rieff implied that, at its best, it also subjected some of those very ideals to a searching and potentially devastating scrutiny, for, as he pointed out, it was not in liberal individualism or republican citizenship but in the "doctrine of the Church"—the principle that Christians were a community living in but not wholly of the world—that Americans possessed a "critical principle of renewal." Since liberal citizenship was now, in Rieff's view, the assertion of claims to consumer comforts, only religion remained as a "guardian critic" capable of steadfast remonstrance against the impending secular and therapeutic cultural order. And since moral authority was now largely vested among cultural, scientific, and technological professionals, the prime object of religious criticism had to be the battery of expertise indispensable to American power. If "in our time, not science but religion must carry once again the power of criticism, if not that of love," then only religious intellectuals could speak harsh and redemptive truth to the new mandarins.[13]

GOD IN TECHNOPOLIS: THE NEW BREED AND SECULAR THEOLOGY

Many Christian intellectuals shared Rieff's conviction that the civil rights movement marked both a crisis in religious authority and a watershed in the nation's cultural history. In his "Letter from Birmingham Jail," Martin Luther King, Jr., warned that the churches would comprise "an irrelevant social club" if they failed to "recapture the sacrificial spirit of the early church" and support the crusade. As King chastised the mainline Protestant churches for their lukewarm support, his summons to recover the moral purity and courage of the catacombs galvanized a younger cohort of theologians, lay intellectuals, seminarians, and clergy—a "new breed," as they were baptized by Harvey Gallagher Cox, professor at Harvard Divinity School and one of their leading luminaries.[14]

The new breed was, in fact, the current crop of intellectuals in the echelons of Protestant and Catholic institutions, resembling their counterparts among the new class in the professional-managerial bloc. There was nothing sociologically new about the new breed. As academics, journalists, urban or campus clergy, and church bureaucrats, they joined a lineage of progressive religious professionals that extended back to

Rauschenbusch, Ryan, and Scudder. Yet the novelty of the new breed was genuine in two related and fateful respects. As Cox observed in 1967, the new breed enjoyed a degree of "bureaucratically secured freedom" from lay criticism and control that was, if not unprecedented, then certainly unmatched. The managerial revolution in American Protestantism, together with the clerical bureaucratization and lay *embourgeoisement* of American Catholicism, had created numerous posts from which a mobile and militant religious clerisy could venture into rent strikes, picket lines, and protest marches. From ecumenical entrepôts such as Clergy and Laity Concerned about Vietnam and the Southern Christian Leadership Conference, the new breed's theologians and clergy—King, Cox, the Southern minister Will Campbell, the Yale chaplain William Sloane Coffin, Jr., theologian Robert McAfee Brown, the Catholic priests Daniel and Philip Berrigan, journalist Michael Novak, the Episcopal priests Malcolm Boyd and Paul Moore, Jr., the Episcopal bishop of California James Pike—launched its forays against racism, segregation, and the Vietnam war.[15] However, because their freedom depended on insulation from the laity, the new breed's independence pointed to a widening separation of intellectuals and people that threatened prospects for a popular religious left.

Another novelty resided in the theology that arose as the new breed's theoretical navigation of contemporary currents. In the myriad varieties of "secular theology"—secular city, openness, open church, maturity—the new breed registered its impatience with middle-class religious conventions and the desire to escape from the gospel of containment. In *The Secular City* (1965), the bona fide new breed manifesto, Cox renarrated the trek from *gemeinschaft* to *gesellschaft* as a victory march to the postindustrial "technopolis." However, while technopolis stood at the endpoint of the biblically sanctioned process of secularization—"the loosing of the world from religious and quasi-religious understandings of itself"—secularity doubled as a covert persistence of religious conviction, a determination to evade conscription into middle-class life. Gibson Winter, eager to end *The Suburban Captivity of the Churches* (1962), recoiled from a suburban pastorate reduced, he felt, to "a supplement to the didie service." In *The Noise of Solemn Assemblies* (1961), the religious sociologist Peter Berger called on "insurrectionary spirits, adventurers, rebels" to topple the "religio-political cult" and deliver the churches from a gray flanneled Babylon. Calling for greater *Honesty in the Church* (1965), *Commonweal* editor Daniel Callahan demanded that the glaze of "contrived advertising campaigns" be removed from the brick and mortar church. Another Catholic editor, Donald Thorman, in *The Emerging Layman* (1962), merged the democratic promise of Vatican II with the revolutionary nationalism of the postcolonial world. Laymen, he asserted, were "newly formed nations who have just won independence from a colonial power." The young Rochester theologian William Hamilton encapsulated the *enrage* spirit in his celebrated 1964 essay "From Prufrock to Ringo." "Old Niebuhrians," he cracked in an acrid farewell to neoorthodoxy, now shuffled off "to the back pages of the *National Review* to die." Good riddance, he snorted. Draped in the gabardine wisdom of the tragic sense, Niebuhr and his epigoni had cloaked their political fatigue and ideological exhaustion in "good manners, nice clothes . . . and a good conscience about the rat race." Fed up with moral men mortgaged to an immoral society, Hamilton urged younger religious intellectuals to abrogate the old testament of containment.[16]

The new breed's testament of liberation began with a recognition of its own liminal state. Distant from congregations yet not fully absorbed into the secular milieus of postindustrial professionals, members of the new breed saw themselves as living between times, between a waning epoch of Christian cultural establishment and a future of complete disestablishment. Hamilton described a typical young theologian in 1961 as "a displaced person, in hiatus between the dead certainties of the past and a future that attacks and frightens." Yet Hamilton finally welcomed an "end of special privilege for religious men and institutions." In *The Secular City*, Cox berated his fellow religious for dwelling in an intellectual ghetto, a "subculture of humanistic academia," and urged them to come out from the groves and march in the streets. Thomas Merton, echoing the German theologian Karl Rahner's belief that Catholicism was in diaspora from the era of Christendom, applauded the undoing of those entangling alliances with power that corrupted the Church. Catholics, he wrote in the early 1960s, no longer had to reside in "a ghetto of antiquated customs, outworn rituals, and censorious theological rigidity."[17]

Present at the conjuncture of civil rights agitation, the mythos of the New Frontier, the *aggiornamento* ("updating") promised by Pope John XXIII and the Second Vatican Council, and radical currents in Protestant theology, new breed clerics indeed felt a season of favor from the Lord. Vatican II's deliberations—distilled in encyclicals such as *Lumen gentium* (1962) and *Pacem in terris* (1963)—ordained liturgical innovation, promoted a new respect for the pacifist witness, committed the Church to racial and sexual equality, endorsed accelerated technical progress and the welfare state, and replaced "Mystical Body" with the more democratic "People of God" as the regnant ecclesial nomenclature. As conservatives correctly suspected, Vatican II raised revolutionary expectations among North Atlantic Catholics straining in the starched collar of tradition. (The British "Slant" group of Catholic radicals, for instance, called for a "New Left Church" to be the "sacrament of a socialist society.") The Vatican's reforms also coincided with an effective *aggiornomento* among liberal Protestant intellectuals. While the Anglican bishop John A. T. Robinson mostly rehashed modernist rejections of the Virgin Birth, the Trinity, and conventional ideas about God, the candor and accessibility of his *Honest to God* (1963) betokened a popular appropriation of modernist religious thought. At the same time, a small but media-hyped ring of theologians announced the death of God. Varying by coroner, the autopsies revealed either genuine metaphysical demise (Thomas Altizer's account of Christ's "kenotic" death and immersion into history), a cultural event (Gabriel Vahanian), or an admission of God's unreality that Christians should celebrate as the moment of humanity's assumption of responsibility for its fate (Hamilton). In any case, God's expiration released energies for social and political transformation. "When we greet our chaos with a total Yes-saying," Altizer proclaimed in *The Gospel of Christian Atheism* (1966), then "we too can become open to a new and total epiphany of light," an epiphany that Hamilton saw as a step into the adult world of "new forms of technology, of mass media, of great danger and great experiment."[18] Vatican openness and Protestant secularity formed an explosive compound that, in detonating, blew the windows and spires from the churches of containment.

Hamilton's reference to adulthood, replicated in innumerable assertions of maturity and coming of age, conveyed both the largely male new breed's search for masculinity through moral heroism and a claim of relevance to a world in which religious learning seemed less and less germane. As prototypes of maturity and coming of age, new breed intellectuals often invoked the martyred German theologian Dietrich Bonhoeffer and the cryptic French Jesuit Teilhard de Chardin. Bonhoeffer's prison letters "were just the kind of thing my generation was looking for," the Protestant theologian Paul Van Buren recalled in 1965. Indeed, Bonhoeffer's musings about a "religionless Christianity" for a "world come of age" seemed to legitimate the new breed's dismissal of outmoded conventions and its entrance into politics. However, while enthusiasm for Bonhoeffer authorized participation in the civil rights and antiwar movements, it also sanctioned technocratic modes of governance. Bonhoeffer's "holy worldliness" was best exemplified, for Cox, in the pragmatism of President Kennedy. "An artist with a flair for bringing together experts," Kennedy incarnated, in Cox's view, the utilitarian profaneness that Bonhoeffer portended. New breed Catholics beheld in Bonhoeffer, but especially in Teilhard de Chardin, a benediction of professional prowess and power. Mixing theology and biology in an arcane and ungainly lexicon—"cephalization," "the Omega point," "the noosphere," "complexification"—the Teilhardian discursive tableau provided admirers from Marshall McLuhan to Robert MacNamara with a heady ideological repertoire. The abundant encomiums in Robert Francoeur's *The World of Teilhard* (1961) to interdependence, complexity, and the age of technology all conjured a world of professional credentials, cooperation, and mobility.[19]

Despite the hymnody to technopolis, "church" still occupied a central place in the new breed's moral and political imagination. Cox discussed the church in *The Secular City* in passages redolent of guerrilla mobility and vanguard adventure. As a community dedicated to "permanent revolution"—a term Cox borrowed from his Yale mentor H. Richard Niebuhr—the church was "God's *avant-garde*," an "outrider for the secular city" scouting and settling new arable lands for human possibility. As a "cultural exorcist" engaged in an incessant enterprise of social and cultural exorcism (the theology of culture broached by Cox's Harvard mentor Paul Tillich), the church cast out the demons still haunting the streets of technopolis. Moreover, the church in the secular city spoke of God in terms of politics rather than metaphysics. Metaphysics, Cox sniffed, was a boring, obscurantist discourse about "ultimate reality" with incorrigibly conservative political implications. For the new breed in the secular city, "politics replaces metaphysics as the language of theology."[20] Rather than wail in the twilight of Christendom, Cox advised, the church should appropriate the enormous redemptive potential of technopolis and become the agent of authentic postindustrial revolution sought by the New Left.

If not among the suburban Babylonians, who or where was this church? Wherever God's redemptive and hence revolutionary action was in progress, the new breed testified. Rosemary Ruether, a lay Catholic theologian at Howard University, described the church in 1967 as a "happening," a transubstantiation of marches, sit-ins, and other political acts into genuine "eucharistic events." "Sometimes the church is in the churches," theologian Joseph Washington observed in his study of black religious life, *The Politics of God* (1967); "more often it is in the world." "What is the Church anyway?" Daniel Berrigan asked in a 1965 *Commonweal* piece on the Selma march. "Is it where we come from, or is it here, being created by Negroes and their white acolytes?" Daniel's brother Philip, writing from prison after his conviction for the 1968 Catonsville draft file burnings, concluded that Christian communities "form today under pressure of events and around the issues which prompt the events." And as the theologian Richard Schaull told the 1966 Geneva conference of the World Council of Churches, the church flourished as the conscience of revolutionaries, drawing on its biblical and theological heritage to discipline the lines of march traveled by otherwise secular political forces. Churches, Schaull said, should live "in sharp tension both with the revolutionary movements in which they participate" and with "the established order of which they are a part." Schaull doubted that a purely secular politics could produce much beyond a more benevolent species of management. Revolutions degenerated into bureaucracy or worse, he warned, "unless the technical analysis of reality is confronted with a witness to the dimensions of that reality."[21]

Yet what were the dimensions of that reality, especially since secularity appeared to erase the formerly religious contours of the Christian moral imagination? Daniel Berrigan and Thomas Merton, two of the new breed's most revered figures, consistently warned their admirers away from the pitfalls of secularity. In an early collection of essays in theology and cultural criticism, *The Bride* (1959), Berrigan had anticipated much of the tumult and even some of the phraseology that characterized religious thinking in the 1960s. Science had indeed supplanted theology as the premier discourse of Western culture, he conceded, but it promised peace and abundance within the narrow confines of whatever was " 'sensible,' pragmatic, and monolithic"—whatever built up, in his words, "the secular city" of money and power. Merton, irritated by the praise lavished on *Honest to God,* complained in *Commonweal* in 1963 that the book's facile secularity merely repackaged "the old amalgam of agnosticism, laissez-faire, and bourgeois hopefulness" that religious liberals had marketed for a century. Later, questioning the very existence of the modern man who constituted one of the key shibboleths of secularity, Merton argued that the mind of the ordinary person was a "mixture of mental clichés," a creole of mass culture, science, religion, and other tidbits "picked up at random without knowing where they come from or what they imply." Indeed, the whole death-of-God episode struck Merton as a "new-bourgeois movement" emanating from the "muzak-supermarket complex."[22]

For Merton, the impoverishment of moral and political vision caused by secularity was evident in the Vietnam war. The very technopolis that Cox celebrated was the "white-collar murder machine" that, Merton wrote in *Faith and Violence* (1968), dictated "the systematically organized bureaucratic and technological destruction of man." A close student of Herbert Marcuse, Merton grew more acutely sensitive to the gargantuan technocratic features of one-dimensional civilization, sketching in his essays and poetry a harrowing portrait of America as a labyrinth of surveillance, illusion, and commodity glut. In *Raids on the Unspeakable*

(1966), Merton indicted the craving for "inexorable consistency" and control abetted by technical reason, a drive that imposed even on the sidewalk trees a "precise reason for existing." In Berrigan's view, the cold war technology of automation and atomic weapons, harnessed to the capitalist mode of production, exacerbated America's already enormous technological hubris. Yet, even if capitalism could be superseded, as many of the new breed hoped, Berrigan doubted that a more just secular order would be any more humble or free. Inspecting the "blueprints of the social architects" in *They Call Us Dead Men* (1966), Berrigan saw a new host of air-conditioned nightmares: artificial insemination, chemical manipulation of the brain and nervous system, euthanasia—"control of life from the test tube to the grave." Even apart from capitalism, modernity's "loosening of human slaveries" might precede incarceration in "a larger prison yard" of ego, pride, and envy. This concentration on technology as the Goliath of modernity—exemplifed in works such as the French Protestant intellectual Jacques Ellul's *The Technological Society* (1964)—occluded the specifically capitalist context of technical development.[23] Yet, while Merton and Berrigan were perfectly aware of this context, they were more concerned that the secular desire to acquire unlimited control of nature and society ultimately betrayed and confined humanity.

The only escape from this carceral modernity lay in the virtues of mercy and love. Apart from the love enjoined by Christ, Berrigan asserted, no social movement, "no matter what its nobility or greatness," could reach its promised land. In a remarkable 1966 essay, "To Each His Own Darkness," Merton warned those demanding social justice that they were asking for more than they imagined. The proverbial blindness of justice, he implied, could be a curse as well as a blessing. Do we really want to give everyone his just deserts, Merton asked—do we want to be consistent? If so, then we must apply this standard to ourselves—a distinctly unpleasant prospect, for sure. Moreover, as justice thus "damns each man to his own darkness," it precluded, by itself, the creation of a genuinely different future. "Justice is not the final word," Merton concluded; mercy and grace are, since their emancipatory power derives precisely from their preemption of law and their invulnerability to purchase by money, wisdom, or goodness.[24]

With or without attending to these strictures, members of the new breed crusaded on a number of fronts. They grounded their racial gospel in Christian faith and hope. "Without replacing racial identity with the identity of faith in community," Joseph Washington argued in *Black Religion* (1964), "there can be neither openness to the Christian tradition, nor renewal." New breed writers often asserted that the liberation of blacks and other racial minorities was not just a matter of justice but a step toward the emancipation of whites from the oppressive role of oppressor. Washington believed that the civil rights movement had bestowed on "Negro folk religion" a new mission to be a "revelation to white religion" of its need for redemption. Indeed, history, Philip Berrigan intoned in 1961, had "marked the Negro as a sacrament for the white man." Later, in *No More Strangers* (1965), Berrigan highlighted the therapeutic significance of racial upheaval, its provocation toward moral selfhood. "The Negro voice," he declared, spoke in terms of "diagnosis and therapy." Whites, he suspected, feared "more than Negroes freed from their past"; they trembled also at freedom for themselves, emancipation from the racial identity and property ownership they erected as barricades against beloved community. Like the specter of communism, the prospect of black liberation exposed the "burlesque" of whiteness and the "assumed identity" of middle-class Christian propriety.[25]

In his "Letter to a White Liberal," Merton argued that neither white liberals nor many black leaders had even begun to comprehend the enormity of the *kairos* embodied in the civil rights movement. "If the Negro enters wholly into white society, then that society is going to be radically changed," Merton predicted, for the fundamental structures and assumptions of American life were challenged by what he considered to be the "spiritual insight [of blacks] into our common crisis": the naïveté and danger of faith in a rational and orderly universe. The insistence of white liberals on prudence and legality partook of a wider belief among the affluent in the supreme efficacy of a scientific, secular mentality. And if racial justice and even the eradication of race itself required the abolition of class structures from which white liberals profited handsomely, they would have to make a choice between power and charity, over which, Merton feared, they would equivocate. Salvation from race would come only from love, Merton argued, the sort of love that James Baldwin had invoked in the conclusion of *The Fire Next Time* (1963) as the only force capable of dispelling the nation's racial nightmare. Baldwin's trust in the power of love expressed faith, Merton thought, in "a spiritual dynamism with which man freely creates his own history," not as "autonomous, titanic self-affirmation" but as obedience to a force at work "under the surface of human events."[26]

Christian propriety in sexual life and gender conventions also came under assault from the new breed. Finally coming to terms with the sexual revolution of modernity, new breed writers sought to affirm and even enlarge the revolution's benefits by linking them to the creation of a beloved community. Some of the more prominent religious controversies over sexual morality—the "new morality" of "situation ethics," supported by the Episcopal ethicist Joseph Fletcher in *Situation Ethics* (1967), the bitter Catholic debate over artificial contraception occasioned by Vatican II and intensified by Paul VI's *Humanae vitae* (1968)—took place in this larger discourse on "beloved sexuality." Although Cox agreed that humanity had indeed been liberated from the old sexual estate by contraception and penicillin, he warned in *The Secular City* that a new form of bondage awaited those cavorting in the new morality. In an incisive chapter on *Playboy*, Cox argued that the philosophy most indelibly inscribed in the magazine was not sexual freedom but corporate managerialism. Playboy encouraged men to treat women as they treated other men: as "commodified" accessories, "detachable and disposable." Since the bodily nature of personality involved sexual life in community, Cox reasoned, then sexual ethics were bound up with the kind of community that sexual customs helped to create. Any new morality had to promote sexual relations that prefigured the kingdom of God. Glad to be rid of the old sclerotic sexual mores, Cox perceived in the new morality little more than the extension of market individualism from the boardroom to the bedroom.[27]

Catholics such as Rosemary Ruether and Mary Daly accentuated Cox's eschatological note. Moving quickly beyond the careful gender liberalism of Vatican II, they interlaced liberal feminist appeals to merit with more overtly religious invocations of the "covenant community" or "eschatological community" where merit and genitalia had no purchase on redemption. Daly's *The Church and the Second Sex* (1968), the watershed work in American Catholic gender reflection, exemplified this religious brand of feminism. Despite her clear debt to the "rigor and clarity" of Simone de Beauvoir, Daly called attention to her secular limitations. Espousing a personalism, Daly urged a sacramental understanding of sexual life as a material sign of God. Though repelled by the sexism and misogyny of the Church, Daly remained hopeful that the institution's prestige could still be used to exorcise "the demon of sexual prejudice."[28]

Another candidate for exorcism was the rage to accumulate. Like other postindustrial critics, many new breed writers assumed that they inhabited a land of milk and honey where postmaterialist concerns could flourish as never before. "In a culture of increasing leisure," Michael Novak hoped that Christians could finally learn "how to contemplate and how to explore important depths of the human spirit." Yet Novak saw the corporate genesis of abundance as the chief obstacle to this impending spiritual breakthrough. Echoing the personalist tradition, Novak underscored the existential damage wrought by capitalism. "Capitalism deprives a man of his humanity by degrees rather than by violence," he wrote in *A New Generation* (1964). Professionals in particular marketed their souls for prestige and discretionary income and exchanged the "mysteries of contingency and transitoriness" for the illusory certainties of "research, production, and consumption." True to the personalism he had espoused since the 1940s, Merton condemned capitalism in *Seeds of Destruction* (1964) as a cultic economy in which men believed that material objects and even their own personalities had no reality save as sources of capital. "What has no price has no value . . . what cannot be sold is not real." Merton insisted that Christian love and not accumulative acumen knew the score in the real world. "The ritual that surrounds money transactions, the whole liturgy of marketing and profit, is basically void of reality and meaning."[29] For Merton and Novak, dancing on the grave of God was the prelude to digging the grave of humanity and covering the corpse with a surfeit of consumer goods.

Although this infernal vision resembled that of Marcuse's "one-dimensional society," their religious commitments dictated a different path of deliverance. Even if the secular left deplored the injustice, mechanization, and philistinism of American culture, Novak observed that its members still affirmed the Enlightenment ideal of mastery over nature that inevitably "makes man a technician." On secular grounds, the left could neither generate the political will nor summon the moral imagination necessary for authentic liberation. The revolution in which "one man, then another, makes himself into a person and refuses to be a technician" would come only as the professional estate turned to "the traditions of the Gospels" and joined the Church as "a sign raised up among the nations."[30]

Yet the "church" that the new breed invoked bore all the signs of a new professional-managerial culture that valued the flexibility and mobility mandated by the post-Fordist political economy. The content of the new breed's ecclesiology sheds light on the symmetry of New Left ideology and the emerging professional culture. Like the rest of the New Left, the new breed identified knowledge workers as the postindustrial vanguard and upheld an ideal of participatory democracy that expressed desires for personal and professional autonomy. New breed writers saw the new catacombs in the suites, seminars, and homes of cultural, technical, and managerial workers. In *The Open Church* (1964), before railing against the existential depredations of professional life, Novak had located the ground of any future social witness among "the articulate laymen" in "the university, in the business world, and among the professional men of the parish." In *The Secular City*, Cox lauded "the research-oriented, highly skilled bands of specialists" foraging the postindustrial landscape of Boston's Route 128. Calling for "new forms of church life commensurate with new social arrangements," Cox envisioned churches that revolved around "business and communications groups," universities, and social services. These new church structures, Novak and Ruether believed, would be both more flexible and mobile than the old parish settings and emulate the democracy of "the Quakers and other Free Churches."[31]

This participatory ideal pervaded "the underground church," a loose menagerie of people, groups, and ideas that surfaced in the late 1960s. Often seceding from regular parishes, congregants of the underground wrote and performed their own liturgies, experimented with new prayers, and enlisted in political campaigns, open housing protests, and antiwar demonstrations. Its most "mediagenic" cleric, the itinerant Episcopal priest Malcolm Boyd, typified the new breed's underground style in *Are You Running with Me, Jesus?* (1965), a collection of prayers and vignettes that recalled Rauschenbusch's *Prayers of the Social Awakening*. Determined to "quit playing this blasphemous game of religion," Boyd mocked the evasive banality of conventional churches and extolled the sanctifying grace obtainable in marches, coffeehouses, and gay bars. ("If they knew how," Boyd wrote to Jesus of one bar's churchgoing patrons, "they would ask you to be with them in both places.") As a nexus of movement camaraderie and the counterculture, the underground prompted new breed theorists such as Cox to ponder its potential as a new religious political culture. In a series of multimedia lectures at Harvard in the spring of 1968 (published a year later as *Feast of Fools*), Cox harkened to the medieval feast of fools as the template for a politics of "festivity." Anticipating the corporate incarceration of the counterculture in the "predictable and politically impotent" prison of commodity fetishism, Cox challenged Christians to rise to "the level of true fantasy" in their liturgies and other festive events. Emanating from the church's "polis within a polis," Christian festivity—the giving of gifts without thought of return—could, he argued, stimulate the vision and will to extend the festive spirit throughout society. Cox looked to the "Prague Spring" in Czechoslovakia and the May student uprisings in Paris as models for a ludic religious offensive.[32]

However, Cox's weary advice to forgo the "tired and useless task" of transforming existing churches pointed to the fateful limitation of the new breed: its lack of a broad base in the still largely working-class churches. The new breed often dismissed existing churches as unredeemable, insisting on the obsolescence and tedium of denominationally defined residential parishes. "The sharp edge" of the contemporary social gospel, Peter Berger predicted, was "not likely to be in the parish" but rather in "supraparochial" settings such as workplaces and college campuses. Rosemary Ruether captured the restlessness and disgust felt by new breed Christians with what they considered the rotting, hollow hulk of the residential congregation. The new believer, she wrote in the aptly titled *The Church Against Itself* (1967), "endures the non-event of church assemblies as part of his bearing of the dying form of this alienated world."[33]

Yet the alienation and insulation of members of the new breed from lay control—undeniably the conditions of their visionary and political audacity—also sealed them off from popular support. Novak asserted in 1966 that if the Church was "too valuable to entrust to the clergy," it also was too precious to give to a ghettoish and fundamentalist—not to mention blue-collared—laity. The new breed, he continued headily, had dispensed with the conventional churches as so much "useless paraphernalia." Even the new breed's sympathizers noted with unease the preponderance of middle-class professionals in the underground church. Early in 1968, *Commonweal* criticized the "affluent introversion" of an underground that was all too well stocked with "middle-class, well-educated, professional white men and women." Partisans themselves drew a clear connection between the underground church and the emergence of a new corporate culture. "The new style of Christianity," one supporter wrote in *Commonweal* in 1968, was rooted in "small intimate groups" whose vibrancy contrasted with the fatigue of the "massive church membership" in an institution that was "more like General Motors than a prophetic community." This analogy captured perfectly the unsuspected affinity of underground discourse with an embryonic corporate ideology that valorized elasticity. As Andrew Ross has argued, flexibility and mobility were the mantras of a small but influential coterie of postindustrial social theorists—Alvin Toffler in particular—who provided, in Ross's words, a "popular ideological vehicle" for the abrogation of the postwar social settlement.[34]

Just as the rhetoric of flexibility informed the creation of a more physically decentralized but more politically consolidated corporate order, the "flexibilist" argot of the new breed heralded a more fragmented and purely therapeutic religious discourse. As the New Left would discover when its participatory lexicon was ransacked by managerial ideologues, the new breed's liturgical and moral innovations could harmonize well with a revitalized and rationalized accumulative ethos. Uncoupled from a clear and broad-based political project, religious experimentation could be incorporated easily into existing church arrangements, especially among professionals whose religious life featured a more selective adherence to traditional codes and doctrines—a flexibility that also could preclude commitment to social justice.

Novak and Merton augured this purely therapeutic turn. In their writings, personalism was clearly coming untethered from its Christian religious foundations. Asking in *Belief and Unbelief* (1965) if indeed it made "any difference to our identity whether there is a God, a heaven," Novak was arguing by 1968 that Catholics could "safely forget ecclesiastical language." The key issues, he wrote, were "what it is to be alive in our time" and whether or not Catholicism was "obstructive to one's development as a man." Though never as modish as Novak, Merton nonetheless looked to Zen Buddhism for a promise of religious renewal. Sparked by his disenchantment with Trappist life in the late 1950s, Merton's interest in Zen intensified over the next decade. He translated the work of Buddhist monks such as Chuang Tzu, studied Chinese ideograms and calligraphy, and sampled Zen contemplative and meditative techniques. "Much is to be learned from a study of the techniques and experiences of Oriental religions," he wrote in 1967. Chuang Tzu, for instance, was "not concerned with words and formulas about reality," he explained, but with "the direct existential grasp of reality in itself." Similarly, Zen was "outside all structures and forms"; the Zen master enjoyed "direct and pure experiences . . . liberated from verbal formulas and linguistic conceptions." Zen spoke to modern man and to Christianity, Merton believed, because it dispensed with "party platforms in politics, religion, science, or anything else." Here was Paul Tillich's "absolute faith," an abstract expressionist canvas of the spirit. In his frequent avowals that the quest for authenticity led beyond culture and social life, Merton obscured the reliance of his own moral and political positions on a multitude of "party platforms."[35] Like other new breed Christians, Merton assumed too easily that loosening the bonds of authority, leaving the corner church, and shelving the Baltimore Catechism would usher in some new Pentecost.

Merton's final speech, "Marxism and Monastic Perspectives" (delivered to a gathering of monks in Bangkok only hours before his death), illustrated the purely therapeutic preemption of the social gospel. While the monk stood with Marxists in a "critical attitude toward the world and its structures," Merton cautioned that monks—and all radical Christians—would be "relevant . . . in proportion as we are simply monks—simply what we are." Becoming "what we are"—the discovery of authenticity—required a "monastic therapy." "The period of monastic formation is a period of cure, of convalescence," Merton said, a recovery from self-centered love into charity. Marxism, in defining communism as reception according to need and giving according to ability, represented a secularized mutation of the monastic therapeutic ideal. However, in secularizing this ideal, Marxists had sundered the branches from their nourishing vine. "It is my personal opinion," Merton reflected, that "monastic community life is really the only place in which this can be realized," For Christian radicals, "the essential thing," Merton concluded, was the unity of religious intellectuals and people, "the formation of spiritual masters" to cultivate faith, hope, and charity "in the hearts of people who are as yet unformed." Yet Merton then opined that "you cannot rely on structures. The time for relying on structures has disappeared." In an address devoted to the prospect of a new kind of religious politics, Merton inserted a Tibetan adage that could be taken as a creedal statement of the triumph of the purely therapeutic. "From now on, Brother, everybody stands on his own feet."[36]

By the late 1960s, some new breed partisans had belatedly realized the errors of their ways. Made increasingly conscious of working-class resentment through his coverage of George Wallace's 1968 presidential campaign, Novak soon implored radical students and clergy in *A Theology for Radical Politics* (1969) to empathize with "the lower middle class, with firemen, gas station attendants, meter men." The working and lower middle classes were "our teachers," he wrote, "men of flesh" uncorrupted by the haughty rationalism of academics and other professionals. At the same time, Protestant sociologists conducted a spate of studies detecting what Jeffrey K. Hadden called *The Gathering Storm in the Churches* (1969). Although impeccably new breed, Hadden advised his comrades to evangelize the choir on the need to witness in the streets. Even if "converting the Christians" was "a more difficult task than carrying a picket sign," the only way new breed clergy could maintain and extend their political activity was to develop "a strategy for engaging laity in the struggle."[37]

Yet this counsel arrived too late to rescue the new breed from its prophetic folly. If the new breed believed, as Daniel Berrigan opined in *Night Flight to Hanoi* (1968), that "to be radical is to habitually do things that society at large despises," then it fostered a permanent estrangement and not a permanent revolution. As guardians of religious traditions still sacred to millions of students, workers, professionals, and poor, the new breed was uniquely positioned to shape a distinctive political consciousness. Still, harboring an often unconcealed contempt for the mores of working-class and lower-middle-class Americans; romanticizing small, flexible groups and thereby retarding the formation of enduring strategies and institutions; ignoring the need for theory and for a political education of the existing churches; idealizing an authenticity defined in melodramatic terms—the new breed shared in those failures of the larger New Left that seriously dimmed the prospects for a popular progressive movement.[38]

As an ex-Jesuit seminarian who traveled on a press pass from the *National Review* to *Nixon Agonistes* (1970), Garry Wills chronicled the twin declines of the new breed and the New Left. Wills's first book, *Chesterton: Man and Mask* (1961), read at points like an anticipation of the *aggiornomento*. Because "the deepest radicalism" was always conservative—"a return to roots, not simple deracination"—Wills welcomed reform of the Church on conservative grounds. "Killing it," he wrote, "is a new task in each generation." But this creative destruction entailed an eschewal of detached criticism and a fidelity to the intellectual and communal requisites of tradition. "Catholic thought," he explained in 1965, was "an endless tracing of different strands in the traditional teaching"—strands strong enough to bear perpetual scrutiny and extension into "a complex of thoughts, experiences, stresses, institutions, and inner tensions." Thus Wills defended much of the kitschy but, in his eyes, venerable ghetto Catholicism anathematized by new breed Catholics. He refused, he told *Commonweal* in 1969, to join "demented teachers" who stripped the insignia from popular religious culture: novenas, fish on Fridays, May processions, "the sign of the cross before the foul shot." Later, in *Bare Ruined Choirs* (1972), Wills concluded his "memories of a Catholic boyhood"—the sights, sounds, and smells that comprised the sensual texture of faith—by admitting that his Atlanta parish was "a ghetto, undeniably. But not a bad ghetto to grow up in."[39]

Thus Wills was well prepared to see the 1960s as a twilight of the gods—or of idols. Together, *Nixon Agonistes* and *Bare Ruined Choirs* depicted the trembling of American liberalism and American Catholicism as moments in a single religious crisis: "all our religions are empty," as he wrote in *Nixon Agonistes*. With its mythology of selfhood forged in competition, "the Market," most hallowed of liberal deities, marked "a cruel reversal of biblical paradox, that he who would make a self must lose it." By the same token, opponents of welfare for the poor—"of getting something for nothing"—forgot Jesus's maxim that God's bestowal of blessings and misfortunes was morally indiscriminate. Hard work, self-improvement, meritocracy, pluralism—all fell in Wills's serial demolition of liberal totems and taboos. Whether laissez-faire purists or New Deal reformers, liberals were Pharisees "scoring a game of spiritual effort and merit badges." Likewise, the American Church (too many of whose members were, in Wills's view, the most ardent devotees of the liberal faith) stood implicated in a plot of falsity and pretense. Throughout *Bare Ruined Choirs*, Wills blasphemed treacly and rotting piety—the "cheap faith" that Bonhoeffer despised—with the new breed's abrasive but cleansing refusal of sentimentality. Just as he belittled the "chromium graces" of Wallace's resentful and racist supporters in *Nixon Agonistes,* Wills castigated "the mother too pious to be intimidated into mere goodness," the ways for "the family that prays together to prey upon itself." The bloated body of American Catholicism (of American Christianity, Wills implied) had feasted for too long at the tables of the military-industrial order. "Thus did the preconciliar church prosper and grow fat." Like the rest of America, the Church, "to know life," had to die; it had, in fact, "a lot of dying to catch up on." Slaughtering this sacred cow was thus "a holy task, the destroying of idols."[40]

Wills also critiqued the New Left and the new breed. He was unimpressed by the intellectual caliber both of SDS (the Port Huron Statement he dismissed as "unoriginal and derivative" (derivative in part, he might have added, from undigested theological sources) and of theologians such as Cox, whose work struck him as a farrago of fads, a "confession of lost energies." More pointedly, Wills perceived that both the New Left and the new breed reflected as much as they opposed their nemeses. The New Left's ideal of authenticity, of complete mastery of the self, revealed its essentially liberal conception of selfhood as "an interiorization of the market." Indeed, it caricatured consumer culture and business ideology, wherein maximum expansion and the free play of forces ensured fulfillment. Likewise, Cox delivered his ode to Camelot, Wills wrote sardonically, in "the voice of confident research." Wills saw the gravest threat to both movements in self-absorption and therapeutic drift. Without standards of evaluation and self-criticism outside of personal engagement, the New Left's enshrinement of experience, he pointed out, "drastically *limits* experience"—a retardation Wills noted among renegade Jesuits on the upper West Side. Begun with the best intentions, their liturgical innovations had become ill-prepared, "quick prepandial get-togethers," while their mission to the poor, unconnected to any doctrinal coherence or organizational discipline, had degenerated into "therapy for themselves" rather than "a field for any coordinated apostolate." Much of post-Vatican II religious culture, larded with "sermons as lifeless as before, but with different clichés," moved Wills to disappointment rather than celebration.[41]

Still, after a decade of newfangled clichés, Wills turned to one of the oldest Christian verities as the final hope for the nation's future. Though he loathed Nixon's duplicity and meanness, Wills affirmed that the only way to fight fire was with the water of the spirit. "We must not," he admonished, "despise Nixon, but forgive him," for in doing so we also would "absolve ourselves."[42] Wills urged a magnanimity that, in ever shorter supply as the turn of the decade approached, did not appear to be summoned by calls to secularity.

"Exodus, Immersion, and Resurrection": People's Religion, Liberation Theology, and Identity Politics

By the late 1960s, the vogue for secularity had crested and passed, and some new breed intellectuals sought expiation and clemency among their brethren in the pews. They embarked on what Cox dubbed a search for "people's religion," varieties of religious experience and practice that, they hoped, possessed critical and political resources neglected in the rush for secularity. Their quests converged with the appearance of "liberation theology" from Latin America, a broad and amorphous effort among theologians to integrate Christian theology and Marxist praxis. Rooted in seminaries and universities and in base communities of the rural poor, liberation theology seemed to promise both intellectual novelty and the prospect of a religious-popular front of intellectuals and the people.[43] Yet, while liberation theology and people's religion revived this ideal, it also reflected the metamorphosis of authenticity into therapeutic identity politics.

The turn to people's religion was in part a response to the conservative disaffection of churches. The gathering storm arrived in the early 1970s, and reports of its scope and intensity proliferated. Asking *Why Conservative Churches Are Growing* (1972), the Protestant sociologist Dean Kelley attributed the appeal of "evangelical" or "fundamentalist" churches, especially among the young, to the very doctrinal clarity and ecclesial discipline that repelled the new breed. Though not oblivious to the sexual and racial conservatism that characterized these churches, Kelley confirmed Hadden's view that liberal parishes and clergy lacked both integrity of purpose and effective mobilization. The erosion of liberal Protestantism was, Kelley concluded tersely, "probably not reversible." Catholic conservatives—many of whom were disappointed acolytes of Vatican II—were more acerbic. Yet, while magazines such as *Triumph* printed eloquent dementia about hordes of guitar-strumming vandals desecrating sanctuaries, some conservatives made more sophisticated analyses. Chronicling *The Decline and Fall of Radical Catholicism* (1971), historian James Hitchcock indicted new breed Catholics for their use of "a democratic rhetoric to mask an elitist conception of religious reform."[44]

People's religion also partook of an adverse shift in postindustrial discourse. Waves of dissent from more liberal and technocratic forms of postindustrial theory—the counterculture, Black Power, women's liberation, the "discovery" of the working class—struck at the authority of a white, male professional-managerial elite, demanding that the world not, in Todd Gitlin's words, be "signed, sealed, and delivered over to the powers of instrumental reason." The new visibility of the working class in particular revealed the persistence of very unsecular modes of religion. Directed, humiliated, and embittered by professional power, the protagonists of Robert Coles's *The Middle Americans* (1971), Studs Terkel's *Working* (1972), and Richard Sennett and Jonathan Cobb's *The Hidden Injuries of Class* (1972) all spoke for a working-class world of stubborn devotion to family, neighborhood, and religion—loyalties compromised and threatened by the secularity of the postindustrial world.[45]

Intellectuals experienced yet another round of disenchantment with science and technology. Peering uneasily into a future of technologically ingenious nihilism, Daniel Bell leavened *The Coming of Post-Industrial Society* (1973) with moral critique. The "social alchemist's dream" of a rational and humane society had been confounded, in his view, by the cantankerousness of human nature and politics. Later, seeking resolutions to *The Cultural Contradictions of Capitalism* (1976), Bell looked longingly to "religions of incorporation"—communities with strong sacral codes—to moderate desire and champion social justice in liberal democracies. Lewis Mumford ended his assault on "the myth of the machine" in 1970 with a plea for a religious conversion analogous to the Christian transformation of a decrepit imperial Rome. "The God who saves us" from nuclear and ecological havoc, he speculated, "will not descend from the machine; he will rise up again in the human soul." The more even-tempered economist Robert Heilbroner gestured toward religion in his bleak *Inquiry into the Human Prospect* (1974). Conceding the manifest failure of capitalist civilization to "satisfy the human spirit," Heilbroner doubted that the secular left could uproot the system without plumbing "the nature of man in ways much more courageous" than those traced by humanism. A more humane postindustrial world needed a recovery of preindustrial elements, he thought, especially the practices of tradition and ritual.[46]

Other intellectuals produced a more explicitly religious brand of postindustrial dissent. While debunking "the myth of objective consciousness"—the secular and pragmatic mentality of experts—Theodore Roszak rummaged through spiritual history in search of alternative traditions. Yet, if Roszak enlisted William Blake, Zen masters, and tribal shamans as guides out of the waste land, he offered no clear alternative symbolic or political economy to replace those of "objective consciousness," whereas his desperate eclecticism typified the commodity spirituality then ascending in American religious culture. Often mentioned with, but very different from Roszak, the renegade priest Ivan Illich, director of the Center for Intercultural Documentation in Cuernavaca, Mexico, rooted his celebrated diatribes against schooling, industrial technology, and modernization schemes in an ideal of popular religion. The "convivial society" Illich evoked in *Celebration of Awareness* (1970) and *Tools for Conviviality* (1973) featured a spiritually and technically literate people, brethren-artisans possessing the means of salvation and production. Just as "management could be done away with" by "eliminating the machinery . . . and the demands for output that give it sway," so the "vanishing clergyman" could disappear forever by handing more of his pastoral and liturgical duties to the laity. In a convivial workplace and a democratic church, Illich wrote, "there is little need for replacing the chairman of the board."[47]

Illich cleared the way for the British Labour economist E. F. Schumacher, whose oft-maligned but popular *Small Is Beautiful* (1973) provided a sustained religious argument against centralization, technical progress, and expertise. Though noted for his chapter on "Buddhist economics," Schumacher defended smallness in a manner more befitting Catholics such as Chesterton, Gill, and Day, peppering his book with references to the Epistles, the Beatitudes, scholastic philosophy, and papal encyclicals. Although committed to politics and social reconstruction, Schumacher insisted that "metaphysical reconstruction"—the clarification of fundamental convictions—was primary. Indifference to metaphysics, he argued, caused rapacious and reckless action, enshrined the false virtues of "avarice and precaution," and sanctioned the accumulation that despoiled the natural world and degraded the skills of workers. Attention to metaphysics revealed the world's divine origins and promoted health, beauty, dexterity, and charity. Turning to Aquinas's definition of a person as one "creatively, usefully, and productively employed with both his hands and his brains," Schumacher called for the replacement of mass production with "production by the masses" and the development of an intermediate or "democratic people's technology" that joined technical sophistication and artisanal artistry. Often derided as a sage of the granola set, Schumacher relied on Catholic principles of personalism and subsidiarity to suggest a basis for a popular religious politics of ecology, technics, and culture.[48]

Created by new breed black theologians and religious officials, "black theology" both indicated their frustration with the freedom movements and represented their hope for a popular religious politics uniting intellectuals and the churches—a front of "theologians, preachers, and others in the oppressed community," as James H. Cone of Union Theological Seminary described it. Black theology arose in part out of what many among the younger black religious intelligentsia considered the exhaustion of King's moral and political energy. Advocates of "Black Power," they believed, confronted more realistically the stubbornness of white racism, recognized an implicit whiteness in the ideal of integration, and demanded the hard currency of power over the bad credit of love. (James Forman's 1969 "Black Manifesto," in which he called for "reparations" from white churches, made this demand concrete.) Joseph Washington had broached suspicion of King's appeal to the white middle class in 1964, warning that racism's "demonic irrationality" might well run deeper than the civil rights movement could fathom. Indeed, the historian Vincent Harding surmised four years later, white racism was a "night of terror" that "seems too dark for King to enter." In the white secular city—in "the bowels of the technological society" that white theologians hosannaed—King's God, Harding noted acridly, "seems no less dead than anyone else's."[49]

God lived in black theology as the judge and liberator leading blacks on their exodus from an American Egypt. The central message of the biblical tradition was liberation, black theologians argued, the deliverance of oppressed peoples from bondage. Since God always stood by the lowly and smote the oppressor, then God became "black" in the circumstances of American history, as did those who joined blacks in their revolutionary struggles. "To receive God's revelation," Cone wrote in *Black Theology and Black Power* (1969), was to "become black with God by joining with God in the work of liberation." Furthermore, God's deliverance commenced "in the history of a particular community": the church, a people "called into being," Cone argued in *A Black Theology of Liberation* (1970), "by the power and love of God to share in his revolutionary activity for the liberation of man."[50]

Cone's assertion that this church now existed only among blacks marked black theology as an ambiguous religious form of identity politics. Black theologians insisted on the corrupting whiteness of the inherited Protestant social tradition and placed African-American experience at the center of theology. Black identity was "the ground out of which we spring," as Harding put it. Yet black life and history could endow black theology with an imagery whose power shattered racial boundaries, as when Cone jolted readers with his comparison of the infant Jesus's manger to "a beer case in a ghetto alley." Numerous references to Barth, Tillich, Niebuhr, and other white theologians testified to the continuity of black theology with the Protestant social gospel tradition. Moreover, since black theologians often defined "blackness" as a historical condition and not as an ontological or physiological reality, they implied a fluidity to racial identity that permitted whites to join the ranks of the revolutionary church. "To be black," Cone explained in *Black Theology*, meant "your heart, your soul, your mind, and your body are where the dispossessed are." Whites could become black by virtue of a "conversion wherein they are given, by the Holy Spirit, a new way of thinking and acting in the world."[51] Thus, at its most generous, black theology pointed toward the transcendence of racial identity through a spiritual agency present only in religious community.

To the degree that black theology essentialized race, however, it plunged into the therapeutic quicksand that mired identity politics. If blackness required, as Cone asserted further, immersion in "the totality of black experience," then whites faced an almost impossibly exacting standard. Indeed, Cone insisted on a racial standard not only for religious inclusion but also for God as well. "Black theology refuses to accept a God who is not identified totally with the goals of the black community." Aside from Cone's facile assumption of a monolithic black community, this aggressively raced ecclesiology melted Christian faith into racial identity, undermining the religious foundation of black theology and delivering it, in white Niebuhrian fashion, to the world of *realpolitik*. In Fanonian tones, Cone wrote of the emancipatory exhilaration of heaving "a live Molotov cocktail into a white-owned building"—with or without people inside, Cone did not specify. ("There is more to getting rid of evil than burning buildings," Cone shrugged, but "one must start somewhere."[52])

Fearing such a descent into chauvinism and bitterness, other black theologians pleaded with their comrades to remember the promised land beyond race. God, Major Jones reminded Cone in 1971, redeemed the mighty as well as the weak, joining the struggle "on both sides, seeking to transform both the oppressed and the oppressor." Harding urged reliance on God's indiscriminate grace to cultivate more enduring and cosmopolitan loyalties than those summoned in Cone's incendiary gospel. Grace, he predicted, would allow blacks and whites to discern "the reality of [those] creative, healing forces" that harnessed "the power of resurrection" to those of passion and death. The Kingdom, Harding wrote, awaited not those who sought "the glory of blackness" but those who fought "for the sake of the Lord."[53]

In a manner similar to black theologians, the Catholic Michael Novak ordained ethnicity as a new vessel for the social gospel. Taking to the road as a journalist and working as a campaign aide for Sargent Shriver in 1972, Novak settled on the "great unwasped"—the non-Anglo-Saxon, non-Protestant, mostly white working and lower middle classes—as the vanguard of a more humane postindustrial world, the catalysts for a union of intellectuals and people. God no longer spoke, to Novak at least, in the cadences of cultural and managerial professionals. Trying to steer between an emerging populist conservatism and a discredited left, Novak now identified not the publishers but "the hard hats," as he put it in *Christianity and Crisis* in 1971, as the "closest matrix of his revelation."[54]

Novak explored this new matrix in a spate of books that appeared in the early 1970s: *Ascent of the Mountain, Flight of the Dove* (1971), *All the Catholic People* (1971), and the remarkable *The Rise of the Unmeltable Ethnics* (1972). "The new industrial state," he claimed in *Ascent of the Mountain,* was now "a type of religion," a "religion of modernity" busily constructing a "new type of person, a new sense of reality, a new kind of story, . . . a new set of symbols." This faith, an individualized spirituality bereft of institutional embodiment but indispensable for the frictionless functioning of the market, had as its clerics the technical and managerial corps of capitalism. If postindustrial capitalism was a religion, it could be resisted only by another religion, and so Catholics, he wrote in *All the Catholic People,* "must elaborate the political consequences of their personal and communal positions; they cannot pretend that political expression and theological position are separate and independent."[55]

Novak himself elaborated his position in *Unmeltable Ethnics*. Determined to counter conventional wisdom about the chauvinism of ethnic identity, Novak argued that modernity itself was a project of covert ethnic particularism. The culture of modernization inhabited by professional elites—the culture of "specialization, objectivity, and technical proficiency"—was the imperious culture of the white Anglo-Saxon Protestant, a "superculture" that routinely "disguises [its] ethnicity." Whether demolishing black neighborhoods to build superhighways or napalming Vietnamese villages to build liberal capitalist democracies, the avatars of progress—the "political project of the professional classes" and "the operating mythology of experts"—exacted an escalating toll for the provision of knowledge, comfort, and freedom.[56]

Yet, in Novak's view, most intellectuals maintained a haughty distance from the lives of ordinary people. Even if liberals recoiled from their own superculture, they sought redemption in the social planning and psychological expertise that were case studies in supercultural pride and insensitivity. New Left radicals struck Novak as no less fantastical than adherents of fundamentalist theology, right down to their increasingly sanguinary visions of apocalypse. Both liberals and the New Left suffered from the peculiar "bigotry of the intellectual," a detestation of the values and customs of the less educated. Vice President Spiro Agnew's alliterative sound bites would never have resonated as strongly and widely as they did, Novak believed, had intellectuals spoken "for those to whom it is their vocation to give voice."[57]

The only effective challenge to the superculture lay among "the great unwasped": Poles, Italians, Greeks, and Slovaks—"PIGS" as Novak fondly, if infelicitously, dubbed them—as well as blacks, Hispanics, and Jews. (Novak also gestured weakly but politely toward the women's movement, with its critique of male medical professionals, as a potential ally in the revolution of the "unwasped.") Still largely working class, and still resistant to immersion in the melting pot simmered and stirred by cultural and managerial professionals, these unmeltable ethnics would bring salvation to the desiccated land of the WASP. Novak's claims for the superior wisdom of the "unwasped" turned pivotally on the religious, particularly Catholic, component of these identities. The "pagan quality" he loved in the religious cultures of southern and eastern European ethnics—"communion with God through the things that are—red soil upon the fingers, white clouds across vast skies"—Novak figured as "Catholic." "Perhaps no belief about man is more deeply Catholic than a fundamental and radical trust in the goodness of creation." Novak's "politics of smallness" to reorganize the political and technical structures of postindustrial society recalled the decentralist, sacramental radicalism of British distributists and Catholic Workers. Calling for decentralized industries, workers caucuses, and dispersed technology to disassemble the inhuman scales of modern factory life, Novak envisioned the restoration of the sacramental and artisanal character of labor and techniques. Since technology "is, after all, an art," workers should be artists. Such a "Catholic" program suggested that the only way to reunite intellectuals and people was to erase their social and political distinction through the fusion of mental and manual labor, of physical and imaginative life.[58]

Still, Novak's desire to effect a common front of the people and an intelligentsia reborn in the waters of populism left him without critical principles and thus prey to the rhetoric and politics of malice. "Genuine hatred as a political phenomenon," he thought, "is easier to make constructive than feigned compassion, condescension, or morality." Novak need only have looked at the ineffectual nihilism of Black Power to see the folly of this assertion. Penetrating when directed at the dehumanizing impact of professional expertise and bureaucratic homogenization, Novak's insistence on the truth of the senses and emotions could sanction malevolence as well. Cone's use of the Molotov index of blackness found its parallel in Novak's endorsement of an "unwasped bloody law" to complement the blue laws of the WASP superculture. For the "feeling of changing history and mastering the environment," WASP ladies, Novak suggested, should strangle cats with their bare hands,

WASP gentlemen should behead chickens, and women who procured abortions should "publicly grind an aborted fetus underfoot."[59] Grounding politics in the mores of the subaltern could unleash the demons as well as the better angels of our nature.

The conceptual and political flaws in Novak's search for a postindustrial populism stemmed from a failure of religious imagination, especially his indifference to American Catholicism as an alternative site of politics and culture. Throughout *Unmeltable Ethnics*, Novak—like Cone— viewed religion more as a constitutive element of ethnic identity than as an identity in its own right, consonant with but also critical of other loyalties and commitments. The idea that a people's religion should be the conscience as well as the partner of populism—and that therefore religious intellectuals had a legitimately critical role to play in a revival of popular politics—disappeared in Novak's newfound enthusiasm for the people. Novak explicitly downgraded the critical and prophetic talents of religious intellectuals, urging them instead to become humble tribunes. The Catholic intellectual should "not enlighten," he wrote in *All the Catholic People* but should "give tongue to," be a "*vox populi,* not [an] *avant-garde.*" The religious intellectual, in this view, became a ventriloquist's doll, not a "connected critic" in Michael Walzer's formulation, who educated and upbraided his people into new possibilities.[60]

Moved by their own sense of frustration and promise, female theologians roused by the women's liberation movement composed "feminist theology" as another avenue from the academy to the subaltern. As Rosemary Ruether asserted in *Liberation Theology* (1972), feminist theology originated among members of a larger alienated intelligentsia who served as a "crucial mediating force for translating the protest of the oppressed into an opportunity for repentance in the dominant society." "Women of all 'types,' " Daly announced in *Beyond God the Father* (1973), now formed a "sisterhood for liberation." Like Rauschenbusch at the dawn of the social gospel, feminist theologians conceived their work as a democratic enterprise that flowed "not downward from the experts," Yale's Letty Russell wrote in 1974, but "upward and outward from collective experience."[61]

Feminist theologians resembled black theologians in a number of ways, placing the experience of oppression at the center of the social gospel and accenting liberation as the theme of the Christian tradition. Ruether, for instance, argued that "the sexual model" was "the basic model for all types of social oppression." Also, like the "blackness" that was not exclusively black, femininity did not always reside in women. The desire for the abolition of gender rested on the acknowledgment of gender as a social and historical, not ontological, reality. Yet most feminists balked at making sexual oppression and gender the regulative concerns of the social gospel. Like all genuine revolutionaries, feminists, Ruether cautioned, must "affirm a universal humanity as the ground of their own self-identity." This universalist affirmation was commitment to the church, "the place," Ruether claimed in *Liberation Theology*, "where a new humanity is begun."[62]

This universalist commitment contributed to feminist theology's remarkably generous and reparative political imagination, one that contrasted with the sometimes sanguinary visions of Cone or Novak. (Daly, for one, considered black theology too "fiercely biblical and patriarchal," too much "religion as a gun.") Ruether urged women to remember that the oppressed, perhaps especially the oppressed, lived under God's judgment. In fact, she argued in *Liberation Theology*, "the dehumanization of the oppressor is really their primary problem." Christians who engaged in vituperation and bloodshed "abort their possibilities as a liberating force for the oppressors, and derail their own power to liberate themselves." Feminist recasting of traditional imagery, especially of the Virgin Mary, reflected this position. While the dogma of Mary's immaculate conception certainly reflected male sexual anxiety, Ruether asserted, it also recalled the "unfallen state of humanity." Far from enjoining submission to male authority, the Magnificat prefigured "the beloved community and its anticipation of final redemption."[63]

Yet feminist theology wavered between religion and gender as the centerpiece of Christian political identity. The very strength of feminist theology—the recovery and transfiguration of the experience of oppression—could be its weakness—the substitution of that oppression into the fulcrum of identity. As Ruether and Russell realized, sisterhood could not by itself provide the moral imagination pivotal to the eradication of sexual oppression. "All ideologies," Russell emphasized, "must be subject to constant critique in the light of the gospel," and that gospel remained, in Ruether's words, "the social mandate of human history." Only through a religious commitment outside the bounds of sisterhood could feminist Christians effect the reparative liberation they promised. The danger that a purely therapeutic—and therefore unnecessarily divisive—identity politics would ensue from an exclusive emphasis on gender became evident in Daly. In *Beyond God the Father*, Daly flatly repudiated Christianity in favor of the "cosmic covenant of sisterhood," carried in an ark borne through history by witches and goddess devotees. Modern adherents to the covenant would reject the "rigidly structured" codes and "phallic morality" of Christianity, Daly exulted, insisting on their "individuality and diversity"—keywords soon to be siren sweet to the ears of (mostly male) corporate leaders.[64] If in Ruether the feminist vision drew vitality and strength from a broader vision of redemption, in Daly it withered into solipsism.

Even Cox, former enthusiast for secularity, traveled far and wide in search of a people's religion. Beginning in the late 1960s, Cox visited churches, cities, and villages in southwestern United States, Latin America, sub-Saharan Africa, and India, noting the persistence of Marian devotion, popular festivals, holy men, spirit possessions, and other doggedly unsecular practices. Expecting premodern religious life to be a reactionary opiate, Cox found instead an effortless mixture of traditional religion and popular radicalism. In Santa Fe, for instance, Jesus shared mural space with Emiliano Zapata, Our Lady of Guadalupe, and Che Guevara. The popular religion of Santa Fe, Cox speculated, was linked with those of black pentecostals praising King and Malcolm and Appalachian fundamentalists singing hymns as they marched against the mine owners. Perhaps, he realized, liberal Protestants and Catholics had "adjusted too quickly to the categories of modernity" and had become too hasty in hosing down the "occasional tongue of fire."[65]

Dividing the wheat from the chaff in premodern religion—separating the "use and abuse of people's religion" as he categorized them in *The Seduction of the Spirit* (1973)—Cox played variations on themes rehearsed in black and feminist theology. If "to be radical," he wrote, meant to be "touched by the pain and hope of the poor," then being a radical *theologian* meant "to listen to the singing and the sobbing in the religions of the poor." Cox partially recanted his allegiance to the secular technopolis, imploring Christians to retrace their steps and reclaim what they could of "the Christianity that informed Western culture before the rise of mercantilism, capitalism, or industrialization"—the Christianity of the Middle Ages, reconfigured in quasi-monastic communities that were "co-ed" and "ecologically balanced." Looking for release from the increasingly intolerable burdens of the secular city, people would flock, Cox believed, to updated versions of Cluny and Monte Cassino, communities "explicitly based on the rites and ethics" of churches. These liberated communities, Cox hoped, would blur the liberal demarcation between church and state and avoid the internecine identity politics he discerned in black and feminist theologies. He shrewdly observed how identity politics narrowed the range of human sympathy and compounded rather than resolved the dilemmas of liberal individualism. As more groups emerge to define the self, Cox wrote, "the less power any one of them has to give . . . a full identity or claim full loyalty." In Cox's view, this unsorted multiplicity of identities issued not in some postmodern state of *jouissance* but rather in a dull ache of homelessness. "No one owns my soul, but I want to belong somewhere." Selves and communities grounded in race or sexuality were at best transitional, Cox hoped, "forms the struggle for liberation takes, not the form of the liberated community itself."[66]

Like feminist theologians such as Ruether, Cox could envision the transcendence of identity politics because he retained some conviction of the political priority of religious identity and therefore of the critical primacy of theology. Just as the former celebrant of secularity now contended that "outside the church, *some* church, there is no salvation," so he endorsed theology as a "stubborn holdout" in the intellectual life of the West, a great refusal to accept subordination in the "one-dimensional flatland" of technical and managerial power. Theology's most important contribution to contemporary culture lay precisely in its "intractable irrelevance," its "downright inconvenience" to those obsessed with pragmatism and efficiency. Because theology remained so apparently mired in the past, it stood as a mocking, genuinely subversive reminder that "the present moment is not all there is" and thereby occupied the best position from which a truly different future could be imagined.[67] For theology posed the question not of what was humanly possible but of what was divinely ordained for human nature and destiny.

Yet, like other champions of people's religion, Cox could not overcome the lack of popular American roots. The dearth of American figures in Cox's cosmopolitan pantheon foreshadowed the preoccupation of American acolytes of liberation theology with non-American peoples, a romance that compensated for their political impotence at home. The rootless, abstract quality of Cox's people's religion also indicated its therapeutic import. Agreeing at one point with George Santayana that "to try to be religious 'in general' is like trying to speak language in general. It cannot be done," Cox hinted at the grammar and syntax of just such a religious vernacular. The religious person of the future, Cox thought, must be a versatile actor, adept at playing and relinquishing a variety of equally expendable roles. Like "a vaudeville trouper or a repertory player," the new religious man would "master the technique of moving in and out of different religious traditions without losing his psyche in the process." Unencumbered by fidelity to a single tradition, he could be "a Sioux brave, . . . a neolithic hunter, . . . a Krishna, . . . a sixteenth-century Carmelite nun."[68] Cox's protean religious ideal pointed to a purely therapeutic selfhood, a personality increasingly detached from ever more rickety institutional foundations, engaged in a commodity spirituality, jostling in a moral and existential marketplace.

If Cox reflected the happy transformation of faith into the consuming vision—the fruition of the Jamesian "will to believe"—Wills articulated the melancholy hope of a critic connected to a popular religious tradition. Looking for heroes in *Bare Ruined Choirs*, Wills lit on the unlikely figure of Daniel Berrigan. Although the Jesuit's pronounced disdain for most American Catholics would earlier have put off Wills, Berrigan's newly cultivated self-criticism (occasioned in part by his trials as a fugitive from the FBI in 1970) and his resolute traditionalism prompted Wills to elevate him into a model Christian. "How shall we speak to our people, to the people everywhere?" Berrigan asked in the *Village Voice* in 1971. Reproving radicals (and especially the Weathermen) for their alienation, Berrigan warned that "we must never refuse, in spite of their refusal of us, to call them our brothers and sisters." For Wills, Berrigan came to embody the traditional basis of prophetic politics, the insistence on "roots instead of rockets, tradition over progress, tragedy over arrogance." In looking not to Teilhard de Chardin but to St. John of the Cross as his guide through the dark night of the nation's soul, Berrigan reminded Wills that "prophecy looks simultaneously backwards and forwards, assigns men fresh tasks with an urgency born of ancient obligation."[69]

But prophets, Wills remembered, also were obliged to and from a people; they could not discharge their "ancient obligation" in the desert. "Responsibility to a people certifies the prophet," Wills asserted, and Berrigan, in his view, met this standard. Here Wills's admiration got somewhat the better of his critical acumen. Berrigan's career illustrated the modern American tension between progressive intellectuals—prophets, in Christian terms—and the people they desire to educate, chastise, embrace. If Berrigan had a witness to share, he also had a people to engage, and it was not at all clear that Berrigan's belated recognition of accountability fulfilled the popular requirements of his mission. However, as Wills implied, Berrigan's prophetic mandate, like that of the whole new breed, had come at a moment when the churches themselves were in a state of decomposition, revival, and recombination. Perhaps, Wills hoped, the people themselves were slowly becoming ready to receive Berrigan and his descendants. The new attention to the Bible in Protestant and Catholic churches—to the "close public study of the scripture" that constituted a "meditation on the community's biblical origins"—might, he speculated, generate a new political culture. Reflecting on "Exodus, and Immersion, and Resurrection," Americans might rebuild from the rubble of their bare ruined choirs. "One lives, if at all, by parturition, the pangs and sundering; by successive resurrections, life out of death."[70]

Yet Wills sensed that the bare ruined choirs would never be rebuilt to their former stature. Which was just as well; rebirth implied that the social gospel of the future would resemble but not mirror its ancestor. Besides, having seen through the threadbare vestments of evasion and accommodation, and having taken the measure of the anguish that would attend the death and rebirth of the social gospel, Wills knew that the institutions of American Christianity were living on borrowed time and that the moment was not propitious for a full renaissance: "it is time," Wills concluded, "to go underground."[71] With Wills, Berrigan, and others, the communion of American saints entered a new time, as rich in promise as it was shrouded in shadow.

†

Epilogue

In his *City of God*, St. Augustine told a tale of two cities which, in the wake of liberal and socialist narratives of progress, might still read well as the fundamental account of history. The story of humanity, Augustine explained, unfolded as the sometimes peaceful, sometimes antagonistic, always tense relationship between the "earthly city" and the "heavenly city." Epitomized in the state (for Augustine, the Roman Empire), the earthly city encompassed the entire range of human institutions and achievements—all, however, marked by a "lust of domination" kindled by a lack of trust in God. Always troubled, the peace and justice of this city could be neither genuine nor lasting, since they rested on practices of compromise and coercion that mimicked true harmony and postponed the next round of conflict. Even its magnificent cultural, scientific, and technological artifacts—evidence, Augustine argued, of "the blessings [it] enjoys" from God—only compounded the city's vexations, since they so often slaked the lust for power and tantalized humanity with glimpses of a perfect world. The earthly city's corrupted marvels reflected the state of sin, a perversion or misdirection of our divinely bestowed powers. The sorrow of the sinful earthly city lay, in Augustine's view, not in a deliberate commitment to evil but in a futile aspiration to goodness. "We commit sin to promote our welfare, and it results instead in our misfortune."[1]

Because the city understands its welfare wrongly, the residents will acquiesce in any social order as long as they enjoy "material prosperity . . . the glory of victorious war, [and] the security of peace." Bored by politics and enthralled by commodities, the earthly city is, in its purest form, a managerial paradise and a boundless marketplace. The rulers cultivate not the morality but "the docility of their subjects," and legitimize themselves not as ethical models but as "providers of material satisfactions." Augustine noted that, among the wealthy and the poor, affluence bolstered a belief in self-possession, the individualist distillation of the larger city's lust for power. "Anyone should be free to do as he likes about his own, or with his own, or with others, if they consent."[2] As a pure culture of secularity, the unfettered market in goods and selves soon became, in Augustine's view, the shallow grave of religious and republican virtue.

Living in the midst of this imperium were the citizens of another realm—the "heavenly" or "celestial city" whose peace and justice the earthly city strove unsuccessfully to emulate. Born in the earthly city, they had discovered the sickness of its lust for dominion and self-possession and embarked on a therapeutic journey that would never end on this side of paradise. Salvation was a form of therapy, Augustine argued, a "healing and restoration" that cures the soul of sin and sets it on its proper course. Always migrants, Christians were a caravan of convalescents whose life on the road anticipated the heavenly city whose fullness would flourish only at the end of time. "The City," Augustine sighed, "is on pilgrimage until the time of its kingdom comes." While on earth, however, its citizens lived in a spirit far different from the one that prevailed among their prodigal brethren. Renouncing self-possession, they created a beloved community where the self expanded and healed through its own effacement and dispersal, for goodness, being a "possession enjoyed more widely by the united affection of partners," was enjoyed by any one person "in ampler measure in proportion to his ability to love his partner in it." Thus the pilgrim city should not divide into warring factions and states as did its earthly imitators. Instead, calling out "citizens from all nations," they formed a cosmopolitan family, "a society of aliens speaking all languages." Though resident aliens in their secular abodes, Christians obey the laws and participate in all the mundane activities of the earthly city, making "use of the earthly peace . . . [only] so far as may be permitted without detriment to true religion and piety." That qualification made Christians potential critics and dissenters in their earthly homes. Yet, even when they had to oppose the ways of the earthly city, Christians had to defy them in a manner that itself prefigured heaven's "perfectly ordered and perfectly harmonious fellowship in the enjoyment of God." Heaven itself, Augustine asserted, was in part a renewed and healed earth, "a material and spiritual paradise" where with "physical bodies" we "observe God in utter clarity and distinctness," and where unbounded trust assured a psychic transparency that allowed our minds to "lie open to mutual observation." In the heavenly city, all things and selves are enjoyed in common.[3]

As citizens of the two cities, American Christian intellectuals drafted two charters of coexistence between the earthly and celestial realms in the twentieth century. They lived in the earthly regime of liberal, corporate capitalist modernity. Faced with the ingenuity and magnitude of this earthly city, many Christian intellectuals generated a critical lineage that looked toward a "Christianized," democratic reconstruction of corporate modernity. But in relying on an intellectual gospel unencumbered by religious convictions, they began the attrition of theology as a form of social and cultural criticism, folded the ideals of "personality" and "beloved community" into the expertise of social and psychological specialists, and ensured the secularization of the American left. When Harvey Cox asserted in 1965 that "the church has no power to heal" he stated boldly what Reinhold Neibuhr had only implied, and what Walter Rauschenbusch had never imagined—that the heavenly city had lost and even transferred its therapeutic powers to the earthly metropolis.[4]

Other Christian critics comprised a lineage for whom theology remained the master language of selfhood, social thought, and cultural criticism. Insisting on the divine likeness of selfhood, these critics resisted or sought to modify secular therapeutic practices, contested the reduction of "personality" to a monad of market individualism, and advanced forms of personalism that located the regeneration of self and society under the aegis of religion. They recycled the artisanal critique of industrial capitalism through theology, and rearticulated demands for worker's control secularized in the language of anarchism, syndicalism, or participatory democracy. They contended that this artisanal, therapeutic, and democratic order that erased the lines separating mental and manual labor could flourish only is so far as it arranged its affairs on the basis of faith, hope, and charity. The heavenly city was, in their view, neither a chamber of the private self nor an ideal to come "after the revolution," but a present, anticipatory reality. "All the way to heaven is heaven," as Dorothy Day put it.[5]

The history of the American Christian critical tradition contains lessons that are all the more urgent as the disarray of the contemporary left becomes more visible every day. The fractious condition of the left has not resulted entirely from the disintegration of the New Deal, the discrediting of socialism, the rise of "identity politics," and the resurgence of the right. Although the secular left has relied heavily on the traces of a moral language and sensibility baptized in the Christian tradition, it has now adopted a moral libertarianism that enshrines a purely therapeutic ideal of "choice." As the religious traces have diminished in number and strength, the shift in moral imagination denoted by "choice" has won the left a Pyrrhic victory—a widespread deference to those shibboleths of the marketplace that denature the passion necessary to confront social injustice. For moral libertarianism—the ideology of "self-possession" endemic in the earthly city—partakes of the very market ethos the left otherwise vilifies. One could even argue that the discursive and ethical proximity of this libertarianism to late-capitalist business ideology has made the left into a cultural subsidiary of the corporate order. Struggles for justice, freedom, and peace can be waged only by those willing to assert judgments and demands that are more substantive and uncompromising than the hollow ideal of choice can sustain.[6]

Yet even a recovery of this moral language would still leave unresolved "that unhappy ambiguity as to just how values were created" that Randolph Bourne identified long ago. The post-modernist left might reflexively (and not unjustifiably) dismiss such a concern as the residue of "essentialism." Andrew Ross, for instance, mounts an assault on "humanism" that is symptomatic of the post-modernist repudiation of universalist ideals. Providing a bill of depredations traceable to the raced and gendered ideals of scientific rationality and technological control—ecological devastation, male supremacy, ethnocentrism, genocide—Ross pronounces humanism "corrupt" and opposes its nomination as "the ideal candidate for contesting the claims of technocracy." But Ross presents his incontrovertible evidence without the exculpatory material that might redeem it.[7] The harshest rebukes to Western pride have come from religious injunctions to humility, forgiveness, and love that are inseparable from the Western humanist tradition. I would invite Ross and other post-modernist critics to consider many of this book's subjects, if not quite as comrades, then surely as precursors and sympathizers. If St. Francis, Las Casas, and the Jesuits of Paraguay were Christian critics of their brethren's hubris and bigotry, then Vida Scudder, Richard Niebuhr, Dorothy Day, and Martin Luther King, Jr. merit places of honor in the lineage of humanism. Immune to the narcissism of difference that has become identity politics, Christian critics asserted universalist, essentialist claims about the human likeness unto God.

Many of those weary of identity politics display indifference and hostility to Bourne's fundamentally metaphysical challenge. Richard Rorty, for instance, rejecting "the whole idea of holding reality and justice in a single vision," attempts to retain simulacra of Christian values without affirming the metaphysical claims on which they rest. Rorty's "post-modernist bourgeois liberalism," with its vision of the good life as a "Kuwaiti bazaar" of lifestyles, sanctions the sort of self-possession at the heart of the earthly metropolis. At the same time, Rorty espouses the broad-minded and generous "civic religion" expounded by Walt Whitman and John Dewey. The "common faith"—a revival of the progressive religiosity that inspired Dewey, Josiah Royce, and other Progressives—could, Rorty believes, leaven a democratic nationalism that links left intellectuals and other Americans in a project of social reconstruction. But to do so, Rorty asserts, we must separate "the fraternity and loving kindness urged by the Christian Scriptures from the idea of supernatural parentage, immortality, providence, and—most important—sin." These theological antiques must be consigned, in his view, to the flea market of "privatized religious belief, not the sort of religious belief that produces churches, especially churches which take political positions."[8] We might even, he writes generously, think of St. Francis and Eugene Debs as "members of a single movement."

As this book suggests, however, Christian ethics, Christian theology, and Christian churches cannot be divorced without trivializing and disabling all three. Rorty's meager and misleading renderings of Christian ideas indicate as much. "Loving kindness" is not quite the same as charity; "fraternity" is not quite the same as church. And sin (which Rorty lamely psychologizes into "self-loathing"), because it denotes the perversion of blessings, is actually an ironic testament to human possibility, for any being who can violate the will of God must surely partake of divinity.[9] Indeed, the Christian conviction that men and women represent the image and likeness of God speaks more forcefully to the problems of "identity politics" than Rorty's call to remount the barricades of class. As Protestant and Catholic acolytes of "personality" and "personalism" realized, *all* politics is identity politics, and their claim that Christianity embraced the whole of life—and therefore disciplined any politics of class, race, gender, sexuality: the whole array of "subject positions,"—was a claim that the fundamental issue was the basis of human selfhood. Bourne's question about origins leads inexorably to the question of God.

The need to pose this impertinent question has been recognized by a number of intellectuals. Cornel West, for instance, aims to reinvigorate the left through a "prophetic pragmatism," one that avoids the foundering of Deweyan and Jamesian varieties "on the rocks of cultural conservatism and corporate liberalism." At the same time, bemoaning "the severing of ties to churches, synagogues, temples, and mosques by the left intelligentsia," West affirms a public role for religion and locates sites where a grand alliance of intellectuals and other Americans could be consummated. Yet after offering a glimpse of how theology could reconstruct the pragmatist and left traditions, West retreats from the implication that the secular left has some learning to do from religion. Prophetic pragmatism, while it "harks back to the Jewish and Christian prophets," neither "requires a religious foundation nor entails a religious perspective"—an assertion about the nature of prophecy that would have puzzled Amos and Isaiah, not to mention Jesus.[10]

Others, such as Christopher Lasch, urged the introduction of sophisticated religious ideas into the nation's public intellectual culture. Well aware that most of what passes for "religion" in public life is either pabulum or drek—"family values," school prayers, avowals of piety offensive primarily for their blandness—Lasch desired the sort of vigorous theological disputation that Orestes Brownson thought indispensable to both religion and democracy. Lasch appreciates (more clearly than "communitarian" friends of religion like Robert Bellah's *Habits of the Heart* group) that religious conviction necessarily chafes under protocols of "civility," and that only contention could sharpen the mind, humble the fanatic, and avoid the moral vacuity to which liberal societies were especially prone. "Politics," Lasch wrote in an approving gloss on Brownson, "ought to address moral issues of transcendent importance, even at the risk of disturbing the peace."[11] Because it would surely direct attention to the inequities and inanities of our Kingdom of Customer Service, a high quality of religious controversy probably would disturb the peace of those committed, whether out of contentment or fatigue, to keeping our politics as titillating and brainless as possible.

However, even Lasch's political imagination, defined by "limits and hope," will not, I think, suffice as the basis for a renewal of religious and especially Christian social thought in our time. Beholden to a halfway covenant that kept him poised uneasily between his secular vocation as a social critic and his growing attraction to theology, Lasch remained reluctant to address the metaphysical claims that grounded the work of Brownson, Jonathan Edwards, Reinhold Niebuhr, and other Christian intellectuals he admired. Although "limits and hope" restated Christian convictions about human finitude and the goodness of creation, they did not do justice to two other articles of faith—humanity's likeness to God and the social recovery of that likeness from sin. The principle of divine likeness underwrites the varieties of human possibility, while the assertion that faith thrives only in the practice of communities and traditions guards against the abstraction into which even Lasch's notion of "religion" often fell.[12]

More promising, perhaps, will be the search among a growing number of Anglo-American religious intellectuals for a renewal of "church" that resurrects the largest ambitions and quandaries of the Christian critical tradition. The church "does not *have* a social ethic," as one of the more acerbic of their number writes; "the church *is* a social ethic." The church is a "polis," in their view, a community with a distinctive way of life—hence, a distinctive politics and culture. Recalling the "Black International" envisioned by H. Richard Niebuhr, the personalist "cells of good living" and the "base communities" lauded by liberation theologians, the partisans of "radical orthodoxy" see the church as a disciplined historical agent on an emancipatory mission, a cosmopolitan movement that does not acknowledge nation, race, gender, or class as the ultimate ground of identity. Although sometimes chained to militantly (and ahistorically) anti-liberal stances (especially on sexual matters), orthodox radicals swear fidelity first to principles and historical communities, not to encrusted moral and political positions.[13]

I suspect that any renewal of the Christian critical tradition—as well as any worthwhile reformulation of the left's cultural and political responsibilities—will depend greatly on these orthodox radicals. Still, they have yet to articulate a coherent and popular agenda of their own, as Alasdair MacIntyre's *After Virtue* (1981) portended. Like the earliest Christians who forswore allegiance to the Roman Empire and "ceased to identify the continuation of civilization and moral community with the maintenance of that imperium," a new moral vanguard must, MacIntyre argued, reject the secularizing dominion of capitalism, declare the bankruptcy of secular oppositional movements, and construct "new forms of community" in which "the intellectual and moral life can be sustained." However, despite MacIntyre's claim that this position entails a "contemporary politics of relevance"—a politics that fuses the virtues of "Trotsky and St. Benedict"—orthodox radicals have yet to translate their sacramental vision into sketches of technology, political economy, or sexuality.[14] At the same time, their critique of modernity still needs to be leavened by an appreciation of how Christianity has been a mainstay and beneficiary as well as a casualty of modern science and culture. Otherwise, they risk the fate of becoming a beloved clique.

Building the beloved communities demanded by orthodox radicals is made all the more difficult by the separation of religious intellectuals from their brethren, a gulf that covers much the same distance between secular left academics and their potential publics. As Leon Fink writes, intellectuals "have trouble dislodging themselves from their own sheltered perches to make honest, let alone efficacious, contact with the world of ordinary citizens." Along with their secular counterparts, most of the critical religious intelligentsia work as symbolic professionals of post-Fordist capitalism. Teaching in universities or seminaries, writing primarily for academic readers, and attending conferences in agreeable and occasionally sumptuous settings, they live the lives of mobile, harried, e-mail–deluged professionals whose commitments curtail the time and labor available for a "religious-popular" front. At the same time, the proliferation of "theologies"—"liberation theologies" based on sexuality, race, or gender, as well as "post-liberalism" or "radical orthodoxy"—parallels the creative and debilitating multiplication of identity politics. Besides, all of these approaches remain concentrated in the academy, with only the most diluted impact in the pulpits or the pews.[15]

The gulf between the classrooms and the pews exacerbates the decomposition of religious institutions and their replacement by privatized, purely therapeutic collages of belief and practice. American religious life increasingly reflects the most powerful centrifugal forces of late capitalist culture—the elevation of "personal choice" as the *summum bonum* of the good life, and the attendant dislodging of moral and religious symbols from historical traditions. Both liberal Protestantism and Roman Catholicism have been shaken and remade by these disintegrative forces. Liberal Protestantism lives in genteel spiritual poverty, a wheezing *rentier* entailed to a dilapidated estate and a dwindling historical capital. It shows, even sympathetic observers write, "many signs of tired blood—levels of orthodox belief are low, doubt and uncertainty in matters of faith common, knowledge of the Scriptures exceedingly low." At the same time, the condition of American Catholicism is only a little less critical. Beneath much of the post-Vatican II period's bland and reflexive optimism about the "laity," one can discern a growing uneasiness about the capacity of that laity to undertake the social reconstruction to which they have been exhorted by papacy, hierarchy, and reformers. As one of the American Church's more astute observers has written, the post-Vatican II generation displays a "meager knowledge of Catholicism," speaks "an impoverished religious vocabulary," and knows little or nothing of papal encyclicals and pastoral letters on economics, racism, or nuclear weapons.[16]

As post-modern America's two premier religious cultures hemorrhage in numbers and authority, they produce what one writer has dubbed a "generation of seekers." Exemplified in the array of New Age practice or in the "Sheilaism" examined in *Habits*, these freelance montages of religious beliefs increasingly characterize the American religious landscape.[17] On the one hand, the triumph of this therapeutic mode of spirituality—of "commodity spirituality"—while it lessens the social and political tensions introduced by more "orthodox" claims to exclusive moral legitimacy, also depletes the evangelical energy necessary for any social gospel. And yet, in the scented candles, Zen gardens, and personal disciplines, the seeking betokens an irrepressible longing for a different world—one that is fulfilling as well as peaceful, enchanting as well as abundant, cinnamon-sweet as well as just. If social Christianity ever again bears the hope treasures of the heavenly city, it will have revived not only the language of repentance, self-sacrifice, and justice, but also the language of possibility, personality, regeneration, and transfiguration. For the therapeutic ethos so terribly deformed by consumer culture is deserving, not only of ridicule and summary dismissal, but of repair and redemption.

Therefore, despite the embarrassment of riches it continues to shower on ignorance, credulity, and superstition, and despite its dreadful record of subservience to the sinister interests of the earth, Christianity remains a motherlode of the moral imagination essential for deliverance from the glittering imperium of American capitalism. Against the hubris of secular skepticism, it counterpoises faith—not a facile and uncritical security, but "intelligence illuminated by love," as Simon Weil described it. Against the fragile enthusiasm of optimism, it offers hope—the conviction that creation is good, and that human history will have a glorious denouement. Against the ascendant corporate regime, its plenitude guarded by the sentries of meanness and merit, its subjects whipped with the riding crops of profit and production, it sets charity—the practice of making and giving without thought of return, the demolition of all principles and orders of birth, anatomy, and desert. In the mundane routines of the earthly city, it awaits those redemptive moments when, in struggle and love, we glimpse the heavenly metropolis. For the clouds of Good Friday always part for the clear light of Easter.

+

NOTES

INTRODUCTION

1. Ralph Adams Cram, *The Great Thousand Years* (Boston: Jones, 1918), 30–35.
2. On the professional-managerial class, see Barbara and John Ehrenreich, "The Professional-Managerial Class," in *Between Labor and Capital,* ed. Pat Walker (Boston: South End Press, 1979), 5–45, Barbara Ehrenreich, "The Professional-Managerial Class Revisited," in *Intellectuals: Aesthetics, Politics, Academics,* ed. Bruce Robbins (Minneapolis: University of Minnesota Press, 1990), 173–185. On the cultural apparatus, see C. Wright Mills, "The Cultural Apparatus," in *Power, Politics, and People: The Collected Essays of C. Wright Mills,* ed. Irving Louis Horowitz (New York: Oxford University Press, 1963), 405–22. "Secular vocations" comes from Bruce Robbins, *Secular Vocations: Intellectuals, Professionalism, Culture* (New York: Verso, 1993). Although he acknowledges that "the modern concept of vocation has its roots in theology" and that professionalism "has taken over some of its associations with religious or charismatic authority," Robbins considers it "an error both about the past and about the present" to characterize professional expertise as a substitute for religious authority (24). Yet, if a secular vocation is a practice that "appeals to (and helps refashion) public values," then it is surely a mode of cultural authority that depends, to a large degree, on some religious residue. See, on this score, Edward Shils, "The Intellectuals and the Powers: Some Perspectives for Comparative Analyses," in *The Intellectuals and the Powers and Other Essays* (Chicago: University of Chicago Press, 1968), 3–23, and Andrew Ross, *No Respect: Intellectuals and Popular Culture* (New York: Routledge, 1989), 215–223.
3. Jackson Lears, *No Place of Grace: Antimodernism and the Transformation of American Culture, 1880–1920* (New York: Pantheon, 1981), sets American antimodernism clearly but not exclusively in the context of liberalizing religious trends. Among historians of American religion in the antimodernist camp, see especially the evangelical Protestant George M. Marsden, *The Soul of the American University: From Protestant Establishment to Established Unbelief* (New York: Oxford University Press, 1994), and George M. Marsden, *The Outrageous Idea of Christian Scholarship* (New York: Oxford University Press, 1996). Among Catholics, see Christopher Shannon, *Conspicuous Criticism: Tradition and the In-*

dividual in American Social Thought, From Veblen to Mills (Baltimore: Johns Hopkins University Press, 1996), Alasdair MacIntyre, *After Virtue: A Study in Moral Theory* (South Bend, Ind.: University of Notre Dame Press, 1981), 222–223; see also Alasdair MacIntyre, *Whose Justice? Which Rationality?* (South Bend, Ind.: University of Notre Dame Press, 1988).

4. Casey Nelson Blake, *Beloved Community: The Cultural Criticism of Randolph Bourne, Van Wyck Brooks, Waldo Frank, and Lewis Mumford* (Chapel Hill: University of North Carolina Press, 1990), Alan Wald, *The New York Intellectuals: The Rise and Decline of the Anti-Stalinist Left from the 1930s to the 1980s* (Chapel Hill: University of North Carolina Press, 1987), Gregory Sumner, *Dwight Macdonald and the politics Circle: The Challenge of Cosmopolitan Democracy* (Ithaca, N.Y.: Cornell University Press, 1996), Daniel Horowitz, *Vance Packard and American Social Criticism* (Chapel Hill: University of North Carolina Press, 1994).

5. James T. Kloppenberg, *Uncertain Victory: Social Democracy and Progressivism in European and American Thought, 1870–1920* (New York: Oxford University Press, 1986), James T. Kloppenberg, "Pragmatism: An Old Name for Some New Ways of Thinking?" *Journal of American History* 83 (June 1996), 100–140, Robert B. Westbrook, *John Dewey and American Democracy* (Ithaca, N.Y.: Cornell University Press, 1991), Andrew Feffer, *The Chicago Pragmatists and American Progressivism* (Ithaca, N.Y.: Cornell University Press, 1993), James Livingston, *Pragmatism and the Political Economy of Cultural Revolution, 1850–1940* (Chapel Hill: University of North Carolina Press, 1993); see also Cornel West, *The American Evasion of Philosophy: A Genealogy of Pragmatism* (Madison, Wisc.: University of Wisconsin Press, 1988), Richard Rorty, *Achieving Our Country: Leftist Thought in the Twentieth Century* (Cambridge, Mass.: Harvard University Press, 1998). For an overview, see Richard J. Bernstein, "The Resurgence of Pragmatism," *Social Research* 59 (Winter 1992), 813–840. Less favorable historical evaluations of the pragmatist tradition include Edward Purcell, *The Crisis of Democratic Theory: Scientific Knowledge and the Problem of Value* (Lexington: University of Kentucky Press, 1973), and John P. Diggins, *The Promise of Pragmatism: Modernism and the Crisis of Knowledge and Authority* (Chicago: University of Chicago Press, 1994).

6. Christopher Lasch, *The True and Only Heaven: Progress and Its Critics* (New York: W. W. Norton, 1991), Christopher Lasch, *The Revolt of the Elites and the Betrayal of Democracy* (New York: W. W. Norton, 1994), esp. 213–246. See also Michael Kazin, *The Populist Persuasion* (New York: Basic Books, 1995).

7. Blake, *Beloved Community*, 142, Jackson Lears, *Fables of Abundance: A Cultural History of Advertising in America* (New York: Basic Books, 1994), 403.

8. Leon Fink, *Progressive Intellectuals and the Dilemmas of Democratic Commitment* (Chapel Hill: University of North Carolina Press, 1998), 9; see also Leon Fink, Stephen T. Leonard, and Donald M. Reid (eds.), *Intellectuals and Public Life: Between Radicalism and Reform* (Ithaca, N.Y.: Cornell University Press, 1996), Michael Walzer, *The Company of Critics: Social Criticism and Political Commitment in the Twentieth Century* (New York: Basic Books, 1987), Kevin Mattson, *Creating a Democratic Public: The Struggle for Urban Participatory Democracy in the Progressive Era* (University Park: Pennsylvania State University Press, 1998), and Russell Jacoby, *The Last Intellectuals: American Culture in an Age of Academe* (New York: Basic Books, 1987).

9. Philip Rieff, *The Triumph of the Therapeutic: Uses of Faith after Freud* (New York: Harper and Row, 1966); see also the collection of Rieff's writings in *The Feeling Intellect: Selected Writings of Philip Rieff*, ed. Jonathan Imber (Chicago: University of Chicago Press, 1990). Jean-Christophe Agnew, "The Consuming Vision of Henry James," in *The Culture of Consumption: Critical Essays in American His-*

tory, 1880–1980, eds. Richard Wightman Fox and T. J. Jackson Lears (New York: Pantheon, 1983), 69–74, 97. I have dealt with these issues at somewhat greater length in "Heal Me: 'Personality,' Religion, and the Therapeutic Ethic in Modern America," *Intellectual History Newsletter* 21 (Fall 1999), 31–40.

10. H. Richard Niebuhr, "Towards a New Other-Worldliness," *Theology Today* 1 (April 1944), 85.

1. "This Day Is the Scripture Fulfilled"

1. Frank Mason North, "The Church and Modern Industry," cited in Elias Sanford, *The Origin and History of the Federal Council of Churches* (Hartford, Conn.: Scranton Press, 1916), 494–503.
2. John Ireland, "The Mission of Catholics in America" (1889), in *The Church and Modern Society,* vol. 1 (Chicago: D. H. McBride, 1897), 79; John A. Ryan, *A Living Wage: Its Ethical and Economic Aspects* (New York: Macmillan, 1906), 48.
3. John Ireland, "The Church and the Age" (1893), in *The Church and Modern Society,* vol. 1 (Chicago: D. H. McBride, 1897), 121.
4. G. K. Chesterton, *What I Saw in America* (New York: Dodd, Mead, 1922), 11–12; Henry F. May, "The Religion of the Republic," in *Ideas, Faiths, and Feelings: Essays on American Intellectual and Religious History, 1952–1982* (New York: Oxford University Press, 1983), 171–80. For the broad historical sketch in this paragraph I have drawn on Robert T. Handy, *A Christian America: Protestant Hopes and Historical Realities* (New York: Oxford University Press, 1971), and George M. Marsden, *Understanding Fundamentalism and Evangelicalism* (Grand Rapids, Mich.: William B. Ferdmant, 1991), 9–50. On Protestant hegemony in higher education, see George M. Marsden, *The Soul of the American University: From Protestant Establishment to Established Nonbelief* (New York: Oxford University Press, 1994), and Julie A. Reuben, *The Making of the Modern University: Intellectual Transformation and the Marginalization of Morality* (Chicago: University of Chicago Press, 1996), 36–43. On evangelical sponsorship of American science, see George M. Marsden, "Evangelicals and the Scientific Culture: An Overview," in *Religion and Twentieth-Century American Intellectual Life,* ed. Michael J. Lacey (New York: Cambridge University Press, 1989), 23–48. On the evangelical character of populist radicalism after the Civil War, see Herbert G. Gutman, "Protestantism and the American Labor Movement: The Christian Spirit in the Gilded Age" (1966), in *Work, Culture, and Society in Industrializing America* (New York: Vintage, 1976), 79–117, John L. Thomas, *Alternative America: Edward Bellamy, Henry George, Henry Demarest Lloyd, and the Adversary Tradition* (Cambridge, Mass.: Harvard University Press, 1983), 34–36, 212–215, and Bruce Palmer, *"Man Over Money": The Southern Populist Critique of Industrial Capitalism* (Chapel Hill: University of North Carolina Press, 1980), 37–38, 127–128.
5. This portrait of theological liberalism and modernism relies on William R. Hutchison, *The Modernist Impulse in American Protestantism* (Durham, N.C.: Duke University Press, 1991 [1976]), and Bruce Kuklick, *Churchmen and Philosophers: From Jonathan Edwards to John Dewey* (New Haven: Yale University Press, 1985). On Protestant thought at this time, see Claude Welch, *A History of Protestant Thought in the Nineteenth Century,* 2 vols. (New Haven: Yale University Press, 1972, 1985). On the Protestant establishment, see William R. Hutchison, "Protestantism as Establishment," in *Between the Times: The Travail of the Protestant Establishment in America, 1900–1960* ed. William R. Hutchinson (Cambridge, Mass.: Harvard University Press, 1989), 3–18. I have borrowed the term

"covenant theology" from Perry Miller, *The New England Mind: From Colony to Province* (Boston: Beacon Press, 1961 [1953]), esp. 21–26.

6. On the "intellectual gospel," see David Hollinger, "Justification by Verification: The Scientific Challenge to the Moral Authority of Christianity in Modern America," in *Religion and Twentieth-Century American Intellectual Life* ed. Michael J. Lacey (New York: Cambridge University Press, 1989), 116–135. Marsden, "Evangelicals and the Scientific Culture," in Lacey, *Religion and Twentieth-Century American Intellectual Life*, 41, emphasizes the affinity between liberals and evangelicals. On professionalism, see Burton J. Bledstein, *The Culture of Professionalism: The Middle Class and the Development of Higher Education in America* (New York: W. W. Norton, 1976),Thomas Haskell, ed. *The Authority of Experts: Studies in History and Theory* (Bloomington: Indiana University Press, 1984). Reuben, *The Making of the Modern University*, 61–187, discusses the new "secular" curricula that facilitated the emergence of professionalism.

7. Livingston, *Pragmatism*, 83; Robert Crunden, *Ministers of Reform: The Progressive Achievement in American Civilization, 1889–1920* (New York: Basic Books, 1982), 90. The classic account of the formation of the American intellectual is Christopher Lasch, *The New Radicalism in America, 1889–1965: The Intellectual as a Social Type* (New York: Vintage, 1965). I have consulted the following historiography of the Social Gospel: James Dombrowski, *The Early Days of Christian Socialism in America* (New York: Columbia University Press, 1936), C. Howard Hopkins, *The Rise of the Social Gospel in American Protestantism, 1865–1915* (New Haven: Yale University Press, 1940), Henry F. May, *Protestant Churches and Industrial America* (New York: Harper and Row, 1949), and Peter J. Frederick, *Knights of the Golden Rule: The Intellectual as Christian Social Reformer in the 1890s* (Lexington, Ky.: University of Kentucky Press, 1976). David B. Danbom, *"The World of Hope": Progressives and the Struggle for an Ethical Public Life* (Philadelphia: Temple University Press, 1987), 80–111, 187–191, discusses "Christian Progressivism"; Susan J. Curtis, *A Consuming Faith: The Social Gospel and Modern American Culture* (Baltimore: Johns Hopkins University Press, 1991). Robert T. Handy, ed. *The Social Gospel in America* (New York: Oxford University Press, 1966), is a well-selected anthology. On social gospelers as Progressives, see David W. Noble, *The Paradox of Progressive Thought* (Minneapolis: University of Minnesota Press, 1958), 103–124, 157–173, 228–245, Jean B. Quandt, *From the Small Town to the Great Community: The Social Thought of Progressive Intellectuals* (New Brunswick, N.J.: Rutgers University Press, 1970), 10–20, 67–75, Richard Wightman Fox, "The Culture of Liberal Protestant Progressivism, 1875–1925," *Journal of Interdisciplinary History* 23 (Winter 1993), 639–660, Daniel T. Rodgers, *Atlantic Crossings: Social Politics in a Progressive Age* (Cambridge, Mass.: Harvard University Press, 1998), 62–65.

8. See Jackson Lears, *No Place of Grace: Antimodernism and the Transformation of American Culture, 1880–1920* (New York: Pantheon, 1981), 7–47, esp. 43, on liberal Protestantism as a "religion *banalise*." See also Josiah Royce, *The Philosophy of Loyalty* (New York: Macmillan, 1908), 241–242, 245–248; on Royce's work, see R. Jackson Wilson, *In Quest of Community: Social Philosophy in the United States, 1860–1920* (New York: Wiley, 1968), 159–169. Walter Lippmann, *Drift and Mastery: An Attempt to Diagnose the Current Crisis* (New York: Greenwood Press, 1977 [1914]), 113–119, Randolph Bourne, "This Older Generation" (1915), in *The Radical Will: Selected Writings, 1911–1918* ed. Olaf Hansen (Berkeley: University of California Press, 1992 [1977]), 161, 167. On Bourne's religious life in Bloomfield, see Walzer, *Company of Critics*, 41–43.

9. George C. Coe, "Can Religion Be Taught?" (1909), cited in William McGuire King, "An Enthusiasm for Humanity: The Social Emphasis in Religion and Its

Accommodation in Protestant Theology," in Lacey, *Religion and Twentieth-Century American Intellectual Life,* 57; Eugene Lyman, in King, "Enthusiasm for Humanity," 67. On "expressive-experiential" conceptions of religion, see George Lindbeck, *The Nature of Doctrine: Religion and Theology in a Post-Liberal Age* (Philadelphia: Westminster, 1984), 31–49. Talal Asad, *Genealogies of Religion: Discipline and Reasons of Power in Christianity and Islam* (Baltimore: Johns Hopkins University Press, 1993), 27–54, discusses the invention of "religion" in anthropological discourse.

10. Frances Willard, *Women and Temperance* (Hartford: Park Publishing, 1884), 42; George Herron, *Social Meanings of Religious Expression* (New York: Johnson Reprint, 1969 [1896]), 178; Walter Rauschenbusch, *A Theology for the Social Gospel* (New York: Macmillan, 1917), 100, 102–103, 142. For discussions of "personality" that aim to recover it from consignment to consumer culture, see Blake, "The Young Intellectuals and the Culture of Personality," *American Literary History* 1 (Fall 1989), 510–534, Blake, *Beloved Community,* 51, Fox, "Liberal Protestant Progressivism," and Eugene McCarraher, "Heal Me."

11. On social selfhood, see Livingston, *Pragmatism,* 72–83, Marshall J. Cohen, *Charles Horton Cooley and the Social Self in American Thought* (New York: Garland, 1982). Josiah Royce, *The Problem of Christianity,* 2 vols. (New York: Macmillan, 1913), I: xix–x, 163–213. Bruce Kuklick, *The Rise of American Philosophy: Cambridge, Massachusetts, 1860–1930* (New Haven: Yale University Press, 1977), 385–398, provides a clear but technical critical exposition of this work; Randolph Bourne, "Trans-National America" (1915), in Hansen, *The Radical Will,* 264. On the meaning of "beloved community" to the "young Americans," see Blake, *Beloved Community,* 76–156. Jane Addams, *Democracy and Social Ethics* (Cambridge: Harvard University Press, 1964 [1902]), 69–70, 276–277; see also Jane Addams, "The Subjective Necessity of Social Settlements" (1892), in *The Social Thought of Jane Addams* ed. Christopher Lasch (Indianapolis, Ind.: Bobbs-Merrill, 1965), 40–42. On Addams's religious views, see Crunden, *Ministers of Reform,* 22–25, and Jean Bethke Elshtain, "A Return to Hull House: Reflections on Jane Addams," in *Power Trips and Other Journeys: Essays in Feminism as Civic Discourse* (Madison: University of Wisconsin Press, 1990), 5; Addams later noted that the "household service" held for a time by Hull House residents quickly became a "diluted form of worship" in *Twenty Years at Hull House* (New York: Signet, 1981 [1910]), 307–308; Lippmann, *Drift and Mastery,* 152–157; Herbert Croly, *Progressive Democracy* (New York: Macmillan, 1914), 397. On Croly's spiritual odyssey, see David W. Levy, *Herbert Croly of the New Republic: The Life and Thought of an American Progressive* (Princeton, N.J.: Princeton University Press, 1985), 32–37, 65–67, 290–295; C. Lasch, *The New Radicalism,* 11, seems to argue against a connection of Progressivism and religion by asserting that Protestant moralism existed "in a theological void."

12. Royce, *The Problem of Christianity,* vol. 1: xix, vol. 2: 430–431. Lasch, *True and Only Heaven,* 356–359, makes a powerful but unconvincing case for the "religion of loyalty" as the model for a politics of "particularism." Where Lasch commends "appreciation of loyalty for its own sake, without regard to the ends on behalf of which it was enlisted," I would think that the ends are precisely what dictate any "appreciation."

13. John Dewey, "Christianity and Democracy" (1892), cited in Westbrook, *John Dewey,* 79. Westbrook discusses Dewey's brief career as a liberal Protestant philosopher (22–36). William James, *The Varieties of Religious Experience* (New York: Penguin, 1985 [1902]), 31, 110–113, 175, 455–456; *The Will to Believe and Other Essays in Popular Philosophy* (Cambridge, Mass.: Harvard University Press, 1979 [1897]), 150; William James, *Pragmatism* (New York: Prometheus Books,

1991 [1907]), 132. George Santayana referred to pragmatism as a "new theology" in "The Genteel Tradition in American Philosophy," in *The Genteel Tradition and Nine Other Essays* (Lincoln, Neb.: Bison Books, 1998 [1922]), 59–60. The discussions of James that inform my view of his work on religion are found in West, *American Evasion*, 54–68, Diggins, *Promise of Pragmatism*, 148–156, and Alfred Kazin, *God and the American Writer* (New York: Alfred A. Knopf, 1997), 161–175. The promise of pragmatism as a medium for religion's readmission into intellectual and public life has elicited considerable but, I think, far too hopeful interest among historians; see, for example, James Kloppenberg, "Knowledge and Belief in American Public Life," in *The Virtues of Liberalism* (New York: Oxford University Press, 1998), 38–58. In my view, Kazin puts the matter best. Stressing that "no one seriously interested in the actual content of religion can doubt that James finally wins us as a fellow soul, not as a believer," Kazin observes that "if you ask James for bread in this matter [of religion], he gives you a stone—meaning an hypothesis" (*God and the American Writer*, 174–175).

14. Randolph Bourne, "Twilight of Idols" (1917), in Hansen, *The Radical Will*, 338–339, 342–343, 346–347. For discussions of this essay, see Blake, *Beloved Community*, 161–164, and Westbrook, *John Dewey*, 186–187, 202–212, 367–369. Westbrook takes refuge in the "obscurity" of Dewey's prewar reflections on the question of values and concludes, in effect, that it was all just a big misunderstanding.

15. On the Protestant lineage of American social science, see Jean B. Quandt, "Religion and Social Thought: The Secularization of Postmillennialism," *American Quarterly* 25 (October 1973), 390–409, Arthur J. Vidich, *American Sociology: Worldly Rejections of Religion and Their Directions* (New Haven: Yale University Press, 1985), Dorothy Ross, *The Origins of American Social Science* (New York: Cambridge University Press, 1991), esp. 102–104, Cecil I. Greek, *The Religious Roots of American Sociology* (New York: Garland, 1992), Susan Henking, "Sociological Christianity and Christian Sociology: The Paradox of Early American Sociology," *Religion and American Culture* 3 (Winter 1993), 49–67, Richard T. Ely, *The Social Aspects of Christianity* (London: Thomas Y. Crowell, 1889), 9, Dombrowski, *The Early Days of Christian Socialism*, 12, Walter Rauschenbusch, *Christianizing the Social Order* (New York: Macmillan, 1907), 144, and Rauschenbusch, *Theology for the Social Gospel*, 5.

16. Willard, *Women and Temperance*, 43; Ely and Bliss, cited in Dombrowski, *The Early Days of Christian Socialism*, 51, 103; Reverdy Ransom, quoted in Calvin Morris, *Reverdy C. Ransom: Black Advocate of the Social Gospel* (Lanham, Md.: University Press of America, 1990), 54; Kevin Gaines notes Ransom's dissent from the philosophy of "racial uplift" in *Uplifting the Race: Black Leadership, Politics, and Culture in the Twentieth Century* (Chapel Hill: University of North Carolina Press, 1996), 97–98; George Woodbey, "The Bible and Socialism" (1904), in *Black Socialist Preacher: The Teachings of Reverend George Washington Woodbey* ed. Philip Foner (San Francisco: Synthesis, 1983), 193–201. On the social gospelers and race, see Ronald C. White, *Liberty and Justice for All: Racial Reform and the Social Gospel, 1877–1925* (New York: Harper and Row, 1990), and Ralph Luker, *The Social Gospel in Black and White: American Racial Reform, 1885–1912* (Chapel Hill: University of North Carolina Press, 1991).

17. Herron, *Social Meanings of Religious Expression*, 111, 117, 122; Leon Fink, *Progressive Intellectuals*, 9.

18. Rauschenbusch, *Theology for the Social Gospel*, 2. On "labor churches," see Elizabeth Fones-Wolf and Ken Fones-Wolf, "Trade Union Evangelism: Religion and the AFL in the Labor Forward Movement, 1912–1916," in *Working-Class Amer-*

ica: Essays on Labor, Community, and American Society Michael H. Frisch and Daniel J. Walkowitz, eds. (Urbana: University of Illinois Press, 1983), 153–184, and Ken Fones-Wolf, *Trade Union Gospel: Christianity and Labor in Industrial Philadelphia, 1865–1915* (Philadelphia: Temple University Press, 1989); on one "people's church," see Kathryn J. Oberdeck, "Religion, Culture, and the Politics of Class: Alexander Irvine's Mission to Turn-of-the-Century New Haven," *American Quarterly* 47 (June 1995), 236–279. For a list of institutional churches, see W. D. P. Bliss, *The New Encyclopedia of Social Reform: Including All Social-Reform Movements and Activities, and the Economic, Institutional, and Sociological Facts and Statistics of all Countries and all Social Subjects* (New York: Funk and Wagnalls, 1908), 629–631; see also Rauschenbusch's comments on institutional churches in *Christianity and the Social Crisis*, 354–355. On the social gospel origins of the settlement movement, see Mina Carson, *Settlement Folk: Social Thought and the American Settlement Movement, 1885–1930* (Chicago: University of Chicago Press, 1990), 10–50, and Elizabeth Lasch-Quinn, *Black Neighbors: Race and the Limits of Reform in the American Settlement House Movement, 1890–1945* (Chapel Hill: University of North Carolina Press, 1993), 47–74. Robyn Muncy, *Creating a Female Dominion in American Reform 1890–1935* (New York: Oxford University Press, 1991), 3–37, overlooks the religious concerns of settlement founders.

19. Rauschenbusch, *Theology for the Social Gospel*, 119–120; Max L. Stackhouse, ed. *The Righteousness of the Kingdom* (Nashville, Tenn.: Abingdon Press, 1968), 149–162. On Rauschenbusch, see Paul Minus, *Walter Rauschenbusch: American Reformer* (New York: Macmillan, 1988). I have also benefited from Lasch's perceptive "Religious Contributions to Social Movements: Walter Rauschenbusch, The Social Gospel, and Its Critics," *Journal of Religious Ethics* 18 (Spring 1990), 7–23.

20. Walter Rauschenbusch, "The New Evangelism," *The Independent* 56 (June 1904), 1057; *Theology for the Social Gospel*, 16–17; *Christianity and the Social Crisis*, 119–120; *Prayers for the Social Awakening* (1910), cited in *Walter Rauschenbusch: Selected Writings* ed. Winthrop Hudson (New York: Paulist Press, 1984), 207–239. On the Rochester meetings, see Matson, *Creating a Democratic Public*, 52.

21. Rauschenbusch, *Christianity and the Social Crisis*, 14–16, 388–400, 409, *Christianizing the Social Order*, 367–368, and contribution to *The Christian Socialist* 11 (March 1914), 12. Lasch, "Religious Contributions," 21, while noting that Rauschenbusch "feared that a proletarian movement uninformed by religious faith would degenerate into bitterness and recrimination," overlooks his emphasis on the church.

22. Rauschenbusch, *Christianity and the Social Crisis*, 409–410, and *Theology for the Social Gospel*, 16–17.

23. Cited in Philip Gleason, *Contending with Modernity: Catholic Higher Education in the Twentieth Century* (New York: Oxford University Press, 1995), 113.

24. Paula Kane, *Separatism and Subculture: Boston Catholicism, 1900–1920* (Chapel Hill: University of North Carolina Press, 1994), 108–144, is a rich description of Catholic medievalism, despite the author's final dismissal of it as a species of "escapism." The most nuanced and even sympathetic account of medievalism is Philip Gleason, "American Catholics and the Mythic Middle Ages," in *Keeping the Faith: American Catholics Past and Present* (South Bend, Ind.: University of Notre Dame Press, 1987), 11–34.

25. The text of *Rerum novarum* can be found in *Catholic Social Thought: The Documentary Heritage*, David O'Brien and William Shannon, ed. (Maryknoll, N.Y.: Orbis, 1992), 14–39.

26. On "Catholic domesticity" and "evangelical Catholicism," see Colleen McDannell, *The Christian Home in Victorian America, 1840–1900* (Bloomington, Ind.: Indiana University Press, 1986), 52–76, 116–126, 136–149, and Jay P. Dolan, *Catholic Revivalism* (South Bend, Ind.: University of Notre Dame Press, 1976), esp. 164–184. On the devotional aspects of this domestic, evangelical Catholic piety, see Ann Taves, *The Household of Faith: Roman Catholic Devotions in Mid-Nineteenth Century America* (South Bend, Ind.: University of Notre Dame Press, 1986). George Santayana, *Character and Opinion in the United States* (New York: Macmillan, 1967 [1923]), 48.

27. Santayana, *Character and Opinion*, 47. On "solidarism," a German-American Catholic form of moral economy, see Philip Gleason, *The Conservative Reformers: German-American Catholics and the Social Order* (South Bend, Ind.: University of Notre Dame Press, 1968), esp. 130–138; on Italian-American anxiety about capitalism, see Robert Anthony Orsi, *The Madonna of 115th Street: Faith and Community in Italian Harlem, 1880–1950* (New Haven: Yale University Press, 1985), 155–160, 191–192. Kane, *Separatism and Subculture*, 104–107, is a brief but lucid discussion of Catholic ambivalence about accumulation.

28. Kane, *Separatism and Subculture*, 145–199, examines Catholic gender ideology. On turn-of-the-century medievalism as an element of "anti-modernism," see Lears, *No Place of Grace*, 142–215; Henry Adams is cited in Lears, *No Place of Grace*, 279–280.

29. John McGreevy, *Parish Boundaries: The Catholic Encounter with Race in the Twentieth-Century Urban North* (Chicago: University of Chicago Press, 1996), 10, 24–25, discusses this "sacramental" quality of ethnic neighborhoods. Dorothy M. Brown and Elizabeth McKeown, *The Poor Belong to Us: Catholic Charities and American Welfare* (Cambridge, Mass.: Harvard University Press, 1997), 51–85, provide an overview of the parish-based Catholic charitable network at the turn of the century.

30. Robert Cross, *The Emergence of Liberal Catholicism in America* (Cambridge, Mass.: Harvard University Press, 1958); Thomas T. McAvoy, *The Americanist Heresy in Roman Catholicism, 1895–1900* (South Bend, Ind.: University of Notre Dame Press, 1963); R. Scott Appleby, *"Church and Age Unite!" The Modernist Impulse in American Catholicism* (South Bend, Ind.: University of Notre Dame Press, 1992). See also R. Laurence Moore, *Religious Outsiders and the Making of Americans* (New York: Oxford University Press, 1986) 51–71, for an exceptionally clear and perceptive discussion, one in which Moore goes so far as to defend the "non-Americanist" position (67–68).

31. John Ireland, "Human Progress" (1892), in *Church and Modern Society*, vol.1: 142; "Labor and Capital" (1903), in *Church and Modern Society*, vol. 2: 357–358.

32. Ireland, "The Church and the Age," in *Church and Modern Society*, vol. 1: 119–121, "Human Progress," in *Church and Modern Society*, vol 1: 153–154, and "The Catholic Church and Liberal Education" (1895), in *Church and Modern Society*, vol 1: 252.

33. On lay trustees, see Patrick Carey, *People, Priests, and Prelates: Ecclesiastical Democracy and the Tensions of Trusteeism* (South Bend, Ind.: University of Notre Dame Press, 1987), and Ireland, "The Mission of the Church in America," in *Church and Modern Society*, vol 1: 99.

34. Ireland, "The Mission of the Church in America," in *Church in Modern Society*, vol 1: 93. Histories of Catholic social thought and action before World War I include Aaron Abell, *American Catholicism and Social Action: A Search for Social Justice, 1865–1950* (Garden City, N.Y.: Doubleday, 1960), 90–188, David O'Brien, *Public Catholicism* (New York: Macmillan, 1989), 124–57, and Mel Piehl, *Break-*

ing Bread: The Catholic Worker and the Origins of Catholic Radicalism in America (Philadelphia: Temple University Press, 1982), 33–52. The best anthology of American Catholic social writing is Aaron Abell, ed. *American Catholic Thought on Social Questions* (Indianapolis: Bobbs-Merrill, 1968).

35. William Kerby, quoted in O'Brien, *Public Catholicism*, 145; "The Priesthood and the Social Movement" (1900), cited in Abell, *American Catholic Thought*, 274–275.

36. John A. Ryan, *Social Doctrine in Action* (New York: Macmillan, 1941), 52–54, and *A Living Wage*, 44–66, 69–70, 188; reviews cited in Patrick Geary, "The Economic Thought of Monsignor John A. Ryan" (Ph.D. dissertation, Catholic University of America, 1953), 27–28; Ely, foreword to *A Living Wage*, xii. On the "living wage" as a sign of a shift in working-class identity from producer to consumer, see Lawrence B. Glickman, *A Living Wage: American Workers and the Making of Consumer Society* (Ithaca, N.Y.: Cornell University Press, 1997), 57–128. Francis L. Broderick, *Right Reverend New Dealer: John A. Ryan* (New York: Macmillan, 1963), is the only biography of Ryan. For an illuminating discussion of Ryan's social thought, see Charles E. Curran, *American Catholic Social Ethics: Twentieth-Century Approaches* (South Bend, Ind.: University of Notre Dame Press, 1982), 26–91.

37. Rauschenbusch, *Christianizing the Social Order*, 26; Bourne, "Socialism and the Catholic Ideal" (1912), quoted and discussed in Blake, *Beloved Community*, 79–82; Bourne, "The Uses of Infallibility" (1917), in Hansen, *The Radical Will*, 502, 503.

38. John A. Ryan, *Distributive Justice: The Rights and Wrongs of Our Present Distribution of Wealth* (New York: Macmillan, 1916), 304–336, *The Church and Socialism and Other Essays* (Washington: Catholic University Press, 1919), 43–44; Joseph Husslein, *The World Problem: Capital, Labor, and the Church* (New York: P. J. Kenedy and Sons, 1919), 209, *Democratic Industry: A Practical Study in Social History* (New York: P. J. Kenedy and Sons, 1919). On the centrality of neoscholasticism to all dimensions of American Catholic intellectual life, see Gleason, "Neoscholasticism as Preconciliar Ideology," *U.S. Catholic Historian* 7 (Fall 1988), 401–411.

39. Husslein, *The World Problem*, 201–231, *Democratic Industry*, 135, 359.

40. Husslein, *Democratic Industry*, 248–249, *The World Problem*, 272–284.

41. On "cultural citizenship," see Blake, *Beloved Community*, 5–6, 76–121, 268. Guild socialist writings include G. D. H. Cole, *Guild Socialism Re-Stated* (London: Methuen, 1920), Mary Parker Follett, *The New State: Group Organization the Solution to Popular Government* (New York: Longmans, Green, 1918), and Croly, *Progressive Democracy*. I follow Lasch's inclusion of Follett and Croly in the "guild socialist" camp in *The True and Only Heaven*, 317–328, 340–342, where he argues that the guild socialist-syndicalist tradition represented the most democratic solution to the problems of "industrial self-government." Lasch notes but does not discuss the contribution of distributists such as Hilaire Belloc and A. J. Penty to this debate. Distributism can be sampled in Hilaire Belloc, *The Servile State* (London: Foulis, 1912) (quote on 150–151), and G. K. Chesterton, *Utopia of Usurers and Other Essays* (Freeport, N.Y.: Books for Libraries, 1967 [1917]). Jay P. Corrin, *G. K. Chesterton and Hilaire Belloc: The Battle Against Modernity* (Athens: Ohio University Press, 1981), is the best study to date of distributism. On Figgis, see Peter D'Arcy Jones, *The Christian Socialist Revival, 1877–1914: Religion, Class, and Social Conscience in Late-Victorian England* (Princeton, N.J.: Princeton University Press, 1968), 275–295.

42. Ryan, *Church and Socialism*, 44; John A. Ryan and Morris Hillquit, *Socialism: Promise or Menace?* (New York: Macmillan, 1914), 41; John A. Ryan, "A Program of Social Reform by Legislation," *Catholic World* 89 (August 1909), 613.

43. Husslein, *Democratic Industry*, 141, 311–330; see also Husslein, *The World Problem*, 209–213. On prewar and wartime debate over "industrial democracy," see Joseph A. McCartin, *Labor's Great War: The Struggle for Industrial Democracy and the Origins of Modern American Labor Relations, 1912–1921* (Chapel Hill: University of North Carolina Press, 1997). See also David Montgomery, *The Fall of the House of Labor: The Workplace, the State, and American Labor Activism, 1865–1925* (New York: Cambridge University Press, 1987), 306–310, which includes a sympathetic discussion of Catholic social thought.

44. Husslein, *Democratic Industry*, 122–124, 135–143, 325–327.

45. Ryan, "A Program of Social Reform," 614; Husslein, *Democratic Industry*, 178–179, 285–286, and *The World Problem*, 272–280.

46. On Scudder, see Frederick, *Knights of the Golden Rule*, 115–140, Lears, *No Place of Grace*, 209–215, Theresa Corcoran, *Vida Dutton Scudder* (Boston: Twayne, 1982), and Susan Lindley, " 'Neglected Voices' and *Praxis* in the Social Gospel," *Journal of Religious Ethics* 18 (Spring 1990), 77–84. Mari Jo Buhle mentions Scudder only briefly in *Women and American Socialism, 1870–1920* (Urbana: University of Illinois Press, 1981), 60. Lears, *No Place of Grace*, 209, acknowledges that Scudder "used Anglo-Catholic sacramentalism as the basis for an assault on Protestant individualism," but does not explore her religious brand of socialist theory.

47. Vida Dutton Scudder, *On Journey* (Boston: J. M. Dent, 1937), 84; on Toynbee Hall, see Standish Meachem, *Toynbee Hall and Social Reform, 1880–1914* (New Haven: Yale University Press, 1987), esp. 37–44; on the Church Socialist League, see Jones, *The Christian Socialist Revival*, 225–302.

48. Vida Dutton Scudder, *The Life of the Spirit in the Modern English Poets* (Boston: Houghton Mifflin, 1896), 143, 145, "A Hidden Weakness in Our Democracy," *Atlantic Monthly* 89 (May 1902), 641, "Woman and Socialism," *Yale Review* 3 (April 1914), 456, and *Socialism and Character* (Boston: Houghton Mifflin, 1912), 187.

49. Scudder, *Socialism and Character*, vii, 134, 176, 350–352, and Vida Dutton Scudder, *Social Ideals in English Letters* (Boston: Houghton Mifflin, 1898), 306–309.

50. Scudder, *Social Ideals*, 7–45, 166, 249, *A Listener in Babel* (Boston: Houghton Mifflin, 1902), 316, and "A Hidden Weakness," 641. See also "Democracy and Society," *Atlantic Monthly* 90 (September 1902), 349, and "Democracy and the Church," *Atlantic Monthly* 90 (October 1902), 524.

51. Michael Williams, *American Catholics in the War, 1917–1921* (New York: Macmillan, 1921), 89, 91–92, 159, 249; on Williams and American Catholicism after the war, see William M. Halsey, *The Survival of American Innocence: American Catholicism in An Age of Disillusionment, 1920–1940* (South Bend, Ind.: University of Notre Dame Press, 1981), 37–60. On the National Catholic War Council, see Elizabeth McKeown, *War and Welfare: American Catholics and World War I* (New York: Garland, 1988).

52. The Bishops' Program forms an appendix to John A. Ryan, *Social Reconstruction* (New York: Macmillan, 1920), 217–237; for an analysis, see Joseph McShane, S.J., *"Sufficiently Radical": Catholicism, Progressivism, and the Bishops' Program of 1919* (Washington: Catholic University Press, 1986). The Federal Council of Churches of Christ, *The Church and Industrial Reconstruction* (New York: Macmillan, 1920), 172. For an analysis, see Donald Meyer, *The Protestant Search for Political Realism, 1919–1941* (Middletown, Conn.: Wesleyan University Press, 1988 [1960]), 19–25.

53. On World War I as a "pentecost of calamity" for Protestant social gospelers, see Curtis, *A Consuming Path*, 179–227.

1. T. S. Eliot, "Gerontion" (1920), in *Collected Poems, 1909–1962* (New York: Harcourt, Brace, and World, 1963), 30, F. Scott Fitzgerald, *This Side of Paradise* (New York: Charles Scribner's Sons, 1920), 260. On the disappearance of God as a theme in modern American literature, see Kazin, *God and the American Writer* 194–253.
2. Reinhold Niebuhr, "The Twilight of Liberalism," *New Republic* 19 (June 14, 1919), 218, John Ryan, "The Bishops' Program of Social Reconstruction," 217.
3. Sherwood Eddy, cited in Handy, *A Christian America* 193. On the demise of industrial democracy and the rise of welfare capitalism, see McCartin, Epilogue, Montgomery, 454–57, Lizabeth Cohen, *Making a New Deal: Industrial Workers in Chicago, 1919–1939* (New York: Cambridge University Press, 1990), 184–211. The following three books offer the standard view of social gospel inertia: Paul A. Carter, *The Decline and Revival of the Social Gospel: Social and Political Liberalism in American Protestantism, 1920–1940* (Ithaca, N.Y.: Cornell University Press, 1956), 29–95, Robert Moats Miller, *American Protestantism and Social Issues, 1919–1939* (Chapel Hill: University of North Carolina Press, 1958), 17–62, and Meyer, *Protestant Search*, 76–165.
4. King, " 'An Enthusiasm for Humanity,' " 49–77, provides an invaluable corrective to the perspectives cited above.
5. Detlev Peukert, *The Weimar Republic* (New York: Hill and Wang, 1990), Joseph Wood Krutch, *The Modern Temper: A Study and a Confession* (New York: Harcourt Brace Jovanovich, 1957 [1929]), Modris Eksteins, *Rites of Spring: The Great War and the Birth of the Modern Age* (Boston: Houghton Mifflin, 1989), 255–261, quote on 256. Perry Anderson, *Considerations on Western Marxism* (London: New Left Books, 1976), 24–37, 49–94, explains "Western Marxism" as the product of revolutionary defeat.
6. Karl Barth, *The Epistle to the Romans* (London: Oxford University Press, 1933 [1919]), Paul Tillich, *The Socialist Decision* (New York: Harper and Row, 1977 [1932]), Jacques Maritain, *Bergsonian Philosophy and Thomism*, trans. Mabelle Andison and J. Gordon Andison (New York: Philosophical Library, 1955 [1913]). On Maritain, see Bernard Doering, *Jacques Maritain and the French Catholic Intellectuals* (South Bend, Ind.: University of Notre Dame Press, 1983). On the new Catholic left, see John Hellman, *Emmanuel Mounier and the New Catholic Left in France, 1930–1950* (Toronto: University of Toronto Press, 1981).
7. Paul Tillich, *The Protestant Era* (Chicago: University of Chicago Press, 1948), 47, Jacques Maritain, *Art and Scholasticism*, trans. J. F. Scanlon (New York: Charles Scribner's Sons, 1949 [1920]), 16, R. H. Tawney, *The Acquisitive Society* (New York: Harcourt, Brace, 1948 [1920]), 161–179; see also R. H. Tawney, *Religion and the Rise of Capitalism* (New York: Mentor Books, 1963 [1926]), 227–235. Thomas J. Haskell, "Professionalism versus Capitalism: R. H. Tawney, Emile Durkheim, C. S. Pierce, and the Disinterestedness of Professional Communities," in *The Authority of Experts: Studies in History and Theory* (Bloomington, Ind.: Indiana University Press, 1984), 185–221, is a useful discussion of Tawney as an acolyte of professionalism.
8. Warren Susman, "Culture and Civilization: The Nineteen-Twenties," in *Culture as History: The Transformation of American Society in the Twentieth Century* (New York: Pantheon, 1985), 105–121, John Dewey, *The Public and Its Problems* (Athens, Ohio: Swallow Press, 1954 [1927]), 142, Walter Lippmann, *Public Opinion* (New York: Macmillan, 1922), 233–249. Other useful accounts of cultural conflict in the 1920s include Lawrence Levine, "Progress and Nostalgia: The

Self-Image of the Nineteen-Twenties," in *The Unpredictable Past: Explorations in American Cultural History* (New York: Oxford University Press, 1993), 189–205, and Lynn Dumenil, *The Modern Temper: American Culture and Society in the 1920s* (New York: Hill and Wang, 1995), 98–249.

9. Charles Beard, "Introduction," in *Whither Mankind? A Panorama of Modern Civilization* (London: Longmans, Green, 1928), v, Charles Beard, "Summary: The Planning of Civilization," in *Toward Civilization* (London: Longmans, Green, 1930), 302, 305, James Harvey Robinson, "Religion," in *Whither Mankind?* 286.

10. Paul Conkin, *When All the Gods Trembled: Darwinism, Scopes, and American Intellectuals* (Lanham, Md.: Rowman and Littlefield, 1998), 141–167. Dumenil, *The Modern Temper*, is better at conveying the ambivalence of secular intellectuals. H. L. Mencken, *Treatise on the Gods* (New York: Alfred A. Knopf, 1930), Sinclair Lewis, *Elmer Gantry* (New York: Harcourt, Brace, 1927), Harry Elmer Barnes, *The Twilight of Christianity* (New York: Vanguard Press, 1929), Edmund Wilson, "T. S. Eliot and the Church of England" (1929), in *The Shores of Light: A Literary Chronicle of the Twenties and Thirties* (New York: Farrar, Straus, and Strong, 1952), 438.

11. Walter Lippmann, *Men of Destiny* (New York: Macmillan, 1927), 45–60, Walter Lippmann, *A Preface to Morals* (New York: Macmillan, 1929), 87–88, 191–210, 326–330.

12. John Dewey, "The American Intellectual Frontier" (1922), quoted in Robert Westbrook, *John Dewey*, 316, n. 39, Dewey, *The Public and Its Problems* (Boulder, Col.: Swallow Press, 1956 [1927]), 143, 184, John Dewey, *The Quest for Certainty* (New York: Minton, Balch, and Co., 1929), 304, John Dewey, *Individualism Old and New* (New York: Minton, Balch, and Co., 1930), 131. On Dewey's work in the 1920s, see Westbrook, *John Dewey*, 231–373, esp. 309–318. See also the deft and insightful discussion in Shannon, *Conspicuous Criticism*, 62–86. Alfred North Whitehead, *Science and the Modern World* (New York: Macmillan, 1925), 265, 269–270, Alfred North Whitehead, *Religion in the Making* (New York: Macmillan, 1926), 15–16, 88.

13. Lippmann, *Preface to Morals*, 47, Krutch, *Modern Temper*, esp. 39–57, John Crowe Ransom, *God without Thunder: An Unorthodox Defense of Orthodoxy* (Hamden, Conn.: Archon Books, 1965 [1930]), 5, 20, 28, 81, 170–171, 299–328; on Ransom, see Daniel Joseph Singal, *The War Within: From Victorian to Modernist Thought in the South, 1919–1945* (Chapel Hill: University of North Carolina Press, 1982), 212–216.

14. Harry Emerson Fosdick, *Adventurous Religion and Other Essays* (New York: Harper and Brothers, 1926), 16. Robert Moats Miller, *Harry Emerson Fosdick* (New York: Oxford University Press, 1985), is the only biography. On the religious depression, see Robert T. Handy, "The American Religious Depression, 1925–1935," *Church History* 29 (Summer 1960), 3–16. For a discussion of American Catholics at this time, see Charles Shanabruch, *Chicago's Catholics: The Evolution of an American Identity* (South Bend, Ind.: University of Notre Dame Press, 1981), 155–187.

15. Dorothy C. Bass, "Ministry on the Margin: Protestants and Education," in *Between the Times*, ed. Hutchison, 48–71, Marsden, *Soul of the American University*, 332–356, Gleason, *Contending with Modernity* , 62–145. For an illustration of centralizing trends in one city, see Edward R. Kantowicz, *Corporation Sole: Cardinal Mundelein and Chicago Catholicism* (South Bend, Ind.: University of Notre Dame Press, 1983); Cohen, *Making a New Deal*, 83–94, discusses Mundelein's war on ethnic religious customs and institutions.

16. Shailer Mathews, *The Faith of Modernism* (New York: Macmillan, 1924), 4, 21–22, 90, Harry Emerson Fosdick, *Christianity and Progress* (New York: Fleming H. Revell, 1922), 175; see also Harry Emerson Fosdick, *Twelve Tests of Character* (New York: Association Press, 1923), 35. Hutchison, *Modernist Impulse*, 257–282, is a judicious account of liberal Protestant theologians' postwar ambivalence about progress. George Shuster, *The Catholic Spirit in America* (New York: Dial Press, 1927), 12–19. On Shuster, see Halsey, 84–98.

    See also Joan Shelley Rubin, *The Making of Middlebrow Culture* (Chapel Hill: University of North Carolina Press, 1991).

17. J. Gresham Machen, *Christianity and Liberalism* (New York: Macmillan, 1934 [1922]), esp. 11–14; on Machen, see D. G. Hart, *Defending the Faith: J. Gresham Machen and the Crisis of Conservative Protestantism in Modern America* (Baltimore: Johns Hopkins University Press, 1994), esp. 59–107. Fosdick, *Adventurous Religion*, 73–74, 258–274, Harry Emerson Fosdick, *The Meaning of Faith* (New York: Association Press, 1921), 313; see also Fosdick, *Twelve Tests of Character*, 67, Mathews, *Faith of Modernism*, 3, Shailer Mathews, *Contributions of Science to Religion* (Chicago: D. C. Appleton, 1924), 374, Harry F. Ward, *Which Way Religion?* (New York: Macmillan, 1931), 108, 186–189. On the fundamentalist-modernist controversy in the 1920s, see George M. Marsden, *Fundamentalism and American Culture: The Shaping of Twentieth-Century Evangelicalism, 1870–1925* (New York: Oxford University Press, 1980), 141–195, and Hutchison, *Modernist Impulse*, 257–287. Bradley J. Longfield, *The Presbyterian Controversy: Fundamentalists, Modernists, and Moderates* (New York: Oxford University Press, 1991), studies the conflict within one denomination.

18. Fosdick, *Twelve Tests of Character*, 8, "The True Economy," editorial, *Commonweal* 2 (June 3, 1925), 92, Shuster, *Catholic Spirit*, 226–229, Michael Williams, *Catholicism and the Modern Mind* (New York: Macmillan, 1928), 222.

19. Fosdick, *Adventurous Religion*, 28, "Organized Womanhood," editorial, *Commonweal* 10 (October 23, 1929), 632–633. On the new woman, Dumenil, *The Modern Temper*, 98–144, esp. 143–144, is a lucid survey. Nancy Cott, *The Grounding of Modern Feminism* (New Haven: Yale University Press, 1987), 237, argues that "professional ideology . . . encouraged professional women to see a community of interest between themselves and professional men and a gulf between themselves and nonprofessional women."

20. Fosdick, *Adventurous Religion*, 35–36; John Ryan, *Declining Liberty and Other Essays* (New York: Macmillan, 1927), 336–337; G. K. Chesterton, *Eugenics and Other Evils* (London: Cassell, 1922), vi, 76–77, 150–151; see also G. K. Chesterton, "Religion and Sex," *Commonweal* 1 (November 12, 1924), 8–10. On eugenic thought at this time, see Charles Rosenberg, *No Other Gods: On Science and American Social Thought* (Baltimore: Johns Hopkins University Press, 1976), 89–97, and Daniel J. Kevles, *In the Name of Eugenics: Genetics and the Uses of Heredity* (New York: Alfred A. Knopf, 1985), 96–147.

21. Ward, *Which Way Religion?* 210–211, John Ryan, "False and True Welfare," in *The Church and Socialism*, 184–186, and Ryan, *Declining Liberty*, 325. On Veblen's hostility to ornament, see Theodor Adorno, "Veblen's Attack on Culture" (1941), in *Prisms* (Cambridge: MIT Press, 1990 [1967]), 73–94. Lasch, *True and Only Heaven*, 52–55, 69–70, features Smith and Patten as exemplars of the modern rehabilitation of desire.

22. The trope "salvation to self-realization" appears in Jackson Lears, "From Salvation to Self-Realization: Therapeutic Roots of the Consumer Culture, 1880–1930," in Fox and Lears, eds, 3–38, and E. Brooks Holifield, *A History of Pastoral Care in America: From Salvation to Self-Realization* (Nashville: Abingdon

Press, 1983). Francis J. McConnell, *Humanism and Christianity* (New York: Macmillan, 1928), 141, Kirby Page, *The Personality of Jesus* (New York: Association Press, 1932), 147, Fosdick, *Twelve Tests*, 87, Ward, *Which Way Religion?* 155–156; see also Harry F. Ward, *The New Social Order: Principles and Programs* (New York: Macmillan, 1919), 131–153, on the supremacy of personality, and Edgar S. Brightman, *Moral Laws* (Nashville: Abingdon Press, 1933), 223–242.

23. Fosdick, *Twelve Tests*, 51–52, Fosdick, *Adventurous Religion*, 26, Kirby Page, *Jesus or Christianity: A Study in Contrasts* (New York: G. H. Doran, 1929), 305–318; see also *Fellowship for a Christian Social Order* (FSCO pamphlet, 1923), Harry F. Ward, *New Social Order*, 148, 152–153. On the fate of industrial democracy in the 1920s, see Steve Fraser, "The Labor Question," in *The Rise and Fall of the New Deal Order, 1930–1980*, eds. Steve Fraser and Gary Gerstle (Princeton, N.J.: Princeton University Press, 1989), 59–62.

24. R. Laurence Moore, "Secularization: Religion and the Social Sciences," in Hutchison, *Between the Times*, 236–239. On the turn toward objectivity in sociology in the twenties, see Robert C. Bannister, *Sociology and Scientism: The American Quest for Objectivity, 1880–1940* (Chapel Hill: University of North Carolina Press, 1987), and Edward A. Purcell, Jr., *The Crisis of Democratic Theory: Scientific Naturalism and the Problem of Value* (Lexington: University of Kentucky Press, 1973). Westbrook, *John Dewey*, 280–286, is a lucid critical discussion of social and political science in the 1920s (quote on 282). William Graebner, *The Engineering of Consent: Democracy and Authority in Twentieth-Century America* (Madison: University of Wisconsin Press, 1987), brings these developments under the rubric democratic social engineering. Mathews, *Contributions* passim; Mathews, *Faith of Modernism*, 7, Ward, *Which Way Religion?* 69–70, Ward, *New Social Order*, 78, 374.

25. Kirby Page, *Living Creatively* (New York: Farrar and Rinehart, 1932), 92–95. On the secularization of liberal Protestant counseling in the 1920s, see Holifield, *History of Pastoral Care*, 210–231.

26. Williams, *Catholicism and the Modern Mind*, 153. On the formation of the National Catholic Welfare Council (NCWC), see Douglas Slawson, *The Foundation and First Decade of the National Catholic Welfare Council* (Washington: Catholic University Press, 1992); on the professionalization of Catholic social services in the 1920s, see Brown and McKeown, *Poor Belong to Us*, 86–119. Paul Hanly Furfey, "From Catholic Liberalism to Catholic Radicalism," *American Ecclesiastical Review* 166 (December 1972), 680–681; see also Paul Hanly Furfey, *The Gang Age: A Study of the Preadolescent Boy and His Recreational Needs* (New York: Macmillan, 1928); William Kerby, *The Social Mission of Charity: A Study of Points of View in Catholic Charities* (New York: Macmillan, 1921), 139, 168.

27. John Ryan, "Fascism in Theory and in Practice," in *Declining Liberty*, 83–100. On American Catholic reactions to Italian fascism, see John P. Diggins, *Mussolini and Fascism: The View from America* (Princeton, N.J.: Princeton University Press, 1972), 182–197.

28. Shuster, *Catholic Spirit*, 250; John Ryan, *Social Reconstruction*, 143–149, Ryan, "Democratizing Industry," in *Declining Liberty*, 224–238; see also Ryan, "Americanism in Industry," *Annals of the American Academy of Political and Social Science* 90 (June 1920), 126–130, Ryan, *Industrial Democracy from a Catholic Viewpoint*, pamphlet (Washington, 1925). Proposals similar to Ryan's appeared regularly in *Commonweal*: David A. McCabe, "Catholics and Economics," *Commonweal* 2 (July 15, 1925), 244, Raymond McGowan, "A Catholic Economic Program," *Commonweal* 3 (November 28, 1925), 48, Henry Somerville, "A Guild Plan for Industry," *Commonweal* 3 (February 10, 1926), 375.

29. Williams, *Catholicism and the Modern Mind*, 126–127.
30. Reinhold Niebuhr, "The Attitude of the Church toward Present Moral Evils" (1911), cited in *Young Reinhold Niebuhr: His Early Writings, 1911–1931*, ed. William G. Chrystal (New York: Pilgrim Press, 1977), 43, Reinhold Niebuhr, *Beyond Tragedy: Essays in the Christian Interpretation of History* (New York: Charles Scribner's Sons, 1937), 289, Reinhold Niebuhr, "The Validity and Certainty of Religious Knowledge" (B.D. thesis, Yale Divinity School, 1915), cited in Richard Wightman Fox, *Reinhold Niebuhr: A Biography* (New York: Pantheon, 1985).

    The literature on Niebuhr is voluminous. Meyer, *Protestant Search*, esp. 217–269, makes the strongest case for Niebuhr as the paragon of Christian social and political wisdom. Fox's biography is a penetrating, critical, even moving portrait of its subject. John Murray Cuddihy, *No Offense: Civil Religion and Protestant Taste* (New York: Seabury Press, 1978), 31–49, is an acerbic account of Niebuhr as a social climber and political opportunist. Though discomforting, Cuddihy's polemic conveys more uncomfortable truths than Niebuhr's defenders care to acknowledge. Other useful studies of Niebuhr include Charles W. Kegley (ed.), *Reinhold Niebuhr: His Religious, Social, and Political Thought* (New York: Macmillan, 1956), Paul Merkley, *Reinhold Niebuhr: A Political Account* (Montreal: McGill-Queen's University Press, 1975), and Dennis McCann, *Christian Realism and Liberation Theology* (Maryknoll, N.Y.: Orbis, 1981). Charles C. Brown, *Niebuhr and His Age: Reinhold Niebuhr's Prophetic Role in the Twentieth Century* (Philadelphia: Westminster, 1992), and Ronald H. Stone, *Professor Reinhold Niebuhr: A Mentor to the Twentieth Century* (Louisville, Ky.: John Knox Press, 1992), are largely uncritical.
31. Reinhold Niebuhr, *Leaves from the Notebook of a Tamed Cynic* (New York: Meridian, 1960 [1929]), 187–188, 193–194, 216, 224, Reinhold Niebuhr, "Why I Am Not a Christian," *Christian Century* 44 (December 15, 1927), 1483; see also "To Whom Shall We Go?" *Christian Century* 44 (March 10, 1927), 299–301. On Niebuhr's years in Detroit, see Fox, *Reinhold Niebuhr*, 41–110.
32. Reinhold Niebuhr, "A Reformationsfest Sermon" (1915) and "Tyrant Servants" (1926), cited in Chrystal, *Young Reinhold Niebuhr*, 73, 169, Niebuhr, "Why I Am Not a Christian," 1482; see also Reinhold Niebuhr, "Henry Ford and Industrial Autocracy," *Christian Century* 43 (November 4, 1926), 1355. On Bethel's class composition, see Fox, *Reinhold Niebuhr*, 67.
33. Reinhold Niebuhr, "Shall a Minister Have an Education?" (1921), cited in Chrystal, *Young Reinhold Niebuhr*, 121, Reinhold Niebuhr, *The Contributions of Religion to Social Work* (New York: Columbia University Press, 1932), 44, 57, 65, 69.
34. Reinhold Niebuhr, *Does Civilization Need Religion?*, 4, 36, 200, 206–207.
35. Ibid., 146, 226, 228–229, 233, Niebuhr, *Leaves*, 157.
36. Bryan's speech is contained in an appendix to Mary Baird Bryan (ed.), *The Memoirs of William Jennings Bryan* (Chicago: John C. Winston, 1925), 530, 537, 554–556. On Bryan's democratic conception of science, see James Gilbert, *Redeeming Culture: American Religion in an Age of Science* (Chicago: University of Chicago Press, 1997), 23–35. As its subtitle indicates, Edward Larson's *Summer for the Gods: The Scopes Trial and America's Continuing Debate Between Science and Religion* (New York: Basic Books, 1997), is another tiresome pitting of science versus religion. A much more valuable discussion is Garry Wills, *Under God: Religion and American Politics* (New York: Simon and Schuster, 1990), 98–107, in which the author suggests that the real victim of the Dayton trial was Bryan's fusion of evangelical Protestantism and progressive politics.
37. Lewis Mumford, *Sticks and Stones: A Study of American Architecture and Civilization* (New York: Dover, 1955 [1924]), 113, Lewis Mumford, *The Golden Day: A*

Study in American Experience and Culture (New York: Horace Liveright, 1926), 193, 255–256, 268, Lewis Mumford, *The Story of Utopias* (New York: Viking, 1962 [1922]), 232–233. For a discussion of these works, see Blake, *Beloved Community*, 208–228.

38. Lewis Mumford, "Architecture and Catholicism," *Commonweal* 1 (April 15, 1925), 623–624, Ralph Adams Cram, *Great Thousand Years*, 31, Jacques Maritain, *The Angelic Doctor: The Life of St. Thomas Aquinas*, trans. J. F. Scanlon (New York: Sheed and Ward, 1931 [1930]), 108, H. Richard Niebuhr, "Back to Benedict," *Christian Century* 42 (July 2, 1925), 680–682. While always recognized as intellectually superior to Reinhold ("I think before I write," he once snapped when asked why he was not as prolific), Richard has been an obscure figure to historians, known primarily as the author of *The Social Sources of Denominationalism* (New York: Henry Holt and Co., 1929), and *The Kingdom of God in America* (Middletown, Conn.: Wesleyan University Press, 1988 [1937]). Jon Diefenthaler, *H. Richard Niebuhr: A Lifetime of Reflections on the Church and the World* (Macon, Ga.: Mercer University Press, 1986), provides much revealing information and shrewd psychological insight (as does Fox, *Reinhold Niebuhr*, 11–12, 17), but it fails to consider Niebuhr in a broader context. Of the many studies of Niebuhr's work in sociology, history, and theology, the best are Paul Ramsey (ed.), *Faith and Ethics: The Theology of H. Richard Niebuhr* (New York: Harper and Row, 1957), James W. Fowler, *To See the Kingdom: The Theological Vision of H. Richard Niebuhr* (Nashville: Abingdon Press, 1974), Linnell E. Cady, "A Model for a Public Theology," *Harvard Theological Review* 80 (April 1987), 192–212, Ronald F. Thiemann (ed.), *The Legacy of H. Richard Niebuhr* (Philadelphia: Fortress, 1989). William Stacy Johnson's introduction to an edition of Niebuhr's papers, *Theology, History, Culture: Major Unpublished Writings* (New Haven: Yale University Press, 1996), vii–xxxvii, is especially illuminating.

39. H. Richard Niebuhr, "Theology and Psychology: A Sterile Union," *Christian Century* 44 (January 13, 1927), 48, H. Richard Niebuhr, *Social Sources of Denominationalism*, 263, Maritain, *Angelic Doctor*, 98.

40. Christopher Dawson, "Christianity and The New Age," in *Essays in Order*, eds. Christopher Dawson, Jacques Maritain, and Peter Wurst (New York: Macmillan, 1931), viii, x, Maritain, *Bergsonian Philosophy*, 95, H. Richard Niebuhr, "Back to Benedict," 680, H. Richard Niebuhr, "The Social Gospel and the Liberal Theology, *Keryx* 22 (May 1931), 13, H. Richard Niebuhr, "Theology in a Time of Disillusionment" (1931), in *Theology, History, Culture*, 110–111, Howard Thurman, "The Task of the Negro Ministry" (1928), in *A Strange Freedom: The Best of Howard Thurman on Religious Experience and Public Life*, eds. Walter Earl Fluker and Catherine Tumber (Boston: Beacon Press, 1998), 1–17, 197, 198–199. Tumber's introduction to Thurman's life, work, and significance is elegant and informative.

41. Christopher Dawson, *Progress and Religion: An Historical Enquiry* (London: Sheed and Ward, 1931 [1929]), 244, H. Richard Niebuhr, *Social Sources*, 271–284, H. Richard Niebuhr, "Back to Benedict?" 860–861.

42. Mystical body theology can be sampled in Karl Adam, *The Spirit of Catholicism* (Garden City, N.Y.: Doubleday, 1954 [1924]), and Emile Mersch, *The Whole Christ: The Historical Development of the Doctrine of the Mystical Body of Christ in Scripture and Tradition* (Milwaukee: Bruce Co., 1938). Dawson, Maritain, and Wurst, *Essays in Order*, 28, Shuster, *Catholic Spirit*, 255–264. Shuster's idea was not fantastical. By the early 1930s, the Amalgamated Clothing Workers Union had constructed an apartment complex on Grand Street in lower Manhattan that featured what Daniel Rodgers calls "an inner hive of collective endeavors"; see Daniel Rodgers, *Atlantic Crossings*, 402, and photos following 408.

43. On the liturgical renaissance, see Ernest B. Koenker, *The Liturgical Renaissance in the Roman Catholic Church* (Chicago: University of Chicago Press, 1954); on the Liturgical Arts Society, see Susan J. White, *Art, Architecture, and Liturgical Reform: The Liturgical Arts Society, 1928–1972* (New York: Pueblo Publishing, 1990), esp. 78–118. Eric Gill, *Beauty Takes Care of Herself* (New York: Sheed and Ward, 1933 [1930]), esp. 180–203, was his best-known work at this time. On Gill, see Donald Attwater, *A Cell of Good Living: The Life, Work, and Opinions of Eric Gill* (London: Geoffrey Chapman, 1969), esp. 52–141, on the 1920s; Fiona MacCarthy, *Eric Gill: A Biography* (London and Boston: Faber and Faber, 1989), relates more about Gill than many will want to know.

44. Chesterton's influence in America is discussed in Halsey, 13–14, and Arnold Sparr, *To Promote, Defend, and Redeem: The Catholic Literary Revival and the Transformation of American Culture, 1920–1960* (New York: Greenwood Press, 1990), 71–78. Oddly, neither author discusses *What I Saw in America*. For a sympathetic discussion of Chesterton's observations on consumer culture, see William Leach, *Land of Desire: Merchants, Power, and the Rise of a New American Culture* (New York: Pantheon, 1993), 346–348.

45. G. K. Chesterton, *What I Saw in America*, 33–34, 38–40.

46. Ibid., 34, 40, 44, 46.

47. Ibid., 286–287, 291–293.

48. Ibid., 293, 296.

49. On Virgil Michel and the liturgical movement, see Paul Marx, *Virgil Michel and the Liturgical Movement* (Collegeville, Minn.: St. John's University Press, 1957), and R. W. Franklin and Robert L. Spaeth, *Virgil Michel: American Catholic* (Collegeville, Minn.: St. John's University Press, 1988).

3. THE PERMANENT REVOLUTION

1. H. Richard Niebuhr, "The Grace of Doing Nothing," *Christian Century* 49 (March 23, 1932), 378–379.

2. Reinhold Niebuhr, "Must We Do Nothing?" *Christian Century* 49 (March 30, 1932), 416–417.

3. John Ryan, "The New Things in the Encyclical," *American Ecclesiastical Review* 85 (July 1931), 1–14, John Ryan, "A New Social Order," *Catholic Action* 14 (October 1932), 15. For the text of *Quadragesimo anno*, see O'Brien and Shannon, 42–79.

4. Dorothy Day, "The Real Revolutionists," *Commonweal* 17 (January 11, 1933), 293–294, Dorothy Day, *The Long Loneliness* (New York: Harper and Row, 1952), 163–166. On Day, see William Miller, *Dorothy Day: A Biography* (San Francisco: HarperCollins, 1982), and James T. Fisher, *The Catholic Counterculture in America, 1933–1962* (Chapel Hill: University of North Carolina Press, 1989), 1–69.

5. Day, *The Long Loneliness*, 166–171. On Maurin, see Marc H. Ellis, *Peter Maurin: Prophet in the Twentieth Century* (New York: Paulist Press, 1981).

6. Meyer, *Protestant Search*, 166–348, David J. O'Brien, *American Catholics and Social Reform: The New Deal Years* (New York: Oxford University Press, 1968), 148. O'Brien is more critical of Ryan and other Catholic moderates in *Public Catholicism* (Maryknoll, N.Y.: Orbis Books, 1996 [1988]), 194. On the question of realism in Popular Front culture, see Michael Denning, *The Cultural Front: The Laboring of American Culture in the Twentieth Century* (New York: Verso, 1996), 118–123.

7. Fraser and Gerstle, *Rise and Fall of the New Deal Order*; Denning, *The Cultural Front*, 21–37, dubs the 1930s "the age of the CIO." Warren Susman, "Culture and Commitment," in *Culture as History*, 207.

8. Antonio Gramsci, "Notes for an Introduction and an Approach to the Study of Philosophy in the History of Culture," in *An Antonio Gramsci Reader: Selected Writings 1916–1935*, ed. David Forgacs (New York: Schocken Books, 1988), 330, 333.

9. Walter Benjamin, "The Work of Art in the Age of Mechanical Reproduction" (1936), in *Illuminations: Essays and Reflections*, ed. Hannah Arendt (New York: Schocken Books, 1969), 223–224, 242, Walter Benjamin, "Theses on the Philosophy of History" (1940), *Illuminations*, 253–255, 264. On the messianic preoccupations of these unorthodox Marxists, see Richard Wolin, *Labyrinths: Explorations in the Critical History of Ideas* (Amherst: University of Massachusetts Press, 1995), 43–54.

10. League of Professional Groups for Foster and Ford, *Culture and the Crisis* (New York: Workers' Library Publishers, 1932), 18.

11. Kenneth Burke, "Revolutionary Symbolism in America" (1935), in *Perspectives on Modern Literature*, ed. Frederick J. Hoffman (Evanston, Ill.: Row, Peterson, 1962), 183–184, Kenneth Burke, *Permanence and Change: An Anatomy of Purpose* (Indianapolis: Bobbs-Merrill, 1965 [1935]), 71–82, 125–147, 155–158, 179–187, Kenneth Burke, *Attitudes Toward History*, vol. 2 (New York: New Republic Books, 1937), 44–45, 68, 233, Kenneth Burke, *The Philosophy of Literary Form: Studies in Symbolic Action* (Baton Rouge: Louisiana State University Press, 1967 [1941]), 55–60, 304, 447–451. The phrase "secular prayer" is cited in Denning, *The Cultural Front*, 439. Burke took a serious intellectual interest in religion, exploring the religious language of St. Augustine with great erudition and subtlety in *The Rhetoric of Religion* (Boston: Beacon Press, 1961).

12. John Dewey, *A Common Faith* (New Haven: Yale University Press, 1934), 31–33, 41, 62, 87. Westbrook, *John Dewey*, 418–428, discusses *A Common Faith* in the context of an ideal of "consummatory experience," whereas Bruce Kuklick argues that Dewey "transformed religious concerns into a new language": a "lingua franca for those in the knowledge professions who sought power," especially the "social-scientific epigoni." "John Dewey, American Theology, and Scientific Politics," in Lacey, 90, 92.

13. Thurman Arnold, *The Symbols of Government* (New Haven: Yale University Press, 1935), 125–127; see also Thurman Arnold, *The Folklore of Capitalism* (New Haven: Yale University Press, 1937), 230–237, on corporate receivership as a form of "vicarious atonement." For a discussion of Arnold as a quintessential New Deal technocrat, see Lasch, *True and Only Heaven*, 429–435.

14. Editorial, "Why No Revival?" *Christian Century* 52 (September 18, 1935), 1168–1170. Burke, *Permanence and Change*, 64–65, James Rorty, *Where Life Is Better* (New York: New Republic Books, 1936), 157.

15. Walter Marshall Horton, *Realistic Theology* (New York: Harper and Bros., 1934), 120, F. Ernest Johnson, *The Church and Society* (Nashville: Abingdon Press, 1935), 136, Samuel C. Kinchloe, *Research Memorandum on Religion in the Depression* (Westport, Conn.: Greenwood Press, 1970 [1937]), 1.

16. Meyer, *Protestant Search*, 217–269, articulates the classic neoorthodox position. Fox, *Reinhold Niebuhr*, 142–192, covers Niebuhr's career in the 1930s. Fox, "Tragedy, Responsibility, and the American Intellectual, 1925–1950," in *Lewis Mumford: Public Intellectual*, eds. Thomas and Agatha Hughes (New York: Oxford University Press, 1989), 329–330, discuses the shift from "personality" to "responsibility" in Niebuhr's work. Though Fox is much more critical of Niebuhr's work than Meyer, he still purveys a somewhat misleading assessment of Niebuhr's significance both for American Protestantism and for American liberalism.

17. Reinhold Niebuhr, *Moral Man and Immoral Society* (New York: Charles Scribner's Sons, 1932), 44–45, Reinhold Niebuhr, *Beyond Tragedy*, 127, Reinhold Niebuhr, "Ten Years That Shook My World," *Christian Century* 56 (April 26, 1939), 542, Reinhold Niebuhr, *Reflections on the End of an Era* (New York: Charles Scribner's Sons, 1934), ix.

18. Reinhold Niebuhr, letter to Harry Emerson Fosdick, cited in Miller, *Harry Emerson Fosdick*, 393, H. Richard Niebuhr, cited in Fox, *Reinhold Niebuhr*, 145, Robert L. Calhoun, "A Liberal Bandaged but Unbowed," *Christian Century* 56 (May 31, 1939), 901–904, John C. Bennett, "A Changed Liberal—But Still a Liberal," *Christian Century* 56 (February 8, 1939), 178–181, Georgia Harkness, "A Spiritual Pilgrimage," *Christian Century* 56 (March 15, 1939), 348–351. Hutchison, *Modernist Impulse*, 288–310, covers the reaction of liberal Protestants to "crisis theology" in the 1930s.

19. Niebuhr, *Moral Man*, 277, Niebuhr, *Reflections*, 88, Reinhold Niebuhr, "The Truth in Myths," in *The Nature of Religious Experience*, eds. J. S. Bixler, H. Richard Niebuhr, and Robert L. Calhoun (New York: Harper and Bros., 1937), Reinhold Niebuhr, "A Reply to Professor Macintosh," *Review of Religion* 4 (Summer 1940), 304–308, Reinhold Niebuhr, "A Footnote on Religion," *Nation* (September 26, 1934), 358. Westbrook, *John Dewey*, 523–532, astutely analyzes the running battle—and the unacknowledged affinity—between Niebuhr and Dewey. On Niebuhr's association with "middle-of-the-road Militants" in the Socialist party, see Fox, *Reinhold Niebuhr*, 157. Denning, *The Cultural Front*, 423–462, discusses American socialist theory but does not mention Niebuhr at all. On pragmatism in the 1930s see Denning, *The Cultural Front*, 428–434, and Christopher Phelps, *Young Sidney Hook: Marxist and Pragmatist* (Ithaca, N.Y.: Cornell University Press, 1997).

20. Niebuhr, *Moral Man*, 53, 81, Niebuhr, *Reflections*, 122, 193.

21. Niebuhr, *Moral Man*, 263.

22. Ibid., 274, *Reflections*, 73–74, 104.

23. Niebuhr, *Moral Man*, 23–50, quote on 32, Reinhold Niebuhr, *An Interpretation of Christian Ethics* (New York: Charles Scribner's Sons, 1935), 149, 184, Niebuhr, *Reflections*, 210, Reinhold Niebuhr, "After Capitalism—What?" *World Tomorrow* 16 (March 1, 1933), 203–204, Reinhold Niebuhr, "The Idea of Progress and Socialism," *Radical Religion* 1 (Spring 1936), 28. See also Reinhold Niebuhr, "Religion and Marxism," *Modern Quarterly* 8 (February 1935), 714–715, Reinhold Niebuhr, "The Creed of Modern Christian Socialists," *Radical Religion* 3 (Spring 1938), 16.

24. Reinhold Niebuhr, "Reflections from Mississippi," *Christian Century* 54 (February 10, 1937), 183–184. For a description of Delta, see Sherwood Eddy, "The Delta Cooperative's First Year," *Christian Century* 54 (February 3, 1937), 139–140.

25. Niebuhr, *Moral Man*, 115, 211, 215–216; see also Reinhold Niebuhr, "The Professional Union," *Radical Religion* 3 (Spring 1938), 6. On Niebuhr's support for a farmer-labor party, see Fox, *Reinhold Niebuhr*, 170–171.

26. Francis Miller, letter to Reinhold Niebuhr, January 27, 1933, cited in Fox, *Reinhold Niebuhr*, 142, John C. Bennett, *Christian Realism* (New York: Macmillan, 1941), 152.

27. Niebuhr, *Moral Man*, 81, 231–256, Reinhold Niebuhr, "Why I Leave the FOR," *Christian Century* 51 (January 3, 1934), 255.

28. On the flourishing of evangelical and fundamentalist churches at this time, see Joel Carpenter, *Revive Us Again: The Reawakening of American Fundamentalism* (New York: Oxford University Press, 1997), 110–140. Howard Kester, *Revolt*

Among the Sharecroppers (Knoxville: University of Tennessee Press, 1997 [1936]), Liston Pope, *Millhands and Preachers: A Study of Gastonia* (New Haven: Yale University Press, 1942). Carter, *Decline and Revival of the Social Gospel*, 123–231, and Miller, *American Protestantism and Social Issues*, 63–112, 274–313, provide thorough overviews of liberal Protestant social activism at this time, whereas Elizabeth and Ken Fones-Wolf, "Lending a Hand to Labor: James Myers and the Federal Council of Churches, 1926–1947," *Church History* 68 (March 1999), 79–85, cover liberal Protestant support for the labor movement.

29. On the prominence of the idea of Catholicism as culture—intertwined with that of a Catholic revival in the 1930s—see Halsey, *Survival of American Innocence*, 152–168, Sparr, *Promote, Defend, and Redeem*, 99–121; Gleason, *Contending with Modernity*, 146–166, Gleason, "In Search of Unity," James Hitchcock, "Postmortem on a Rebirth: The Catholic Intellectual Renaissance," *American Scholar* 49 (Spring 1980), 211–225. Calvert Alexander, *The Catholic Literary Revival: Three Phases in Its Development from 1845 to the Present* (Milwaukee: Bruce, 1935), was the scholarly lodestone of the movement. The New York publishing house of Sheed and Ward became a major entrepôt of Catholic intellectual life at this time. On Frank Sheed and Maisie Ward, see Wilfred Sheed, *Frank and Maisie: A Memoir with Parents* (New York: Simon and Schuster, 1985), and Dana Greene, *The Living of Maisie Ward* (South Bend, Ind.: University of Notre Dame Press, 1997).

30. Francis X. Talbot, "Reflections on the Plebiscite," *America* 54 (March 21, 1936), 573, Calvert Alexander, "Fall Operations on the Literary Front," *America* 54 (October 12, 1935), 18, Robert Pollack, "The Challenge of Secularism to Modern Man," in *Man and Modern Secularism*, ed. National Catholic Alumni Federation (New York: National Catholic Alumni Federation, 1940), 72–82, Luigi Ligutti, *Rural Roads to Security: America's Third Struggle for Liberty* (Milwaukee: Bruce, 1940), xi, 39.

31. The ACTU citation is from O'Brien, *Public Catholicism*, 185, *Organized Social Justice* (New York: n.p., n.d.).

32. Jacques Maritain, *Integral Humanism: Temporal and Spiritual Problems of a New Christendom* (South Bend, Ind.: University of Notre Dame Press, 1973 [1936]), 9–22, 78–80, Jacques Maritain, *Freedom in the Modern World* (New York: Sheed and Ward, 1936 [1935]), 60, 97, 211. On French personalism, see John Hellman, *Emmanuel Mounier and the New Catholic Left in France, 1930–1950* (Toronto, Canada: University of Toronto Press, 1981).

33. Maritain, *Freedom*, 204, 211. On corporatism, see Ellis Hawley, *The New Deal and the Problem of Monopoly: A Study in Economic Ambivalence* (Princeton, N.J.: Princeton University Press, 1966), Wyn Grant (ed.), *The Political Economy of Corporatism* (New York: Cambridge University Press, 1983). While Michael Novak, *The Catholic Ethic and the Spirit of Capitalism* (New York: Free Press, 1992), 32–33, enlists Maritain in his cohort of "democratic capitalists"—not without reason, if my analysis is valid—he misses the strongly corporatist dimension of Maritain's ideal.

34. Jacques Maritain, *The Twilight of Civilization* (London: Centenary Press, 1942 [1939]), 31.

35. John Ryan, quoted in Broderick, *Right Reverend New Dealer*, 242. On Ryan's career in the 1930s, see O'Brien, *American Catholics*, 120–149.

36. Joseph Schrembs, D.D., "The Basis and Aims of Catholic Action," in *A Call to Catholic Action*, ed. Charles Callan, O.P. (New York: Joseph F. Wagner, 1935), 16, 19, "ACTU Statement of Principles," *Labor Leader* 1 (January 3, 1938), 6. On Rice, see Patrick J. McGeever, *Reverend Charles Owen Rice: Apostle of Contradiction* (Duquesne, Pa.: Duquesne University Press, 1989). Steve Rosswurm, "The

Catholic Church and the Left-Led Unions," in *The CIO's Left-Led Unions*, ed. Steve Rosswurm (New Brunswick, N.J.: Rutgers University Press, 1992), 121–123, discusses the labor schools and the dependence of the ACTU on clerical leadership and ideology. For two very different accounts of the ACTU, see the laudatory tale told by Neil Betten, *Catholic Activism and the Industrial Worker* (Gainesville, Fla.: University Presses of Florida, 1976), 33–145, and the condemnation by Douglas P. Seaton, *Catholics and Radicals: The ACTU and the American Labor Movement from Depression to Cold War* (Lewisburg, Pa.: Bucknell University Press, 1981), 53–140. On the Young Christian Workers, see Steven Avella, "Reynolds Hillenbrand and Chicago Catholicism," *U.S. Catholic Historian* 9 (Fall 1990), 353–370, and Mary Irene Zotti, *A Time of Awakening: The Young Christian Worker Story in the United States, 1938–1970* (Chicago: Loyola University Press, 1991), 5–97.

37. Raymond McGowan, "Property—Organization—Government Action," *Catholic Action* 14 (January 1932), 25, Raymond McGowan, "Reconstructing the Social Order," *Proceedings of the American Catholic Philosophical Association* 9 (1933), 187; see also Raymond McGowan, "The Church and the Problems of Democracy," *Catholic Action* 18 (August 1936), 7–8, Raymond McGowan, "Government Action and Social Justice," *Catholic Mind* 26 (June 8, 1938), 222–226. Philip Murray presented the "Victory Plan" in "CIO Looks Forward," *Christian Social Action* 6 (January 1941), 9–12. Murray has yet to receive serious biographic attention.

38. John Ryan, *Seven Troubled Years, 1930–1936: A Collection of Papers on the Depression and on the Problems of Recovery and Reform* (Ann Arbor, Mich.: University of Michigan Press, 1937), 89–91, 195; see also John Ryan, "Economics and Ethics," *Commonweal* 18 (October 6, 1933), 521–522, John Ryan, Letter, *Christian Front* 1 (January 1936), 2, John Ryan, "Are We on the Right Road?" *Commonweal* 20 (October 12, 1934), 548, and John Ryan, "Ethics and Political Intervention in the Field of Social Action," *Review of Politics* 3 (July 1941), 301. On Ryan's advisory relationship to the New Deal, see Broderick, *Right Reverend*, 212–218, and Gearty, 49–53. Ryan says nothing about his role as an advisor in his autobiography.

39. National Catholic Welfare Council, "The Church and Social Order" (1940), in *Pastoral Letters of the American Hierarchy 1789–1970*, ed. Hugh J. Nolan (Indianapolis: Our Sunday Visitor, 1971), 338–353, quote on 339.

40. Ligutti, *Rural Roads*, 65, 72, John Ryan, "Looking Forward II," *Christian Front* 3 (April 1938), 60, Steve Fraser, "The Labor Question," in Fraser and Gerstle, *Rise and Fall of the New Deal Order*, 72–78. Cohen, *Making a New Deal*, 323–368, illuminates the significance of mass culture in the shift from ethnicity and religion to class and consumption as the foci of working-class political consciousness.

41. Gary Gerstle, *Working-Class Americanism: The Politics of Labor in a Textile City, 1914–1960* (New York: Cambridge University Press, 1989), esp. 174–195, Cohen, *Making a New Deal*, 314–321.

42. A. J. Muste, *Non-Violence in an Aggressive World* (New York: Macmillan, 1940), 176; see also A. J. Muste, "The True International" (1939), in *The Essays of A. J. Muste*, ed. Nat Hentoff (Indianapolis: Bobbs-Merrill, 1967), 207–214. Jo Ann Robinson, *Abraham Went Out: A Biography of A. J. Muste* (Philadelphia: Temple University Press, 1981), is the only biography. H. Richard Niebuhr (in collaboration with Francis Miller and Wilhelm Pauck), *The Church Against the World* (Chicago: Willett, 1935), 142–144, H. Richard Niebuhr, *The Meaning of Revelation* (New York: Harper and Bros., 1941), ix, Paul Hanly Furfey, *Fire on the Earth* (New York: Macmillan, 1936), 39–40, Paul Hanly Furfey, *Three Theories of Society* (New York: Macmillan, 1937), 232, 235, Dorothy Day, "Catholic

Church Stands Alone Today as Always—The True International," *Catholic Worker* 2 (May 1, 1934), 1, Dorothy Day, *From Union Square to Rome* (New York: Arno Press, 1978 [1938]), 150, Peter Maurin, "Maurin's Program," *Catholic Worker* 1 (June-July 1933), 4; see also Edward Day Stewart, "Christianity and Communism," *Orate Fratres* 9 (May 18, 1935), 307–312. On Muste and Niebuhr, see Meyer, *Protestant Search*, 283–284, 361–370. On the Catholic Workers, see O'Brien, *American Catholics*, 182–211, Piehl, *Breaking Bread*, 57–143; Fisher, *The Catholic Counterculture*, 25–99.

43. Niebuhr, *Meaning of Revelation*, 74, 103, H. Richard Niebuhr, *The Kingdom of God in America* (New York: Harper and Bros., 1937), 196–197, Furfey, *Three Theories*, 3–16, 57–61, Furfey, *Fire on the Earth*, 68–70.

44. Niebuhr, *Church Against the World*, 153–154, Niebuhr, *Meaning of Revelation*, 18, 37, Furfey, *Fire on the Earth*, 8–10, 27, Virgil Michel, "Natural and Supernatural Society," *Orate Fratres* 10 (July 25, 1936), 394–398. On democratic social engineering, see Graebner, On the Lynds in the 1930s, see Fox, "Epitaph for Middletown: Robert S. Lynd and the Analysis of Consumer Culture," in *Culture of Consumption*, eds. Fox and Lears, 129–141.

45. Niebuhr, *Meaning of Revelation*, 110, Charles Clayton Morrison, *The Social Gospel and the Christian Cultus* (New York: Harper and Bros., 1933), 42, 44, 101, 251.

46. Federal Council of Churches, *The Christian Year: A Suggestive Guide for the Worship of the Church* (New York: Federal Council of Churches of Christ in America, 1937), 8, Fred Winslow Adams, "For a Modern Church Year," *Christian Century* (May 25, 1938), 651–653; Morrison, *The Social Gospel*, 101.

47. Gerald Ellerd, S.J., *Men at Work at Worship* (New York: Longmans, Green, 1940), 146–167, Eric Gill, "Mass for the Masses," in *Sacred and Secular* (London: J. M. Dent, 1940), 143–155, Ade Bethune, "Small Churches," *Orate Fratres* 12 (October 2, 1938), 487–488.

48. Furfey, *Fire on the Earth*, 92–95, Furfey, *Three Theories*, 184, 222; see also Paul Hanly Furfey, "Liturgy and the Social Problem," *National Liturgical Week 1941* (Newark, N.J.: Benedictine Liturgical Conference, 1942), 181–186, and Paul Hanly Furfey, "The Positive Society," *Commonweal* 25 (January 22, 1937), 353–354, John Griffin, "The Liturgical Economy and Social Reconstruction," *Orate Fratres* 11 (December 27, 1936), 73, Virgil Michel, "The Liturgy, the Basis of Social Regeneration," *Orate Fratres* 9 (November 2, 1935), 542–544.

49. Niebuhr, *Meaning of Revelation*, 5–6, 65–72, Carl Becker, cited in Peter Novick, *That Noble Dream: The Objectivity Question and the American Historical Profession* (New York: Cambridge University Press, 1988), 265, W. E. B. Du Bois, *Black Reconstruction* (New York: Harcourt, Brace and Co., 1935), Herbert Aptheker, *American Negro Slave Revolts* (New York: Columbia University Press, 1943). Denning, *The Cultural Front*, 135, interprets the works of Du Bois and Aptheker as efforts to identify the conditions for a national-popular movement.

50. Niebuhr, *Meaning of Revelation*, 116–117. Benedict Anderson, *Imagined Communities: Reflections on the Origins and Spread of Nationalism* (London: Verso, 1983), 14–16, 20–25, discusses religious tradition as a form of imagined community. Gramsci theorizes the national-popular in Forgacs, *An Antonio Gramsci Reader*, 364–370.

51. Joseph Haroutunian, *Piety versus Moralism: The Passing of the New England Theology* (Hamden, Conn.: Archon Books, 1964 [1932]), Perry Miller, *Orthodoxy in Massachusetts 1630–1650* (Cambridge, Mass.: Harvard University Press, 1933), xi–xii, Perry Miller, *Jonathan Edwards* (New York: W. Sloane, 1949), xii–xiii. Miller's account of his epiphany is in *Errand into the Wilderness* (New York: Harper and Row, 1964 {1956]), vii–x. Miller later wrote of Roger Williams that his "mind was

much too theological: therein consists his challenge to the twentieth century" in *Roger Williams: His Contribution to the American Tradition* (Indianapolis: Bobbs-Merrill, 1953), 27. On Miller as a cultural critic, see David Harlan, *The Degradation of American History* (Chicago: University of Chicago Press, 1997), 32–52. See Niebuhr's criticism of Vernon Parrington in *Kingdom of God*, 199, n. 2.

52. Niebuhr, *Kingdom of God*, xix, 10, 43, 111. Fox has argued that Niebuhr's inattention to social forces in *Kingdom*—an apparent repudiation of his stance in *Social Sources of Denominationalism*—was a surrender of "hard-won theoretical ground without a fight." I suspect that Niebuhr might reply that such a success had been a pyrrhic victory for the social gospel. Richard Fox, "H. Richard Niebuhr's Divided Kingdom," *American Quarterly* 42 (April 1990), 93–101.

53. Niebuhr, *Kingdom of God*, 69, 74–75. Richard confided to Reinhold in the mid-1930s that he felt "at home in a friar's gown" and might even "end up in Catholicism." Fox, *Reinhold Niebuhr*, 156.

54. Niebuhr, *Church Against the World*, 130, n. 1, Niebuhr, *Kingdom of God*, 42, review of *Church Against the World*, cited in Hutchison, *Modernist Impulse*, 301.

55. Dorothy Day, "Reflections on Work," *Catholic Worker* 13 (January 1947), 2, Day, *The Long Loneliness*, 55, Nicholas Berdyeav, *The End of Our Time* (New York: Sheed and Ward, 1933), Constance Mary Rowe, "Meeting of St. Dominic and St. Francis," *Christian Front* 1 (February 1936), 25, Graham Carey, "Art and Reconstruction," *Christian Front* 1 (February 1936), 26, Graham Carey, "The Christian as Artist," *Christian Front* 1 (March 1936), 42, Virgil Michel, "The Corporative Order," *Christian Front* 3 (December 1938), 155. Alden Brown, *The Grail Movement and American Catholicism, 1940–1975* (South Bend, Ind.: University of Notre Dame Press, 1989), 8–10, 32, 58, relates that children attending Grailville, a summer camp established by the Grail, a Catholic women's group, lived in dormitories named Galahad, Percival, Gawaine, and Gareth. For a list of books recommended for study groups by the *Catholic Worker* (which includes Kropotkin, Gill, and Maritain), see *Catholic Worker* 1 (December 1933), 2.

56. Susman, "Culture and Commitment," 179, Dorothy Day, *Loaves and Fishes* (New York: Harper and Row, 1962), 44, Furfey, *Fire on the Earth*, vii, 152–153.

57. Stanley Vishnewski, quoted in Ellis, *Peter Maurin*, 73–74, Day, *Long Loneliness*, 149–150. See also Dorothy Day's remarks to Robert Coles in *Dorothy Day: A Radical Devotion* (Boston: Addison-Wesley, 1987), 82.

58. Day, *Long Loneliness*, 216, Furfey, *Fire on the Earth*, 107–108.

59. Furfey, *Fire on the Earth*, 107–108, Paul Hanly Furfey, "Art and the Machine," *Catholic Art Quarterly* 7 (Pentecost 1944), 1–6, Ade Bethune, "Can Secularism Effect Technique?" *Catholic Art Quarterly* 12 (Pentecost 1949), 108. Eric Gill, "Art in Relation to Industrialism" (1935), *Blackfriars* 17 (January 1936), 6–23, was widely read by intellectuals in the nexus of liturgical, arts and crafts, and Catholic Worker circles. See also Eric Gill, "All Art Is Propaganda" (1935), in *It All Hangs Together* (London: Faber and Faber, 1941), 158–162. Colleen McDannell, *Material Christianity: Religion and Popular Culture in America* (New Haven: Yale University Press, 1995), 167–186, claiming that "Catholic critics joined modernist artists" in rejecting realism and in believing that "good art was separated from mass culture and everyday life" (177), misses the point of the Catholic radical critique: that everyday life itself needed to be revolutionized so as to reunite art and work.

60. Day, *The Long Loneliness*, 204, Furfey, *Fire on the Earth*, 107–108. On the roundtable discussions, see Piehl, *Breaking Bread*, 74–75.

61. Peter Maurin, "Outdoor Universities," *Catholic Worker* 4 (January 1937), 1, 7. Hutchins elaborated his view of university education in *The Higher Learning in*

America (New Haven: Yale University Press, 1936). Marsden, *Soul of the American University*, 368–397, covers the debate over religion in higher education in the 1930s.

62. Day, *The Long Loneliness*, 220–228, Peter Maurin, "Back to Christ! Back to the Land!" *Catholic Worker* 3 (November 1935), 1, 8, Richard Deverall, "Co-Operation and Private Property," *Christian Front* 1 (October 1936), 153. See also Cyril Echele, "An Idea of a Farming Commune," *Catholic Worker* 4 (February 1936), 1, 6, Echele and Dorothy Weston Coddington, "Cult, Culture, and Cultivation," *Liturgy and Sociology* 1 (Summer 1936), 15. Furfey's critique of Catholic Worker agrarianism is in "There Are Two Types of Agrarians," *Catholic Worker* 7 (October 1939), 1, 8. Rodgers, *Atlantic Crossings*, 446–461, examines the New Deal's greenbelt suburbs. Anthony Novitsky, "Peter Maurin's Green Revolution: The Radical Implications of Reactionary Social Catholicism," *Review of Politics* 37 (January 1975), 83–103, is a valuable examination of Maurin's ideas.

63. Dorothy Day, Editorial, *Catholic Worker* 14 (May 1947), 1, Dorothy Day, "Reflections on Work," *Catholic Worker* 13 (November 1946), 4, Day, *From Union Square to Rome*, 150.

64. Fisher, *The Catholic Counterculture*, 121, Peter Maurin, unpublished "Easy Essay," cited in Ellis, *Peter Maurin*, 131, Day, *The Long Loneliness*, 228–229. On the revival of interest in rural life in the 1930s, see David Shi, *The Simple Life: Plain Living and High Thinking in American Culture* (New York: Oxford University Press, 1985), 222–247. Agar and Borsodi often were cited approvingly by Catholic writers on rural issues. The National Catholic Rural Life Conference published numerous essays on the religious philosophy, economics, and technology of agriculture, many of which are collected in *Catholic Rural Life Objectives*, 3 vols. (St. Paul, Minn.: National Catholic Rural Life Conference, 1935–1937). Ligutti, *Rural Roads to Security*, 41, 217–221. On the NCRLC, see David Bovee, "Luigi G. Ligutti: Catholic Rural Life Leader," *U.S. Catholic Historian* 8 (Fall 1989), 143–162.

65. Lewis Mumford, *Technics and Civilization* (New York: Harcourt Brace and Co., 1934), 227, 267, 286, Simone Weil, *Oppression and Liberty*, trans. Arthur Wills and John Petrie (Amherst, Mass.: University of Massachusetts Press, 1973), 54–124.

66. Day, "Reflections on Work," *op. cit.; Long Loneliness*, 195.

67. Dorothy Day, "Catholic Worker States Stand on Strikes," *Catholic Worker* 4 (July 1936), 2, Day, *The Long Loneliness*, 222. Betten, *Catholic Activism*, 72, acknowledges that Catholic Workers fumbled their chance to engage the CIO but asserts that they galvanized *liberals* to support the labor movement—galvanized, in other words, those who accepted the Fordist order the Catholic Workers abhored.

68. John Ryan, quoted in Broderick, *Right Reverend*, 242–243, Paul Hanly Furfey, "The New Social Catholicism," *Christian Front* 1 (December 1936), 182–183.

4. Rendering Unto Caesar

1. Henry Luce, *The American Century* (New York: Farrar and Rinehart, 1941), 6–7, 19, 23–24, 34, 39.

2. Daniel Bell, *The End of Ideology: On the Exhaustion of Political Ideas in the Fifties* (New York: Collier Books, 1962 [1960]), 300, 313. On this postwar new class of cultural professionals, see Jackson Lears, "A Matter of Taste: Corporate Cultural Hegemony in a Mass-Consumption Society," in *Recasting America: Culture*

and Politics in the Age of Cold War, ed. Larry May (Chicago: University of Chicago Press, 1989), 48–54, Ross, No Respect, 42–64, Denning, The Cultural Front, 107–114.

3. Bell, The End of Ideology, 405; on Bell's own postwar journey, see Howard Brick, Daniel Bell and the Decline of Intellectual Radicalism: Social Theory and Political Reconciliation in the 1940s (Madison: University of Wisconsin Press, 1986).

4. Bell, The End of Ideology, 278–279, 301–302, Adolf A. Berle, Jr., Power without Property: A New Development in American Political Economy (New York: Harcourt Brace, 1959), 6–7, David Hollinger, "The Canon and Its Keepers" (1981), in In the American Province: Studies in the History and Historiography of Ideas (Bloomington: Indiana University Press, 1985), 85–88. Hollinger emphasizes that the surge of interest in religion among secular intellectuals did not, in his words, occasion any "sacrifices to ancient gods." Modernist critics and writers appreciated "novelties and liberties that the theologians did not." R. P. Blackmur, for instance, played "Augustine to Gide's St. Paul" (88).

5. Bell, The End of Ideology, 300, Morton White, Religion, Politics, and the Higher Learning (Cambridge, Mass.: Harvard University Press, 1959), 88–89 (see also White's trenchant critique of Niebuhr, 112–123), Richard Rovere, The American Establishment: And Other Reports, Opinions, and Speculations (New York: Harcourt, Brace, and World, 1962), 13.

6. Robert J. Griffith, "Dwight D. Eisenhower and the Corporate Commonwealth," American Historical Review 87 (February 1982), 87–122.

7. Jacques Maritain, Christianity and Democracy (New York: Charles Scribner's Sons, 1944), 10–11, John Cort, "Are We Missing a Bus?" Commonweal 46 (August 14, 1942), 392, 394, H. Norman Silbey, "The War as the Gospel's Opportunity," Christianity and Crisis 3 (August 9, 1943), 5, Francis Miller, "The Christian Church in the Latter Half of the Twentieth Century," Christianity and Crisis 2 (December 14, 1942), 4, Reinhold Niebuhr, "Anglo-Saxon Destiny and Responsibility," Christianity and Crisis 3 (October 4, 1943), 2. Mark Hulsether, Building a Protestant Left: Christianity and Crisis Magazine, 1941–1993 (Knoxville: University of Tennessee Press, 1999), 24–48, is an indispensable study of Christianity and Crisis at this time.

8. H. Richard Niebuhr, Meaning of Revelation, 122, H. Richard Niebuhr, "War as the Judgment of God," Christian Century 59 (May 13, 1942), 630–633, H. Richard Niebuhr, "Is God in the War?" Christian Century 59 (August 5, 1942), 953–955, H. Richard Niebuhr, "War as Crucifixion," Christian Century 60 (April 25, 1943), 513–515, John Hugo, "The Immorality of Conscription," Catholic Worker 11 (November 1944), 3, John Hugo, "Pacifist Problems," editorial, Catholic Worker 9 (February 1942), 2, Dorothy Day, "Random Reflections," Catholic Worker 11 (June 1944), 1–2. On the opposition of religious women to the war, see Rachel Waltner Goossen, Women against the Good War: Conscientious Objection and Gender on the American Home Front, 1941–1947 (Chapel Hill: University of North Carolina Press, 1999).

9. Reinhold Niebuhr, The Nature and Destiny of Man, vol. 1: Human Nature (New York: Charles Scribner's Sons, 1941), 226, Reinhold Niebuhr, "The End of the Beginning," Christianity and Crisis 2 (November 30, 1942), 1–2.

10. On Niebuhr's journey to the Fortune station, see Fox, Reinhold Niebuhr, 193–223; on Maritain's, see Julie Kiernan, Our Friend, Jacques Maritain: A Personal Memoir (Garden City, N.Y.: Doubleday, 1975), 120–135.

11. Reinhold Niebuhr, The Children of Light and the Children of Darkness (New York: Charles Scribner's Sons, 1944), 117–118, 146. On the wartime apprehensiveness about totalitarianism among liberals and radicals, see Alan Brinkley, The End of

Reform: New Deal Liberalism in Recession and War (New York: Alfred A. Knopf, 1995), 154–164.

12. Maritain, Christianity and Democracy, 22, 66, 77.

13. John Brophy, "The Industrial Council Plan," Commonweal 49 (November 12, 1948), 110–112, National Catholic Welfare Conference, "The Churches in Action," (November 21, 1948), in Nolan, Pastoral Letters, 411, John Cort, "Reform Begins at the Plant Level," Commonweal 48 (October 1, 1948), 597, John Cort, "Is Christian Industrialism Possible?" Commonweal 49 (October 29, 1948), 62–63.

14. Cort, "Is Christian Industrialism Possible?" 62, Cort, "Reform Begins," 597.

15. Reinhold Niebuhr, "Frontier Fellowship," Christianity and Society 13 (Autumn 1948), 4, Reinhold Niebuhr, "Democracy and World Responsibilities," Christianity and Society 14 (Autumn 1949), 7–8.

16. Reinhold Niebuhr, "The Anomaly of European Socialism," Yale Review 42 (December 1952), 167, Edwin Silcox, "The Christian Attitude Toward Capitalism and Socialism," Christianity and Crisis 10 (March 6, 1950), 19.

17. Editorial, "Democracy in Color," Christianity and Crisis 2 (March 23, 1942), 2, Niebuhr, Children of Light, 140–144, Jacques Maritain, "On Anti-Semitism," Commonweal 46 (September 28, 1942), 537; see also Maritain's piece in the same title in Christianity and Crisis 1 (October 6, 1941), 2–4. Brinkley, The End of Reform, 164–170, examines the renewed liberal attention to race.

18. Mark Silk, Spiritual Politics: Religion and America since World War II (New York: Simon and Schuster, 1988), 15–53. We are only beginning to understand the dynamics of postwar religious rapprochement. Will Herberg, Protestant, Catholic, Jew: An Essay in Religious Sociology (Garden City, N.Y.: Doubleday, 1960 [1955]), is the classic departure for this discussion; for a more recent assessment, see Martin E. Marty, Modern American Religion, vol. 3: Under God, Indivisible, 1941–1960 (Chicago: University of Chicago Press, 1996), 89–101. John T. McGreevey, "Thinking on One's Own: Catholics in the American Intellectual Imagination, 1928–1960," Journal of American History 84 (June 1997) 127–30, notes the easing of hostilities but does not explain it.

19. Niebuhr, Nature and Destiny of Man, 202; see also Reinhold Niebuhr, "The Roman Question Again," editorial, Christianity and Crisis 3 (October 18, 1943), 1, Niebuhr, Children of Light, 134, Maritain, Christianity and Democracy, 21, 31, 39.

20. H. A. Reinhold, "Let Us Give Thanks for Our Colored Brethren," Orate Fratres 17 (February 21, 1943), 174, Paul Hanly Furfey, "letter to the editor," Theological Studies 4 (September 1943), 467–472. Furfey was responding to John Courtney Murray, "On the Problem of Cooperation," American Ecclesiastical Review 112 (March 1945), 211.

21. Mortimer Adler, "God and the Professors," Vital Speeches 7 (December 1, 1940), 99–103, Jacques Maritain, Education at the Crossroads (New Haven: Yale University Press, 1943), 115. On the Conference on Science, Philosophy, and Religion, see Gilbert, Redeeming Culture, 70–93.

22. Sidney Hook, "The New Failure of Nerve," Partisan Review 10 (January–February 1943), 2–23, Philip Rahv, "The Sense and Nonsense of Whittaker Chambers," Partisan Review 19 (July–August 1952), 480–481, Lionel Trilling, The Liberal Imagination: Essays on Literature and Society (Garden City, N.Y.: Doubleday, 1953 [1950]), 7, 216–217, Lionel Trilling, "Our Country and Our Culture," Partisan Review 19 (May–June 1952), 324.

23. On the republic of science, see Gilbert, Redeeming Culture, 37–61. James B. Conant, On Understanding Science (New York: New American Library, 1951 [1947]), 18–19, James B. Conant, Science and Common Sense (New Haven: Yale University Press, 1951), 262.

24. Trilling, "Our Country and Our Culture," 320. See also Mills, "The Cultural Apparatus." Although Lears, "A Matter of Taste," 53, rightly argues that we should make an analytical distinction between "technicians and literati"—the first favoring the language of expertise and power and the second favoring that of taste and style—this seems to me to obscure the expertise and power of cultural professionals such as Trilling. On the growth of the military-industrial-educational complex after World War II, see David Noble, *Forces of Production: A Social History of Industrial Automation* (New York: Alfred A. Knopf, 1984), David Dickson, *The New Politics of Science* (New York: Pantheon, 1984), 22–162, Roger Geiger, *Research and Relevant Knowledge: American Research Universities since World War II* (New York: Oxford University Press, 1993).

25. Leslie Fiedler, "Our Country and Our Culture," *Partisan Review* 19 (May–June 1952) 295, 298, Trilling, *The Liberal Imagination,* 7; on Shapley, see Gilbert, *Redeeming Culture,* esp. 278–279.

26. Lewis Mumford, *Faith for Living* (New York: Harcourt, Brace, 1940), 46, 88, 166, 168.

27. Gilbert, *Redeeming Culture,* 80, Reinhold Niebuhr, *The Nature and Destiny of Man,* vol. 2: *Human Destiny* (New York: Charles Scribner's Sons, 1943), 287–321, Reinhold Niebuhr, *Faith and History: A Comparison of Christian and Modern Views of History* (New York: Charles Scribner's Sons, 1949), 167, Maritain, *Christianity and Democracy,* 23.

28. Editors' introduction to "Religion and the Intellectuals," *Partisan Review* 17 (February 1950), 103–105, William Barrett, *Partisan Review* 17(May 1950), 456–461, Allen Tate, *Partisan Review* 17(February 1950), 123, Alfred Kazin, *Partisan Review* 17(March 1950), 235, 237.

29. Theodor Adorno, *Minima Moralia: Reflections from Damaged Life,* trans. E. P. H. Jephcott (London: New Left Books, 1974 [1951]), 155, James Agee, "Religion and the Intellectuals" *Partisan Review* 17 (May 1950), 452–456, Barrett, *Partisan Review* 17, H. Stuart Hughes, "On Social Salvation," *Saturday Review* 34 (March 3, 1951), 14. The religious revival among secular intellectuals deserves more attention. Silk, *Spiritual Politics,* 28–39, and James Hudnot-Beumler, *Looking for God in the Suburbs: The Religion of the American Dream and Its Critics, 1945–1965* (New Brunswick, N.J.: Rutgers University Press, 1994), 65–71, are good starting points.

30. Tate, *Partisan Review* 17 (February 1950), 123.

31. H. Richard Niebuhr, "Towards a New Other-Worldliness," *Theology Today* 1 (April 1944), 85; see also H. Richard Niebuhr, "The Gift of the Catholic Vision," *Theology Today* 4 (June 1948), 513.

32. H. Richard Niebuhr, *Christ and Culture* (New York: Harper and Row, 1951), 188, 220, 236–237.

33. Ibid., 117, 130.

34. On containment as the dominant mode of postwar domestic life and social criticism, see Ross, *No Respect,* 42–64, Stephen J. Whitfield, *The Culture of the Cold War* (Baltimore: Johns Hopkins University Press, 1991), and Elaine Tyler May, *Homeward Bound: American Families in the Cold War Era* (New York: Basic Books, 1988), esp. 16–36, 114–134.

35. Lears, "A Matter of Taste," Hollinger, "Ethnic Diversity, Cosmopolitanism, and the Emergence of the American Liberal Intelligentsia," in *In the American Province,* 56–73; see also Terence Ball, "The Politics of Social Science in Postwar America," in May, Recasting America, 76–92. David Riesman, *The Lonely Crowd: A Study of the Changing American Character* (New Haven: Yale University Press, 1950), William H. Whyte, *The Organization Man* (New York: Simon and Schuster, 1956), Russell Lynes, *A Surfeit of Honey* (New York: Harper, 1957). For a deft

critique of this literature, see Harold Rosenberg, "The Orgamerican Phantasy," in *The Tradition of the New* (New York: Horizon Press, 1959), 269–285.

36. Daniel Bell, "Interpretations of American Politics," in *The Radical Right*, ed. Daniel Bell (Garden City, N.Y.: Anchor Books, 1964 [1955, entitled *The New American Right*]), 154–155, Richard Hofstadter, *Anti-Intellectualism in American Life* (New York: Vintage Books, 1963), 154–155, Richard Hofstadter, *The Age of Reform: From Bryan to FDR* (New York: Alfred A. Knopf, 1955), 152, 316–328. David W. Noble, "The Reconstruction of Progress: Charles Beard, Richard Hofstadter, and Postwar Historical Thought," in May, *Recasting America*, 71–74, discusses Hofstadter's optimism about the social sciences.

37. Robert J. Wuthnow, *The Restructuring of American Religion: Society and Faith since World War II* (Princeton, N.J.: Princeton University Press, 1988), 80–83, 100–131, quote on 127; the description of mainline Protestantism's managerial revolution comes from Paul Harrison's classic *Authority and Power in the Free Church Tradition: A Social Case Study of the American Baptist Convention* (Princeton, N.J.: Princeton University Press, 1959), 149. H. Richard Niebuhr, *The Purpose of the Church and Its Ministry* (New York: Harper and Row, 1956), 90–91.

38. John Cogley, "The Religious Revival," *Commonweal* 65 (January 18, 1958), 407, Andrew Greeley, *The Church and the Suburbs* (New York: Sheed and Ward, 1959), 46, Andrew Greeley, *Strangers in the House: Catholic Youth in America* (New York: Sheed and Ward, 1961), 147.

39. Greeley, *Church and the Suburbs*, 55, Daniel Callahan, *The Mind of the Catholic Layman* (New York: Charles Scribner's Sons, 1963), 127, Donald Thorman, *The Emerging Layman: The Role of the Catholic Layman in America* (Garden City, N.Y.: Doubleday, 1962), 109, Walter Ong, S.J., *Frontiers in American Catholicism: Essays in Ideology and Culture* (New York: Macmillan, 1957), 24–34. I examine the emergence of the layman in postwar Catholic intellectual life in "The Saint in the Gray Flannel Suit: The Professional-Managerial Class, 'The Layman,' and American Catholic Religious Culture, 1945–1965," *U.S. Catholic Historian* 15 (Summer 1997), 99–118.

40. The *Christian Century* vented its spleen at Billy Graham and the broader religious revival in a fusillade of editorials over the late spring and summer of 1957; see *Christian Century* 74 (May 8, May 15, June 19, and September 18, 1957), 582, 614–615, 749–751, 1095–1096. Callahan's dismissal of devotional piety is in *Mind of the Catholic Layman*, 129. The editors of *Commonweal* offered their jaundiced view of the revival in "Religion and Popular Culture," *Commonweal* 63 (October 7, 1955), 5–6. Cultural historians must begin paying more attention to the religious revival after World War II. The best studies of the revival by contemporaries—Herberg, *Protestant, Catholic, Jew*, A. Roy Eckhardt, *The Surge in Piety in America: An Appraisal* (New York: Association Press, 1958), and Martin E. Marty, *The New Shape of American Religion* (New York: Harper and Row, 1959)—were all written under the Niebuhrian shadow and have set the terms of almost all subsequent historical discussion of postwar popular religion. James Gilbert, *Another Chance: Postwar America, 1945–1968* (Philadelphia: Temple University Press, 1981), 233–241, Whitfield, *The Culture of the Cold War*, 77–100, Marty, *Under God, Indivisible*, 277–330, and the postmodernist Alan Nadel, "God's Law and the Wide Screen: *The Ten Commandments* as Cold War Epic," in *Containment Culture*, 90–116, all bear the marks of the Herberg-Eckhardt interpretation. Only the shrewd discussion of the Billy Graham controversy in Silk, *Spiritual Politics*, 54–69, manages to break the neoorthodox shackles.

41. Reinhold Niebuhr, "Pious and Secular America," *Atlantic Monthly* 200 (November 1957), 180–184, Ong, *Frontiers*, 10–11, Herberg, *Protestant, Catholic, Jew*, 2–3, 55.

42. Reinhold Niebuhr, "Editorial," *Christianity and Crisis* 16 (March 5, 1956), 18, Reinhold Niebuhr, *Pious and Secular America* (New York: Charles Scribner's Sons, 1958), 20–21; see also Reinhold Niebuhr, "After Comment, the Deluge," *Christian Century* 74 (September 4, 1957), 1034–1035. Herberg, *Protestant, Catholic, Jew*, 74–90, 260, 266–267.

43. John Courtney Murray, *We Hold These Truths: Catholic Reflections on the American Proposition* (New York: Sheed and Ward, 1960), 14, Reinhold Niebuhr, *Christian Realism and Political Problems* (New York: Charles Scribner's Sons, 1953), 68–72, Reinhold Niebuhr, *The Irony of American History* (New York: Charles Scribner's Sons, 1952), 7.

44. Ong, *Frontiers*, 31, Niebuhr, *Irony*, 90, 113, 116, 120. On postwar theories of modernization, see Michael J. Adas, *Machines as the Measure of Men: Science, Technology, and Ideologies of Western Dominance* (Ithaca, N.Y.: Cornell University Press, 1989), 411–412.

45. Niebuhr, *Christian Realism*, 119–146, Murray, *We Hold These Truths*, 285–289.

46. John Courtney Murray, "Catholics in America—A Creative Minority—Yes or No?" *Catholic Mind* 53 (October 1955), 594–595, Murray, *We Hold These Truths*, 7, 13, 42–43, 117–122. Murray bears a close resemblance to the Walter Lippmann of *Essays in the Public Philosophy* (Boston: Little, Brown, 1955). Murray's life and career receive perceptive scrutiny in Peter McDonough, *Men Astutely Trained: A History of the Jesuits in the American Century* (New York: Free Press, 1993), 219–233, and especially Cuddihy, *No Offense*, 64–100.

47. Ed Marciniak, "Catholics and Labor-Management Relations," in *The American Apostolate: American Catholics in the Twentieth Century*, ed. Leo Ward (Philadelphia: Westminster, 1952), 81, Ong, *Frontiers*, 30, 32, John Bennett, *Christians and the State* (New York: Macmillan, 1958), 277. Perry Miller lamented how Ong, his former student, reflected "just how 'American' the Catholicism of this country has become" in "Sinners in the Hands of a Benevolent God" (1958), in *Nature's Nation* (Cambridge, Mass.: Harvard University Press, 1967), 286. Jacques Maritain, *Reflections on America* (New York: Charles Scribner's Sons, 1958), 87, 108–109, 110. For examples of this strain of managerial ideology, see Peter Drucker, *The New Society: The Anatomy of the Industrial Order* (New York: Harper, 1950), R. W. Davenport (ed.), *U.S.A.: The Permanent Revolution* (New York: Prentice-Hall, 1951), Adolf A. Berle, *The Twentieth-Century Capitalist Revolution* (New York: Harcourt Brace, 1954), David Lilienthal, *Big Business: A New Era* (New York: Harper, 1953). See also Bell, *End of Ideology*, 39–94, and John Kenneth Galbraith, *American Capitalism: The Concept of Countervailing Power* (Boston: Houghton Mifflin, 1952), as arguments for the existence of a more responsible corporate order. On Hutchins, Adler, and the Great Books Program, see James Sloan Allen, *The Romance of Commerce and Culture: Capitalism, Modernism, and the Chicago-Aspen Crusade for Cultural Reform* (Chicago: University of Chicago Press, 1983), 78–109, and Joan Shelley Rubin, *The Making of Middlebrow Culture* (Chapel Hill: University of North Carolina Press, 1992), 186–197.

48. David J. Southern, *John LaFarge and The Limits of Catholic Interracialism* (Baton Rouge, La.: Louisiana State University Press, 1996), 289–325. On the shift from class to race as the pivot of liberal politics in the 1940s and 1950s, see Gary Gerstle, "The Protean Character of American Liberalism," *American Historical Review* 99 (October 1994), 1070–1072.

49. Reinhold Niebuhr, "The Sin of Racial Prejudice" (1948), cited in *A Reinhold Niebuhr Reader: Selected Essays, Articles, and Book Reviews*, ed. Charles C. Brown (Philadelphia: Trinity Press, 1992), 71, Reinhold Niebuhr, "Stevenson, the Democrats, and Civil Rights," *New Leader* (July 9, 1956), 11, Niebuhr, *Pious and Secu-*

lar America, 76; Reinhold Niebuhr, "The Desegregation Issue," *Christianity and Society* 21 (Spring 1956), 3–4. See Irving Howe's sharp criticism of Niebuhr, "Reverberations in the North," *Dissent* 3 (Spring 1956), 121–123, where he observes that Niebuhr does not let his "theological right hand" know what his "worldly political left hand does." Hulsether, *Building a Protestant Left*, 51, notes that the Protestant left, while committed to integration in theory, "failed to endorse even mild activism by African Americans" and viewed the problem "almost exclusively from the standpoint of government policymakers and white southern clergy." On the Catholic racial gospel in the first two decades after World War II, see Southern, *John LaFarge*, 289–325, from which the quotes are taken on 313 and 318. On the new liberal orthodoxy concerning race—one that focused on prejudicial attitudes rather than on structures and communities—see Walter A. Jackson, *Gunnar Myrdal and America's Conscience: Social Engineering and Racial Liberalism, 1938–1987* (Chapel Hill: University of North Carolina Press, 1990), 279–293, and Walter A. Jackson, "White Liberal Intellectuals, Civil Rights, and Gradualism, 1954–1960," in *The Making of Martin Luther King and the Civil Rights Movement*, ed. Brian Ward and Tony Badger (New York: New York University Press, 1996), 96–114. David W. Wills, "Black Americans and the Establishment," in *Between the Times*, ed. Hutchison, 182–188, examines the uneasy and incomplete incorporation of black Protestants into mainstream circles in the 1950s.

50. William H. Kirkland, "Needed: A Culture Ethic," *Christian Century* 74 (December 18, 1957), 1510–1512, esp. 1511, where the author asserts that postwar challenges "cannot be met by the revival of a social gospel movement." See also Ralph B. Thompson, "Christian Virtues in an Age of Abundance," *Christian Century* 74 (December 18, 1957), 1508–1510. Niebuhr, *Irony*, 46. The persistence of the producer ethic in postwar social criticism is noted in Lears, *Fables of Abundance*, 255–256, and Daniel Horowitz, *Vance Packard and American Social Criticism* (Chapel Hill: University of North Carolina Press, 1994), esp. 122–131, 177–178 (Horowitz notes Niebuhr's influence on Packard on 127).

51. Ong, *Frontiers*, 10, Marshall McLuhan, *The Mechanical Bride: The Folklore of Industrial Man* (New York: Vanguard Press, 1951), v, 11, 33–34, 102, William Lynch, *The Image Industries* (New York: Sheed and Ward, 1959), 6, 10, 26, 113–125, 131, 141. On McLuhan, see Philip Marchand, *Marshall McLuhan: The Medium and the Messenger* (New York: Ticknor and Fields, 1989), and Patrick Allitt, *Catholic Converts: British and American Intellectuals Turn to Rome* (Ithaca, N.Y.: Cornell University Press, 1997), 313–316.

52. Ong, *Frontiers*, 101, 121–123, Walter Ong, "Wired for Sound: Teaching, Communication, and Technological Culture," in *The Barbarian Within: And Other Fugitive Essays and Studies* (New York: Macmillan, 1962), 226.

53. A. J. Muste, "Saints for This Age" (1962), in *Essays of A. J. Muste*, ed Hentoff, 410–411, 412, 418, A. J. Muste, *Not By Might: Christianity the Way to Human Decency* (New York: Harper and Brothers, 1947), 43, 118, Dorothy Day, "We Go on Record," *Catholic Worker* 13 (December 1946), 4.

54. James J. Farrell, *The Spirit of the Sixties: The Making of Postwar Radicalism* (New York and London: Routledge, 1997), 5–136, is the most comprehensive discussion of the personalist brand of postwar social and cultural criticism. There is as yet no serious biography of Goodman. On Macdonald, see Michael Wreszin, *Rebel in Defense of Tradition: The Life and Politics of Dwight Macdonald* (New York: Basic Books, 1994), and Sumner. Rexroth's cultural criticism can be sampled in Kenneth Rexroth, *Assays* (New York: New Directions, 1961); on Rexroth's spirituality, the meager discussion by Linda Hamalian, *A Life of Kenneth Rexroth*

(New York: W. W. Norton, 1991), 76, 125–126, is disappointing, especially given Rexroth's pronounced interest in Catholicism and Buddhism.

55. "Tract for the Times," *Liberation* 1 (March 1956), 6, Paul Goodman, "Reflections on Drawing the Line" (1945), in *Drawing the Line: The Political Essays of Paul Goodman*, ed. Taylor Stoehr (New York: E. P. Dutton, 1979 [1977]), 5, Paul Goodman, with Percival Goodman, *Communitas: Means of Livelihood and Ways of Life* (Chicago: University of Chicago Press, 1947), 14, 171, Paul Goodman, *Growing Up Absurd: Problems of Youth in the Organized System* (New York: Random House, 1960), 141–143. Dwight Macdonald, "Dorothy Day" (1952), in *Memoirs of a Revolutionist: Essays in Political Criticism* (New York: Farrar, Straus, and Cudahy, 1957), 349–368. Harrington relates Macdonald's observation about the Catholic Worker in Michael Harrington, *Fragments of the Century* (New York: E. P. Dutton, 1973), 19. Weil's pieces in *politics* were Simone Weil, "Reflections on War," *politics* 2 (February 1945), 55, Simone Weil, "The Iliad—A Poem of Force," *politics* 2 (November 1945), 328, and Simone Weil, "Factory Work," *politics* 3 (December 1946), 369–375. On Macdonald's interest in Weil, see Sumner, *Dwight Macdonald*, 55–60. Weil's work and life attracted the interest (not all of it admiring) of a number of postwar intellectuals. Leslie Fiedler referred to her as "our kind of saint" in his introduction to Weil's *Waiting for God* (New York: Harper and Row, 1973 [1951]), 3, whereas Rexroth would have advised her, as he wrote in *Assays*, "to put some meat on your bones and get a husband" (201).

56. On Muste, Day, and their pacifist activism, see Maurice Isserman, *If I Had a Hammer: The Death of the Old Left and the Birth of the New Left* (New York: Basic Books, 1987), 144–147, 174–180. Dee Garrison, " 'Our Skirts Gave Them Courage': The Civil Defense Protest Movement in New York City, 1955–1961," in *Not June Cleaver: Women and Gender in Postwar America, 1945–1960*, ed. Joanne Meyerowitz (Philadelphia: Temple University Press, 1994), 201–226, examines the strong maternalist dimension of the civil protests.

57. A. J. Muste, "Theology of Despair: An Open Letter to Reinhold Niebuhr" (1948), in Hentoff, 303–307, Muste, "Pacifism and Perfection" (1948), 312; see also Muste, *Not By Might*, 170–171, 179–180.

58. Thomas Merton, *Seeds of Contemplation* (New York: New Directions, 1949), 26, 28, Thomas Merton, *Disputed Questions* (New York: Farrar, Straus, and Cudahy, 1960), 179, 188, 206, Thomas Merton, *The Silent Life* (New York: Farrar, Straus, and Cudahy, 1957), 42. Merton's life and work have become a veritable cottage industry. I have relied mainly on Fisher, *Catholic Counterculture*, 206–247, and Michael Mott, *The Seven Mountains of Thomas Merton* (Boston: Houghton Mifflin, 1984). Merton's autobiography, *The Seven Storey Mountain* (New York: Harcourt, Brace, 1948), is an extraordinary personal account of religious conversion, even though it obscures or conceals some of the more unsavory episodes of his life.

59. Howard Thurman, "The Fellowship Church for All Peoples" (1945), in Fluker and Tumber, eds., *Howard Thurman*, 226, James Farmer, memorandum to Muste (spring 1942), included in Francis Broderick and August Meier (eds.), *Negro Protest Thought in the Twentieth Century* (Indianapolis, Ind.: Bobbs-Merrill, 1966 [1965]), 212, 215, 216–217. See James Farmer, *Lay Bare the Heart: An Autobiography of the Civil Rights Movement* (New York: Arbor House, 1985), 101–116, on the early years of CORE.

60. Howard Thurman, *With Head and Heart: The Autobiography of Howard Thurman* (New York: Harcourt Brace Jovanovich, 1979), 144–145, 151–153, 159, 161, Howard Thurman, *Jesus and the Disinherited* (Nashville, Tenn.: Abingdon Press, 1969 [1949]), 22–23.

61. David Dellinger, *From Yale to Jail: The Life Story of a Moral Dissenter* (New York: Pantheon, 1993), 62–63, 145–152. On Dellinger's influential reportage on the Cuban Revolution for the *Catholic Worker*, see Van Gosse, *Where the Boys Are: Cuba, Cold War America, and the Making of a New Left* (New York: Verso, 1993), 255–256. Staughton Lynd, *Living Inside Our Hope* (Ithaca, N.Y.: Cornell University Press, 1997), 48–50.

62. Dorothy Day, "The Church and Work," *Catholic Worker* 13 (September 1946), 8; other pieces in the series were Dorothy Day, "Reflections on Work," *Catholic Worker* 13 (November 1946), 1, 4, and Dorothy Day, "Reflections on Work," *Catholic Worker* 13 (December 1946), 1, 4.

63. Ed Willock, "Toward Peace in the Lay Apostolate," *Integrity* 3 (December 1948), 19–20. On the *Integrity* circle and its abortive Marycrest farm commune, see Fisher, *Catholic Countercultures*, 101–129. Claire Hutchet Bishop, *All Things Common* (New York: Harper and Brothers, 1950), Elizabeth Rogers, review of Melford Shapiro, *Venture in Utopia* (1956), *Catholic Worker* 25 (February 1959), 4–5. Another sympathetic discussion of the *communités du travail* is Erich Fromm, *The Sane Society* (New York: Fawcett World Library, 1967 [1955]), 267–279. See also Michael Harrington, "Review of Martin Buber's *Paths in Utopia*" (1949), *Catholic Worker* 18 (July–August 1951), 3, 6, Michael Harrington, "Review of Frank Tannenbaum's *A Philosophy of Labor*" (1951), *Catholic Worker* 18 (October 1951), 5, Michael Harrington, "Social Democracy," *Catholic Worker* 19 (December 1952), 4.

64. Merton, *Seeds of Contemplation*, 26, 106–107.

65. Robert Ludlow, "Constructive Anarchism," *Catholic Worker* 18 (July–August 1952), 4; see also Robert Ludlow, "Personalist Revolution," *Catholic Worker* 18 (November 1952), 1, 4–5.

66. Robert Ludlow, "Pax Column," *Catholic Worker* 15 (June 1948), 7, Robert Ludlow, "Pax Column," *Catholic Worker* 14 (June 1947), 6, Robert Ludlow, "Pax Column," *Catholic Worker* 14 (March 1947), 3.

67. Robert Ludlow, "Pax Column," *Catholic Worker* 14 (April 1947), 3, Robert Ludlow, "Pax Column," *Catholic Worker* 15 (July–August 1948), 7, Robert Ludlow, "The State and the Christian," *Catholic Worker* 15 (October 1948), 6, 8, Robert Ludlow, "Eternal Man," *Catholic Worker* 16 (June 1949), 5–6.

68. Robert Ludlow, "Christian Anarchism," *Catholic Worker* 16 (September 1949), 5.

5. The Gospel of Eros

1. Taylor Branch, *Parting the Waters: America in the King Years, 1954–1963* (New York: Simon and Schuster, 1988), 102, 118, 363, Martin Luther King, Jr., "Letter from Birmingham Jail," in *Why We Can't Wait*, ed. Martin Luther King, Jr. (New York: Dell, 1964), 82–83.

2. Richard Fox, *Reinhold Niebuhr*, 257–258.

3. Paul A. Carter, *Another Part of the Fifties* (New York: Columbia University Press, 1983), 141–146, is a brief account of Tillich's impact on the intellectual scene. Doug Rossinow, *The Politics of Authenticity: Liberalism, Christianity, and the New Left in America* (New York: Columbia University Press, 1998), 64–68, outlines Tillich's thought and assesses his impact on the New Left.

4. Fox, *Reinhold Niebuhr*, 257, Philip Rieff, *Triumph of the Therapeutic*, 223. Rieff did not always feel this way about Tillich: see, for instance, "Paul Tillich's Systematic Theology," (1952) in Imber, ed. *The Feeling Intellect*, 134–36.

5. On Tillich's early life, see Paul Tillich, *On the Boundary: An Autobiographical Sketch* (New York: Charles Scribner & Sons, 1966), 14–15, Paul Tillich, *My Search*

for Absolutes (New York: Simon and Schuster, 1967), 23–33, Wilhelm Pauck and Marion Pauck, *Paul Tillich: His Life and Thought,* vol. 1: *Life* (New York: Harper and Row, 1976), 1–5. See also Rollo May, *Paulus: Reminiscences of a Friendship* (New York: Harper and Row, 1973), 77–79. There is no definitive biography of Tillich. The Paucks' volume is informative but uncritical. May (a former student and friend of Tillich's) is psychologically astute but protective. Both books were written, I suspect, with Hannah Tillich's painful and revealing memoirs in mind. In *From Time to Time* and *From Place to Place* (New York: Stein and Day, 1973, 1976), Hannah Tillich recounts her life with Tillich with excruciating candor.

6. The poem is quoted in May, *Paulus,* 41.

7. Tillich, *On the Boundary,* 17–19, Tillich, *My Search,* 25, Wilhelm and Marion Pauck, *Paul Tillich,* 6–9.

8. Tillich, *On the Boundary,* 19–24, Tillich, *My Search,* 33–38, Paul Tillich, *The Protestant Era* (Chicago: University of Chicago Press, 1948), ix–xi; Wilhelm and Marion Pauck, *Paul Tillich,* 16–20. On German youth and student movements, see George L. Mosse, *The Crisis of German Ideology: Intellectual Origins of the Third Reich* (New York: Schocken Press, 1981 [1964]), 171–217, Fritz Stern, *The Politics of Cultural Despair* (Berkeley: University of California Press, 1961), 223–227.

9. Wilhelm and Marion Pauck, *Paul Tillich,* 20–29, Tillich, *On the Boundary,* 31–32, Tillich, *My Search,* 38, Paul Tillich, "Autobiographical Reflections," in *The Theology of Paul Tillich,* ed. C. W. Kegley and R. W. Bretall (New York: Macmillan, 1952), 7. The psychosexual dynamics reflected in these rituals are explored best in Klaus Theweleit, *Male Fantasies* (Minneapolis: University of Minnesota Press, 1987).

10. Tillich, *My Search,* 39, Wilhelm and Marion Pauck, *Paul Tillich,* 40–56, quote on 56.

11. Detlev Peukert, *The Weimar Republic,* 164–190, Peter Gay, *Weimar Culture: The Outsider as Insider* (New York: Harper and Row, 1968), 70–101, on the hunger for wholeness, see also Anson Rabinbach, *In the Shadow of Apocalypse: German Intellectuals Between Apocalypse and Enlightenment* (Berkeley: University of California Press, 1997), esp. part 1.

12. On the *Kairos* circle, see Tillich, *On the Boundary,* 33–36, Wilhelm and Marion Pauck, *Paul Tillich,* 70–75, Ronald H. Stone, *Paul Tillich's Radical Social Thought* (Atlanta, Ga.: John Knox Press, 1980), 46–53. On Tillich's relationship to the Frankfurt Marxists (he supervised Adorno's dissertation and helped Horkheimer secure an academic position), see Martin Jay, *The Dialectical Imagination: A History of the Frankfurt School and the Institute for Social Research, 1923–1950* (Boston: Houghton Mifflin, 1973), 24–25, 66–68. Martin Buber's religious socialism can be sampled in Martin Buber, *I and Thou,* trans. Walter Kaufmann (New York: Charles Scribner's Sons, 1970 [1922]); on Buber, see Maurice Friedman, *Martin Buber's Life and Work: The Middle Years, 1923–1945* (New York: Dutton, 1983), 95–119. On Bloch and Benjamin, see Rabinbach, *In the Shadow of the Apocalypse,* 27–65.

13. Paul Tillich, "The Protestant Message and the Man of Today" (1929), Paul Tillich, "Kairos" (1922), and Paul Tillich, "Realism and Faith" (1929), in *The Protestant Era* (Chicago: University of Chicago Press, 1948), 44–46, 69, 192, 200, Paul Tillich, "Basic Principles of Religious Socialism" (1923), in *Political Expectation,* trans. and ed. Franklin Sherman (New York: Harper and Row, 1971), 85, Paul Tillich, *The Socialist Decision,* trans. and ed. Franklin Sherman (New York: Harper and Row, 1977 [1933]), 150.

14. Paul Tillich, "On the Idea of a Theology of Culture" (1919), in *What Is Religion?* ed. James Luther Adams (New York: Harper and Row, 1969), 159–160, Tillich,

The Socialist Decision, xxxii, 150–160, Tillich, "Basic Principles," 78–79, and Tillich, "Religious Socialism" (1930), in *Political Expectation*, 53.

15. Paul Tillich, "The Idea and Ideal of Personality" (1930), in *Protestant Era*, 115–117, 130–131, Hannah Arendt, *The Origins of Totalitarianism* (New York: Harcourt, Brace, 1951).

16. Tillich, "Ideal of Personality," 134–135, Paul Tillich, *The Religious Situation*, trans. H. Richard Niebuhr (New York: Harper and Brothers, 1932 [1925]), 104–105, 107.

17. Tillich, *Religious Situation*, 58–59; on the *neue Sachlichkeit*, see John Willett, *Art and Politics in Weimar Germany: The New Sobriety, 1917–1933* (London: Macmillan, 1978).

18. Tillich, *The Religious Situation*, 201, Tillich, "On the Idea of a Theology of Culture," 172–173. On Weimar's sexual revolution, see Renate Bridenthal, Atina Grossman, and Marion Kaplan (eds.), *When Biology Became Destiny: Women in Weimar and Nazi Germany* (New York: Monthly Review Press, 1984), esp. 66–197.

19. Hannah Tillich discusses her marriage at this time in *From Time to Time*, 99–156; quotes are from 103–104, 115, 190. Tillich himself made veiled references to his sexual life in some of his sermons and speeches; see, for example, Paul Tillich, "God's Pursuit of Man," in *The Eternal Now* (New York: Charles Scribner's Sons, 1963), 106: "I speak of the ecstasy of living that includes participation in the highest and the lowest of life in one and the same experience." The most judicious discussion of the Tillichs' erotic life is Alexander C. Irwin, *Eros Toward the World: Paul Tillich's Theology of the Erotic* (Minneapolis: University of Minnesota Press, 1991), 99–120.

20. Colin Campbell, *The Romantic Ethic and the Spirit of Modern Consumerism* (Oxford, England: Basil Blackwell, 1987), 195–201. On Weimar Germany's consumer culture, see Peukert, *The Weimar Republic*, 174–177. Tillich, "The Protestant Message," 200, Tillich, "On the Idea of a Theology of Culture," 178.

21. Wilhelm and Marion Pauck, *Paul Tillich*, 159–161.

22. Tillich, *My Search*, 47–49, Hannah Tillich, *From Time to Time*, 169–173. Fox, *Reinhold Niebuhr*, 160–164, 257–259, relates the deterioration of Tillich's friendship with Niebuhr, which appears to have resulted from a combination of professional rivalry, theological difference, and Niebuhr's revulsion at Tillich's sexual behavior.

23. Wilhelm and Marion Pauck, *Paul Tillich*, 183–186. On the Columbia Seminar and the New York Group, see Holifield, *History of Pastoral Care*, 324–325, and Seward Hiltner, "Tillich the Person," *Theology Today* 30 (December 1974), 383. Influential works by Protestant members of the New York Group include Seward Hiltner, *The Context of Pastoral Counseling* (Nashville, Tenn.: Abingdon Press, 1961), and David Roberts, *Psychotherapy and a Christian View of Man* (New York: Harper and Row, 1950).

24. Erich Fromm, *Escape from Freedom* (New York: Farrar and Rinehart, 1941), 56–122, Erich Fromm, *Man for Himself* (New York: Rinehart, 1947), 18–46, Erich Fromm, *Psychoanalysis and Religion* (New Haven: Yale University Press, 1950), Karen Horney, *The Neurotic Personality of Our Time* (New York: W. W. Norton, 1939). (Fromm's first book, published in Germany in 1930, was entitled *The Dogma of Christ*.) Holifield, 284–88, covers Fromm's impact on pastoral counseling. For critiques of the revisionists, see Herbert Marcuse, *Eros and Civilization: A Philosophical Inquiry into Freud* (Boston: Beacon Press, 1955), 217–251, Russell Jacoby, *Social Amnesia: A Critique of Conformist Psychology from Adler to Laing* (Boston: Beacon Press, 1975), 19–45, Ellen Herman, *The Romance of American Psychology: Political Culture in the Age of Experts* (Berkeley: University of Cal-

ifornia Press, 1995), 264–275. Recent defenses of the neo-Freudians include Marcia Westcott, *The Feminist Legacy of Karen Horney* (New Haven: Yale University Press, 1986), and Daniel Burston, *The Legacy of Erich Fromm* (Cambridge, Mass.: Harvard University Press, 1991.)

25. Paul Tillich, "Ethics in a Changing World" (1941), in *The Protestant Era*, 158, Paul Tillich, "Man and Society in Religious Socialism," *Christianity and Society* 8 (Winter 1943), 17.

26. Paul Tillich, "Spiritual Problems of Post-War Reconstruction," *Christianity and Crisis* 2 (August 10, 1942), 3–5.

27. Paul Tillich, "You Are Accepted," in *The Shaking of the Foundations* (New York: Charles Scribner's Sons, 1948), 154–162, Melanie Klein, "Love, Guilt, and Reparation" (1937), in *Love, Guilt, and Reparation and Other Works 1921–1945* (New York: Delacorte Press, 1975), 306–343.

28. Tillich, "You Are Accepted," 162–163, Fox, *Reinhold Niebuhr*, 257, Blake, *Beloved Community*, 289.

29. Tillich, "Spiritual Problems," 6, Tillich, "Born in the Grave," in *Shaking of the Foundations*, 165, Tillich, *The Protestant Era*, xvii, 230.

30. Tillich, *The Protestant Era*, 227–233. On Macdonald, Goodman, and others, see Chapter 4.

31. Paul Tillich, "Protestant Principles," *The Protestant Digest* 4 (April–May 1942), 17; see also Paul Tillich, "The Post-Protestant Era," *Protestant Digest* 4 (August–September 1941), 4.

32. Paul Tillich, "The Transmoral Conscience" (1945), in *The Protestant Era*, 136–149; see also Paul Tillich, "The Yoke of Religion," in *Shaking of the Foundations*, 93–103. Historians and theologians have assumed routinely that neoorthodoxy's tough-mindedness about the human capacity for evil necessarily translated into an equally stringent moral code. However, Holifield, 276–280, writes of the neoorthodox "revolt against legalism."

33. On other-direction, see Riesman, *Lonely Crowd*, 19–24; on the social ethic, see Whyte, *Organization Man*, 7–8, 22–59; on the hipster, see Norman Mailer, "The White Negro: Superficial Reflections on the Hipster," in *Advertisements for Myself* (New York: G. P. Putnam's Sons, 1959), 41–59.

34. Hannah Tillich, *From Time to Time*, 176–177. On Small's Paradise, see David Levering Lewis, *When Harlem Was in Vogue: The Harlem Renaissance in the 1920s* (New York: Vintage, 1981), 320.

35. James Baldwin, *The Fire Next Time* (New York: Dell, 1988 [1963]), 49–50. On Baldwin's *Go Tell It on the Mountain* as a tale of redemption, see Albert Raboteau, "The Conversion Experience," in Raboteau, *A Fire in the Bones: Reflections on African-American Religious History* (Boston: Beacon Press, 1995), 157–65.

36. Hannah Tillich, *From Time to Time*, 14, Janine Chasseguet-Smirgel, "Some Thoughts on the Ego Ideal: A Contribution to the Study of the 'Illness of Ideality,' " *Psychoanalytic Quarterly* 45 (Autumn 1976), 345–373, Melanie Klein, "Envy and Gratitude" (1957), in *Envy and Gratitude and Other Essays 1946–1963* (New York: Delacorte, 1975), 176–235.

37. Paul Tillich, "The Shaking of the Foundations," in *Shaking of the Foundations*, 3, 7, 9, Paul Tillich, "Beyond Religious Socialism," *Christian Century* 66 (June 15, 1949), 732–733.

38. Wilhelm and Marion Pauck, *Paul Tillich*, 246–285, Hannah Tillich, *From Time to Time*, 197–243, quote on 198, Paul Tillich, "The Ambiguity of Perfection," speech delivered at *Time* magazine banquet, quoted in *Time* (May 17, 1963), 69.

39. Carl Schorske, "A Life of Learning," in May, ed., *Recasting America*, 101–102 and Carl Schorske, *Fin-de-Siecle Vienna: Politics and Culture* (New York: Alfred A.

Knopf, 1980), xxiii–xxv recounts this shift in intellectual life. Dorothy Dinner-
stein, *The Mermaid and the Minotaur: Sexual Arrangements and Human Malaise* (New
York: Harper and Row, 1976), 258–262, 265–266, also evokes this moment well.

40. Herbert Marcuse, *Eros and Civilization*, 63–70, quote on 66, Erik H. Erikson,
Young Man Luther: A Study in Psychoanalysis and History (New York: W. W. Norton, 1958), 20–21, Norman O. Brown, *Life Against Death: The Psychoanalytical
Meaning of History* (Middletown, Conn.: Wesleyan University Press, 1985
[1959]), xvii, 13, 227, 307–322.

41. Brown, *Life Against Death*, 202–233.

42. Erikson, *Young Man Luther*, 219, 265, Paul Goodman, *Growing Up Absurd: Problems of Youth in the Organized System* (New York: Random House, 1960), 133–143.

43. For an overview, see Walter Kaufmann, "The Reception of Existentialism in the
United States," *Salmagundi* 10–11 (Fall 1969–Winter 1970), 69–96. The most
widely read works on existentialism were Walter Kaufmann (ed.), *Existential-
ism from Dostoevsky to Sartre* (New York: Meridian Books, 1966 [1956]), William
Barrett, *Irrational Man: A Study in Existential Philosophy* (Garden City, N.Y.: Dou-
bleday, 1958), and Will Herberg (ed.), *Four Existentialist Theologians: Jacques
Maritain, Nicholas Berdyaev, Martin Buber, and Paul Tillich* (Garden City, N.Y.:
Doubleday, 1958).

44. On existentialism among college students, see Rossinow, *The Politics of Authenticity*, 53–84. Existentialism, Rossinow writes, "validated the complaints of college
students by asserting that material deprivation was not the only legitimate source
of unhappiness, that in fact it was not the most politically salient one" (194).

45. Paul Tillich, *The Courage to Be* (New Haven: Yale University Press, 1952), 4, Paul
Tillich, "Psychoanalysis, Existentialism, and Theology," *Pastoral Psychology* 9
(1958), 16, Paul Tillich, *Systematic Theology*, vol. 1 (Chicago: University of Chicago Press, 1951), 99. On the use of religion and values by existentialist psychologists, Jacoby, *Social Amnesia*, 54–58, is especially acute. Tillich's remarks
on psychology are cited in Robert Coles, "In Paul Tillich's Seminar," in *Harvard
Diary: Reflections on the Sacred and the Secular* (New York: Crossroad, 1990), 164.

46. Tillich, *Courage to Be*, 123–154.

47. Ibid., 186–188, Paul Tillich, "To Whom Much Is Forgiven," in *The New Being*
(New York: Charles Scribner's Sons, 1955), 6, Paul Tillich, *Systematic Theology*,
vol. 3 (Chicago: University of Chicago Press, 1963), 178, Paul Tillich, "The Person in a Technical Society," in *Christian Faith and Social Action*, ed. John A.
Hutchison (New York: Oxford University Press, 1953), 151.

48. Paul Tillich, "Holy Waste," in *The New Being*, 46–49.

49. On the influence of religion (particularly of Christian existentialism) on student radicals, see Sara Evans, *Personal Politics* (New York: Vintage, 1980 [1979]),
29–36, Todd Gitlin, *The Sixties: Years of Hope, Days of Rage* (New York: Bantam
Books, 1987), 105–109, and especially Doug Rossinow, " 'The Break-Through to
New Life': Christianity and the Emergence of the New Left in Austin, Texas,
1956–1964," *American Quarterly* 46 (September 1994), 309–340, Rossinow, *The
Politics of Authenticity*, 53–114, and Farrell, *Spirit of the Sixties*, 137–154. For examples, see the Student Non-Violent Coordinating Committee (SNCC) charter,
cited in Clayborne Carson, *In Struggle: SNCC and the Black Awakening of the
1960s* (Cambridge, Mass.: Harvard University Press, 1981), 23–24, *Student Voice*
1 (1960), 3, Tom Hayden"The Port Huron Statement," Appendix to James
Miller, *Democracy Is in the Streets: From Port Huron to the Siege of Chicago* (New
York, 1987), 331–333. Martin Luther King, Jr., *Stride toward Freedom: The Montgomery Story* (New York: Harper and Row, 1958), 17, 218. On King's theological
development, Keith Miller, *Voice of Deliverance: The Language of Martin Luther*

King, Jr., and Its Sources (New York: Free Press, 1991), is indispensable. I dissent from Lasch's enlistment of King as a promoter of petty bourgeois virtues in *True and Only Heaven*, 394–395.

50. Martin Luther King, Jr., *Strength to Love* (New York: Harper and Row, 1963), 120–121; Martin Luther King, Jr., "The Most Durable Power," *Christian Century* 74 (June 5, 1957), 708, King, *Stride toward Freedom*, 90–107.

51. King, *Stride toward Freedom*, 86.

52. Paul Tillich, "Religion as a Dimension in Man's Spiritual Life," in *Theology of Culture*, ed. Robert C. Kimball (New York: Oxford University Press, 1959), 3–9, Tillich, *Courage to Be*, 177, 186–190. See also Paul Tillich, "Beyond the Usual Alternatives," *Christian Century* 75 (May 8, 1958), 558, and interview with Ved Mehta, *The New Theologian* (New York: Farrar, Straus and Giroux, 1966), 45–54.

53. On the method of correlation, see Tillich, *Systematic Theology*, vol. 1, 59–66. Tillich's remarks at the Union art exhibition are cited in Carter, *Another Part of the Fifties*, 142–143. Tillich, "Protestantism and Artistic Style" (1957), in Kimball, Theology of Culture, 68–75.

54. The citations from Newman and Rothko can be found in Annette Cox, *Art-as-Politics: The Abstract Expressionist Avant-Garde and Society* (Ann Arbor: University of Michigan Press, 1982), 68–69, and in Lears, *Fables of Abundance*, 367. Historians are beginning to see in the abstract expressionists more than a simple retreat from the social concerns of the 1930s: Lears, *Fables*, 364–367, and Daniel Belgrad, *The Culture of Spontaneity: Improvisation and the Arts in Postwar America* (Chicago: University of Chicago Press, 1998), esp. 105–119.

55. H. Richard Niebuhr, "Reformation: Continuing Imperative," *Christian Century* 77 (March 2, 1960), 250–251, H. Richard Niebuhr, Cole Lectures (1961), in *Theology, History, Culture*, 3–49, quotation on 42.

56. Niebuhr, Cole Lectures, 32, H. Richard Niebuhr, *Radical Monotheism and Western Culture* (New York: Harper and Row, 1960), 39, 44, 52. Frederic Jameson captures the significance of this abstracting and purely therapeutic turn. In this hermeneutic dispensation, the gospel, he writes, can be "translated into existential or ontological experiences, whose essentially abstract language and figuration . . . can now, much like the 'open works' of aesthetic modernism, be offered to a differentiated public of Western city-dwellers to be recoded in terms of their own private situations": Frederic Jameson, *Postmodernism; Or, The Cultural Logic of Late Capitalism* (Durham, N.C.: Duke University Press, 1991), 390.

57. Joseph Campbell, *Hero with a Thousand Faces* (Princeton, N.J.: Princeton University Press, 1949), 388–391.

58. Paul Tillich, "Waiting," in Tillich, *Shaking of the Foundations*, 149–152.

59. Tillich, *From Time to Time*, 223.

60. Ibid., 242–243.

6. THE TWILIGHT OF THE GODS

1. Paul Goodman, "Post-Christian Man" (1961), in *Utopian Essays and Practical Proposals* (New York: Vintage Books, 1962), 80–82, 86, 89.

2. Ibid., 85, 90–91.

3. Paul Goodman, *New Reformation: Notes of a Neo-Lithic Conservative* (New York: Vintage Books, 1971 [1970]), 62–63.

4. James Miller, *Democracy Is in the Streets: From Port Huron to the Streets of Chicago* (New York: Simon and Schuster, 1987), Todd Gitlin, *The Sixties*, esp. 420–438, Howard Brick, *The Age of Contradiction: American Thought and Culture in the*

1960s (Boston: Twayne, 1998),Doug Rossinow, *Politics of Authenticity*, Rossinow, "The New Left and the Counterculture: Hypotheses and Evidence," *Radical History Review* 67 (Winter 1997), 79–120. If only because of its attention to religion in the emergence of the New Left, Rossinow's work itself constitutes a breakthrough in our understanding of postwar liberalism and radicalism. See also *The Sixties: From Memory to History*, David Farber (ed.) (Chapel Hill: University of North Carolina Press, 1994). Wini Breines, "Whose New Left?" *Journal of American History* 75 (September 1988), 528–545, while it poses a valuable corrective to the rise and fall scenario set forth in both Miller and Gitlin, does not address the argument that the women's and gay liberation movements—fissionary products, she argues, of the male, heterosexual New Left's declension—escaped a therapeutic ethos. On this score, see Rossinow, *Politics of Authenticity*, 291–295.

5. Save for Rossinow, none of the works cited earlier more than glance at religion, but see Farber's suggestive remarks in his introduction to *The Sixties*, 4–5, 10, n. 9. See Wuthnow, *Restructuring of American Religion*, 133–214; see also Robert Wuthnow, *The Consciousness Reformation* (Berkeley: University of California Press, 1976), on the rising interest in therapies and Eastern religions. Steven Tipton, *Getting Saved from the Sixties: Moral Meaning in Conversion and Cultural Change* (Berkeley: University of California Press, 1982), Walter Anderson, *The Upstart Spring: Esalen and the American Awakening* (Reading, Mass.: Addison-Wesley, 1983), Peter Clecak, *America's Quest for the Ideal Self: Dissent and Fulfillment in the 60s and 70s* (New York: Oxford University Press, 1983). Robert S. Ellwood, *The Sixties' Spiritual Awakening: American Religion Moving from Modern to Postmodern* (New Brunswick, N.J.: Rutgers University Press, 1994), is a good point of departure despite the facile interpretive trope announced in the subtitle.

6. Howard Brick, "Optimism of the Mind: Imagining Post-Industrial Society in the 1960s and 1970s," *American Quarterly* 44 (September 1992), 348–380, is a seminal essay on the notion of postindustrial society. Brick's bibliography provides a wide-ranging introduction to the literature. For examples, see David Bazelon, *Power in America: The Politics of the New Class* (New York: New American Library, 1967), John Kenneth Galbraith, *The New Industrial State* (Boston: Houghton Mifflin, 1967), and Daniel Bell, *The Coming of Post-Industrial Society: An Essay in Social Forecasting* (New York: Basic Books, 1973). I also would include under this rubric the new working class analysis, originating in French Marxism, that influenced Students for a Democratic Society (SDS); on its American impact, see Rossinow, *Politics of Authenticity*, 187–196. Christopher Lasch, "After the New Left," in *The World of Nations* (New York: Alfred A. Knopf, 1973), 133–139, offers a deft critique of postindustrial theory.

7. Michael Harrington, *Toward a Democratic Left: A Radical Program for a New Majority* (New York: Macmillan, 1968), 291, Michael Harrington, *The Accidental Century* (New York: Macmillan, 1965), 301. On the early 1960s as the "golden age" of the professional-managerial class, see Barbara Ehrenreich and John Ehrenreich, "The Professional-Managerial Class," 7. Galbraith, *The New Industrial State*, 399, Bazelon, *Power in America*, 332.

8. Bazelon, *Power in America*, 172, Miller, *Democracy Is in the Streets*, 204–208, 332–335, 365, 373–374, Gitlin, *The Sixties*, 105–109, and Rossinow, *Politics of Authenticity*, 53–84, discuss the significance of this language of love and authenticity among the early New Left. Rossinow, 184, notes that New Left radicals, like many college youth, entered the university system believing that they would receive "culture," only to find that higher education now existed to train a corps of well-paid technical and managerial functionaries.

9. Harrington, *Accidental Century*, 41, 146, 174, 301, 305.

10. Philip Rieff, *The Triumph of the Therapeutic*, 12–13, 27, Philip Reiff, *Freud: The Mind of the Moralist* (New York: Harper and Row, 1959), 293.

11. Rieff, *Triumph of the Therapeutic*, 18, 23.

12. Ibid., 240–241.

13. Ibid., 211, 250.

14. Martin Luther King, Jr., "Letter from Birmingham Jail," 92; Harvey Gallagher Cox, "The New Breed in American Religion: Sources of Social Activism in American Religion" (1967), in *On Not Leaving It to the Snake* (New York: Macmillan, 1967), 124–140, first published in *Daedalus* 96 (Winter 1967).

15. Cox, "The New Breed," 127, 131–132. On religious and especially clerical participation in the civil rights and antiwar movements, see Mitchell K. Hall, *Because of Their Faith: CALCAV and Religious Opposition to the Vietnam War* (New York: Columbia University Press, 1990), James Findlay, "Religion and Politics in the Sixties: The Churches and the Civil Rights Act of 1964," *Journal of American History* 77 (June 1990), 66–92, James Findlay, *Church People in the Struggle: The National Council of Churches and the Black Freedom Movement, 1950–1970* (New York: Oxford University Press, 1993), Murray Polner, *Disarmed and Dangerous: The Radical Lives and Times of Daniel and Philip Berrigan* (New York: Basic Books, 1997), Michael Friedland, *Lift Your Voice Like a Trumpet: White Clergy and the Civil Rights and Antiwar Movements, 1954–1973* (Chapel Hill: University of North Carolina Press, 1998), Hulsether, *Building a Protestant Left*, 114–134.

16. Harvey Gallagher Cox, *The Secular City: Secularization and Urbanization in Theological Perspective* (New York: Macmillan, 1965), 2, Gibson Winter, *The Suburban Captivity of the Churches* (Garden City, N.Y.: Doubleday, 1962), 25, Peter Berger, *The Noise of Solemn Assemblies: Christian Commitment and the Religious Establishment in America* (Garden City, N.Y.: Doubleday, 1961), 165, 178, Daniel Callahan, *Honesty in the Church* (New York: Charles Scribner's Sons, 1965), 42–70, Donald Thorman, *The Emerging Layman*, 114, William Hamilton, "The New Optimism: From Prufrock to Ringo" (1966), in *Radical Theology and the Death of God*, ed. William Hamilton and Thomas J. J. Altizer (Indianapolis, Ind.: Bobbs-Merrill, 1966), 157–158.

17. William Hamilton, *The New Essence of Christianity* (New York: Association Press, 1961), 25, William Hamilton, "Dietrich Bonhoeffer," *Nation* (April 9, 1965), also in Hamilton and Altizer, *Radical Theology and the Death of God*, 114, Cox, *Secular City*, 247, Thomas Merton, "The Church in Diaspora," in *Seeds of Destruction* (New York: Farrar, Straus and Giroux, 1964), 93–220, quote on 188.

18. The texts of these encyclicals are in O'Brien and Shannon, 84–128. The Slant group of New Left Catholics can be sampled in Terry Eagleton (ed.), *The New Left Church* (Baltimore: Helicon Books, 1966), and Adrian Cunningham, Terry Eagleton, and Brian Wicker, *Catholics and the Left: The "Slant" Manifesto* (Springfield, Ill.: Templegate, 1967). John A. T. Robinson, *Honest to God* (Philadelphia: Westminster, 1963). The claims in Robinson's book are tame compared with those of Altizer and Hamilton, who collected their miscellaneous pieces in *Radical Theology*. Thomas J. J. Altizer, *The Gospel of Christian Atheism* (Philadelphia: Westminster, 1966), 102–131, 147–157, Hamilton, "Dietrich Bonhoeffer," 114, Gabriel Vahanian, *The Death of God: The Culture of Our Post-Christian Era* (New York: Braziller, 1961). Paul Van Buren, *The Secular Meaning of the Gospel* (New York: Macmillan, 1963), is a more technical work of exegesis and theology. Ved Mehta interviewed a number of distinguished European and American theologians (among them Barth, Tillich, and Reinhold Niebuhr) on Bonhoeffer, the death of God, and other topics for the *New Yorker* and later turned the inter-

views into *The New Theologian* (New York: Harper and Row, 1985), 52. *Time*'s celebrated "Is God Dead?" issue (February 8, 1966)—complete with funereal black cover and satanic red lettering—covered the movement "none-too insightfully" (Hulsether, *Building a Protestant Left*, 109).

19. Paul Van Buren, interview in Mehta, *The New Theologian*, 65, Cox, *Secular City*, 62–70, quote on 63. The most important of Dietrich Bonhoeffer's works are *The Cost of Discipleship* (New York: Macmillan, 1959) and *Letters and Papers from Prison* (London: SCM Press, 1967). Martin E. Marty (ed.), *The Place of Bonhoeffer* (New York: Association Press, 1962), was an early assessment of Bonhoeffer's impact; Rossinow, *Politics of Authenticity*, 62–63, 69, discusses Bonhoeffer's reputation among student radicals. Teilhard de Chardin's oeuvre includes *The Divine Milieu* (New York: Harper, 1960) and *The Phenomenon of Man* (New York: Harper and Row, 1965). Walter J. Ong refers to Teilhard's work as a "major anthropological and religious breakthrough" in *In the Human Grain: Further Explorations in Contemporary Culture* (New York: Macmillan, 1967), 144. Garry Wills, *Bare Ruined Choirs: Doubt, Prophecy, and Radical Religion* (Garden City, N.Y.: Doubleday, 1972), 97–117, relates McNamara's interest in Teilhard in the midst of an eviscerating critique of Teilhardian fashion.

20. Cox, *Secular City*, 105–163, 241–269; see also Harvey Gallagher Cox, *On Not Leaving it to the Snake*, 108–110.

21. Rosemary Ruether, *The Church against Itself* (New York: Herder and Herder, 1967), 159–172, Joseph Washington, *The Politics of God* (Boston: Beacon Press, 1967), 182, Daniel Berrigan, "Report from Selma," *Commonweal* 82 (April 9, 1965), 73, Philip Berrigan, *Prison Journals of a Priest Revolutionary* (New York: Holt, Rinehart, and Winston, 1970), 22, Richard Schaull, "Revolutionary Change in Theological Perspective" (1966), in *The Church Amid Revolution*, ed. Harvey Gallagher Cox (New York: Association Press, 1967), 36–37, 47.

22. Daniel Berrigan, *The Bride: Essays in the Church* (New York: Macmillan, 1959), 3–4, Thomas Merton, "Honest to God" (1963) and "The Death of God and the End of History, " in *Faith and Violence: Christian Teaching and Christian Practice* (South Bend, Ind.: University of Notre Dame Press, 1968), 236, 243–244, 247.

23. Merton, "Toward a Theology of Resistance," in *Faith and Violence*, 7, Thomas Merton, "To Each His Own Darkness" and "Rain and the Rhinoceros," in *Raids on the Unspeakable* (New York: New Directions, 1966), 11, 31, Daniel Berrigan, *They Call Us Dead Men: Reflections in Life and Conscience* (New York: Macmillan, 1966), 68, 170–172. Merton's poetic criticism can be sampled in Thomas Merton, *Cables to the Ace; Or, Familiar Liturgies of Misunderstanding* (New York: New Directions, 1968). David Cooper, *Thomas Merton's Art of Denial: The Evolution of a Radical Humanist* (Athens, Ga.: University of Georgia Press, 1989), 251–269, is a splendid analysis of Merton's cultural criticism.

24. Berrigan, *Dead Men*, 67, Merton, "To Each His Own Darkness," 31–33.

25. Joseph Washington, *Black Religion: The Negro and Christianity in the United States* (Boston: Beacon Press, 1964), 255, 289, Philip Berrigan, "The Challenge of Segregation," *Interracial Review* 34 (February 1961), 30, Philip Berrigan, *No More Strangers* (New York: Macmillan, 1965), 68, 102, 109, 115, 118.

26. Thomas Merton, "Letters to a White Liberal," and "The Legend of Tucker Caliban," in *Seeds of Destruction*, 8, 69, 83–84, 87.

27. Joseph Fletcher, *Situation Ethics* (Philadelphia: Westminster Press, 1967); Cox, *Secular City*, 192–216.

28. Mary Daly, *The Church and the Second Sex* (Boston: Beacon Press, 1968), 31, 124–136, 150, 179. On Daly's significance in the women's liberation movement, see Alice Echols, *Daring to Be Bad: Radical Feminism in America, 1967–1975* (Min-

neapolis: University of Minnesota Press, 1989), 250–253. See also "The Woman Intellectual and the Church," *Commonweal* 85 (January 27, 1967), 446–458, a symposium that included Daly, Ruether, and other Catholic feminists. Philip Berrigan's analysis of the new social context of marriage in *No More Strangers*, 31–68, could be read as a prolegomena to a new Catholic sexual ethic.

29. Michael Novak, *A Time to Build* (New York: Macmillan, 1967), 95, Michael Novak, *A New Generation: American and Catholic* (New York: Sheed and Ward, 1964), 15, 141, 196. See also Novak's contribution to "The Secular City: An Exchange of Views," *Commonweal* 83 (November 12, 1965), 186, where he notes that Cox's *Secular City* "read like the rationalization of a busy, harried man." Merton, "Letters to a White Liberal," 24. Terry Anderson, "The New American Revolution: The Movement and Business," in Farber, *The Sixties*, 175–205, notes the lack of a radical critique of corporate business in the 1960s.

30. Novak, *A New Generation*, 235.

31. Michael Novak, *The Open Church* (New York: Macmillan, 1964), 130–147, 338, Novak, *A Time to Build*, 367–369; see also Michael Novak, "The Underground Church," *Saturday Evening Post* (December 28, 1968), 43, Michael Novak, *A Theology for Radical Politics* (New York: Herder and Herder, 1969), 96, Cox, *Secular City*, 6–13, 97, 180–191, Rosemary Ruether, "Schism of Consciousness," *Commonweal* 88 (May 31, 1968), 326–331.

32. Cox, *Feast of Fools*, 96.

33. Berger, *Noise of Solemn Assemblies*, 167, Ruether, *Church Against Itself*, 215.

34. Michael Novak, "Where Is Theology Going?" *Christian Century* 90 (November 3, 1965), 291, Editorial, *Commonweal* 88 (May 31, 1968), 317, George J. Hafner, "A New Style of Christianity," *Commonweal* 88 (May 31, 1968), 332–333. On flexibility and mobility as corporate code words, see Andrew Ross, *Strange Weather: Culture, Science, and Technology in the Age of Limits* (New York and London: Verso, 1991), 172–181. Thomas Frank, *The Conquest of Cool: Business Culture, Counterculture, and the Rise of Hip Consumerism* (Chicago: University of Chicago Press, 1997), discusses the convergence of countercultural sensibility and corporate advertising.

35. Michael Novak, *Belief and Unbelief: A Philosophy of Self-Knowledge* (New York: Macmillan, 1965), 11, Thomas Merton, *Zen and the Birds of Appetite* (New York: New Directions, 1968), 21–32; see also Thomas Merton, *The Way of Chuang Tzu* (New York: New Directions, 1965), and Thomas Merton, *Mystics and Zen Masters* (New York: New Directions, 1967). On Merton's interest in Zen, his old friend Edward Rice, *The Man in the Sycamore Tree: An Entertainment* (Garden City, N.Y.: Doubleday, 1970), 91–96, is especially informative. Merton appears to have confided to Rice and others that he intended to leave Gethsemani.

36. Thomas Merton, "Marxism and Monastic Perspectives" (1968), in Thomas Merton, *The Asian Journal of Thomas Merton* (New York: New Directions, 1973), 328–342.

37. Novak, *Theology for Radical Politics*, 12–13, 125; see also Michael Novak, "Why Wallace?" *Commonweal* 89 (October 18, 1968), 79–80. Jeffrey K. Hadden, *The Gathering Storm in the Churches* (Garden City, N.Y.: Doubleday, 1969), esp. 221–235, quotes on 228, 231.

38. Daniel Berrigan, *Night Flight to Hanoi: War Diary with 11 Poems* (New York: Macmillan, 1968), 49. On the New Left's fatal shortcomings, see Christopher Lasch, *New Radicalism in America*, 180–188, Miller, *Democracy Is in the Streets*, 326. Alan Brinkley, "The Therapeutic Radicalism of the New Left," in *Liberalism and Its Discontents* (Cambridge: Harvard University Press, 1998), 221–236, while repeating legitimate complaints about the personal and therapeutic char-

acter of postwar radicalism, relies on narrow conceptions of personalism and therapy.

39. Garry Wills, *Chesterton: Man and Mask* (New York: Sheed and Ward, 1961), 240, Garry Wills, "Liberals Convert a Cardinal," *National Review* 6 (February 25, 1961), 120, Wills, *Bare Ruined Choirs*, 37. See also Garry Wills, "Conservatism and Change," *National Catholic Reporter* (June 30, 1965), 8. Wills's career in the 1960s can be tracked in his Garry Wills, *Lead Time: A Journalist's Education* (Garden City, N.Y.: Doubleday, 1983), ix–50, as well as in Patrick Allitt, *Catholic Intellectuals and Conservative Politics*, 243–282, passim., which is a superb comparison of Wills and Michael Novak.

40. Garry Wills, *Nixon Agonistes: The Crisis of the Self-Made Man* (Boston: Houghton Mifflin, 1970), 53, 184, 244; Wills, *Bare Ruined Choirs*, 6, 212, 260.

41. Wills, *Nixon Agonistes*, 356, 362, 376–377, Wills, *Bare Ruined Choirs*, 94, 201, 208.

42. Wills, *Nixon Agonistes*, 601.

43. The ur-text of liberation theology is Gustavo Gutiérrez, *A Theology of Liberation*, trans. Caridad Inda and John Eagleson (Maryknoll, N.Y.: Orbis, 1973). For a judicious historical discussion of liberation theology and base communities, see Jorge Castaneda, *Utopia Unarmed: The Latin American Left after the Cold War* (New York: Alfred A. Knopf, 1993), 205–217.

44. Dean Kelley, *Why Conservative Churches Are Growing* (New York: Harper and Row, 1972), 154. On the Catholic conservative resurgence, see Allitt, *Catholic Intellectuals*, 121–142.

45. Gitlin, *The Sixties*, 202. On the discovery of the working class, see Barbara Ehrenreich, *Fear of Falling: The Inner Life of the Middle Class* (New York: Pantheon, 1989), 97–143. Writing of government bureaucrats and corporate managers, Farber observes that many Americans "rightfully saw that these rigidly secular agents of centralized power challenged the meaning and security of their lives" (*The Sixties*, 4).

46. Bell, *Coming of Post-Industrial Society*, 147, Daniel Bell, *The Cultural Contradictions of Capitalism* (New York: Basic Books, 1976), 146–171, Lewis Mumford, *The Pentagon of Power* (New York: Harcourt Brace Jovanovich, 1970), 413, Robert L. Heilbroner, *An Inquiry into the Human Prospect* (New York: W. W. Norton, 1991 [1974]), 19, 148, 164–166, 189.

47. Theodore Roszak, *The Making of a Counterculture* (Garden City, N.Y.: Doubleday, 1969), Ivan Illich, "The Vanishing Clergyman" (1967) and "The Powerless Church" (1967), in *Celebration of Awareness: A Call for Institutional Revolution* (New York: Pantheon, 1970 [1969]), 69–103, Ivan Illich, *Tools for Conviviality* (New York: Harper and Row, 1973), 15.

48. E. F. Schumacher, *Small Is Beautiful: Economics as if People Mattered* (New York: Harper and Row, 1973), 86, 91–94, 141, 146–149, 230, 280–281. Schumacher followed up this book with two others: *A Guide for the Perplexed* (New York: Harper and Row, 1977) and *Good Work* (New York: Harper and Row, 1979).

49. James Cone, *Black Theology and Black Power* (New York: Seabury, 1969), 17, Washington, *Politics of God*, 5, Vincent Harding, "The Religion of Black Power," in *The Religious Situation: 1968*, ed. Donald R. Cutler (Boston: Beacon Press, 1968), 8, 34. James Forman, "The Black Manifesto" (1969), in *Black Theology: A Documentary History*, vol. 1: *1966–1979*, eds. James Cone and Gayraud Gilmore (Maryknoll, N.Y.: Orbis, 1993 [1979]), 27–36. Other seminal works in the black theology movement are Albert Cleage, *The Black Messiah* (New York: Sheed and Ward, 1968), Major J. Jones, *Black Awareness: A Theology of Hope* (Nashville, Tenn.: Abingdon Press, 1971), Major J. Jones, *Black Christian Ethics* (Nashville, Tenn.: Abingdon Press, 1974), J. Deotis Roberts, *Liberation and Reconciliation: A Black Theology* (Philadelphia: Westminster, 1971), J. Deotis Roberts, A Black Political Theology (Philadelphia: Westminster, 1974), Gayraud Gilmore, *Black Re-*

ligion and Black Radicalism: An Interpretation of the Religious History of African-Americans (Maryknoll, N.Y.: Orbis, 1997 [1973]). The Cone and Gilmore volume is an indispensable collection of black theology. For an analysis, see Hulsether, *Building a Protestant Left,* 191–195.

50. Cone, *Black Theology and Black Power,* 63, James Cone, *A Black Theology of Liberation* (Philadelphia: J. B. Lippincott, 1970), 30–34, 53–81, 228–249. Cone was the principal drafter of "Black Theology: Statement by the National Committee of Black Churchmen," June 13, 1969, in Cone and Gilmore, *Black Theology,* 37–39, a much more modest declaration of principles.

51. Harding, "Religion of Black Power," 9–10, Cone, *Black Theology of Liberation,* 204, Cone, *Black Theology and Black Power,* 151.

52. Cone, *Black Theology of Liberation,* 40, 57.

53. Jones, *Black Awareness,* 129, Harding, "Religion of Black Power," 36–37.

54. Michael Novak, "A Planetary Culture," *Christianity and Crisis* 30 (March 29, 1971), 29. On the ambiguities and contradictions of populist conservatism, see Jonathan Reider, "The Rise of the 'Silent Majority,' " in *Rise and Fall of the New Deal Order,* eds. Fraser and Gerstle, 243–268.

55. Michael Novak, *Ascent of the Mountain, Flight of the Dove* (New York: Harper and Row, 1971), 28–29, 152, Michael Novak, *All the Catholic People* (New York: Macmillan, 1971), 181.

56. Michael Novak, *The Rise of the Unmeltable Ethnics: Culture and Politics in the Seventies* (New York: Macmillan, 1972), 35–38.

57. Ibid., 70, 131, 167–189.

58. Ibid., 190–191, 242–249.

59. Ibid., 195–196. In his review, "New Material for Archie Bunker," *New York Times Book Review* (April 23, 1972), 27–29, Garry Wills pronounced *Unmeltable Ethnics* "an immoral book" written by a "very moral man."

60. Novak, *All the Catholic People,* 160, Walzer, *Company of Critics,* see also Walzer, *Exodus and Revolution.*

61. Rosemary Ruether, *Liberation Theology* (New York: Paulist Press, 1972), 14, Mary Daly, *Beyond God the Father: A Philosophy of Women's Liberation* (Boston: Beacon Press, 1973), 1, Letty Russell, *Human Liberation in a Feminist Perspective: A Theology* (Philadelphia: Westminster, 1974), 55. Hulsether, *Building a Protestant Left,* 184–191, is a valuable examination of the feminist turn in theology.

62. Ruether, *Liberation Theology,* 12, 16, 154–155.

63. Daly, *Beyond God the Father,* 25, Ruether, *Liberation Theology,* 200, Rosemary Ruether, *New Woman, New Earth: Sexist Ideologies and Human Liberation* (New York: Seabury, 1975), 52. See also Daly, *Beyond God the Father,* 81–92, and Phyllis Trible, "Good Tidings of Great Joy: Biblical Faith without Sexism," *Christianity and Crisis* 33 (February 4, 1974), 12–16.

64. Russell, *Human Liberation,* 60, Daly, *Beyond God the Father,* 98–178, quote on 131.

65. Harvey Gallagher Cox, *The Seduction of the Spirit: The Use and Abuse of People's Religion* (New York: Simon and Schuster, 1973), 115–122, 144–196.

66. Ibid., 86–88, 170, 246–250.

67. Ibid., 327–329.

68. Ibid., 317, 320–221.

69. Daniel Berrigan, "Letter to the Weathermen" (1971), in *Daniel Berrigan: Poetry, Drama, Prose,* ed. Michael True (Maryknoll, N.Y.: Orbis Books, 1988), 284. See also Berrigan's interviews with Robert Coles while a fugitive from the FBI in Robert Coles and Daniel Berrigan, *The Geography of Faith: Conversations between Daniel Berrigan, When Underground, and Robert Coles* (Boston: Beacon Press, 1971). Wills, *Bare Ruined Choirs,* 249–250.

70. Wills, *Bare Ruined Choirs,* 212, 267–272.

71. Ibid., 272.

1. Augustine, *City of God*, intro by John O'Meara (London and New York: Penguin Books, 1984), 5, 548–558, 1070–1076. On the political dimensions of Augustine's thought, see the excellent discussions in John Milbank, *Theology and Social Theory: Beyond Secular Reason* (Oxford: Basil Blackwell, 1990), 403–431, and Jean Bethke Elshtain, *Augustine and The Limits of Politics* (South Bend, Ind.: University of Notre Dame Press, 1995), esp. 19–48, 89–112.
2. Ibid., 71–75.
3. Ibid., 569, 601, 870, 878, 1087.
4. Cox, *The Secular City*, 163.
5. Day, *The Long Loneliness*, 219.
6. For an example of this left libertarianism, see Ellen Willis, *Don't Think—Smile! Notes from a Decade of Denial* (Boston: Beacon Press, 1999). George Scialabba's review of this book, "Entrapments of Modernity," *Dissent* 45 (Fall 1999), esp. 103–105, ably critiques this moral sensibility.
7. Ross, *Strange Weather*, 165–167.
8. Richard Rorty, *Philosophy and Social Hope* (New York: Penguin, 1999), 12, 203; "Post-modernist Bourgeois Liberalism" *Journal of Philosophy* 80 (Summer 1983), 583–589; see also Richard Rorty, *Contingency, Irony, and Solidarity* (Cambridge: Cambridge University Press, 1989) 44–69, on the "contingency of liberal community." Richard Rorty, *Achieving Our Country: Leftist Thought in Twentieth-Century America* (Cambridge, Mass.: Harvard University Press, 1998) 15–17, 35, 142 n. 8. In his most recent work, Rorty goes so far as to envision a time when "the social gospel theology of the early twentieth century has been rediscovered": *Philosophy and Social Hope*, 249. Although there are compelling critiques of Rorty's claim to descent from Dewey advanced by Westbook, *John Dewey*, 539–542 and Kloppenberg, "Pragmatism," loc. cit., 123–125, his connection to Dewey on the question of "religion" is, I think, plain. I second Kloppenberg's observation that despite both his support for social democracy and his eschewal of the left academy's concerns with identity, Rorty's "liberal ironism encourages selfishness, cynicism, and resignation;" Kloppenberg, "Pragmatism," 125. Still, despite his greater openness to religion in the pubic sphere, I do not find Kloppenberg's less ironic pragmatism any more inspiring. See Kloppenberg, "Knowledge and Belief in American Public Life," in *The Virtues of Liberalism* (New York: Oxford University Press, 1998), 38–58.
9. Rorty, *Achieving Our Country*, 30.
10. Cornel West, *American Evasion of Philosophy*, 211–239; see also *Prophesy Deliverance: An Afro-American Revolutionary Christianity* (Philadelphia: Westminster Press, 1982) *and Keeping the Faith: Philosophy and Race in America* (New York and London: Routledge, 1993).
11. Lasch, *True and Only Heaven*, 184–194; Robert Bellah, William Sullivan, Steven Tipton, et al., *Habits of the Heart: Individualism and Commitment in American Life* (Berkeley: University of California Press, 1985), and *The Good Society* (New York: Knopf, 1991). Wilfred McClay's criticisms of the Bellah group in *The Masterless: Self and Society in Modern America* (Chapel Hill: University of North Carolina Press, 1994), 280–283, 287–288, are compelling, especially his description of their catalogue of virtues-without-disciplines as a list of "insubstantial word combinations" (282).
12. Lasch, *True and Only Heaven*, 530–532; *Revolt of the Elites*, 230–246. I discussed Lasch's views on religion in "A World Full of Prophets: Populism and Religion

in Christopher Lasch's Critique of Progress," paper given at the annual meeting of the American Historical Association in Chicago, January 7, 2000.

13. Stanley Hauerwas, *The Peaceable Kingdom: A Primer in Christian Ethics* (South Bend, Ind.: University of Notre Dame Press, 1983), 99–102. The most thoughtful representatives of "radical orthodoxy" are John Milbank, *Theology and Social Theory*; John Milbank, *The Word Made Strange: Theology, Language, Culture* (Oxford: Basil Blackwell, 1997); Catherine Pickstock, *After Writing: The Liturgical Consummation of Philosophy* (Oxford: Basil Blackwell, 1997); Milbank, Pickstock, and Graham Ward, eds., *Radical Orthodoxy* (London: Routledge, 1999). On the "church as polis," see Hauerwas, *In Good Company, The Church as Polis* (South Bend, Ind.: University of Notre Dame Press, 1995).

14. MacIntyre, *After Virtue*, 262–263.

15. Fink, *Progressive Intellectuals*, 258.

16. On the current state of liberal Protestantism, see Wade Clark Roof and William McKinney, *American Mainline Religion: Its Changing Shape and Future* (New Brunswick, N.J.: Rutgers University Press, 1987), quote on 86; Roof and Jackson W. Carroll, *Beyond Establishment: Protestant Identity in a Post-Protestant Age* (Louisville, Ky.: Westminster/John Knox, 1993); Dean R. Hoge and David A. Roazen, *Understanding Church Growth and Decline, 1950–1978* (New York: Pilgrim Press, 1979); Hoge, Benton Johnson, and Donald A. Luidens, *Vanishing Boundaries: The Religion of Protestant Baby Boomers* (Louisville, Ky.: Westminster/John Knox, 1994). Randall Balmer, *Grant Us Courage: Travels on the Mainline of American Protestantism* (New York: Oxford University Press, 1996) is a brief but penetrating study of several liberal churches. All of these studies paint a gloomy picture of mainline Protestant church life and of the prospects for some renewal of the social witness. On Catholics, see Peter Steinfels, "The Pollsters Look at U. S. Catholics," *Commonweal* 123 (September 13, 1996), 19.

17. Roof, *A Generation of Seekers: Spiritual Journeys of the Baby Boom Generation* (San Francisco: HarperSanFrancisco, 1993).

INDEX

Sheen, Bishop Fulton J., 104
Shuster, George, 41–42, 53–54, 59
Silk, Mark, 96
"Slant group," 156
Small's Paradise, 134
Social Action Department, 46
"The Social Creed of the Churches"
    (1908), 7
social gospel, 16–20
socialism
    Christian, 17–20, 30–32
    religious, 1'25–27
    secular, 19, 31, 125
Susman, Warren, 36, 60, 82

Talbott, Fr. Francis, 70
Tate, Allen, 101–102
Tawney, R. H., 36
Teilhard de Chardin, Pierre, 156–57
theology of culture, 126–28, 143–44
therapeutic ethic, 5–6, 133–34, 143–46, 189
Thorman, Donald, 106, 154–55
Thurman, Howard, 52, 115
Tillich, Hannah, 123, 127–28, 131, 134–35,
    146
Tillich, Johannes, 121–22
Tillich, Paul, 36, 120–46, 157
tolerance, 96–97
transmoral conscience, 133–34
Trilling, Lionel, 98–99

ultimate concern, 143
underground church, 163–64
Union for Democratic Action, 93,
    100

Vahanian, Gabriel, 156
"Victory Plan" (1941), 73, 88

Ward, Harry, 41, 44–45
Washington, Joseph, 157, 159
Weil, Simone, 85–87, 113, 190
Weimar culture, 124–29
West, Cornel, 186–87
Westbrook, Robert, 45, 62
White, Morton, 91
Whitehead, Alfred North, 38–39
Willard, Francis, 13, 16
Williams, Michael, 32, 46
Willock, E d, 116
Wills, Garry, 167–68, 179–81
Wilson, Edmund, 37
Wingolf Fellowship, 123
Winter, Gibson, 139, 154
Woodbey, Rov. Goerge, 17
World Council of Churches, 105
Wuthnow, Robert, 105

Young Catholic Workers (YCW), 73

Zen Buddhism, 165